A LEECHBOOK

OR

COLLECTION OF MEDICAL RECIPES
OF THE FIFTEENTH CENTURY

THE TEXT OF MS. NO. 136 OF THE MEDICAL SOCIETY OF
LONDON, TOGETHER WITH A TRANSCRIPT INTO MODERN
SPELLING, TRANSCRIBED AND EDITED WITH AN INTRODUCTION,
NOTES AND APPENDIX

by

WARREN R. DAWSON
F.R.S.E., F.R.S.L., F.S.A.Scot.

Fellow of the Royal Society of Medicine
Honorary Fellow of the Medical Society of London
Honorary Librarian of Lloyd's

*PUBLISHED FOR THE ROYAL SOCIETY OF LITERATURE
OF THE UNITED KINGDOM UNDER THE TERMS OF THE
DR. RICHARDS TRUST*

MACMILLAN AND CO., LIMITED
ST. MARTIN'S STREET, LONDON
1934

TO

ARTHUR FRANCIS VOELCKER,
M.D., F.R.C.P.

IN FRIENDSHIP

CONTENTS

INTRODUCTION.

§ I.—The Manuscript.

THE manuscript here transcribed is the property of the Medical Society of London, and it is published by the kind permission of the President and Council of that body. Nothing is known of its history : it has been in the library of the Medical Society (founded 1773) since its earliest days, and has been re-bound in recent years. When preparing a catalogue of the Society's manuscripts,[1] I made a complete transcript of this document in March, 1932, and again collated my copy carefully with the original in November, 1933.

The manuscript (hereinafter referred to as M.) bears the number 136, and is a small quarto volume of 98 folios of vellum, measuring $18 \cdot 5 \times 14$ cm. The leechbook which forms the subject of the present work occupies folios 1–95 : the remainder of the manuscript is filled with the beginning of a botanical glossary in Latin. The folios are inscribed on both sides, like the pages of a modern book ; the hand-writing is neat and careful, and it is throughout the work of one and the same scribe. Red and blue inks are used for the decoration of capital letters,[2] and for the paragraph-marks which divide the various prescriptions, recipes, glosses and other contents of the book. The text was written first, and the paragraph-marks (alternately red and blue) were inserted afterwards, but these are often incorrectly placed. In many cases the scribe has omitted to insert these marks in the places where they should have been found, and almost as often he has planted them in the middle of a paragraph, where, if they were regarded, they would stultify the sense. In the transcript here printed, these

---

[1] *Manuscripta Medica : A Descriptive Catalogue of the Manuscripts in the Library of the Medical Society of London*, by Warren R. Dawson. Published for the Society by John Bale, Sons & Danielsson, London, 1932.

[2] Decorated capitals are used at the beginning of §§ 1, 2, 18, 70, 156, 243, 245, 271, 302, 365, 441, 523, 548, 584, 623, 688, 755, 763, 775, 894, 932, 969, 996 and 1006. The letter O (§ 647) has only been drawn, but not decorated.

A

paragraph-marks have been entirely omitted, and for convenience of reading and of reference the sections have been numbered and printed as separate paragraphs, instead of following one another continuously as they do in the original.

The volume is in almost perfect condition, only two blemishes exist to interrupt the continuity of the text. An entire leaf has been cut out after fo. 6 (§ 68), but the pagination must have been made after the removal of this leaf, as its absence makes no interruption in the numbering of the folios. By the removal of this leaf, the end of § 68 is lost, as well as the beginning of § 69, and an unknown number of sections has vanished between these two, probably about twelve, if the average number per folio here applied. That is the first blemish : the second is that a large piece has been torn from the upper part of fo. 26, carrying with it all but the beginnings of the first fourteen lines of the *recto* and the ends of the same number of lines on the *verso*. Fortunately, it has been possible, with the help of another manuscript, to restore the missing part of the text of the *verso*. These are the only defects in the volume, which is otherwise intact. For the numbering of the folios, the Saxon forms of the numerals are employed, but in the text itself, numerals are always expressed in Roman notation.

§ II.—Date of the Manuscript.

A careful comparison of the handwriting of M. with a number of others of known date, and the application of the usual palæographical criteria, has led me to the conclusion that it was written about the middle of the fifteenth century. This general indication of date, which is scarcely open to doubt, is supported by the spelling, syntax and other philological factors, but quite near the end of the text I came upon a striking confirmation of the period to which I had already assigned it. On fo. 94 (§ 1064), John, Duke of Somerset, is mentioned. This is John Beaufort, the first Duke of Somerset, grandson of John of Gaunt, whose daughter Margaret became the mother of Henry VII. John Beaufort was born in 1403, was created Duke in 1443, and, after his recall from Normandy in the following year, died (it is said by his own hand) in May, 1444.[1] He is mentioned in M. in circumstances that suggest that he was at the time of writing still living, and if this inference is correct, the manuscript must have been written at the end of 1443 (after Beaufort's elevation to Dukedom) or the beginning of 1444 (before his death in May). But whether this precise date can be maintained or not, it can be said with certainty that M. was written in the reign of Henry VI, most probably before the commencement of the Wars of the Roses.

§ III.—CONTENTS OF THE MANUSCRIPT.

The manuscript consists mainly of a large collection of recipes (many can scarcely be called prescriptions) for injuries, ailments and affections of all kinds, interspersed with paragraphs defining and discussing, in the manner of glosses, the nature of certain diseases and the properties of herbs. The arrangement purports to be alphabetical, but the grouping of subjects under the letters of the alphabet is often very arbitrary and inaccurate. Thus many of the remedies are assembled in the alphabet under the names of the parts of the body affected, others are classed under the names of the diseases, others under the names of the drugs used in their cure, and others again under such vague terms as " aches," " evils," etc. This arrangement frequently has the effect of separating closely-related remedies : aural troubles, for instance, will be found scattered throughout the book, partly under E (ears), partly under A (aches), partly under D (deafness), and elsewhere, according to their titles. Many similar instances might be quoted. Unlike most other manuscripts of its period and class, M. contains no incantations or charms, and is severely practical in character. The magical element is not completely lacking, but it is nowhere obtrusive, and the patient has generally to rely on the cure provided in the leechbook without magical or divine aid.[2] Nearly all the remedies are for human complaints, but a few scattered veterinary prescriptions are to be found (§§ 307, 558, 727, 781, 942). The drugs are mostly herbal, and consist of common plants easily

---

[1] There is a short notice of John Beaufort in the *Dictionary of National Biography ;* see also James Gairdner, *The Paston Letters,* Vol. i, London, 1872, *Introduction,* p. xxxvii.

[2] The expression " by God's grace " occurs in §§ 61, 102, 607.

obtained, though occasionally foreign herbs are used. Mineral drugs, though fairly frequent, are less commonly met with, and animal preparations (except butter, milk, fat, grease, suet and other common products of animal origin) are rarest of all. Such animals as the toad, snail, earthworm, hare, mole, weasel and raven are used from time to time.

In addition to the purely therapeutic matter of the text, there are some passages devoted to the preparation of drinks, confections, salves and other medicaments, and to the gathering of simples (§§ 386 *et seq.*). The properties of certain particular herbs[1] are dealt with, and two passages are devoted to the *dies nefastae*, or unlucky days of the year (§§ 143–54, 1073–4). There are some interesting surgical directions, such as the use of an anæsthetic drink to render the patient somnolent before operating upon him (§ 852), and the method of stitching large wounds (§ 963). Blood-letting and cupping are frequently mentioned, and there are passages that deal with diet and regimen. It is worthy of note that the effects of brain-injury are observed in relation to the side of the head that is affected (§ 843) : as is well known, injuries to the brain that affect other parts of the body, except in cases of *contre-coup*, have their manifestations on the opposite side to that injured, *e.g.*, an injury to the right side of the brain may produce paralysis of the left leg, and *vice versa*.[2]

The leechbook contained in M. is a compilation, made up of extracts drawn from many different sources, but probably it is a copy of another composite document,[3] and is not the

---

[1] Examples : Borage (§ 226) ; Celandine (§ 241) ; Catmint (§ 643) ; Cockle or Ergot (§ 529) ; Hyssop (§ 1004) ; Mugwort (§ 587) ; Pepper (§ 644), etc.

[2] This also had been perceived, but with less accuracy, by the Egyptians more than a thousand years before the Christian Era. See my paper in the *British Journal of Surgery*, Vol. xx, 1932, p. 39.

[3] Three chapter-numbers are given in M., which suggests that it was copied, at least in part, from a book in which the chapters were numbered. The numbers in M. are i, xiii and xiv. Chapter i comes, logically enough, at the head of letter A, thereafter no numbers are encountered until xiii at the head of letter K and xiv at the head of letter O. If the letters of the alphabet which occur are counted as each representing a chapter, K should be chapter, ix, not xiii ; but if the subheadings at §§ 18, 22, 26 and 243 are each reckoned as chapters, then K does become chapter xiii. But this does not account for the number xiv at the letter O. By the same method of reckoning, this should be xvii.

original redaction of its own writer, as many textual corruptions would seem to indicate. The work as a whole ended with the letter Y on fo. 87 *verso* (§ 1005), and thereafter a collection of addenda follows, not in alphabetical order. These addenda often differ in wording and form from the rest of the text, and they are probably the work of the scribe of M., who gathered them from different sources. Amongst them is the reference to John. Duke of Somerset (*see* above, § II), which may perhaps be taken to indicate that the writer of M. was a member of his household. The origins and sources of the recipes will be considered in a later section of this Introduction.

The work is, on the whole, carefully compiled, and the handwriting maintains its beauty and legibility from the first page to the last, and does not, as so often elsewhere, deteriorate with the progress of the text. There are, however, evidences of negligence from time to time. Dittographies are frequent, even in the middle of a line, as are also omitted words. Latin and Greek words are almost always corrupt, and it is therefore evident that the writer of M. did not know these languages. If he himself is not responsible for the corruptions, at least his ignorance prevented him from detecting the errors in the text or texts from which he copied. Nor did he perceive that he had inadvertently admitted into his book a number of duplicate passages. These duplicates are not always quite verbally identical, another indication of the composite nature of the book. They are as follows :—

§ 18 = § 266.	§ 333 = § 343.
§ 65 = § 766.	§ 340 = § 791.
§ 101 = § 117.	§ 532 = § 619.
§ 161 = § 746.	§ 583 = § 765.
§ 292 = § 633.	§ 680 = § 854.
§ 295 = § 953.	§ 965 = § 1070.

There are no erasures, and in two places only has the scribe discovered his own errors. In each of these cases a word has been wrongly inserted, and it is underlined with dots to indicate that it should be considered as deleted (§§ 236, 1005).

It would appear that the manuscripts copied, or those from which the prototype was made up, were all written in

English. Various differences in dialect can be discerned. The prefix *y* before past participles, for instance, is an indication of the southern dialect, and its relative infrequency suggests that the bulk of the book was derived from originals written in the midland or northern dialects. A careful examination of the text will reveal many points of spelling indicating Norman-French, or Anglo-Norman influence. The frequent insertion of the needless initial aspirate and the use of *ch* for *sh* are other indications of the same nature. As is usual in manuscripts of this period, þ is used side by side with *th*, though the former is naturally more frequent than the latter (the other form of the Anglo-Saxon *th*, namely, ð, had, of course, long since disappeared). With these few observations the philological aspect of the text must be dismissed. Its full discussion would require far more space than is permissible in a publication that is avowedly non-philological in purpose, and it would require far more special knowledge of the subject than I can lay claim to.

It will be observed that in a few passages the writer speaks in the first person (§§ 48, 245, 267, 609, 1042). This must not necessarily be taken literally to indicate that such passages are original observations by the writer of M. The greatest caution must be used in accepting the claims to originality made by early medical writers. Thus in a long manuscript of the ninth-tenth century A.D., written in Coptic, very similar in its general nature and composition to M., there are colophons to some of the remedies written in the first person, of which one or two may be quoted. " We have experimented with this remedy and found it perfect " [1] ; " we have tried it and found it useful for all maladies of the eyes " [2] ; and, " I have experimented with it and found it perfect, it has no equal in efficacy." [3] Similarly the Jewish physician, Shabbethai Donnolo, who settled in Italy in the tenth century and wrote a pharmaceutical work, often makes the same claims, but caution must be used in accepting them too literally. [4]

---

[1] *Cairo Coptic Medical Papyrus*, line 57. E. Chassinat, *Un Papyrus Medical Copte*, Cairo, 1921, p. 130.
[2] *Ibid.*, l. 158, p. 190.
[3] *Ibid.*, ll. 224–5, p. 230.
[4] J. Leveen, *Proc. Royal Society of Medicine*, Vol. xxi, 1928, p. 1399.

§ IV.—SIMILAR TEXTS.

Many similar English manuscripts of earlier, equal and later date are known, but so far as I am aware, no complete leechbook of this age and kind has as yet been fully published in English. In various works dealing with medical history, extracts from such manuscripts have been published, but it is difficult to form any adequate estimate of the nature of mediæval medical ideas and practice from such sparse excerpts. A larger collection of extracts from manuscripts of the fourteenth century, closely similar to M. though a little earlier in date, appeared under the editorship of the Rev. Professor George Henslow (1835–1925) in the year 1894.[1] In Henslow's work extracts are given from four manuscripts : (1) a document in the author's possession (frequently referred to in the present volume as H.) ; (2) the British Museum MS. *Harleian* 2378 ; (3) the MS. *Sloane* 2584, and (4) the MS. *Sloane* 521. There is also appended a valuable, but very incomplete, list of plants used in the fourteenth century, with their identifications. The four manuscripts edited by Henslow contain many parallels of passages in M. In the course of preparing the text of M. for publication, I have consulted these and a number of other manuscripts in the British Museum and elsewhere, and in these latter also some parallels are to be found. In the notes I have indicated passages that are duplicated in the manuscripts published by Henslow, but except in a few instances, I have not inserted references to parallel texts in unpublished manuscripts, as this would have increased the bulk of the book without adding to its utility to general readers.

An interesting series of Anglo-Saxon medical manuscripts belonging to the tenth and eleventh centuries has been published by the Rev. Thomas Oswald Cockayne (1807–73). These are of the greatest interest and importance in the history of medicine, but (apart from those that are direct translations of known Latin works) they belong to a somewhat different category from M. and its analogues ; that is to say, in spite of the similarity of the subject-matter, M. and its class are not the lineal descendants of the Anglo-Saxon manuscripts. Both undoubtedly had to a large

[1] *Medical Works of the Fourteenth Century,* London, 1894.

extent a common origin, but they developed along different lines.

For the purposes of comparison I have consulted a number of later manuscripts. These, as a rule, show much less variation than the earlier ones. The prescriptions were tending to become standardised and to assume the form in which we find them in seventeenth and eighteenth-century printed *Dispensatories*. A manuscript in my own possession (MS. *Dawson*, 19) of the Tudor Period, written about a century later than M., contains many prescriptions that are found in an earlier form in M. and others of its period and class. Forty-six recipes from this manuscript are published as an Appendix to this volume, where also a description of the document will be found. It is referred to in the notes as D.

Many of the analogous manuscripts contain much matter besides medical prescriptions. It is common to find considerable parts of them devoted to agriculture, geometry, astrology, divination and other topics. No such miscellaneous subjects occur in M., which is medical throughout.[2] It may also be noted that these other manuscripts are often written partly in Latin and partly in English. There is no Latin in M., except the names of a few drugs. Nor does M. contain any passages written in verse, as many other manuscripts do.

§ V.—THE TITLE.

The title of M. is very similar in wording to those commonly placed at the head of English mediæval medical manuscripts. All of them purport to be made up of matter drawn from the works of Hippocrates and other ancient medical teachers, and from the non-existent books of the mythical Aesculapius. In the title of M., the recipes are said to be drawn out of the books of "Archippus and Ypocras." The name Archippus is manifestly a corruption of Aesculapius, for Archippus was an Athenian poet of the fifth century B.C., and had not the remotest connection with medicine. In the titles of other manuscripts, we can see the

---

[1] *Leechdoms, Wortcunning and Starcraft of Early England*, 3 vols., London, 1864–6. (Rolls Series.)

[2] Excepting only a passage dealing with the *Dies Nefastae* (§§ 1073–4) and a recipe for making sealing-wax (§ 957).

corruption of the name taking place almost before our eyes. Thus *Sloane* 521 has " Galion, Acclepias and Ypocras," *Harleian* 2378 has " Galien, Asclipius and Ipocras," whilst *Sloane* 610 has " Galio, Aschephus and Ypocras."[1]

It is almost needless to add that the Hippocratic Books and the works of Galen are not laid under contribution at all, except perhaps in some instances very remotely through the medium of countless adaptations, commentaries, and translations.

§ VI.—SOURCES OF THE TEXT.

The title of M., as has just been noted, ascribes the origin of its contents to Aesculapius and Hippocrates. In reality countless different writers have contributed their mite to the whole. A few of the remedies in M. are ascribed to specific medical teachers, and it will be convenient to deal with these first.

Anselm. A medicament for a fractured skull is referred to in § 95 as the " enpleyster capitall of Mayster Anselme of Jene," but, so far as I can discover, no medical writer of this name is known. Possibly the personage referred to may be Bishop Anselm of Havelberg, who is known to have been connected with the medical school of Montpellier in the twelfth century.

Galen. A collyrium for the eyes is attributed to Galen in § 485. As this consists of drugs well known to Greek medicine, it may have been found in Galen's works, or, more probably, in a later Latin work attributed to Galen. In § 1064 is a cure for migraine, of which it is said, " This medecyne vsid Galien the gode philosophir."

Gordianus (Bernard Gordon, of the school of Montpellier, where he began to teach in 1285). An ointment for " scald-head " is attributed to this teacher (§ 776).

Henri de Mondeville (1260–1320 ; surgeon ; studied at Montpellier, Paris and Bologna). At the end of a recipe for an aching shoulder, probably some articular or rheumatoid complaint, it is said (§ 42), " and henre de amanda villa

---

[1] *Sloane* 2584 has the glaring anachronism :—

" Ipocras this boke made ȝere,
And sent it to þe Emperour Cesare."

seith þat he fond no better medecyne amonge such maner medecyns then this."

Hippocrates. Apart from the general statement in the title, Hippocrates is mentioned once only, and that is in connection with a preparation to clear the sight (§ 496) : " this is the medecyne þat ypocras vside." I have searched in vain for this recipe in the Hippocratic Collection.

Peter Bonant. I have not succeeded in identifying this personage. Two recipes for treating a fractured skull are attributed to him (§§ 95, 96), and of one of them it is said : " Mayster pers (Petrus) Bonant seyd that he p⁹vyd it in a houndis heed that was hurt in to the breyne ꝫ hit helid hyme." Another recipe (§ 488, for polypus) is introduced by the words : " Mayster petire Bonant cōmendyd þis medecyne that folowith." Peter Bonant must have been some local celebrity. I have not encountered his name elsewhere.

Peter of Spain (Petrus Hispanicus, a Portuguese physician of the thirteenth century, who wrote a book on the eyes). A lotion for the eyes (§ 484) is called " the watir of mayster peter off Spayn."

These are the only authors mentioned by name : whence, then, was the bulk of the book derived ? There can be no doubt that most of it originated in the works of late Latin writers and in Latin translations of Greek books. A careful examination of the text reveals elements that can be recognised in the writings of Dioscorides,[1] Pliny the Elder,[2] Cassius Felix,[3] Galen, Oribasius,[4] Alexander Trallianus,[5] Pseudo-Apuleius, or Apuleius Barbarus,[6] Sextus Placitus,[7] Paulus Aegineta,[8] and last, but not least, Marcellus Empiricus.[9] The compiler of the book or books from which

---

[1] *De Materia Medica*, and *Euporista*, or *De Medicamentis*.

[2] *Historia Naturalis*.

[3] Sometimes called *Cassius the Iatrosophist*. He flourished in the early part of the second century A.D., and his *De Medicina* was translated from Greek into Latin in A.D. 447.

[4] *De Parabilibus Medicamentis*, or *Euporista*.

[5] *Therapeutica*.

[6] *Harbarius*.

[7] *De Medicina ex Animalibus*.

[8] *Epitomæ Medicæ*.

[9] Marcellus the Empiric, of Bordeaux, flourished early in the fifth century. His book is entitled *De Medicamentis*.

M. is copied drew upon Marcellus to a greater extent than on any of the others named above. Marcellus himself compiled much from the works of his predecessors, and especially from Pliny. Doubtless many other writers, known and unknown, have entered into the complex ; but generations of translation and re-translation, and of adaptation and epitomising, have made it difficult to recognise the prototypes. Whilst it can scarcely be said that any passages of Marcellus can be found entire and unaltered in M. and its analogues, yet the number of derivations, certain or probable, is very considerable and would, if tabulated, occupy a good deal of space. It must never be forgotten that the matter derived from ancient authors was generally obtained through the medium of corrupt and often garbled translations.

Besides the books specifically ascribed by name to the above-mentioned and other writers, there were already in existence many compilations made from the works of Greek, Latin, Arabic and Hebrew authors, such as the *Antidotarium* of Nicolaus Myrepsus of Nicea, drawn up at the end of the twelfth century, and containing over 2,600 prescriptions. Arabic writers made similar synopses, such as Ibn al-Beithar of Malaga (died 1248), who composed a great book of simples compiled from the works of Galen, Dioscorides and various Semitic writers, with many original observations and additions. Such works reached northern Europe through Italy and Spain. Added to all the admittedly borrowed elements, there are some purely local accretions derived from England, France and Germany.

The difficulty in identifying passages in manuscripts such as M. and its fellows is increased by the changes that the originals underwent in the course of their transmission through time and space. The Greek writers in their preparations naturally made use principally of locally-growing herbs. The flora of the eastern Mediterranean region is large and varied, and contains many herbs that do not flourish in more northerly regions. Hence arose the practice of substituting in the English manuscripts native herbs to replace those that were unknown or unobtainable, and of speaking of familiar herbs of the Greek writers by other names. A few distinctively Mediterranean herbs will be found in the recipes, and these, if they were ever used,

must have been obtained in a dried form from apothecaries.
Apothecaries or spicers are several times mentioned in M.
in connection with the rarer drugs.

The identification of plants and minerals in the medical
manuscripts is a subject that cannot be discussed here.
It is a matter of the greatest complexity, and must have been
felt to be so even in the Middle Ages, when glossaries and
nomenclators of plants were drawn up giving the synonymy
of herbs. These glossaries are most interesting subjects of
study, but it must be confessed that they often increase
rather than diminish our difficulties.[1]

§ VII.—EGYPTIAN ELEMENTS.

But in tracing the remedies to the books of Greek and
Latin writers, we have by no means tracked them to their
ultimate sources. There cannot be the slightest doubt that
Greek therapeutics (apart from the scientific medicine of the
Hippocratic School), especially in Byzantine times, drew
very largely on Egyptian, and to a lesser extent on Assyrian
writings.

The Egyptian hieratic medical papyri of Pharaonic
times,[2] succeeded by those written in Demotic Egyptian,[3]
Greek[4] and Coptic,[5] maintained an unbroken tradition both
in substance and form for over three thousand years. The
general make-up of M. and similar manuscripts, no less than
that of the intermediate Greek and Latin texts, resembles
that of the Egyptian papyri to a striking and remarkable
degree. The recipes are drawn up in precisely the same
manner : first comes the title, then the drugs and their
quantities, the directions for preparing them (i.e., bray or
stamp, seethe or boil, mix, make into pills, plasters, powders,

---

[1] Examples of such glossaries have been published by J. L. G.
Mowat in *Anecdota Oxoniensia*, Vol. i, Part i (Oxford, 1882), and
Part ii (1887).

[2] The *Ebers, Hearst, Chester-Beatty, Kahun, Ramesseum, London*
and *Berlin* medical papyri.

[3] *The Demotic Magical Papyrus of London and Leiden*, edited by
F. Ll. Griffith and Sir Herbert Thompson, 3 vols., London, 1904–9.

[4] *Oxyrhynchus Papyri*, Nos. 234, 1088 ; *Tebtunis Papyri*, Nos.
272–3 ; *Rylands Papyri*, Nos. 28, 29, 29B, and others.

[5] *Cairo Coptic Medical Papyrus*, published by E. Chassinat ;
fragments published by Zoëga, Bouriant, Crum and others.

ointments, etc., as the case may be), and directions for administering or applying, whether separately or in a vehicle (such as wine, honey, water, etc.), and the time and manner of application (before or after food, early or late, hot or cold, etc.). Each headed prescription is usually followed by alternatives, the headings of which correspond : [hieroglyphs], " another remedy," or simply [hieroglyph], " another," or again [hieroglyphs], " another like it," or " another for the same." Both the Egyptian and the later series of manuscripts are compilations drawn from different sources, and from time to time groups of prescriptions for a particular organ or region of the body or for a similar class of disease, are brought together with a sub-heading. Thus in M. we have " Now begynneth the medecyns for al maner of swellynge " (§ 795), or " Her begynneth þe makynge of good poudresse for dyurs syknes " (§ 695). With these may be compared the many group-headings in the *Ebers Papyrus*, such as [hieroglyphs], " Beginning of the recipes for making the hair grow " (*Ebers*, 66, 7), or [hieroglyphs], " Beginning of he recipes for treating the liver " (*Ebers*, 67, 7), and many similar instances could be quoted. The first words in the title of M., " Here begynneþe good medecyns for al maner yvellis that every man hath," are closely paralleled by the titles of the *Ebers* and *Hearst* Papyri, [hieroglyphs] [hieroglyphs], " Beginning of the collection of recipes to drive out all sicknesses from the body."

Many of the recipes in M. end with the words " until he be whole." This expression frequently occurs in the Egyptian papyri in the very same words, [hieroglyphs], or [hieroglyphs]. Again, in M. many of the recipes are followed by such remarks as " a good remedy," " a true remedy," or by the colophon *It is proved*, or *Probatum est*. In Egyptian medical papyri we have similar comments : ⳥ 𓀀 [hieroglyphs] , "excellent and true, proved a million times," or simply ⳥ 𓀀 [hieroglyphs] , "excellent and true." Many of the recipes in M. are said to be "good," or "very good," a remark frequently appended to Egyptian recipes, 𓊪 "good," or 𓊪 𓊪 , "good, good," or "very good."

Some of the remedies in M. are specifically stated to be "for a man or a woman" (§§ 71, 712, 1054, 1060). This specification is sometimes made in the Egyptian texts, [hieroglyphs] , "a man or a woman." In the great majority of remedies, both English and Egyptian, this specification is not given, and its relative infrequency is therefore significant.

There are, however, other indications of the Egyptian influence transmitted to later medical manuscripts that are even more striking. In several of the recipes in M., as well as in other manuscripts of its class, there occurs the medicinal use of the milk of a woman who has borne a male child (§§ 93, 299, 300, etc.). This is a characteristically Egyptian element : it occurs twelve times in the *Ebers Papyrus*,[1] three times in the *London Medical Papyrus*,[2] twice in the *Berlin Medical Papyrus*,[3] and once each in the *Hearst Papyrus*,[4] the *Berlin Papyrus* 3027[5] and the *Cairo Coptic Medical Papyrus*.[6] In the hieratic papyri the expression is thus written (transcribed into hieroglyphs), [hieroglyphs] , and in Coptic ⲉⲣⲱⲧⲉ ⲛ̄ⲥϩⲓⲙⲉ ⲉⲥⲙⲟⲥⲉ ⲛ̄ⲟⲩϣⲏⲣⲉ, the identical words. Now in the Hippocratic Collection we find γάλα γυναικὸς κουροτρόφου used in a medicine ;[7] similarly in Dioscorides,

---

[1] *Ebers*, 26, 1 ; 26, 6 ; 59, 8 ; 60, 14 ; 62, 10 ; 62, 17 ; 69, 5 ; 69, 7 ; 74, 13 ; 80, 15 ; 90, 19 ; 90, 21.
[2] *London Med.*, 6, 7 ; 14, 3 ; 15, 1.
[3] *Berlin Med.*, Verso, 1, 3 ; 1, 5. [4] *Hearst*, 8, 12.
[5] *Berlin* 3027, 7, 4. [6] *Cairo Coptic Med. Pap.*, line 373.
[7] *De Morbis Mulierum*, i, 75 (ed. Littré, Vol. viii, p. 166).

γάλα αρρενοτόκου γυναικός,[1] and of human milk generally, Pliny says : *semperque in omni usu efficacius eius quæ marem enixa est*.[2] I have elsewhere collected other instances of the survival of this strange drug.[3]

Perhaps the most striking example of Egyptian influence is afforded by the name of the common complaint *megrim* or *migraine*. The very word is a translation of the ancient Egyptian ⌒ 𓏤 , " half-head." In Greek it is ἡμικρανια, Latinised as *hemicrania*, late-Latin *hemigrania*, Anglo-Saxon *healf-heafod*.[4]

Numerous other examples of Egyptian influence in later medicine might be quoted, but as this section of the introduction has already exceeded its proper limits, only two other cases can be mentioned. In § 523 of M. a barbarous experiment is described to ascertain whether a woman will bear children or not. This is derived from the similar passage in the *Berlin Medical Papyrus* and the *London-Leiden Papyrus*, and it has survived almost to the present day, having passed through the Hippocratic Collection in the treatise on the diseases of women. I have elsewhere collected a number of examples of this and similar experiments.[5] Finally, reference may be made to the use of large numbers of similar substances of a like kind, dictated by a belief in their magical efficacy. Thus in M. § 650, in an ointment for " gowtes," but evidently meaning stiff joints, the medicine contains the grease of the badger, pig, hare, cat, dog, capon, deer and sheep, melted together and applied with the juice of herbs. An Egyptian prescription for the same purpose contains the grease of the oryx (antelope), centipede, hippopotamus, lion, ass, crocodile, mouse, lizard and snake similarly prepared.[6] The prescriptions are exactly alike, except that the animals are altered in accordance with the difference in fauna of the two countries.

---

[1] *De Materia Medica*, V, 99.
[2] *Nat. Hist.*, xx, 51 ; again mentioned, xxviii, 27.
[3] *Ægyptus*, Vol. xii, Milan, 1932, pp. 12–15.
[4] This was first pointed out by C. W. Goodwin in *Zeitschrift für äg. Sprache*, Bd. xi (1873), p. 13.
[5] *Magician and Leech*, pp. 141–146.
[6] *Ramesseum Medical Papyrus* No. 2, § 17.

These examples have been quoted to call attention to the fact that ancient Egyptian medical writings, centuries older than the earliest of any other country, did indeed exert an influence on later medicine. I have discussed the subject fully in my book *Magician and Leech* (London, 1929).

§ VIII.—UNLUCKY DAYS.

Two sections of M. are devoted to unlucky days. The belief in lucky and unlucky days is very ancient, and its origin is to be sought in ancient Egypt. Four Egyptian papyri are known containing calendars of the days of the month, each marked *lucky* or *unlucky*,[1] as the case may be. One of these, *Papyrus Sallier IV*, gives directions and prohibitions very similar to those in § 1072.[2] The Egyptian origin of these tables of days is traditionally preserved in the name they frequently bear in Mediæval manuscripts, *Dies Ægyptiacæ*.[3] Considerable variation occurs in the different lists that are extant, a fact which is easy to understand when it is remembered how widely diffused this calendar-custom is. Traditional unlucky days would in some places coincide with the feasts of local saints, or with other auspicious occasions, and the dates would accordingly be altered.

§ IX.—THE MODERN TRANSCRIPT.

For the convenience of those who are unaccustomed to the orthography of mediæval manuscripts, I have transcribed the text into modern spelling, the original text and the modern transcript being printed on opposite pages. In this transcript, I have followed the wording and phraseology of the original as closely as possible, and only in the case of words now entirely obsolete or completely changed in meaning have I substituted modern equivalents.

---

[1] W. R. Dawson, " Observations on the Egyptian Calendars of Lucky and Unlucky Days," *Journ. of Egyptian Archæology*, Vol. xii, 1926, pp. 260–264.

[2] F. Chabas, *Le Calendrier des Jours fastes et néfastes*, Chalon-sur-Saône, 1870 ; G. Maspero, *Causeries d'Egypte*, Paris, 1907, pp. 149–158.

[3] H. F. Morland Simpson, *Proc. Soc. of Antiquaries of Scotland*, vol. xxix, 1895, pp. 235–6.

Thus I have nearly always retained the word *seethe* in preference to *boil*, and it must be noted that the past participle, *sothen* or *sodden*, means *boiled* and not, as to-day, merely *soaked* or *saturated*. I have retained throughout *temper* in preference to *blend*, *combine*, *work-up*, or *triturate*, for all of which meanings it serves. I have generally substituted *put* for *do*, in such phrases as " do it into a pan," but have retained *do away* in preference to *take away*, *e.g.*, " it will do away the ache." It must also be borne in mind that such common words as *sore* and *ache* do not always convey the meanings we understand by them at the present day. A *sore* in M. and similar texts simply means an affected part, whether there is any external manifestation (such as a wound, inflammation, excoriation, etc.) or not. The same applies to *gout*, *boil*, *fester* and other words.

It is necessary also to call attention to the fact that I have followed the original in its frequent changes of person, regardless of the violence done to concord and syntax according to the modern practice of expression. In the recipes the ingredients are constantly spoken of in the plural, first as *them* (envisaging the several elements), immediately afterwards followed by the singular, *it* (envisaging the resultant mixture or compound). We thus have such combinations as this : " Take the herbs A, B and C, and stamp *them* in a mortar ; and then boil *them* and strain *it* with a slice, then wring *them* through a cloth, and let *it* cool." In the same way the directions for the application of remedies confuse the grammatical persons. Often a hypothetical patient is understood, spoken of in the third person as *he*, *him*, and equally often the directions are addressed directly to the patient in the second person, *thou*, *thee*. The two methods, however, are very frequently used in one and the same remedy, in such expressions as " *thou* shalt lay it to *thy* head, and do this oft till *he* be whole." Scores of similar changes of person could be quoted, but to have corrected them by modern standards would have completely disguised the frank and characteristic expression of the text.

WARREN R. DAWSON.

London,
27th November, 1933.

18

1 Here begynneþe gode medycyns for al man͞
yvellis that eu͡y man hath that gode lechys
drawen owt off þe bokys that men clepe Archippus ꒭
Ypocras ffor thies ware þe best lechis off the world in
her tyme and þ⁹ for who so will do as thys boke wyll
tech hyme he may be sekyr to haue help off all yvellys
and woundys and oþ⁹ desesys and sekeness both wᵗ in
and eke wyth owt. ᴥ

Capitlm̄ primum.

2 Ach off hede · make þ⁹ for lye of verveyne or ellys of
betenye ether of wormod and þ⁹ with wasshe
thyne hede thrise in þe weke

3 An other Take wormod wex and encens and stamp
heme toged͡ wᵗ the whyte of an ay and do it in a lynen
clout and bynd about ym hede

4 An other Take savayn and stamp hitt and tempyr itt
wᵗ oyll off Rosen and seth and anoynt thyne hede þ⁹ wᵗ
agayns the svnne in som͡ and agayns þe fyre in wynt͡. Do
so oft and be hole

5 An other Take mustard seed and Rubb and stamp hem
wele toged͡ and tempre hitt wele wᵗ wat͡ so þat itt be
thykk and lay itt to ym hede

6 An other Take peletre and chew þe rothe iij days and
be hole

7 An oþ⁹ Take bitayne verveyn celidony wormod weybred
Rubb wal wort sawge fyue cornys of pep and hony and seith
all in wat͡ and Drynke hitt fastynge

8 An oþ⁹ hete hilwort ꒭ eysell and do it in yʳ nose threllys
þat þe odour may go to þe brayne and make a playst͡ of
hilworth sodyn and lay itt to yʳ hede

1 Here beginneth good medicines for all manner of evils that every man hath, that good leeches have drawn out of the books of those whom men call Archippus[1] and Hippocrates, for these were the best leeches of the world in their time : and therefore whoso will do as this book will teach him, he may be secure to have help for all evils and wounds and other diseases and sickness both within and also without.

Capitulum Primum.

2 Ache of head. Make therefor lye of vervain or else of betony or of wormwood, and therewith wash thine head thrice in the week.

3 Another. Take wormwood, wax and incense and stamp them together with the white of an egg, and put it in a linen cloth and bind it about his head.

4 Another. Take savin and stamp it, and temper it with oil of roses ; and seethe [it] and anoint thine head therewith in the sun in summer and by the fire in winter. Do so often, and be whole.

5 Another. Take mustard-seed, and rub and stamp it well together, and temper it well with water so that it be thick, and lay it to his head.

6 Another. Take pellitory and chew the root three days, and be whole.

7 Another. Take betony, vervain, celandine, wormwood, waybread ; rub walwort (danewort), sage, five corns of pepper and honey, and seethe all in water and drink it fasting.

8 Another. Heat hillwort (thyme) and aysell (vinegar), and put it in your nostrils that the odour may go to the brain ; and make a plaster of hilwort boiled, and lay it to your head.

---

[1] Corrupt for Æsculapius. *See* Introduction, V.

B 2

9 An other Take an hand full of ruw and an oþ⁹ off
hayhove þᵉ thrid of levys of lorec and seith heme toged⁀
in waꝶ ether in wyne and þᵗ playsꝶ lay on ym hede and
þˡˢ is for ach þᵗ durith longe

10 An oþ⁹ Take sothernwode and hony ⁊ eysell pound it
togedir ⁊ drynk it oft fastyng ⱬ⸺

11 [fo. 1 *verso*]   An oþ⁹ Take ruw wᵗ the thykke gronnde of
Eufras ⁊ enoynt thy tēples

12 An oþ⁹ Take hillwort and pound it with floure and giff
hym to drynke in hoote watꝶ and hold hyme fastynge till
hitt be noone

13 Anoþ⁹ Take agarland for þᵉ hede ach Take surmonnteyn
that spycers haue and bete it wele in a brasyn mortar and
take camamell Dried and make powd⁀ off hitt and then
take thies powdʳs by euen porcions and put hem in a longe
narow pockett þat it may be full of powdre and þᵗ it may go
abowt hys hede and loke þᵗ þᵉ powdre be elych moch in
ech place of þᵉ poket and then seth it in a potell of white
wyne and when it is welle sodyne thrust oute the juse of
þᵉ poket ⁊ sywe it abowt his hede as hote as he may suffre
hitt and do so ech nyght whē you gost to bedde ⁊ while þᵉ
wyne will last pbaꝶ est //

14 An oþ⁹ for the hede ache þᵗ com̄yth of colde · seth
betayn in wyne and washe thyne hede þ⁹in and it is gode
for cold of the stomake ⁊ for fumes þat smyteth vp into þᵉ
hede

15 Anoþ⁹ take encenes ⁊ coluere dunge and whete floure
an vnce of ich and temp hem wᵗ þᵉ white of an ey and wher
so þᵉ hede akyth bynd it and it shall voyd away anone

16 Anoþ⁹ for ache of the hede þᵗ comyth out of þᵉ stomake
Take ffenell solsicle camamyll and roses of ich elich moch
seth heme in white wyne and make a plaisꝶ and lay it
þ⁹to ⱬ⸺

---

¹ *Ammi visnaga,* called *siler montanum,* or *syrmontayne* : a plant
of the Mediterranean region, sometimes called " Spanish toothpick."
    ² Two quarts.

9 Another. Take a handful of rue and another of ground-ivy, the third of leaves of laurel, and seethe them together in water or in wine, and that plaster lay on his head : and this is for an ache that endureth long.

10 Another. Take southernwood and honey and vinegar ; pound it together and drink it often, fasting.

11 Another. Take rue with the thick sediment of eufrasia (eyebright) and anoint thy temples.

12 Another. Take hillwort and pound it with flour and give him to drink in hot water, and keep him fasting till it be noon.

13 Another. Take a garland for the headache. Take ammi[1] that spicers have, and beat it well in a brazen mortar and take camomile dried and make powder of it ; and then take these powders by even portions and put them in a long narrow pocket that it may be full of powder and that it may go about his head, and look [to it] that the powder be of like quantity in each place of the pocket (*i.e.*, evenly distributed), and then seeth it in a pottle[2] of white wine, and when it is well sodden, thrust (squeeze) out the juice from the pocket, and swathe it about his head as hot as he may suffer it, and [do] so each night when thou goest to bed and while (as long as) the wine will last. *Probatum est.*[3]

14 Another for the headache that cometh of cold. Seethe betony in wine and wash thine head therein. And it is good for cold of the stomach and for the fumes that rise up into the head.

15 Another. Take incense and pigeon's dung and wheat flour, an ounce of each, and temper them with the white of an egg ; and whereso the head acheth, bind it, and it shall vanish anon.

16 Another for ache of the head that cometh out of the stomach. Take fennel, solsicle, camomile and roses, of each equally much ; seethe them in white wine, and make a plaster, and lay it thereto.

---

[3] " It is proved " ; the commonest form of colophon in the medical MSS.

17 Anoþ⁹ Take an ay and rost it wele in þᵉ colys and when
it is hard cleue hyme in two and as hote as þou mayste
suffre lay it to þᵉ hede and hitt shall do away þᵉ akynge ᵎᐧ

Eris

18 Take yonge braunchis off asshes when þai bene grene
[fo. 2 *recto*]. and lay hem on a brandyren on þᵉ
fyre and gedir the waᵗ þᵗ comyth owt at þᵉ endys of heme
an ey shall full and of þᵉ juse of the bradys of lekys an ey
shell full and of þᵉ droppynge of elys and medull all thies
toged⁾ and seith hem toged⁾ alytell and clens hem þem
thrugh a cloth · and putt it in a glasen vessell   And when
thow hast nede put this in the hole Ere of þᵉ seke mane
and lat hym lygge on the sore ere   And wᵗ juice ij tymes
he shall be hole and then take wole vnd⁾ a blak shepis
bely and lay itt wete in the same juse and lay it on þᵉ ere
and it restorith herynge and doth away akynge of eres

19 Another ffor akynge of Eres Take þᵉ juse of swynes
Cressis ꝫ put it in hys eres ꝫ it shall do away the akynge
wond⁾ wele

20 An oþ⁹ Take þᵉ juse of Radich and oyle of olyfe even
mesure ꝫ put it in the akynge Ere and this doth away the
akynge and also defenes

21 An oþ⁹ Take juse of reed myntys and hete it a lyttyll ꝫ
put it in þᵉ eres.

Eyen

22 ffor akynge of a mannys eyen/   Take new fresche clese
and lay it vpoñ the eyen and it shall voyd the akynge

23 An other for þᵉ same · who so enoyntith the eyen wᵗ
mylk of ij women that is to say þᵉ mod⁾ and of the
dought it will distroy the akynge of the eyne

24 Anoþ⁹ for eyen that ake and for dirknes of syght Take
may buttur and hony by euen porcion ꝫ seith hem toged⁾

---

¹ This recipe is a duplicate of § 266. A similar passage occurs
in the Anglo-Saxon Leechbook, MS. *Royal*, 12, D, xvii, fo. 15 *verso*.
" Again for the same, take a green ashen staff, lay it on the fire, then
take the juice that issues from it, put it on some wool, wring

17 Another.   Take an egg and roast it well in the coals and when it is hard, cleave it in two and, as hot as thou mayst suffer it, lay it to the head and it shall take away the aching.

Ears.

18 Take young branches of ash when they are green, and lay them on a gridiron on the fire, and gather the water that cometh out at the ends of them, an egg-shell full ; and of the juice of the blades of leeks, an egg-shell full ; and of the dripping of eels.   Mix all these together, and seethe them together a little ; and cleanse them through a cloth, and put it in a glass vessel.   And when thou hast need, put this in the whole ear of the sick man and let him lie on the sore ear.   And with [this] juice [used] twice, he shall be whole ; and then take wool [from] under a black sheep's belly and lay it wet in the same juice, and lay it on the ear, and it restoreth hearing and doth away aching of ears.[1]

19 Another for aching of ears.   Take the juice of swine's-cress (knotgrass), and put it in his ears, and it shall take away the aching wondrous well.

20 Another.   Take the juice of radish and oil of olive, even measures, and put it in the aching ear.   And this takes away the aching and also deafness.

21 Another.   Take the juice of red mint, and heat it a little, and put it in the ears.

Eyes.

22 For aching of a man's eyes.   Take new fresh cheese and lay it upon the eyes, and it shall void the aching.

23 Another for the same.   Whoso anointeth the eyes with milk of two women, that is to say [of] the mother and of the daughter, it will destroy the aching of the eyes.

24 Another for eyes that ache and for darkness of sight. Take may-butter[2] and honey by even portions and seethe

---

into the ear, and stop up the ear with the same wool."   O. Cockayne, *Leachdoms*, Vol. ii, p. 43.   Both are derived from Marcellus.

[2] Butter made in May, and preserved unsalted for medicinal purposes.

and aft put in þe whit of an ey ⁊ all all (*sic*) cold put this
in thin eyen and he shall be hole

25 An oþᵒ Take a gude qūtite of celidoyne and stamp it
wel in a morture ⁊ make þᵒof a lyttill ball and lap it in a
lyttill hemp · or a lyttell flax ⁊ ley [fo. 2 *verso*] it in hote
assches aft wrynge the juse in to a clene basyn and dry it
in the sonne and whenne hitt is driet temp it with a lyttell
alegᵒ of gude alle and put in thyne eyene.

Teth

26 ffor akynge of teth · Take the root of quincfoyle ⁊ seth
it wele in vinakyr or in wyne ⁊ hold it somdelle hote as he
may suffre hitt a gude while in his mouth ⁊ it shall do
away the ach.

27 An oþᵒ schaue hertys horne and seth it wele in wat and
with the wat washe the teth · and hold it hote in thy
mouth a good whille and thou shalt neu have the toth
ach agayne

28 Another Take vynegre and tansay ⁊ a rede onyon salt
and a fewe pep cornys grondyn and boyled toged⁾ ⁊
streyn it ⁊ drop a sponfull of the juse of in to that side of
thi mouth and hold it longe ther in and then spitt out and
lefe þe drasse ther of betwyx the toth and the cheke all
nyght

29 Anoþᵒ Take figges and comyn ⁊ stamp it wele toged⁾
and boyll hem wele in vynegr or rede wyne ⁊ make a
plaist and lay it to þe cheke wᵗ oute forth pƀ est

30 ffor akyng of the holow toth · take a ravennys tord
and put it in the holow toth and coloure hitt wᵗ the juse
of peletre of Spayne that þe syke knaw it not ne wote not
what it be ⁊ þen put it in the toth and it shall breke the
toth and do away þe akynge ⁊ as som men seith it will make
the toth to fall out

31 Anoþᵒ for the same and this is a speciall medecyne and
best of all and wes preved   Take jve beryes and seth heme
wele in vynegr and þe soup of þe licour all hote and hold it
in þe mouth till it be cold and þen kest it owt and take more

them together ; and afterwards put in the white of an egg and, all cold, put this in thine eyes, and he shall be whole.

25 Another. Take a good quantity of celandine and stamp it well in a mortar, and make thereof a little ball, and wrap it in a little hemp or a little flax and lay it in hot ashes. Afterwards wring the juice into a clean basin and dry it in the sun, and when it is dried, temper it with a little aleger[1] of good ale and put thine eyes.

Teeth.

26 For aching of teeth. Take the root of cinqfoil and seethe it well in vinegar or in wine, and hold it as hot as he may suffer it a good while in his mouth. And it shall take away the ache.

27 Another. Shave hartshorn and seethe it well in water, and with the water wash the teeth, and hold it hot in thy mouth a good while. And thou shalt never have the toothache again.

28 Another. Take vinegar and tansey and a red onion, salt, and a few pepper-corns ground and boiled together, and strain it and drop a spoonful of the juice into that side of thy mouth and hold it long there, and then spit out, and leave the dross thereof between the tooth and the cheek all night.

29 Another. Take figs and cumin and stamp it well together, and boil them well in vinegar or red wine ; and make a plaster and lay it to the cheek outside. *Probatum est.*

30 For aching of the hollow tooth. Take raven's dung and put it in the hollow tooth and colour it with the juice of pellitory of Spain that the sick recognize it not nor know what it be ; and then put it in the tooth and it shall break the tooth and take away the aching, and as some men say, it will make the tooth fall out.

31 Another for the same, and this is a special medicine and best of all and was proved. Take ivy-berries and seethe them well in vinegar and [take] the soup of the liquor all hot and hold it in the mouth till it be cold, and then

---

[1] Ale-gill, an infusion made of gill, or ground-ivy, used in brewing. *Cf.* § 495.

And do so iij or iiij tymes and it shall hele the w^t owte
dowte for yt is p̄ncipall medcyn þ^9 for ⚹ [fo. 3 *recto*]

32 An oþ^9 Take the sede of apm̄ a scripull þett is to say a
peny weght of henbane and of the levys of henbane and
of the sed of avance ij scripuls and grynd it small with
aqua vite and make pelettis þ^{9}of of the gretnesse of a fiche
and lay on the toth that akyth and it shall cese anone for
hitt hitt (*sic*) be pv̄yd that hitt hath sesed þe þe (*sic*) ach in
halffe an our.

33 An oþ^9 take henbane sede and leke sede and floure and
lay thies iij thyngys on a glowyng teyle stone that the breth
may com thorow to þe toth and it shall sle the wormes and
do away the ach

34 Who so wil kepe his teth fro akynge vse not to ete
freshe wat͛ fishe for þei gend͛ lyghtly corrupcion abowte
þe teth. Also bewar to ete cold mete after ryght hote or
hoot aft͛ cold ne vse not moch raw onyons and lekys and
kepe the wele fro brakynge if yow may for all þies done
moch harme to þe teth and gendren lyghtly corrupcion of
which comyth akynge //

35 ffor all man͛ of ach wher so eu͛ itt be. Take water
cressen and seth heme wele and then take heme vp and
wrynge oute the wat͛ and schred heme small and take
fresshe gresse and fayr shepis talow and fry it toged͛ and
take fair branne of whete an handfull or ij and straw it þ^{9}on
꒐ has hote as þow mayste wrapp it þ^{9}in and do so ij or iij
and þou shall be hole

36 Anoþ^9 for the same Take hony bores grese or barowes
grese and lylies or the rotis agode quantite and bray heme
and fry heme and anoynte the place w^t the licour agayne
the fire oft and make a playst͛ of thykkyst ther off and lay
it on þe sor place twyes or thrise and thou shalt be hole

37 Ach of stomake and of guttys and and (*sic*) the modre
vse the powdre of calamynt with metys ꒐ [fo. 3 *verso*]
drynke the wyne that it is sodon in for to dry þe supfluitese
of þe modre seth calamynt in wat͛ and þ^{9}w^t wasshe hym
benethe for and he shall be hole

cast it out and take more. And so do three or four times and it shall heal without doubt, for it is a principal medicine therefor.

32 Another. Take the seed of apium (smallage, or wild celery), a scruple, that is to say a pennyweight, of henbane, and of the leaves of henbane and of the seed of avens two scruples, and grind it small with aqua vitæ and make pellets thereof of the size of a vetch and lay on the tooth that acheth and it shall cease anon for it be proved that it hath ceased the ach in half an hour.

33 Another. Take henbane seed and leek seed and flour and lay these three things on a glowing tile-stone that the breath (vapour) may come through to the tooth and it shall slay the worms and take away the ache.[1]

34 Whoso will keep his teeth from aching, be accustomed not to eat fresh-water fish for they readily engender corruption about the teeth. Also beware of eating cold meat after right hot, or hot after cold, nor use much raw onions and leeks, and keep thee well from braking (vomiting) if thou mayst, for all these do much harm to the teeth, and readily engender corruption of which aching cometh.

35 For all manner of aches wheresoever it be. Take water-cresses and seethe them well then take them up and wring out the water, and shred them small; and take fresh grease and fair sheep's tallow and fry it together; and take fair bran of wheat, an handful or two, and strew it thereon as hot as thou mayst, and wrap it therein and do so three or four [times] and thou shall be whole.

36 Another for the same. Take honey, boar's grease and lillies or their roots a good quantity and bray them and fry them and anoint the place with the liquor in front of the fire often, and make a plaster of the thickest [part] thereof and lay it on the sore place twice or thrice and thou shalt be whole.

37 Ach of stomach and of guts and of the mother (womb). Use the powder of calamint with meats (*i.e.,* in the food), and drink the wine that it is sodden in : for to dry the superfluities of the mother, seethe calamint in water and therewith wash him beneath and he shall be whole.

---

[1] Compare § 912, and *see* note thereon.

38 Annothir for the stomake that comyth of cold or of
winde vse to ete þe powdre of philipendula and of þe ffenell
sede

39 Ach of stomach that comyth [of cold] or of wynde and
for colliac passio and strangury   Take peritory and oyle of
olyue and boyle it to gedur and somwhat warme anoynte
the tofore the stomake and the womb and sidys agayns
the fire and wᵗ goddis help þᵘ shall be hole

40 Ach of the modre seth ij littill bundell of anece in
wyne and make þ⁹of a playst and lay abowt his navyl et
sanabitur

41 Ach of shuldur joynt¹   Take v dragmes of gall of an ox
and a dragme of hony and seith hem as thikke and enoynt
þe joynt that akyth ther with til it be hole.   A dragme is
the weght of iij penyes ͻ

42 An other.   Take hempe sede and ry of ech a dragme
and parch hem in a scherde till thei wax blake that thai
may be powdred with vertgresse halue a dragme temper
hem wᵗ hony that sufficith ꝫ it corrodith ryght wele and
levyth the escarþ and jff itt be leyd to oft tymes succe̊syuely
in soch tyme when the escarþ is away hitt helyth ryght
wele old cancry sores and also the same cancres and
[fo. 4 recto] they be new ꝫ malū mortuū and oþ⁹ such //
And henre de amanda villa seith þat he fond no betᵗ
medecyne amonge such mañ medecyns then this //

43 An oþ⁹ medle mazuaton and agrippa toged⁾ wᵗ a littell
aqua vite and anoynt þ⁹with þis is pvyd

44 ffor the kynge off the brest   Take clarified hony and
may butture of of eithere iiij dragms comyn an vnce Anece
ij vnces licorys iij vnces ꝫ medle þies toged⁾ in mañ of a
lettuary and vse this fastynge for this is a principal medecyn
and pvyd

---

¹ In the MS., these words are underlined in red.

² Womb is constantly used in the sense of abdomen generally,
and the Mother is frequently used in the same sense. It never
occurs in this MS. with the meaning *uterus*.

³ Anise, *Pimpinella anisum*, L., is a species of Burnet Saxifrage
growing in Greece and neighbouring countries. In medieval MSS.
the word is often confused with *Anethum*, Dill.

⁴ This colophon, " and he will be cured," is very common in the
medical MSS.

38 Another for the stomach that cometh of cold or of wind. Use to eat the powder of philipendula (dropwort) and of fennel seed.

39 Ache of stomach that cometh [of cold] or of wind and for colica passio and strangury. Take pellitory and oil of olive, and boil it together ; and, somewhat warm, anoint therewith the stomach and the womb[2] and sides before the fire and with God's help thou shall be whole.

40 Ache of the mother. Seethe two little bundles of anise[3] in wine and make thereof a plaster and lay it about his navel. *Et sanabitur.*[4]

41 Ache of the shoulder-joint. Take five drachms of gall of an ox and a drachm of honey, and seethe them till they are thick ; and anoint the joint that acheth therewith till it be whole. A drachm is the weight of three pennies.

42 Another.[5] Take hempseed and rye, of each a drachm, and parch them in a sherd till they become black, that they may be powdered with verdigris, half a drachm ; temper them with honey as much as sufficeth, till it corrodeth quite well and leaveth the scab. And if it be laid to oft-times successively until such time as the scab cometh away, it healeth right well old cancrous sores and also the cankers themselves if they be new, and malum mortuum[6] and other such. And Henri de Mondeville[7] saith that he found no better medicine among such manner of medicines than this.

43 Another. Mix maruaton (an ointment of fennel-seed) and agrippa (an ointment of thyme) together, with a little aqua vitæ and anoint therewith. This is proved.

44 For the kink[8] of the breast. Take clarified honey and may-butter, of each four drachms, cumin an ounce, anise two ounces, liquorice three ounces ; and mix these together in the manner of an electuary and use this fasting. For this is a principal medicine and proved.

---

[5] This recipe has been misplaced, as it has no relation to the preceding, which is for a rheumatoid complaint.

[6] A virulent ulcer, often called *mormal.* Gangrene is often expressed by this term.

[7] A pupil of Theodoric, and a student of Montpellier, Paris and Bologna. He was one of the foremost surgeons of his day, and wrote a treatise on surgery. He died in 1320.

[8] Kynge, kynke, or chinn, is whooping-cough ; but often used of a hacking or persistent cough.

45 An oþᵒ that is a playsᵗ for a kynge of the brest   Take
wormod malows Roses Brane of Whete and temp ham to
gedᵑ wᵗ white wyne and seith heme togedir and make a
plaisᵗ and lay it hote to the breste pbaᵗ est

46 an oþᵒ   Take comyn and pep ꝫ nitrū in even weght and
as moch of ruw as of all all (sic) thies iij wele sokyd in sharp
vynegre and oft dryed vppon an hote plate of yrene and all
thies stamped togedᵑ ꝫ made vp wᵗ hony thys will hele
þe ach of the brest of the sides and of the mawe and of the
reynes iff it be oft etyne.   And iff be etyn oft it auentisith
colora and makyth neshe wombe and confortith þe stomake
and makyth digestion //

47 Ach of women brests or tetys that ben ranclede   Take
growndsceylly and dayse and wasshe heme and stamp hem
and drynke heme first and last

48 Anoþᵒ   Take senvey and stamp wele in a mortere and
take þᵒto the iij part off crommes of white brede take than
and best þᵒto dry fyges hony and vynegre afᵗ that the ach
axith and ye quantite of the sor sufficith ffor the mor þʷ
bestid in dry fyges and hony þe sharper is the playsᵗ but þe
more brede þʷ bestid jnne and vinegre the wayker and the
more feble is þe playsᵗ Jn all wise Jmonyche and counsell
the that thow sett not lyttell by þis confection ffor I prevyd
it full notable in [fo. 4 verso] many cawsis but neuᵑ the
lesse J will not at þʷ lay it on all sores but late and seldyne
to grete and old sores ⤳

49 An other for akynge of tetis that comyth of to moch
mylke · make powder of hempsede and giff it here in all
hir metys and drynkes

50 Ach of wombe and gowte   Take the Clevyd grasse wild
sauge wild tansay columbyne rede mynts of ech v croppes
and pound hame small in a mortar and temp hem wᵗ stalle
ale and drynke it when ther grevyth the any ach.

---

¹ The purport of this somewhat involved passage is this : the
plaster must be made weaker or stronger in accordance with the
intensity of the pain and the size of the area affected.

45 Another that is a plaster for a kink of the breast. Take wormwood, mallows, roses, bran of wheat, and temper them together with white wine ; and seethe them together, and make a plaster and lay it hot to the breast. *Probatum est.*

46 Another. Take cumin and pepper and nitrum (salt-petre), in even weight, and as much of rue as of all these three, well soaked in sharp vinegar and oft dried upon a hot plate of iron ; and all these stamped together and made up with honey, this will heal the ach of the breast, of the sides and of the maw (stomach) and of the reins (kidneys) if it be oft eaten. And if it be eaten oft, it aventith (relieves) colic, and maketh the womb soft, and comforteth the stomach, and maketh digestion.

47 Ach of women's breasts or teats that are rankled (inflamed). Take groundsel and daisies, and wash them and stamp them ; and drink them first and last (*i.e.* morning and evening).

48 Another. Take senvey (mustard-seed) and stamp well in a mortar, and take thereto the third part of crumbs of white bread ; and baste thereto dry figs, honey and vinegar, according as the ache waxeth and the quantity (extent) of the sore sufficeth. For the more thou basteth in dry figs and honey the sharper is the plaster ; but the more bread thou basteth therein and vinegar, the more feeble is the plaster.[1] In anywise I admonish and counsel thee that thou set not little value on this confection, for I proved it full notably in many cases. But nevertheless I wish not that thou lay it on all sores, but lately (*i.e.* as a last resource), and seldom to great and old sores (*i.e.* extensive and chronic inflammation).

49 Another for aching of teats that cometh of too much milk. Make powder of hempseed and give it her in all her meat and drink.

50 Ache of womb and gout. Take the cleaved grass (cleavers, or goose-grass), wild sage, wild tansey, columbine, red mint, of each five crops ;[2] and pound them small in a mortar, and temper them with stale ale. And drink it when there grieveth thee any ache.

---

[2] A bunch or head of flowers, or the greenery exclusive of the root.

51 Ach of womb of man or of woman that hath etyne venym Take grene ruw and wasshe it and temp it w^t wyne and giff hyme to drynke and he shall be hole

52 An oþ⁹ Take tansay ruw and sothernwode and ete heme with salt

53 An oþ⁹ Take yarowe that is noseblede and stamp and temp hitt w^t gode stale ale and giffe the syke to drynke iij sponfull and aft this take piliall royall and bynd it to the wombe as hote as he may suffre it

54 ffor ach and hardnes of wombe Take a sponefull of the juse of fenell and giff hyme to drynke

55 Ach of wounde that is grene or new Take wormod or okes and lynsede of ich elich moch and bete heme wele togedr and fry heme in fresshe gresse and may butture and lay the plaistir on the wounde and kever it with a wort leffe that the grese touch nat ther to

56 Take the floure of ruw and the juse of smalach and the white of an ey and do to that place

57 An oþ⁹ Take nepte and stamp it and temp it w^t wyne and drynke it off and it shall do away the ach ·

58 Ach off [fo. 6 *recto*] woundes and of strokes sone to cese Take lynsede ꝛ bray it in a mortare and take as moch of wormode as of lynesede wiȝt and seth it in saue wat right wele and then poure out the wat and take out the wormod and do the lynesede in to the wat and seith it right wele till it be ropynge as brid lyme and then do the wormod in a mort and stamp it small and put it in to the lynsede and let heme seth both in fere ꝛ do þ⁹to whete branne and barowes gresse and fry heme toged⁹) and make a plaist ꝛ lay to the brusez hote as he may suffre And iff it be a wound lay a cole leffe betwene that the grese enter nat into the wound and it shall cese sone

59 An other for the same Take the rote of holyoke and seth it till it be tend⁹) and grind it in a mortare and do

51 Ache of womb (stomach) of man or of woman that hath eaten venom (poison). Take green rue and wash it, and temper it with wine, and give him to drink. And he shall be whole.

52 Another. Take tansey, rue and southernwood and eat them with salt.

53 Another. Take yarrow, that is nosebleed, and stamp and temper it with good stale ale, and give the sick to drink three spoonfuls ; and after this, take pennyroyal and bind it to the womb as hot as he may suffer it.

54 For ache and hardness of womb. Take a spoonful of the juice of fennel and give him to drink.

55 Ache of wound that is green or new. Take wormwood or hocks (mallows), and linseed, of each equally much, and beat them well together, and fry them in fresh grease and may-butter. And lay the plaster on the wound, and cover it with a cabbage-leaf that the grease touch not thereto.

56 [Another]. Take the flower of rue and the juice of smallage and the white of an egg, and apply it to the place.

57 Another. Take nept (catmint) and stamp it and temper it with wine and drink it often, and it shall do away the ache.

58 Ache of wounds and of strokes (blows), soon to cease [them]. Take linseed, and bray it in a mortar ; and take as much of wormwood as of linseed [by] weight ; and seethe it in save-water,[1] and take out the wormwood and put the linseed into the water and seethe it right well till it be roping (glutinous) as bird-lime. And then put the wormwood in a mortar and stamp it small, and put it into the linseed and let them both seethe together ; and put thereto wheat bran and barrow's grease, and fry them together and make a plaster, and lay it to the bruises as hot as he may suffer. And if it be a wound, lay a cabbage-leaf between, that the grease enter not into the wound, and it shall cease soon.

59 Another for the same. Take the root of hollyhock and seethe it till it be tender, and grind it in a mortar ; and put

---

[1] Save is a medicament for which prescriptions are given in § 872, and in *Sloane* 2584 (Henslow, *op. cit.*, pp. 55, 126). It is mentioned in Chaucer's *Knightes Tale*, l. 1855.

ther to whete floure and medle it wele toged⁾ and do heme
in to a fryynge panne ꝫ temp heme wele wᵗ oyle of olyue
ꝫ fry heme wele togedir as hote as he may suffre skylfully
ley it ther to

60 An othir make crommes of whete brede that is soure
and do it in a skelett and do ther to white wyne and boyl
heme togedir till thei wax thikke as a plaisꝰ ꝫ alyaes styr
it wᵗ a slyce and lay ꝑ⁹to hoote

61 Ach by the bone and al man⁾ brusozs medecyne ꝑ⁹fore
Take agoode quantitee of wormod ꝫ kitt it on iij or iiij
pties and boile it in the best wyne that you may haue a
galon to a potell and then sett it downe and let it kole and
after it is right colde stire in it ꝫ put ther too a good sawser
fulle of hony and let it boille a littel and put ther in a pese
of new wollen cloth iff thow may haue any till it be thorow
wette and as hote as he may suffir wrappe the sore ther in
and do thus oft and alway hote and he shall be hole by
godds gce.

62 [fo. 6 verso.]   An other take hundisburies of the hegge
ꝫ stamp heme ꝫ take ꝑe juse by it selue and the croppys
of nettillis with the seed dried and small powd⁾ and colvere
dunge powdred ꝫ ꝑporcione euen the jusis ꝫ put ꝑ⁹in of
thies powdres so ꝑat it be nat to thikke and fry hem all
in may buttur or in swynys grese and so hote enoynt the
place that alyth agayne the fire and do this oft and bynd
the substance to the sore place and kepe the jusis and ꝑe
powders ech by them selue till ꝑʷ will vse hem pb est

63 Ach by the bone where so euⁱ⁾ it be Take vnguentū
maratū vnguentū aragon vnguentū dialcia calastuū menge
all to gedre and lay it on the pacient and lay a playstur
ꝑ⁹on of diatastos Ciroijnuū is cured as bene oꝑ⁹ fleumatike
empostymes · but a speciall plaisꝰ ꝑ⁹for is the pleisꝰ of
monpeleres made of rede cole soden wᵗ ꝑe leyʒe off wod
asshen and a lyttell vynegre and a littell salt gronden to
gedir.

---

¹ The names of these unguents are corrupt.   In § 43 the word is
written *maruatum*.
² Diaculum (διαχυλον).   *See* below, § 260.
³ A corruption of the name of Cheiron, the Centaur.

thereto wheat-flour, and mix it well together ; and put them into a frying-pan and temper them well with oil of olive, and fry them well together. As hot as he may suffer, skilfully lay it thereto.

60 Another. Make crumbs of wheat bread that is sour and put it in a skillet (stewpan) and put thereto white wine, and boil them together till they wax as thick as a plaster, and always stir it well with a slice, and lay thereto hot.

61 Ache by the bone, and all manner of bruises. A medicine therefor. Take a good quantity of wormwood and cut it into three or four parts, and boil it in the best wine that you may have, a gallon to a pottle (two quarts) ; and then set it down, and let it cool. And after it is right cold, stir it, and put thereto a good saucerful of honey, and let it boil a little. And put therein a piece of new woollen cloth, if thou may have any, till it be thoroughly wet. And as hot as he may suffer it, wrap the sore therein, and do thus oft and always hot, and he shall be whole by God's grace.

62 Another. Take hound's berries (deadly nightshade) of the hedge, and stamp them ; and take the juice by itself and the crops of nettles, with the seed dried and powdered small, and pigeon's dung powdered. And proportion the juices evenly, and put therein of these powders so that it be not thick ; and fry them all in may-butter or in swine's grease, and so hot, anoint the place that aileth before the fire and do this oft. And bind the substance to the sore place and keep the juices and the powders, each by themselves, till you will use them. *Probatum est.*

63 Ache by the bone wheresoever it be. Take unguentum maratum,[1] unguentum aragon, unguentum dialcia,[2] [unguentum] calastuum, mingle all together and lay it on the patient, and lay a plaster thereon of diatastos ciroiinuum[3] [with which it] is cured as are other phlegmatic apostemes. But a special plaster therefor is the plaster of Montpellier,[4] made of red cole (cabbage), boiled with lye of wood-ash and a little vinegar and a little salt, ground together.

---

[4] The school of medicine of Montpellier was established in the twelfth century, and it became one of the most prominent in Europe.

64 ffor ach of lendis or of reynes   Take betayn and stamp it and take an ey shell ther w^t and a sponfull off hony and grynd ix pep cornes and menge al thies in wyne ꝲ geue þe seke

65 An other for ach of reynes that comyth of hete enoynt the reynes with old oyle or with som cold oyntment ꝲ perce a plate of lede and lay on hys reynys ꝲ the powdre off lede is pphetable mengid w^t the oyle þ^t is to say rede lede or white ceruce

66 Ach of reynes and off the bladder   Take the more planteyne and stamp it and drynke the juse w^t alle pb est

67 Anoþ⁹ stampe lorere levys and seith hem in wyne till hit be as thike as guddes ꝲ then stamp it ꝲ make a pleist and lay it to the reynes

68 Another lat þe reynes be open a . . . .

[here a folio has been cut out, although the page-numbering is continuous.]

69 [folio 7 *recto*] and peritory walwort and wat cressis most of all sauge and jsop and boile all thies in wat and vynegre and when thei be boylid enough sett heme vnd ꞁ amannys lymmys so that thei touch nat þe water and stew heme wele to þai swete

70 **B**Ocches Jff thow will remeve heme oute of the place that thei bene jn   Take wormod and mugworte ꝲ roden and stamp heme and drinke the juse ī littell ale and then take a whike oyst and lay it on that place that þ^w wold drawe þe boch to and þiderward it will draw hyme

71 Anothir for the same   Take an herbe þ^t is called o͞cls xpi and verveyne and make a plaist of heme ꝲ lay it fro þe boyle ij fyngur brede and eft put it as fer further ꝲ do so till it come to þ^t place þ⁹ þ⁻ will breke it

64 For ache of loins or of reins. Take betony and stamp it, and take an egg-shell [full] therewith and a spoonful of honey, and grind nine peppercorns and mingle all these in wine, and give to the sick.

65 Another for ache of reins that cometh of heat.[1] Anoint the reins with old oil or with some cold ointment, and pierce a plate of lead and lay on his reins. And the powder of lead is profitable mixed with the oil, that is to say red lead or white ceruse.

66 Ache of reins and of the bladder. Take the more (greater) plantain and stamp it. And drink the juice with ale. *Probatum est.*

67 Another. Stamp laurel leaves, and seethe them in wine till it be as thick as cud. And then stamp it, and make a plaster, and lay it to the reins.

68 Another. Let the reins be open a . . .

. . . .

69 . . . and pellitory, walwort and water-cresses, most of all sage and hyssop ; and boil all these in water and vinegar, and when they be boiled enough, set them under a man's limbs so that they (the limbs) touch not the water, and steam them well till they sweat.

70 Botches. If thou wilt remove them out of the place that they are in. Take wormwood, and mugwort and rods[2] and stamp them and drink the juice in a little ale ; and then take a quick (live) oyster and lay it on the place to where you wish to draw out the botch. And thitherwards it will draw it.

71 Another for the same. Take a herb that is called oculus christi (clary)[3] and vervain, and make a plaster of them ; and lay it from the boil two finger-breadths, and again put it as far further. And so do till it come to the place where you will break it.

---

[1] This remedy is a duplicate of § 766.
[2] Unidentifiable : perhaps the Macedonian herb called Rodia in *Alphita*, the ῥοδια ῥιζα of Dioscorides, iv, 45.
[3] *Salvia verbenaca*, L.

72 An othir for the same   Take columbyne ꜩ stamp it ꜩ
wasshe it wele with þᵉ Juse ꜩ make a longe strake wᵗ the
same juse thid⁾ as þ�“ wilt that it shall breke ꜩ ther lay a
plaister of the same herbe stampid with the juse and it will
breke it

73 Bocches to rype heme//   Seth otemele in mylke and ley
it ther to in a pleisᵗ as hote as he may suffre it and it shall
ripe onone

74 ffor to breke a boch   Take turmentyne hony and salt
ꜩ tempᵽ hem wᵗ the whit of an ey ꜩ lay it on the boch or
byle and it will breke heme

75 An othir   Take tadstoles and rost heme hote and lay
þᵒto also galbanū and it shall breke the boche anone

76 To rote a boch take syngrene mellelotū lynsede and
myntes and seth heme wele in waᵗ and make a pleysᵗ and
lay to þᵉ suellynge and [fo. 7 verso] it shall sone rote away//

77 An oþᵒ   Take sorell and the white bisualue and the lesse
broke lenke and stamp hem in a mortar and fry hem in
shepis talowe and lay it hote to the byle

78 Anothir take þᵉ rotys of the lylye and smalach and
groundswylly figes plantayne and dayse of ech elich but
most of smalach and boyle hem and quen thei bene boylide
presse outè the water of heme saue of the figes ꜩ then
grynd hem small and then boyle hem in oyle ꜩ old grese
and make þᵒof a playsᵗ and lay on the sore

79 An othir   Take rots of lelys and of hokkes ꜩ also dok
rotis wasshe heme clene and kyt hem small and boyll hem
in waᵗ till thei be nesshe ꜩ take out of the waᵗ and bray
hem in a morᵗ ꜩ take halue as moch of sougre dough ꜩ
stamp it þᵒwith and fry it with swynes grese and as hote
as it may be suffrid lay it on the bocche ffor it shall also
gadrè ꜩ breke it

80 To breke a bocche when it is rype wᵗin forth and the
skyne harde and thyke with owte   Stamp sperworte wᵗ
oyle and lay it on the hede of the bocche

72 Another for the same. Take columbine and stamp it, and wash it well with the juice, and make a long streak with the same juice thither (*i.e.* in the direction) that thou wilt it shall break. And there lay a plaster of the same herb stamped with the juice. And it will break it.

73 Botches to ripen them.[1] Seethe oatmeal in milk and lay it thereto in a plaster as hot as he may suffer it. And it shall ripen anon.

74 For to break a botch. Take tormentil, honey and salt, and temper them with the white of an egg, and lay it on the botch or boil. And it will break it.

75 Another. Take toadstools and roast them hot and lay thereto, also galbanum. And it shall break the botch anon.

76 To rot a botch. Take sengreen (houseleek), melilot, linseed and mint, and seethe them well in water ; and make a plaster and lay to the swelling. And it shall soon rot away.

77 Another. Take sorrel and the white bistort (?) and the lesser brooklime, and stamp them in a mortar ; and fry them in sheep's tallow, and lay it hot to the boil.

78 Another. Take the roots of the lily and smallage and groundsel, figs, plantain and daisies, of each equally much, but most of smallage, and boil them ; and when they are boiled press out the water of them, except of the figs. And then grind them small, and then boil them in oil and old grease, and make thereof a plaster and lay on the sore.

79 Another. Take roots of lilies and of hocks (mallows) and also dock-roots ; wash them clean and cut them small, and boil them in water till they be soft. And take them out of the water, and bray them in a mortar ; and take half as much of sugar [and of] dough, and stamp it therewith, and fry it with swine's grease, and, as hot as he may suffer it, lay it on the botch. For it shall also gather and break it.

80 To break a botch when it is ripe within, and the skin hard and thick without. Stamp spearwort with oil, and lay it on the head of the botch.

---

[1] *I.e.*, to bring them to a head.

81 ffor hote bocches in the begynnynge of ther rysynge make a playst of henbane stampyd and of oyle of rosis and it is gode

82 Anoþ⁹ for hote bocchis take violett and stamp it with hony ꝛ vynegre and make þ⁹of a playster ꝛ enoynt the hede in the begynnynge of hys growynge wᵗ the Juse of violett and then lay on the playster

83 ffor hote bocches to rype heme. Seth draganes levys in oyll and lay hem on the boche pb e͛).

84 An other ffor hotte bocches that be brennynge and for byles medle the poudre of litarge and off ceruce wᵗ waꝛ of Rosis and enoynt heme

85 Also litarge strawed on bocches and on [fo. 8 *recto*] byles wastith the whitoʳ and sowdith the bocche togedyr//

86 An othir for byles pounde the rote of lilce ꝛ ꝁof (*sic*) the holihokke and ground swily · vynegre ꝛ lynsede and an onyon rostyde ꝛ an hede of garlyke rostyde medle all theis to gedir with old swynes grese other with oyle of olyue ꝛ hete it ꝛ make a pleystre and lay to the sore pb e͛)

87 ffor boches on eyen Take less planteyne ꝛ stamp it ꝛ lay it ther to wᵗ soft woll and lat it ly þ⁹ ij days

88 ffor colde bocches make a pleystur of turpentyne and barly mele medlede togedir and lay vpon the boche p̄b · e͛)

89 ffor bonys broken in a mannes hede to draw hem owt Take beteyne verveyne and ruw ꝛ stamp hem toged⁹ in a mortar ꝛ medele þ⁹wᵗ hony and flour of ry and of whete ꝛ þᵉ white of an ey ꝛ make a plaist and lay on þᵉ wound//

90 Anoþ⁹ pownde egromoyne ꝛ make a playst and lay on þᵉ sor// Ether drynke betayn and it will kest vp the bones and hele the wounde

91 Anoþ² Take violet ꝛ stamp it ꝛ temp it wᵗ waꝛ and drynke it ꝛ it will kest owte the broken bone of the hede

81 For hot (*i.e.* inflamed) botches, at the beginning of their rising. Make a plaster of henbane stamped and of oil of roses. And it is good.

82 Another for hot botches. Take violet, and stamp it with honey and vinegar, and make thereof a plaster ; and anoint the head [of the botch] in the beginning of its growing with the juice of violet, and then lay on the plaster.

83 For hot botches, to ripen them. Seethe dragance[1] leaves, and lay them on the botch. *Probatum est.*

84 Another for hot botches that are burning, and for boils. Mix the powder of litharge and of ceruse with water of roses, and anoint them.

85 Also litharge strewed on botches and on boils wasteth the quittor (pus) and knitteth the botch together.

86 Another for boils. Pound the root of lilies and of the hollyhock and groundsel, vinegar and linseed and an onion roasted and a head of garlick roasted, mingle all these together with old swine's grease or with oil of olive. And heat it and make a plaster and lay to the sore. *Probatum est.*

87 For botches on the eyes. Take the lesser plantain and stamp it and lay it thereto with soft wool, and let it lie there two days.

88 For cold botches. Make a plaster of turpentine and barley-meal mingled together, and lay upon the botch. *Probatum est.*

89 For bones broken in a man's head, to draw them out. Take betony, vervain and rue, and stamp them together in a mortar ; and mix therewith honey and flour of rye and of wheat, and the white of an egg. And make a plaster and lay on the wound.

90 Another. Pound agrimony and make a plaster and lay on the sore. Or drink betony and it will cast up the bones and heal the wound.

91 Another. Take violet and stamp it, and temper it with water, and drink it. And it will cast out the broken bone of the head.

---

[1] *Arum dracunculus*, L.

92 Anoþ⁹ take pigle bugle sanicle herb R̄ōbt Auence rede
coole tansay hemp croppis of eũych lych moch and take
of madyr as moch as of all thies oþ⁹ ꝫ do þ⁹to Ambres burnet
and crispe hocke and do heme to thies oþ⁹ herbes beforseid
ꝫ if þ⁹ be abone broken and thou darst serche it giff hym
þis to drynke

93 ffor to make a drynke þ⁹fore take þe reed coole tansey
hemp croppis hors mynt rede nettill brambill croppis and
as moch of madyr as of all this herbis stamp heme toged⁹⟩
in white wyne and giff hym to drynke and it com out at the
[fo. 8 verso] wound then it is a tokyn of deth opynly yþ⁹vyd
And iff it com nat owt ne he kest nat than itt is a tokyne
off lyve than do serch the wound and chaufe þe brokyne
bones sotelly and slely · that þou ne tame the taþ of the
breyne and if it be bled fast wyp hyme softly wᵗ
soft lynnēn cloth   And afterward take soft lynnēn
cloth ꝫ wrape and wymple it toged⁹⟩ and lay it oũ þe
wound and take whete floure wele bustyde and straw on
the clowt that lyeth on the wound full softly · and afterward lat a woman that fedith a knawe childe if it be a man
that is wounditt mylke her papp softly on the floure that is
strawed on the clowt ꝫ afterward lay anoþ⁹ cloute þ⁹ vpon
and straw it with floure as þᵘ didest þᵗ othir and of the
mylke till it be evyn wᵗ þe flesshe and hyll þe hed and latt
it be still till on þe morow then on þe morow vnhill the
hede softly   And iff þᵘ se þ⁹ aboue as it was bloburs lyke
to that þᵗ standith on waẗ when it raynyth then it is signe
of deth   And iff thou se before the taþ as it wer a spynnynge
webb or reede that is tokynge that þe reme of the brayne
is brokyn then this is sygne of hasty deth opynly þ⁹vyd
And if þ⁹ none of thies signes be geven hyme ech day twyse
drynke onys at morow a noþ⁹ tyme at eve this drynke ffor
it makyth broken bonys to com owte ꝫ it clensith þe reme
of the breyne of blode and helith the wound   And iff it
was so broke that hit behovyth to do þ⁹in a pece of masere
lat wele than ronge the broken of the hede as hit is before
sayd and sett þ⁹in a pece of maser and enoynt it with this
oyntement her after ywriten

92 Another. Take pigle (stitchwort), bugle, sanicle, herb-Robert, avens, red cole, tansey, hemp-crops, of each equally much ; and take of madder as much as of all these, and put thereto ambrose (wood-sage), burnet and crisp hock (dried marsh mallow), and add them to these other herbs beforesaid ; and if there be a bone broken and thou darest to search for it, give him this to drink.

93 For to make a drink therefor. Take the red cole, tansey, hemp-crops, horsemint, red nettle, bramble-crops and as much of madder as of all these herbs ; stamp them together in white wine and give him to drink. And [if] it (the bone) come out at the wound, then it is a token of death openly proved ; and if it come not out, nor doth he vomit, then it is a token of life. Then search the wound and chafe it delicately with a linen cloth. And afterwards take a soft linen cloth and wrap and wimple it together, and lay it over the wound ; and take wheat flour well sifted and strew on the cloth that lieth on the wound full softly. And afterwards let a woman that feedith a male child, if it be a man that is wounded, milk her pap softly on the flour that is strewn on the cloth. And afterwards lay another cloth thereupon, and strew it with flour as thou didst the other, and with the milk, till it be even with the flesh. And cover the head and let it be still till the morrow. And on the morrow, uncover the head softly, and if thou seest there above as it were bloburs (like pock-marks), like to those that stand on water when it raineth, then it is a sign of death. And if thou see before the membrane as it were a spinning-web or reed, that is a token that the surface of the brain is broken, then this is a sign of rapid death, openly proved. And if there be none of these signs, let there be given him each day twice to drink, once at morn and another time at eve, this drink ; for it maketh broken bones to come out and it cleanseth the surface of the brain of blood and healeth the wound. And if it were so broken that it becomes needful to put therein a piece of gauze, then let the broken [part] of the head be well treated as aforesaid, and set therein a piece of gauze, and anoint it with the ointment hereafter written.[1]

---

[1] The latter part of the directions is very obscure. *Maser* is perhaps a phonetic spelling of the Latin *macer*, meaning here a piece of thin material, web or gauze.

94 Take pyliall royall piliall mounteyn baynwort ambrose
ribwort bugle celydoyne [fo. 9 *recto*] therfoyle weybrede
morell tansey betayn of each elich moch and stamp heme
wele togedir with swynes grese fresshe ꝛ frankyn encens a
lyttyll hony and virgyne wax and when all thies things bene
wele stampid togedir do hem in a clene basyne or a panne
ꝛ þᵘto white wyne and let it stand all a day and all a nyꝫt
ꝛ on the morow do it to the fire ꝛ seth it wele and gif it good
walme afterwarde do it down and draw it thorow a cloth
ꝛ do it vp ꝛ the while it is ought sore enoynt it þᵘ with and
it shall hele hyme full wele

95 An other ffor broken bones in the hede take ij pͭties of
turpentyne on ptye of wex Rosen halue a party · melt heme
at the fire ꝛ cole hem vpon vynegre and lett it stand as a
day ꝛ malax it wele with vynegre þen melt it eft sonys and
best it vpon the juse of thies erbis beteyne ij pties and
verveyne on parte and malax it longe wᵗ those jusis ꝛ wᵗ
womans mylke ꝛ make an enplayſͭ that is clepid enpleyſͭ
capitall of mayster anselme of jene it drawith whiter ꝛ
reysith vp bones ꝛ encarneth ꝛ helith   And mayſͭ pers
Bonant seyd that he þᵘvyd it in an houndis heed that was
hurt in to the breyne ꝛ hit helid hyme

96 A souͤeyn medecyne is appropid for scalis of bones iff
thei will nat come out by the medecyn aforsayde and
mayster pers vsed it   Take on pty of old oyle and of the
filth of wex that is in hyvys as moch o pty of ensordm̄ the
thrid pyte of astrologia longa and a litill of mylke atemall
and make of all thies an oyntement

97 ffor the hede that is broken and the bone hole   Take an
handfull off hockes ꝛ an handfull of wormod ꝛ an handfull
of mugwort ꝛ stamp [fo. 9 *verso*] hem togedir small ꝛ take
iiij vnces of whete flour ꝛ iij vncˢ of hony and red wyne ·
and take iij vncˢ of ꝫaltis grese · ꝛ stamp al togedirs ꝛ do
hony in a panne and scom it wele ꝛ do ther in thin erbis

94 Take pennyroyal, wild thyme, banewort (wallflower), wood-sage, ribwort, bugle, celandine, trefoil, waybread, morell (nightshade), tansey, betony, of each equally much ; and stamp them well together with fresh swine's grease and frankincense, a little honey and virgin wax. And when all these things have been well stamped together, put them in a clean basin or a pan, and [put] thereto white wine and let it stand all one day and all one night ; and on the morrow put it on the fire and seethe it well, and give it a good warming. Afterwards take it down and draw it through a cloth, and do it up, and as long as it is sore, anoint it therewith. And it shall heal him full well.

95 Another for broken bones in the head. Take two parts of turpentine, one part of wax, of rosin half a part ; melt them at the fire and cool them with vinegar and let it stand for a day, and soften it well with vinegar, then melt it as soon as possible, and baste it with the juice of these herbs : betony, two parts and vervain, one part, and soften it long with those juices and with woman's milk. And make an emplaster that is called the " Capital [Remedy] of Master Anselm of Jena " ; it draweth out pus and raiseth up bones, and maketh flesh and healeth. And Master Peter Bonant[1] said that he proved it in a dog's head that was hurt into the brain and it healed him (the dog).

96 A sovereign medicine that is appropriate for scales (*i.e.* fragments) of bone if they will not come out by [means of] the medicine aforesaid, and Master Peter [Bonant] used it. Take one part of old oil and of the filth of wax that is in hives as much, one part of ensordum, the third part of aristolochia longa and a little milk [and] wild bees' honey[2] and make of all these an ointment.

97 For the head that is broken and the bone whole.[3] Take a handful of hocks (mallows), and a handful of wormwood and a handful of mugwort, and stamp them together small ; and take four ounces of wheat-flour and three ounces of honey, and red wine ; and take three ounces of gelt's grease and stamp all together, and put the honey in a pan and

---

[1] Peter Bonant is mentioned again in §§ 96 and 488.
[2] *Atemall*, perhaps a corruption of *Atticum mel*.
[3] That is to say, a scalp-wound, as opposed to a fracture.

ꝫ make it in a playst̃ ꝫ lay it all warme to þe hede

98 A gude enpleyst̃ for broken bones ꝫ sodeyne gowtes for
styches and sodeyne swellyngis wher so it be · take
chikemete sṁalach groundswilly stamp all thies toged⁀
with shepis talow ꝫ swyns grese ꝫ comyn and boyl all hem
in wyne ꝫ þen do þᵒto wyne dregges and white branne ꝫ
stir it wele togedir ꝫ when thou shalt lay it to the soor hete
it

99 Bolnynge of blode letynge let him drynke hertis tunge.

100 An oþᵒ take groundswylly leke ꝫ chekemete myntes
mugwort rubarb pscly ꝫ stamp hem in a mort̃ ꝫ sithen do
hem oũ the fire wᵗ þe juse till thei be wele medylid togedir
ꝫ aft̃ make a pleyst̃ as hote as the sike may suffre ꝫ lay it
on the sore wᵗ all the juse

101 Bolnyng of brest take þe sede of henbane ꝫ breke it
and seth it in wyne and lay it on the brest hote ꝫ it shall do
away þe bolnynge versus Succus que purgat quos gutte
passio turbat

102 ffor bledyng at the foundment make him worthis of
waybrede ꝫ of sanycle ꝫ ete he þᵒof oft and by goddis
grace he shall staunch

103 ffor the blody flux take ȝarow ꝫ weybrede ꝫ stamp hem
in a mort̃ ꝫ take the juse of hem and fair floure of whete ꝫ
temp hem toged⁀ and make a cake and bake it in assches
ꝫ make þe syke to ete it as hote as he may suffre it pb ẽ

104 An oþᵒ ffor the blody menyson Take myllfoill and
waybrede elich moch of both [fo. 10 *recto*] ꝫ stamp it
toged⁀ and temp it wᵗ wyn or wᵗ alle and giff the sike to
drynke et euen hote at morow colde and he shall be sane

105 An oþᵒ for the blody menyson Take a peny wight ꝫ
(*sic*) towncressed and as moch of pcely sede and grynd hem
in a pep wherne with a littell pep than take small hegge
sloue and seith hem in reyn wat̃ and all ꝫ þen take a littell

---

¹ I have here transcribed *bolnyng* by " bulging " rather than
" swelling " in order to conserve the alphabetical sequence.
² Duplicate of § 117.

skim it well, and put therein thine herbs and make it into a plaster and lay it all warm to the head.

98 A good plaster for broken bones and sudden gouts, for stitches and sudden swellings whereso it be. Take chickweed, smallage, groundsel ; stamp all these together with sheep's tallow and swine's grease and cumin, and boil all them in wine. And then put thereto wine-dregs and wheat-bran, and stir it well together ; and when thou shalt lay it to the sore, heat it.

99 Bulging[1] from blood-letting. Let him drink hart's-tongue.

100 Another. Take groundsell, leeks and chickweed, mint, mugwort, rhubarb, parsley, and stamp them in a mortar, and then put them over the fire with the juice till they be well mingled together, and afterwards make a plaster as hot as the sike may suffer it and lay it on the sore with all the juice.

101 Bulging of breast.[2] Take the seed of henbane and break it, and seethe it in wine ; and lay it on the breast hot, and shall take away the bulging. *Versus succus qui purgat quos guttæ passio turbat.*

102 For bleeding at the fundament. Make him worts (infusions) of waybread and of sanicle, and eat he thereof oft. And by God's grace he shall stanch.

103 For the bloody flux. Take yarrow and waybread and stamp them in a mortar, and take the juice of them and fair flour of wheat and temper them together and make a cake and bake it in ashes and make the sick to eat it as hot as he may suffer it. *Probatum est.*

104 For the bloody menison (dysentery). Take milfoil and waybread a like quantity of both, and stamp it together, and temper it with wine or with ale and give the sick to drink at eve hot and at morn cold. And he shall be sane.

105 Another for the bloody menison. Take a pennyweight of towncress[3] (cress), and as much of parsley seed, and grind them in a pepper-quern (hand-mill) with a little pepper ; then take small hedge-sloes and seethe them in rain-water

---

[3] Written *touncressen, tonkarsyn, tuncrissis,* etc. The herb is common cress, *Lepidium sativum,* L.

of that waͭ that the sloon were sodone in as moch as the
syke may drynke at onys ꝫ put þ⁹in iij peny wiȝt of that
powd⁾ forseid ꝫ lat hym drynke it off and do so thrise ꝫ
iff he shall liffe it is lykly that he sall staunch hyme

106 An othir take myntis plantayn mugwort and crabbes
soden till thei be nesshe ꝫ bray all togedyr in a morͭ ꝫ
temp it with floure of benes or ry or of whete ꝫ put þ⁹to
comyn parchid on the fire and boyll armonyake ꝫ gaulis
broke to powdre ꝫ fry all thies with hony ꝫ a littill vynegre
and playsͭ it vpon a cloth about þe pacient reynes ꝫ wombe
as hote as he may suffre

107 An oþ⁹   Take euͤferne ꝫ seith it in waͭ wele ꝫ lat þe
syke sitt þ⁹ouͤ closid aboute with clothis and after wasshe
his feet þ⁹in but nat aboue the ancles ꝫ as men seyn this
shall stop wond⁾fully

108 An othir take swynes grese fresshe ꝫ þe rote of humbloke
and bray hem togedir and enoynt þ⁹wᵗ the hert of his fete
and the pawmes of his handis ꝫ þis will stop it if he be
curabile

109 Anoþ⁹ take the cammoks rots ꝫ all and seth it in waͭ
and wasshe thi fete þ⁹with to the ancle and take the seid
of touncresses a peny wiȝt and drynke it with rede wyne ꝫ
be hoole

110 Blode fallynge in to a mannys legges   Take myghty
tanwost that is clepid wort bifor it hath be walyd a galon
or a halue after the quantite of þe soor ꝫ clence it and
boyle heme to [fo. 10 verso] gedir and skym hem clene and
then take a lynnen cloth but first wasshe the leggis with
this waͭ as hote as thou may suffre a good while ꝫ then
hote lapp the cloute aboute the legge

111 ffor brennynge or schaldynge   Take the rynde of a
tre that men callen Wich ethir elme schaue of the ouͤ
rynd aboue ꝫ kest it away ꝫ take þe jnner rynd ꝫ seith it
in watͭ ꝫ wasshe the sore þ⁹with ꝫ enoynt it wᵗ popilion or

and ale, and then take a little of that water that the sloes were seethed in, as much as the sick may drink at once, and put therein three pennyweight of that powder aforesaid and let him drink it off and do so thrice. And if he shall live it is likely it shall stanch it (the dysentery).

106 Another. Take mint, plantain, mugwort and crabs (crab-apples) seethed till they be soft ; and bray all together in a mortar, and temper it with flour of beans or rye or of wheat, and put thereto cumin parched on the fire, and bol-ammoniac (a gum-resin) and galls broken to powder. And fry all these with honey and a little vinegar, and plaster it upon a cloth about the patient's reins and womb as hot as he may suffer.

107 Another. Take everfern[1] and seethe it in water well, and let the sick sit thereover closed about with cloths ; and after, wash his feet therein but not above the ankles, and as men say, this shall stop wonderfully.[2]

108 Another. Take swine's grease fresh, and the root of hemlock, and bray them together ; and anoint therewith the soles of his feet and the palms of his hands. And this will stop it if he be curable.

109 Another. Take cammocks (restharrow), roots and all, and seethe it in water ; and wash thy feet therewith to the ankle, and take the seed of cress a penny-weight, and drink it with red wine and be whole.

110 Blood falling into a man's legs.[3] Take strong tan-ooze[4] that is called wort before it hath been welled (boiled) a gallon or a half according to the size of the sore, and cleanse it and boil them together ; and skim them clean, and then take a linen cloth, but first wash the legs with this water as hot as thou mayst suffer a good while, and then wrap the cloth hot about the leg.

111 For burning or scalding. Take the rind of a tree that men call wych or elm ; shave off the outer rind above and cast it away, and take the inner rind and seethe it in water and wash the sore therewith and anoint it with popilion[5]

---

[1] *Filix arboratica.*   [2] *Cf.* § 1033.   [3] Perhaps varicose veins.
[4] The liquor from a tanner's vat.
[5] An ointment made of poplar-buds. *See* § 290.

D

with oþᵒ oyntment Ꝫ ley þᵖto a pece of an hares skyn Ꝫ
sanabit.

112 An other for brennynge Take oyle of olyue þat is
new the quantite of a pynte Ꝫ put þᵖto iij sponefull of
rynnynge wat Ꝫ swynge it fast with a spone as þᵘ wold
swynge cawdell Ꝫ swynge it so longe till it wex white and
hard as grese then enoynt þe sor þᵖwith Ꝫ hill it aboute wᵗ
cole levys Ꝫ then bynd it and helith brennynge or scaldynge
fayrist and best of all medycynes pꝑ eᷱ

113 An other take swete creme a quart an handfull of rotis
of ferne and washe hem and kytt hem on small gobettis
and kest heme in the creme and boyle hem togedir in an
erthyn pot Ꝫ assay it on a knyffe for it will torne to a gely
take it then and kepe it for it pᵖcious for all manᷱ of
brennynge chaufe a littell þᵖof at the fire as þᵘ woldist do
papp Ꝫ do þᵖwᵗ enoynt it till you be hole

114 Anothir take oyle of olyue and white wyne or watᷱ a
littell but of the oyle a goode porcion Ꝫ do hem togedir Ꝫ
tꝟeyle hem togedᷱꝪ with a spone or wᵗ an oþᵒ instrument
till it be thike as enoyntment then enoynt the sore often
tymes wᵗ this oyntment after that þe fire is gadird out wᵗ
strect erthe   And iff so be that eny place whelith Ꝫ will nat
come to wark warde than bray lynseed in a mortᷱ vnto
poudᷱꝪ Ꝫ medle it than in brasse panne wᵗ swete cow mylke
Ꝫ seith [fo. 11 *recto*] it Ꝫ make þᵖof a playster and lay it to
þe whelynge place as hote he may suffre Ꝫ that will souke
oute clene the watᷱ Ꝫ make a skyn þᵖon anoñ pꝑ eᷱ

115 Brestis to purge heme of flewme is to take coliandre
and stepe it in vynegre iij days Ꝫ iij nyȝts Ꝫ then take it
owt Ꝫ dry in þe son and ete first and last

116 An othir for narow of the breste Ꝫ streyte Take herts
tunge violet centory endyve peletre peritory fenell ysop
of each lich moch the rote of psyngall Ꝫ iiij sedes of

or other ointment and lay thereto a piece of a hare's skin. *Et sanabitur.*

112 Another for burning. Take oil of olive that is new the quantity of a pint, and put thereto three spoonfuls of running water and whisk it fast with a spoon as you would whisk caudle, and whisk it so long until it wax white and hard as grease. Then anoint the sore therewith and cover it about with cabbage leaves, and then bind it. And [it] healeth burning or scalding fairest and best of all medicines. *Probatum est.*

113 Another. Take sweet cream a quart, and a handful of roots of fern, and wash them, and cut them into small gobbets, and cast them in the cream and boil them together in an earthen pot. And assay it on a knife, for it will turn to a jelly; take it then and keep it for it is precious for all manner of burning. Chafe a little thereof at the fire as thou wouldest do pap, and anoint therewith till you be whole.

114 Another. Take oil of olive and white wine or water a little, but of the oil a good portion, and put them together and work them up together with a spoon or another instrument till it be thick as ointment; then anoint the sore oftentimes with this ointment, [and] after that the fire (inflammation) is gathered out, with fine earth. And if so be that any place putrifies and will not come to workward (respond to treatment), then bray linseed in a mortar unto powder and mix it then in [a] brass pan with sweet cow's milk, and seethe it; and make thereof a plaster, and lay it to the putrid place as hot as he may suffer. And that will soak out and clean the water and make a skin thereon anon. *Probatum est.*

115 Breasts, to purge them of phlegm, is to take coriander and steep it in vinegar three days and three nights, and then take it out and dry [it] in the sun and eat first and last.

116 Another[1] for narrow (congestion) of the breast and [for] straightness (constriction). Take hartstongue, violet, centaury, endive, pellitory [of Spain],[2] pellitory,[3] fennel,

---

[1] A duplicate of this recipe occurs in H. (Henslow, *op. cit.*, p. 47).
[2] *Anacyclus pyrethrum*, DC.
[3] *Parietaria officinalis*, L.

durytikys a quartion of figges seth all thies togedir in a
galon of well wat̃ till it com till a potell Ꝫ then wrynge vp
thyn erbes into a panne Ꝫ than take iij raw eggis Ꝫ stamp
hem schelles and all Ꝫ keele it wᵗ an easy fyre as thou woldist
clene oþᵍ erbis Ꝫ take it down and let it keele Ꝫ do it into a
vessell and stopp wele the mowth Ꝫ let it stand a nyght
and giff it hym to drynke.

117 ffor bolnynge of the brest Take the seed of henbane
and breke it and seith it in wyne and lay on the brest hote
and it shall do away the bolnynge

118 An othir to purge þᵉ brest take the levys and þᵉ tendre
stokkes of the white horehoune Ꝫ stamp hem fast and þen
take thy botre and seth hem toged⁾ and when it is wele
soden wrynge it thorow a cloth and then lett it kele and
then take the powdre of licores and also the powdre of ysop
and medle hem togedir and kep it in a box, and when thou
will vse it take a sponefull and temp it with hote wyne
and vse it when thow goste to bed

119 Anothir take a good quantite of ysop and seith it in a
potell of good wyne till halve be soden away and lat the
[fo. 11 *verso*] Syke vse it first and last at even hote at morow
cold pb ẽ⁾//

120 An oþᵍ for the brest Take the whit horehowne a good
quantite Ꝫ groundeswely a lasse q̄ntite and walwort the
lest quantitee Ꝫ seth hem with fresshe bores grese Ꝫ temp
hem wele togedir Ꝫ make a pleyst̃ and lay abowt the brest
of þᵉ syke in on nyȝt it doth away moch Ꝫ makyth hym
kest owt corrupcion and it is good also for the coughe

121 An oþᵍ for to purge the brest Ꝫ for the rewme Take
clarified hony Ꝫ may botre of ether iiij dragmes · comyn
on vnce Anyse ij vnce licores iij vnces · Ꝫ medle thies
toged⁾ and vse this fastynge for this is a pᵍncipal medecyn
pb ẽ.

---

¹ An unidentified plant.
² *I.e.*, till it evaporates to the measure of a pottle (2 quarts).

hyssop, of each a like quantity ; the root of persingale and four seeds of duritics,[1] a quarton of figs ; seethe all these together in a gallon of well-water till it come to a pottle[2] and then wring up thy herbs into a pan ; and then take three raw eggs and stamp them, shells and all, and cool[3] it with an easy fire, as thou wouldest clean other herbs ; and take it down and let it cool, and put it into a vessel and stop well the mouth (of the vessel). and let it stand a night, and give it him to drink.

117 For bulging of the breast.[4] Take the seed of henbane and break it, and seethe it in wine and lay it on the breast hot. And it shall take away the bulging.

118 Another to purge the breast. Take the leaves and the tender shoots of the white horehound, and stamp them fast ; and then take thy butter, and seethe them together, and when it is well sodden, wring it through a cloth. And then let it cool, and then take the powder of liquorice and also the powder of hyssop, and mingle them together, and keep it in a box. And when thou wilt use it, take a spoonful and temper it with hot wine. And use it when thou goest to bed.

119 Another. Take a good quantity of hyssop and seethe it in a pottle of good wyne till half be boiled away, and let the sick use it first and last, at even hot, at morn cold. *Probatum est.*

120 Another for the breast. Take the white horehound, a good quantity ; of groundsel, a lesser quantity ; of walwort, the least quantity ; and seethe them with fresh boar's grease and temper them well together and make a plaster and lay it about the breast of the sick. In one night it doth away much, and maketh him cast out corruption, and it is good also for the cough.

121 Another for to purge the breast and for the rheum. Take clarified honey and may-butter of each four drachms, cumin one ounce, anise two ounces, liquorice three ounces, and mix these together and use this fasting, for this is a principal medicine. *Probatum est.*

---

[3] *Sic,* " warm " is required by the context. The Henslow duplicate has " do hit a lytel ou) þe fuyre."

[4] Duplicate of § 101.

122 An oþ⁹ for the brest and for to clarifye the pypis Take an handfull of dried ysop ꝫ as moch of the rote of helenacampana ꝫ nat fully so moche of licorysse browsed ꝫ boyle heme in a galone of rennynge waꝉ into halue ꝫ þen streyne it thorow a cloth ꝫ put þ⁹to halue a pynt of clarified hony and drynke þ⁹of first and last ꝫ sanabitur

123 who so haue euell at the brest take rwe and ambrose of eyther lich moch ꝫ stamp hem ꝫ temp hem wᵗ white wyne and giff the syke to drynke fastynge oft

124 An other take ysop and sugur of ether lych moch of licorise and horehowne of eyther elich moch and seth heme wele in waꝉ togedir till the thre pties bene soden in ꝫ giff the syke to drynke at even hote at morow cold

125 ffor the bak that akyth ꝫ is syke and euel at ease Take egmoyn and mogwort both the levys and rots ꝫ stamp hem ī old swynes gresse ꝫ put aysell þ⁹to and lay it to þᵉ bake

126 An oþ⁹ Take peliall riall ꝫ stamp it ꝫ do rosen ꝫ aysell þ⁹to [fo. 12 *recto*] ꝫ oyle of olyue ꝫ do it in a cloute and bynd yᵗ to þᵉ bak

127 Also Anoþ⁹ take smalach Egromoyne ꝫ mowseere both þᵉ leves and the rotis ꝫ stamp hem wele wᵗ bores grese and aysell and do to þᵉ bakk

128 ffor bytynge of an hownd rost garlyke onyons of ech lich moch and stamp hem wᵗ hony ꝫ make enoyntment þ⁹of ꝫ lay on the bytynge ꝫ a pleyst of sothen malews ther vpon

129 An othir make a pıayst of waybrede and wᵗ the whit of an ey ꝫ lay þ⁹to and it will draw owt the venym and hele þᵉ hole

130 An oþ⁹ take town cresses ꝫ piliall riall and seith it in water and giff hym to drynke ꝫ ley of the houndis her þ⁹to if þ~ may haue it

---

¹ The name of this plant, of which there are endless variations of spelling, is corrupted from *enula campana*. The elecampane is the *Inula helenum* of botanists. It is also called scabwort and horseheal.

122 Another for the breast and to clear the pipes, (bronchial tubes, etc.). Take a handful of dried hyssop and as much of the root of elecampane[1] and not quite so much of liquorice bruised, and boil them in a gallon of running water into half. And then strain it through a cloth and put thereto half a pint of clarified honey and drink thereof first and last. *Et sanabitur*.

123 Whoso have evil at the breast. Take rue and ambrose (wood-sage) of each equally much, and stamp them and temper them with white wine, and give the sick to drink fasting, oft.

124 Another. Take hyssop and sugar of each equally much, of liquorice and horehound of each equally much, and seethe them well in water together till the three parts been sodden in.[2] And give the sick to drink at even hot, at morn cold.

125 For the back that acheth and is sick and ill at ease. Take agrimony and mugwort, both the leaves and roots, and stamp them in old swine's grease, and put vinegar thereto, and lay it to the back.

126 Another. Take pennyroyal and stamp it and put rosin and vinegar thereto, and oil of olive, and put it in a cloth, and bind it to the back.

127 Also another. Take smallage, agrimony and mouse-ear, both the leaves and the roots, and stamp them well with boar's grease and vinegar, and lay it to the back.

128 For biting of a dog. Roast garlic [and] onions, of each equally much, and stamp them with honey; and make an ointment thereof, and lay on the bite, and a plaster of sodden (boiled) mallows thereupon.

129 Another. Make a plaster of waybread and the white of an egg, and lay thereto. And it will draw out the venom and heal thee whole.

130 Another. Take cress and pennyroyal and seethe it in water, and give him to drink. And lay of the dog's hair thereto if thou mayest have it.[3]

---

[2] *I.e.* till three-quarters of the mass have been absorbed, and one-quarter has evaporated.

[3] *Cf.* the well-known expression, " A hair from the tail of the dog that bit you."

131 Bytynge of an eddyr grynd centory and botre and gif the syke to drynke ⁊ it will help both man and best

132 An oþ⁹ pound grene ruw and fenell and seth togedir wᵗ botre ⁊ gif hym to drynk

133 An oþ⁹ stamp garlike and lay vpon þᵉ sore and for houndis bitynge take hony ther with and garlyke distroieth venym wᵗ in fore

134 An oþ⁹ for bytynge take detayne ⁊ medle it wᵗ juse of myntis and drynke it and þen make a pleyster and lay vpon þᵉ bytynge

135 An oþ⁹ enoynt þᵉ place wᵗ the juse of peletre and it shall voyd away and vse peletre in the saws ⁊ it shall suffre no venyme with in the (sic) and the juse of smerwort doth the same if it be dronken

136 ffor bytynge of a spither take flies and rub well þᵉ place

137 An oþ⁹ for bytynge and styngynge of any venymous worme   Take an handfull of dragance and half an handfull of centory and halue so moch of ruw and ij cloves of garlyke ⁊ stamp heme small ⁊ wrynge owt the jusse and enoynt the place þat is venymed ⁊ it shall distroy the venym and if thou drynke the [fo. 12 verso] waᵗ of all thies stillid and menged with a littell triacle it wil distroy venym with in

138 ffor hym þat is blastid of vnkynd eyere to do away þᵉ ach and aswage the swellynge   Take an ey and rost is (sic) it harde and do away the yolks and take þᵉ whit ⁊ do it in a brasen mortar and do þ⁹to a quartion of an vnce of copose ⁊ grynd hem wele togedir þat it be as small as oyntment and enoynt þ⁹with the seke face ⁊ that shall cese þᵉ ach ⁊ do away the swellynge for it is kynd þ⁹fore And afterward when it is almost hole enoynt þᵉ syke wᵗ a lyttel popilion for that wil make the skyn soft and easy

139 To breke a sore tete or eny other sore wᵗ an hede Take sourdingh that is clepid bebyn ⁊ the white row of a rede herynge and honey and stamp all yfere ⁊ make a playsᵗ and lay to a sore wᵗ an hede anone

---

¹ " Drink " is clearly an error for " eat."
² " Worm'' is used of any creeping thing, whether reptile, insect or otherwise.

131 Biting of an adder. Grind centaury and butter and give the sick to drink[1] and it will help both man and beast.

132 Another. Pound green rue and fennel and seethe together with butter, and give him to drink.

133 Another. Stamp garlic and lay upon the sore, and for dog's bite take honey therewith. And garlic destroyeth venom from within.

134 Another for biting. Take dittany and mingle it with the juice of mint and drink it. And then make a plaster and lay upon the bite.

135 Another. Anoint the place with the juice of pellitory and it shall void away. And use pellitory in the sores, and it shall suffer no venom within. And the juice of smearwort doth the same if it be drank.

136 For biting of a spider. Take flies and rub well the place.

137 Another for biting and stinging of any venomous worm.[2] Take an handful of dragance and half a handful of centaury and half so much of rue, and two cloves of garlic; and stamp them small and wring out the juice, and anoint the place that is venomed, and it shall destroy the venom. And if thou drinkest the water of all these distilled and mixed with a little treacle, it will destroy venom within.

138 For him that is blasted of unkind air,[3] to do away the ache and assuage the swelling. Take an egg and roast it hard and take away the yolk and take the white, and put it in a brazen mortar and put thereto a quarter of an ounce of copperas and grind them well together that it be as small as ointment, and anoint therewith the sick face, and that shall cease the ache and take away the swelling, for it is kind therefor (*i.e.* appropriate). And afterward when it is almost whole, anoint the sick with a little popilion and that will make the skin soft and easy.

139 To break a sore tetter or any other sore with a head. Take sourdingh that is called beban,[4] and the white roe of a red herring and honey, and stamp all these and make a plaster to lay to a sore with a head anon.

---

[3] A vague expression used for frost-bite, chaps, neuralgia, and many other maladies.

[4] An Arabic drink, made of coagulated sour milk.

140 Brusurs or wennes to hele heme   Take gode figes
and bray hem ryght small till the kernellis be also broke
and then stamp as moch of bores grese ꝫ halff so moch of
yolkys of eyien ꝫ ley þᵒof a pleisͭ to þᵉ sore and it will
breke it and then hele it

141 An othir take drestes of ale and whete branne broke
lempe shepis tallow blake woll and ground swylle ꝫ brisswort
ꝫ hors dunge ꝫ stamp all in a morͭ ꝫ make a pleysͭ ther of
and bynd þᵉ playster to þᵉ sore and be hole.

142 Jff a man be broken he must be wele bounden vpon a
bord and ly so ix days ꝫ ete laxe mete and nat wyndy
neyᵍ right moch ꝫ drynke ech day twyse osmond comfery
and daysye by eueñ porcioñs and grounden and tempeᵭ
wᵗ good stale ale and clene streyned ᴥ ᴥ [fo. 13 recto.]

143 IN the monyth of Jannū) ffastynge white   Ianniᵍ
wyne is goode to drynke and blode to forbere
for vij days of pell bene þerynne þe first the
secund the ferth and þᵉ vᵗʰ and the xᵗʰ the
xv ꝫ xixᵗʰ

144 IN þᵉ monyth of ffeū)yer ete no potage   ffeū)yer
made of hokkes for they bene venyme And on
the hand worst on the vayne on the thowmb lett
the blode two dayes bene of pyll the vj and
the vij and the viij is natt ryght goode and
hote metis vse.

145 IN monyth of march ffyges and Raseyns   March
and oþᵍ swete mets and let the nat blode on
the ry3t arme for ech mañ) of feuer of that
3er.

146 IN the monyth of aprile on the xjᵗʰ day   Aprill
let þᵉ blode on the left arme and that 3ere
shall be nat lese his sight   And in þᵉ iijᵉ day
of aprill lett the blode and that 3ere shall thou

---

¹ Of this corrupt passage there is a parallel, with many variants,
in H., where it is attributed to Galen. (Henslow, op. cit., p. 63.)
See also a passage in the Anglo-Saxon MS., Royal, 12, D, xvii, fo. 55

140 Bruises or wens, to heal them. Take good figs and bray them right small till the kernels be also broken, and then stamp as much of boar's grease and half so much of the yolks of eggs, and lay thereof a plaster to the sore. And it will break it and then heal it.

141 Another. Take dregs of ale and wheat-bran, brook-lime, sheep's tallow, black wool and groundsel and bruisewort and horse-dung, and stamp all in a mortar; and make a plaster thereof, and bind the plaster to the sore, and be whole.

142 Iff a man be broken he must be well bound upon a board and lie so nine days, and eat lax meat and not windy, neither right much, and drink each day twice osmund (a fern), comfrey and daisy by even portions, and ground and tempered with good stale ale and clean strained.

143 In the month of January white wine is   January.[1]
good to drink and blood-letting to forebear.
For seven days of peril are therein : the first,
the second, the fourth, and the 5th and the
10th, the 15th and 19th.

144 In the month of February, eat no pottage   February.
made of hocks (mallows), for they are venomous. And on the hand-wrist [and] on the vein
of the thumb let the blood. Two days are of
peril, the 6th and the 7th ; and the eighth is
not right good. Hot meats use.

145 In the month of March, [use] figs and   March.
raisins and other sweet meats. And let thee not
blood on the right arm for each manner of fever
of that year. [*There be four days of peril, the
10th, the 12th, the 16th and the 18th day.*][2]

146 In the month of April, on the 11th day,   April.
let blood on the left arm, and that year he
shall not lose his sight. And the 3rd day of
April, let thee blood, and that year shalt thou
not have ache of the head. Fresh flesh and

(O. Cockayne, *Leechdoms*, Vol. ii, p. 147). As to the *Dies Nefastæ*, see Introduction, and below, §§ 1073, 1074.

[2] In this and the following sections, the words between asterisks have been restored to the text from the Henslow duplicate.

haue non ach of hede ffresshe flesshe and hoote mete vse

147 IN the monyth of may erly arise and erly ete and drynke ⁊ slepe nat at noone hoote metys vse ete nat the hede ne þe fete of no beste for her brayne wastith and here marye cō (*sic*) consumyth ⁊ all lyuynge thynge feyntith and febleth in this monyth ffoure dayes þꝰ bene of pell the vij xv and þe xx and let the blode in the ende of may on the thrid day ⁊ on the v day or the last day on wheþꝰ arme þ͡u wilt and þ͡u shall be sane from all yuelis that ȝere. May

148 IN the monyth of Jvnne eu͛y day a drawght of wat͛ is good to drynke fastynge ale and mete in mesur ete and drynke and ete letuse and sawge ⁊ for grete nede blede þ͡u maist [fo. 13 *verso*] vij days bene of greet pell þꝰin. Juny

149 IN the monyth of July hod the fro wymmen for thi brayne begynnyth to gedir his humo͛s and latt the natt blode two days there bene of pill the xv and the xix day July

150 IN the monyth of august wortes off hokkes ne of cawles ete thou nat ne blode latt the nat ij days ther bene of perell the xix and the xx day August

151 IN the monyth of Septēbꝛ all froyte ripe is goode to ete and blode is gode to late ffor who so lattith hym blode on the xvij day for the dropsy ne for the frenesy ne the fallynge euyll that ȝere he shall nat haue no dowte Septēbꝛ

152 IN the monyth of october must that nyw wyne is good to drynke and blode for nede to late ⁊ on day þt is of pill ⁊ that is the syxt day Octobꝛ

hot meat use. [*There be two days of peril, the 6th and the 11th.*]

147 In the month of May early arise and   May.
early eat and drink ; and sleep not at noon.
Use hot meats. Eat not the head nor the feet
of any beast, for her brain wasteth and her
marrow consumeth, and all living things
become faint and feeble in this month. There
be four days of peril, the 7th, 15th and the
20th.[1] And let thee blood in the end of May,
on the 3rd day and on the 5th day or [on] the
last day, whichever arm thou wilt. And thou
shall be safe from all evils that year.

148 In the month of June, every day a   June.
draught of water is good to drink fasting.
Ale and meat in [moderate] measure eat and
drink, and eat lettuce and sage. And for
great need [only] mayest thou bleed. Seven
days be of great peril therein [*for blood to
let*].

149 In the month of July, hold thee from   July.
women, for thy brain beginneth to gather its
humors. And let thee not blood. Two days
there be of peril, the 15th and the 19th day.

150 In the month of August neither mallow-   August.
plants nor cabbages eat thee not, nor let thee
blood. Two days there be of peril, the 19th
and the 20th.

151 In the month of September, all fruit that   September.
is ripe is good to eat, and blood is good to let.
For whoso letteth him blood on the 17th day
for the drospy, neither the frenzy nor the
falling-evil that year he shall have, no doubt.

152 In the month of October must, that [is]   October.
new wine, is good to drink, and blood for need
to let, and one day that is of peril, and that is
the sixth day.

---

[1] Only *three* days are here specified. The Henslow duplicate
adds the 16th.

153 IN the monyth of nouembre com þᵘ in no   Nouēb₂↙
bath for then is the blode gederynge gode is
on thi hede veyne ventuse a lyttill for garsynge
and ventusynge is then gode to vse for than
ben all the humós prest and whikk two days
ther bene of pill the xv and xx day

154 IN the monyth of decēbre hote metis vse   Decēb₂↙
and blode for nede þᵘ mayst latt thre days of
pyll ther bene the xv xvj ꝸ xviij day fforbere
then cold worts for þei bene venemôᶘ and
malencoliôᶘ and who so thys lyue lode holdith
of his hele he may be sekyr //

155 But one thynge J werne the vse nat to blede moch for
thies eveles com þᵖoff the Inward it makyth cold ꝸ it
makytt the hete fayll and þe yelow chyll comyth ther of
and it feblyth moch the breyn ꝸ makyth handis moch to
whake and gowtis many com þeroff   And ther of commyth
narownes abowte the hert and evell in the hede ꝸ many
other evylles but blode lattynge ī mesure it clerith thi
thought it closith thi bladder it tēpith þ breyn [fo. 14 recto]
it amendith thyn heerynge it streyngth teres it closith thy
maw it defieth thi mete it clerith thy voyce it sharpith the
witt it easith thi wombe it gedirith thy slepe it drawyth
away angwysshe it norisshith goode blode wykkyd blode
dystroyeth and lenghtith thy lyve.

156 Chardecoynes that is gode for the stomake is thus
     made take a quart of clarified hony and ij vnces
of powdᶘ of pepyr and medle hem togedre and þen take
xx gwyncis and x wardons and payr hem and take owte
the kernellys wᵗ the cores and seith hem in clene wort till
thei be tendyr and then stamp heme in a morᶍ as small
as thow mayst ꝸ then streyne heme thorow a streynyȯ ꝸ
that that will not well thorow put in agayn ꝸ stamp it oft
and oft dryve it thorow a cloth or streynyȯ and iff it be to
dry putt in halue a sawser full or alyttill more for to gett
oute the other þe bettyr ꝸ then put it to the hony and sett

---

¹ The Henslow duplicate gives the 15th and the 19th.
² The duplicate has the 15th and 18th.

153 In the month of November come thou   November.
into no bath, for then is the blood gathering
good (well) in thy head-vein. Ventose a
little ; for garcing (lancing) and ventosing
(cupping) are then good to use, for then be all
the humors pressed (active) and quick. Two
days there be of peril, the 15th and 20th day.[1]

154 In the month of December, hot meats   December.
use, and blood for need thou mayest let.
Three days of peril there be, the 15th, 16th
and 18th day.[2] Forebear then cold worts
for they be venonous and melancholic.
Whoso this regimen (" life-lead ") holdeth,
of his health he may be secure.

155 But one thing I warn thee : use not to bleed much,
for these evils come thereof (*i.e.* from excessive blood-
letting). The inward it maketh cold, and it maketh the
heat fail ; and the yellow chyle cometh thereof and it
enfebleth much the brain, and maketh hands much to
quake, and gouts many come thereof. And thereof cometh
narrowness about the heart and evil in the head, and many
other evils. But blood-letting in measure, it cleareth thy
thought and closeth thy bladder and tempereth thy brain.
It amendeth thine hearing, it restraineth tears, it closeth
thy maw, it defieth[3] thy meat, it cleareth thy voice, it
sharpeth the wit, it easeth thy womb, it gathereth thy
sleep, it draweth away anguish, it nourisheth good blood,
wicked blood destroyeth and lengtheneth thy life.

156 Chardecoynes[4] that is good for the stomach is thus
made. Take a quart of clarified honey and two
ounces of pepper and mingle them together ; and then
take twenty quinces and ten wardens (pears), and pare
them and take out the kernels with the cores, and seethe
them in clean wort till they be tender ; and then stamp
them in a mortar as small as thou mayest, and then strain
them through a strainer. And that which will not pour
through, put in again and stamp it oft ; and oft drive it
through a cloth or strainer, and if it be too dry, put in
half a saucerful or a little more, for to get out the other

---

[3] Obsolete word for *digest.*
[4] *Char (chair) de quince,* quince-pulp.

it on the fyre ⁊ make it to seth wele ⁊ stir fast with a grete
staffe ⁊ iff ther be ij styrreres it is the bettyr for bot if it
be [not] strongly stired it well syet to the vessell ⁊ then it
is lost and seith it till it sothen thik and then take it down
of the fyre and when it is wele nygh cold put in a q̃rt of an
vnce of gynger ⁊ as moch of galyngall and as moch of
canell powdrede and medle hem wele togedre wᵗ a slyce
⁊ then latt it kele and put it in a box thys mañ of makynge
is good and if it þus made it will be blak if thow wilt make
more at onys take more of echon aftur þᵉ pporcions as
moch as the lust

157 An oþ⁹ mañ of makynge and is betᵗ then the firste
ffor to put ij pties of hony and thre pties of sugre and þen
shall this be betᵗ than the oþ⁹ ⁊ in all oþ⁹ thyngis [fo. 14
verso] do as thow did before for thow mayst wele enough
seth thi qwynces in water and it is gode enough though
thow put no wort þ⁹to and iff you wilt þᵚ mayst make it
with owt wardons but it is the bettir with wardons

158 The iij mañ off makynge is this ⁊ is the best of all and
that is for to take sugre and whynces elich moch by weght
and none hony ne perys ⁊ in all oþ⁹ thyngis do as thow
dydist befor and this shall be whitter ant þat oþ⁹ in as moch
as the suger is whitt shall be chardecoyns be

159 Confeccions take a q̃rᵗ of clarified hony ⁊ melt it on
the fyre and skynne it ffayre and loke that thy fyre be
easy and soft for ellys it will wax blake and seth it till it
will be harde and thus shall thow preve itt drop a dropp
upon a cold platyr and anone it will be hard and when it
will do so than straw in a pownd of the floure of ryse lyttell
and littell till it be so thyke þᵗ þᵚ may nat stire it and then
let it kele and when it is colde grynd it to a powd⁹ and
straw þ⁹in other good powders what þᵚ wilt and straw than
all this powder on a fair smoth boord · then make thow
batre of bene floure and of wort · than take the seed of
coliandre or of Annes or anete the which is clepid dyll
chose of thies iij which þᵚ wilt and put in to þᵉ batre what
wight of the seed þat þᵉ lust and than lay it on the borde wᵗ
the powdre afore seid and roll the seede upon the powdre

the better. And then put it to the honey, and set it on the fire, and make it to seethe well, and stir fast with a great staff, and if there be two stirrers, it is the better for both ; if it be [not] strongly stirred, it will stick to the vessel and then it is lost ; and seethe it till it [is] sodden thick. And then take it down from the fire, and when it is well-nigh cold, put in a quarter of an ounce of ginger and as much of galingale and as much of canell (cinnamon) powdered and mingle them well together with a slice ; and then let it cool and put it in a box. This manner of making is good, and if it [is] thus made, it will be black. If thou wilt make more at once, take more of each after the proportions as much as the last.

157 Another manner of making, and [it] is better than the first ; that is to put two parts of honey and three parts of sugar, and then shall this be better than the other. And in all other things, do as thou didst before, for thou mayst well enough seethe thy quinces in water, and it is good enough, though thou puttest no wort thereto ; and if you wilt, thou mayest make it without wardens, but it is the better with wardens.

158 The third manner of making is this, and is the best of all. And that is for to take sugar and quinces, the like amount by weight, and no honey nor pears ; and in all other things do as thou didst before ; and this shall be whiter than that, inasmuch as the sugar being white, so also shall the quince-pulp be.

159 Confections. Take a quart of clarified honey and melt it on the fire, and skim it fair ; and look that thy fire be easy and soft (gentle), or else it will wax black ; and seethe it till it be hard, and thus shalt thou prove it : drop a drop upon a cold platter and anon it will be hard. And when it will do so, then strew in a pound of rye, little by little, till it be so thick that you may not stir it ; and then let it cool, and when it is cold, grind it to a powder, and strew therein [such] other good powders as thou wilt. And strew then all this powder on a fair smooth board. Then make thou batter of bean flour and of wort ; then take the seed of coriander or of anise or [of] anethe, the which is called dill ; choose of these three which thou wilt, and put into the batter what weight of the seed that thou likest ; and then lay it on the board with the powder aforesaid. And roll

E

wᵗ thyn hand vnd꙯ a pawmer till it be round and as of þᵉ
gretnes of pesyn or more as thou wilt heme And this
confeccion is full goode and a prcious thynge for flewm and
for the brest

160 A confeccion ffor the ffeuers Take centory an handfull
of the roote [fo. 15 *recto*] and of the levys of the erthbete
an hanfull of the rote off cloce an handfull of ambrose an
handfull ꝛ make powdyre of heme and than medle hony
þ⁹with and make þ⁹off balles the gretnes of halue a walnot
and giff the syke ech day one of heme fastynge and serue
hyme ix dayes for this is goode confeccion for the fevers
and for the modir of the rysynge at the hert

161 A goode confeccion that is clepid peletis of antioch
take halue a handfull of mowser a handfull of auence and
iij handfull of madyr and stamp hem togedir and do þ⁹to
hony and make þ⁹of balles and dry hem and giff hym ech
day on of hem to drynke in stale ale or in white wyne and
iff thies iij herbis be stilled it is clepid a drynke of antioch

162 Collica paffio. Take Annyce and ȝet it in white
vynegre iij days and iij nyȝts than haue oute the vynegre
ꝛ make powdre of the annece and drynke. it or ete it or
ellys sit in a ffatt of hote waᵗ vp to the navyll · or ellys
take a reede onyone and haue owt þᵉ core and fill it wᵗ
ffresshe gresse and iff it is of a man take barowes grese ꝛ
i f it be a womã take barowes grese and rost it in the fyre
and lay a cloth apon þᵉ navyll and it ouoward as hote as
þᵘ may suffre it

163 An other take rubarb scamony ꝛ mastyke elich moch
and pound heme toged꙯ and make powd꙯ of heme and
take þ⁹of a peny wyght and put it in yolke of an ey and
supp it vpp

164 An oþ⁹ take a quantite of centory as moch as sawge
and as moch of stammarch and as moch of tansey and viij
or ix hedis of garlyke and put hem in to A quantitee of water
and seth it into the haluendele and then dryue it thorow

---

¹ Duplicate of § 746. A confection so named is described in
Harl. 2378 and *Sloane* 2584 (Henslow, *op. cit.*, pp. 77, 128). *Cf.* also
§ 893.

the seed upon the powder with thine hand under a palmer (rolling-pin) till it be round, and as of the size of peas, or more, as thou wilt them. And this confection is full good for phlegm and for the breast.

160 A confection for the fevers. Take centaury a handful ; of the root and of the leaves of the earthbeet (beet-root), a handful ; of the root of cloves a handful ; of ambrose (wood-sage), a handful ; and make powder of them and then mix honey therewith, and make thereof balls of the greatness of half a walnut. And give the sick each day one of them fasting, and serve him nine days. For this is a good confection for the fevers and for the mother and for the rising at the heart (flatulence).

161 A good confection that is called pelotus of Antioch.[1] Take half a handful of mouse-ear, a handful of avens, and three handfuls of madder ; and stamp them together, and put thereto honey ; and make thereof balls, and dry them ; and give him each day one of them to drink in stale ale or in white wine ; and if these three herbs be distilled, it is called a drink of Antioch.

·162 Collica Passio. Take anise, and set it in white vinegar three days and three nights ; then have out the vinegar, and make powder of the anise and drink it or eat it. Or else sit in a vat of hot water up to the navel. Or else take a red onion and have out the core, and fill it with fresh grease. And if it is a man, take barrow's grease, and if it be a woman take sow's[2] grease, and roast it in the fire, and lay a cloth upon the navel, with it (the grease) outward[3] as hot as thou mayest suffer it.

163 Another. Take rhubarb, scammony and mastic, of each equally much, and pound them together ; and make a powder of them, and take thereof a pennyweight in put it in the yolk of an egg, and sip it up.

164 Another. Take a quantity of centaury, as much of sage and as much of stanmarch ; and take as much of tansey, and eight or nine heads of garlic ; and put them into a quantity of water, and seethe it to a half its bulk ;

---

[2] The text has barrow's grease again, in error.
[3] *I.e.* smear the grease on the outside of the cloth.

a cloth and put þᵒto powdꝛ of pepir ꝫ hony [fo. 15 *verso*]
a lyttill and kepe it as longe as thow wilt ꝫ drynke þᵒof
first and laste //

165 An othir take comyne and anyce and stepe heme in
wynegre a day and a nyȝt and dry if aftir in the wynd or
in the sonne and schred þᵒ amonge gynger and licoresse
and ete þᵒof a gud porcion first and last

166 Drynke the juse of brokelemp wᵗ warme ale And he
shall be sane

167 ffor the same take a q̃rẗ of an vnc̃ of skimony halue
an vnce of fresshe botre and j of gall and boyle this till thei
wex thyke as papp and þen take a q̃rt off an vnc̃ of gira
pigra galicua and make of thies a pleysẗ and lay it to the
wombe beneth the navell till he do to prevey ꝫ take it then
awat pᵬ ẽ

168 ffor the same a man shuld drynke his awn vryne all
warme and he shall be sane

169 ffor the same seth small bundellys of mynt in wyne and
pleysẗ hem on hys schare and on his reynes

170 An oþᵒ seth horehown in wyne and oyle and make a
pleysẗ þᵒof ꝫ lay apȯn hys schare.

171 An oþᵒ seth auance in salt waẗ and in oyle and pleisẗ
both behind and bifore and drynke the wyne that auance
is sethen in for it is good to do away ach of the stomake
þat comyth of wynd or of colde ꝫ ach of the guttis and it
makyth a gode digestion

172 A Suppository for the Colyke Take a bladder and put
þᵒin ij sponfull of hony and bynd the mowth of the bladder
to an holow pype of elleme to þᵉ on ende and lat the pype
be as longe as a fyngre and put in hote waẗ till it be lewke
and þen put the pype wele in to þᵉ fundement and thrist
then owt all that is in the bleddꝛ in to the body And he
shall sone haue A seege

173 [fo. 16 *recto*] ffor actua passio[1] Take fyne aqua vite a
pynte and a q̃rt of narvall right wele medled togedꝛ and
enoynt the place at grevyth agayn an hote fyre oft and

---

[1] In the MS. these words are underlined in red.

and then drain it through a cloth, and put thereto powder of pepper, and honey a little ; and keep it as long as thou wilt, and drink thereof first and last.

165 Another. Take cumin and anise, and steep them in vinegar a day and a night ; and dry it after in the wind or in the sun ; and shred thereamong ginger and liquorice ; and eat thereof a good portion first and last.

166 [Another]. Drink the juice of brooklime with warm ale, and he shall be sane.

167 For the same. Take a quarter of an ounce of scammony, half an ounce of fresh butter, and one [ounce] of gall, and boil these till they wax thick as pap ; and then take a quarter of an ounce of gira pigra galicula, and make of these a plaster, and lay it to the womb beneath the navel, till he go to the privy, and then take it away. *Probatum est.*

168 For the same. A man should drink his own urine all warm, and he shall be sane.

169 For the same. Seethe small bundles of mint in wine, and plaster them on his pubes and on his reins.

170 Another. Seethe horehound in wine and oil and make a plaster thereof and lay upon his pubes.

171 Another. Seethe avens in salt water and in oil, and plaster both behind and before ; and drink the wine that the avens was seethed in, for it is good to do away ache of the stomach that cometh of wind or of cold, and ache of the guts, and it maketh a good digestion.

172 A suppository for the colic. Take a bladder and put therein two spoonfuls of honey ; and bind the mouth of the bladder to a hollow tube of elm at the one end ; and let the pipe be as long as a finger, and put it in hot water till it be luke[warm] ; and then put the pipe well into the fundament, and thrust then out all that is in the bladder into the body. And he shall soon have a motion.

173 For actua passio. Take fine aqua vitæ a pint, and a quart of nerval[2] right well mingled together, and anoint the place that grieveth near a hot fire, often ; and then make a

---

[2] A lotion for treating the muscles and nerves.

then make a playster of oxiaccoccion and lay it on continually and he shall be hoole þb est

174 An oþ⁹ take rw and seith in waᵗ and the iiij part vynegre and drynke it for it doth away the disease in þe ribbis þᵗ is clepid actua passio and it distroyethe also the passion that fallith in þe whorle bone and the root of helena campana soden and pleystred ther to will do the same

175 An othir Seth centory in water till it be tendir and bath wele the hipp and the thigh ther with and frote oft the sore place wele agayn the fyre and with in a few dayes he shall be hole

176 An othir ffor þe same seth þe rotis malews and the levys in whit wyne or in waᵗ till thai be nesshe and thike as papp and then lat the waᵗ renne thorow a cloth and of that þat abidith in þe cloth nat streyned pleistre it a brode and lay to the sore place and when it is colde remeve it and lay to an oþ⁹ of the same ꓶ it will take away þe ach with in xij howres

177 ffor cornes in amannes ffete[1] take vnslekkyd lyme and make small powdre ther of and a quantitee of blake sope and medle hem togedir so þat it be som dele harde and payre of the cornes to the whike and ley þ⁹on of this salue ꓶ the brede of the corne and no bredd⁷ for no thynge and it shall frete hyme owt and then take a lyttil oyle of the yolke of an eye and hony but most of oyle and medle heme togedre ꓶ lay þ⁹on ꓶ it shall gedir owte the corne and hele it vp with salue

178 ffor the colorye in the stomake[1]   Take a [fo. 16 verso] greyne of aloes with hony and it clensith the stomake and makyth hyme wele to defye but aloes and mastike shold be stampid and so dyne with whit wyne and so giffen to þe syke. //

179 ffor costyfnes   Take hony and clarify it till it wax hard ꓶ make longe small pelettis and when it is cold put it in his foundment and vse yt iij days ꓶ þen take aloes that is a manꝰ of gwine ꓶ then take the flowres of borage and

---

[1] In the MS. these words are in red.

plaster of oxycroceum[2] and lay it on continually, and he shall be whole. *Probatum est.*

174 Another. Take rue and seethe [it] in water, and the fourth part vinegar, and drink it; for it doth away the disease in the ribs that is called actua passio, and it destroyeth also the passion that falleth in the whorl-bone (hip). And the root of elecampane, sodden and plastered thereto, will do the same.

175 Another. Seethe centaury in water till it be tender, and bathe well the hip and the thigh therewith and rub oft the sore place well by the fire, and within a few days he shall be whole.

176 Another for the same. Seethe the roots [of] mallows and the leaves in white wine or in water until they be soft and thick as pap; and then let the water run through a cloth, and of that which abideth in the cloth, not strained, plaster it abroad (*i.e.* spread it out), and lay it to the sore place; and when it is cold remove it, and lay to another of the same. And it will take away the ache within twelve hours.

177 For corns in a man's feet. Take unslaked lime and make small powder thereof, and a quantity of black soap, and mix them together so that it be somewhat hard; and pare off the corns to the quick, and lay thereon of this salve, to the breadth of the corn, and no broader on any account, and it shall fret them out. And then take a little oil of the yolk of an egg and honey, but most of oil, and mix them together and lay thereon; and it shall gather out the corn. And [then] heal it up with salve.

178 For choler in the stomach. Take a grain of aloes with honey, and it cleanseth the stomach and maketh him well to digest; but aloes and mastic should be stamped, and so done with white wine, and so given to the sick.

179 For Costiveness. Take honey and clarify it till it wax hard, and make long small pellets; and when it is cold, put it in his fundament and use it three days. And then take aloes, that is a manner (kind) of drug, and then take

---

[2] *See* note to § 288.

breke the aloes and ete it w^t clarified hony and with the
flowres as moch as aboue

180 An othire take turmentill a gode quantite and spigernell
and mowsere and v levys of deteyne and scabiouse ꝫ brust-
warte and a grete quantite of mence and seth in wat̅ and
clarfied hony in a new erthen pot and when it is wele boylid
let it kele and hill it clene and drynke ther of first and
last

181 A bath for the same   Take fenell and sauge ꝫ fynit̅
and brustwort and malowes and make a bath twyse or thries
and take of auenes a good bundell and bynd it and put it
in the drynke (*sic*)

182 An othir ffor the same   Take a walnot shall and put
it full of fresshe gresse and bynd it to thi navyll pb est

183 Anoþ⁹   Take fferne that growyth vnd'̅ asshe and
wasshe it wele and take a ffat henne and seth heme wele in
ffayre wat̅ till it be wele Soden and after that stamp heme
wele toged'̅ and wryng thorow a lynnen cloth and drynke
it w^t the broth or ellys take the rote of ferne that growith
on an oke and schred it small and do it in wyne and let it
it aluyȝt by þ⁹jn and on morow drynke it erlich

184 An othir ffor the same   Take sayme and sope and
the floure of whete and the Juse of þe rote [folio 17 *recto*]
off walwort and seth heme togedyr and make a pleyst̅ and
ley on the wombe and he shall haue a sege anoon

185 Anothir ffor þ⁹ same make powd'̅ of laureall and
tempre it w^t as moch hony and vse itt pb est

186 Anothir ffor the same   Take malowes and marcury
and seth heme with a pece of porke and make þ⁹off potage
and lett hym ete þ⁹off wele and lett hym drynke þ⁹with
whyte wyne and this shall help hyme

187 An othir take a mese off porke enterlarde and boyl
it wele it wele (*sic*) in watir and then take off the broth vp
in a disshe and let it kele till it be mylke warme and then
take a quantitee of m̅cury a quantitee of violett a quantite

the flowers of borage, and break the aloes, and eat it with clarified honey and with the flowers, as much as above.

180 Another.   Take tormentil a good quantity, and mouse-ear, and five leaves of dittany and scabious and bruisewort,[1] and a great quantity of mint, and seethe in water and clarified honey in a new earthen pot ; and when it is well boiled, let it cool, and cover it clean (*i.e.* skim it clean), and drink thereof first and last.

181 A bath for the same.   Take fennel and sage and fumitory and bruisewort and mallows, and make a bath twice or thrice.   And take of avens a good bundle and bind it and put it in the drink (*sic*).

182 Another for the same.   Take a walnut-shell and fill it full of fresh grease and bind it to thy navel.   *Probatum est.*

183 Another.   Take fern that groweth under ash-trees, and wash it well ; and take a fat hen, and seethe them well in fair water till it be well sodden ; and after that stamp them well together, and wring through a linen cloth and drink it with the broth.   Or else take the root of fern that groweth on an oak, and shred it small, and put it in wine, and let it lightly lie therein ; and on the morrow drink it early.

184 Another for the same.   Take seam (lard) and soap and the flour of wheat and the juice of the root of walwort, and seethe them together and make a plaster and lay on the womb, and he shall have a motion anon.

185 Another for the same.   Make powder of laurel and temper it with as much honey, and use it.   *Probatum est.*

186 Another for the same.[2]   Take mallows and mercury and seethe them with a piece of pork and make thereof pottage, and let him eat thereof well, and let him drink therewith white wine, and this shall help him.

187 Another   Take a mess of pork-lard, and boil it well in water, and then take off the broth into a dish, and let it cool till it be milk-warm ; and then take a quantity of mercury a quantity of violet, a quantity of borage, a

---

[1] This name is applied to many different herbs, including Comfrey, Daisy and Soapwort.

[2] Duplicates, *Sloane* 521 (Henslow, *op. cit.*, p. 135) and D, § 14.

of borage a quantitee of auence of ech lich moch and make
ther of wortis with the forseid porke and ete broth and
þᵒof a q̃ntite in medle of youre etynge take a quantitee of
stale ale and medle it with þᵉ forseid broth in the disshe and
drynke it in the medle of the potage and vse oft this and
he shall be hole

188 Anoþᵒ   Take a pype of pewtre as grete as a spyndell
end and do þat on end of that pype in a bleddir full of oyle
and that oþᵒ end in his fundement and hold it ther as
longe as the syke may suffre and it shall draw owt the
foule breth and humores

189 An oþᵒ   Take walwort and stamp.it and take the woos
and do þᵒto hony and ete it

190 ffor the pilous coughe   Take sawge rw comyn and pepir
and seith hem togedir with hony and ete þᵒoff eũ)y day at
morow a sponefull at evyn an oþer

191 ffor the dry cough · Take horehounde and camfrey and
ete wᵗ hony thre [folio 17 *verso*] morowes and iij eves

192 who so haue the cough of colde wasshe his fete eũ)y
eve with hote watir and then sett hys fete soles agayne
þᵉ fyre and then take garlyke and a lyttell off horehown
and stamp hem togedir and enoynt the feete vnder the
soles agayne the ffyre at evyne when thow goste to bedde

193 ffor the cough off glett take a dysshefull off vynegre
and boȳle it wele and skymme it weele and put it in a vyall
and soup ther off at eve and morowe

194 An other ffor the cough off fflewme   Take a pownd of
fygges and a q̃rtrou) off a pound off licoresse and an handfull
of ysopp ꝫ stamp hem all togedir and seth it fro a galon
water to a potell and then giff it þᵉ syke oft tyme ffor it is
a principall medecyne and if thou haue ther to anyce and
clarified hony so moch the better with a littell vynegre
but loke that thow skome it wele

195 The cough of rewme in a mannes longes. take origanū
ysop and þᵉ rote of Elena campana of ech a goode quantitee
and seth heme in waꝷ and bray heme wele and seith heme

quantity of avens, of each equally much, and make thereof wort with the aforesaid pork, and eat broth and thereof a quantity ; in the midst of your eating (*i.e.* meal) take a quantity of stale ale and mix it with the aforesaid broth in the dish, and drink it in the midst of the pottage, and use oft this, and he shall be whole.

188 Another.   Take a pipe of pewter as great as a spindle, and put the one end of that pipe in a bladder full of oil, and the other end in his fundament, and hold it there as long as the sick may suffer it, and it shall draw out the foul breath (flatus) and humors.

189 Another.   Take. walwort and stamp it and take the juice and put thereto honey, and eat it.

190 For the parlous (perilous, or persistent) cough.[1]   Take sage, rue, cumin and pepper and seethe them together with honey and eat thereof every day at morn a spoonful, at even, another.

191 For the dry cough.   Take horehound and comfrey, and eat [it] with honey three mornings and three evenings.

192 Whoso have the cough of cold, [let him] wash his feet every eve with hot water, and then set his foot-soles before the fire ; and then take garlic and a little of horehound, and stamp them together and anoint the feet under the soles before the fire at evening when thou goest to bed.

193 For the gleet (ichorous cough).   Take a dishful of vinegar and boil it well and put it in a vial, and sip thereof at eve and at morn.

194 Another for the cough of phlegm.   Take a pound of figs and a quarter of a pound of liquorice and a handful of hyssop ; and stamp them all together, and seethe it from a gallon [of] water to a pottle (two quarts) ; and then give it the sick oftimes, for it is a principal medicine.   And if thou put thereto of anise and clarified honey, so much the better with a little vinegar, but look that thou skim it well.

195 The cough of rheum in a man's lungs.   Take origanum,[2] hyssop and the root of elecampane, of each a good quantity ; and seethe them in water and bray them well ; and seethe

---

[1] Duplicates, D, § 11 ; *Harl.* 2378 (Henslow, *op. cit.*, p. 101).
[2] A variety of *Mentha pulegium*, L., Pennyroyal.

longe in the same water and the streyn it and thenne do
therto halue a pound of anneys and seth it Agayn till it
be thike and then take it ffro the fire and a qrtron of a
pound of gynger and halphe a pynte of hony clarifiede and
an vnce off powder off gete this is a pryncipall lectuary for
the rewme and for the cowgh

196 Anoþ⁹ ffor the cough·ffor the brest for rotchynge for
byles and for sores in the syde for the myst and for the
stomake   Take horshelme groundswylly ysop and centory ·
smalach rwe hilwort piliall of ech lich moch and do ther to
peꝑ and hony and ete þ⁹off at morow [folio 18 *recto*] and at
eve

197 Anothir ffor the dry same   Take a garlike hede and rost
it at the fire then take away the pyllynge and ete it with
goode purid hony

198 Anoþ⁹ take the watir off the juse of horehown and
medle it with diapenidion and ete þ⁹off first and last and
make a pleystre of peritory friede with boture and fresshe
gresse and bynd to the sooles of the feete all hote and the
cough shall cesse and the hede ach also

199 ffor the dry cough.   Take anete smalach seede of ech
lich moch and make powdir of thies and temp with wyne
and seth heme wele till thei begynne to wex thyke and
afterward kep it in a box or in an oþ⁹ clene vessell and vse
it first and last ꝑb est

200 An othir ffor the colde coughe take whit horehown a
good quantitee and growndswylly a lasse quantitee and seth
hem with waꝶ and fresshe bores gresse and aftur temper
hem wele togedir and make a pleyꞩ and lay about the
brest ꝫ i on nyȝt it doth away moch and makyth hyme
to kest out moch corrupcion

201 An othir ffor the same Drynke the juse of lekys wᵗ
wymens mylke ꝫ sanabitʳ for the juse of lekys is a full
goode medecyn

202 A lectuary for the cough and for the fever in the
stomake ꝫ hedeach   Take the juse of horehowne and of

them long in the same water, and then strain it.   And then put thereto half a pound of anise, and seethe it again till it be thick ; and then take it from the fire and [put thereto] a quarter of a pound of ginger and half a pint of clarified honey, and an ounce of powder of jet.   This is a principal electuary for the rheum and for the cough.

196 Another for the cough, for the breast, for retching, for bile, and for sores in the side, for debility[1] and for the stomach.   Take elecampane,[2] groundsel, hyssop, and centaury, smallage, rue, hillwort, wild-thyme, of each equally much , and put thereto pepper and honey, and eat thereof at morn and at eve.

197 Another for the dry same.   Take a garlic head and roast it at the fire, then take away the skin, and eat it with good purified honey.

198 Another.   Take the water of the juice of horehound, and mix it with diapenidion[3] and eat thereof first and last. And make a plaster of pellitory fried with butter and fresh grease, and bind to the soles of the feet all hot ; and the cough shall cease and the headache also.

199 For the dry cough.   Take anete (dill), smallage seed, of each equally much ; and make powder of these and temper with wine, and seethe them well till they begin to wax thick ; and afterwards keep it in a box or in another clean vessel, and use it first and last. *Probatum est.*

200 Another for the cold cough.   Take white horehound a good quantity, and groundsel a less quantity, and seethe them with water and fresh boar's grease.   And afterwards temper them well together and make a plaster and lay about the breast ; and in one night, it doth away much, and maketh him cast out much corruption (phlegm).

201 Another for the same.   Drink the juice of leeks with woman's milk, *et sanabitur.*   For the juice of leeks is a full good medicine.

202 An electuary for the cough and for the fever in the stomach, and headache.   Take the juice of horehound and

---

[1] *Myst, cf.* § 971.
[2] *Horshelne* is another name for elecampane (*cf.* note to § 122), horseheal, or scabwort.   *Cf.* also D, § 12.
[3] A sweet-stuff twisted into a string-like form, for coughs.

fethirfoyle of centory and of horsmynt of betayne rote
and of ffenell and boile al þies togedir with some powdre of
pepir and loke thow haue lich moch off the joycis and of
clarified hony as moch as of all þᵒ and seith it till it be
somwhat harde and euᷓ stir it ffast neuᷓ havynge to grete
a fyre and when it [is] colde kep it in boxis and ete ther of

203 To make A corasife or a generitife for a mormal [fo. 18
verso] that is clepid powdir sotill take vj peny wight of raw
alyme and xij peny wight of snayles howses though the
snayl be þᵍin it is neuᷓ the wors and brenne heme on a tyle
stone and then grynd the alyme and the snayles howses
small in a morᵗ and then fyll the hole of the mormall of
that powdir and so serue hyme ych day till it haue fretide
away the dede flesshe but at ech tyme wash it with aqua
vite and when the dede flesshe is away then dry the sore
with a soft lynen cloth rollyd vnder thyne hande and straw
powdre sotill then þerjnne the sore and ley the pleystir
colman or diaclū malaxid with oile of rosis and roll the legge
wele and remeve it twyes a day at eve and at morowe and
this will hele A mormall hastely and kepe it fro dede flesshe
and wild flesshe

204 An othir ffor the Same[1] ꝫ for oþᵍ sores that is clepid
puluis sine pare ffirst take alome and do it on a rede
glowynge tele stone and do fyre about it and let it liḡḡ þᵍ
till it haue left his boylynge and be white and than that
alom calcyned and then take a lyttill erthyn pott and ffill
it halff full off vitriall and sett þat pott negh an hote fyre
wele stopped and turne hym and wend hyme and after
that sett the pott amyd the fire till it be glowynge rede and
then do hyme fro the fyre and then is that vitriall rubified
and then take xij peny wight of that vitriall rubified and
of orpement añ and xij peny wight of vertgresse and xxiiij
peny wight of alom calcened and then grynd ech of hem

---

    [1] In the MS. these words are underlined in red.
    [2] Febrifugium ; *Pyrethrum parthenium*, L.   The word is cor-
rupted in an endless variety of ways, including febrifu, fetherfoy,
featherfew, fethirfoyle, featherfowl. etc.
    [3] Corruption for *mortuum malum*, an inflamed, or ulcerated, sore ;
also used of gangrene.

of feverfew,[2] of centaury and of horsemint, of betony root and of fennel ; and boil all these together with some powder of pepper, and look that thou hast equally much of the juices, and of clarified honey as much as of all those ; and seethe it till it be somewhat hard, and ever stir it fast, never having too great a fire. And when it is cold, keep it in boxes and eat thereof.

203 To make a corrosive or a generative (regenerative) for a mormal,[3] that is called subtle powder (pulvis subtilis). Take six pennyweight of raw alum and twelve pennyweight of snail's houses (snail-shells), though the snail be therein it is never the worse, and burn them on a tile-stone ; and then grind the alum and the snail-shells small in a mortar, and then fill the hole (sinus) of the mormal with that powder ; and so serve him each day till it [shall] have fretted away the dead flesh, but each time wash it with aqua vitæ. And when the dead flesh is away, then dry the sore with a soft linen cloth rolled under thine hand ; and strew pulvis subtilis then into the sore, and lay the plaster colman[4] or diaculum,[5] softened with oil of roses ; and roll the leg well, and remove it (the dressing) twice a day, at eve and at morn. And this will help a mormal speedily, and keep it [free] from dead flesh and wild (inflamed) flesh.

204 Another for the same, and for other sores, that is called pulvis sine pare. First take alum, and put it on a red (red-hot) glowing tile-stone, and put fire about it, and let it lie there till it have left its boiling (i.e. till it has ceased bubbling) and be[comes] white, and then it [is] alum calcined. And then take a little earthen pot and fill it half full of vitriol, and set that pot nigh a hot fire, well stopped, and turn it about, and after that set the pot in the midst of the fire till it be glowing red ; and then take it from the fire, and then is that vitriol rubified. And then take twelve pennyweight of that rubified vitriol, and of orpement[6] another [twelve dwt.] and twelve pennyweight of verdigris, and twenty-four pennyweight of alum calcined ;

---

[4] Perhaps a corruption of *colmenier*, " heartsease."
[5] A medicament of butter, oil and litharge. *See* § 260, and note thereon.
[6] *Aurum pigmentum*, yellow arsenic.

[fo. 19 *recto*] by hem selff on a molare stone and then medle heme al togedyr and then it is clepid a powdir puluis sine pare · and than ley of that powdir ther in on a mormall but first wasshe þe mormall with aqua vite or with waᵗ of rosis and then dry þe soor with a soft lynnen cloth rollyd in thyne handis and this powdre and aqua vite will do away dede flesshe and make yonge flesshe to wax but thow must ligg trete ouwarde the cloute that keuere the brynkes of the mormall ffor fretynge of the whyke flesshe ꝯ than aboue thi poudre diaclum malaxid and when the dede flessh is away lay colman þ⁹on and wasshe it at ech tyme with ãq vite and dry it as it is afore seyde and strew þ⁹on powdre sotil and eũ roll the legg wele when thọu hast layde on this pleisᵗ Aqua vite is clenser and a helar and suffreth no filth about it

205 A good corrosay to opyne a wound take Alyme calcyned and sañddewere vertgresse and hony and medle hem all togedre and lay þ⁹of on the soore

206 ffor ffestresse a corrosay Take alome that is clepid stobwort or wodesoure a gode quantyteé ꝯ lapp hem in doke levys and rost it and lay it to a sore that is rankeled pᵬ est

207 An othir brenne hen bones and ey shellys and after grynd heme small and make powdre and kest ther the dede flesshe is

208 An othir take a quarte of hony or an halue and halue a quarte of white vynegre and halue a quart of rybwort juys and boile hem to gedir till it be all wastide to the quantitee of the hony and lay it to þe sore and it will frete and also hele at the best pᵬatum est

209 [fo. 19 *verso*] Cramp Take an erbe that grovith on the rote of brome geneste a goode handfull anoþ⁹ off lorec levys an oþ⁹ of lawrall a quart of white wyn and a quart of oyle olyue and boyll itt togedir till the wyne be wastid and clens itt and kepe itt wele for itt is full goode for the cramp iff it be enoynted þ⁹with

---

[1] It has been necessary to paraphrase the latter part of this paragraph owing to its involved construction.

[2] Saline matter obtained from the vitrification of glass.

and then grind each of them by itself on a millstone, and then mix them all together ; and then it is called pulvis sine pare. And then lay of that powder on a mormal, but first wash the mormal with aqua vitæ or with water of roses ; and then dry the sore with a soft linen cloth, rolled in thy hands ; and this powder and aqua vitæ will do away dead flesh, and make young (new) flesh to grow. But you must lay the medicament on the outside of the cloth that covers the edges of the mormal to avoid fretting the quick (live, healthy) flesh, and then above that, thy softened powder diaculum. And when the dead flesh is away, lay colman thereon and wash it at each time with aqua vitæ, and dry it as aforesaid, and strew thereon pulvis subtilis, and ever roll (bandage) the leg well when thou hast laid on this plaster. Aqua vitæ is [a] cleanser and a healer and suffereth no filth (pus) about it.[1]

205 A good corrosive to open a wound. Take alum calcined and sandiver,[2] verdigris and honey ; and mix them all together, and lay thereof on the sore.

206 For festering, a corrosive. Take alum, [and the herb] that is called stubwort or wood-sorrel, a good quantity, and wrap them in dock-leaves ; and roast it, and lay it to a sore that is rankled. *Probatum est.*

207 Another. Burn hen-bones and eggshells, and afterwards grind them small, and make powder, and cast [it] where the dead flesh is.

208 Another. Take a quart of honey or a half, and half a quart of white vinegar, and half a quart of ribwort juice ; and boil them together till it be all wasted (evaporated) to the quantity of the honey ; and lay it to the sore. And it will fret and also heal at the best. *Probatum est.*

209 Cramp. Take a herb that groweth on the root of broom genesta[3] a good handful, another of laurel-leaves, another of laureola (spurge-laurel), a quart of white wine, and a quart of oil of olive ; and boil it together till the wine be wasted ; and cleanse it, and keep it well, for it is full good for the cramp, if it be anointed therewith.

---

[3] The parasitic plant *Orobanche major*, the greater broom-rape, which is commonly found growing on the roots of broom (*Genista*).

210 Stampe Ruw and menge it with fresshe butture and
kepe it so in a vessell ix dayes wele keuᵓyd and then boyle
it and skymme it wele and þen do ther to whill it is hote
encence powdrede and stir it wele and make enoyntment to
enoynt ther with.

211 ffor cankyr in the mowth take alomglasse twey pties
and the iij part of vertgresse powdir heme wele and temp
heme wele with hony in manᵓ of a pleystir and lay it to þe
sore

212 An oþ⁹ Take loueach and anyse and stamp hem
togedir and seth hame wele in wyne and giff hym to drynke
as hoote as he may and anoon he shall kest all the poyson
and the venyme

213 ffor the cancre in the pappis   Take colver dunge hony
vyrgyn wex floure of barly and of benes and lynsede and
seth hem in vynegre or wyne and put ther to rammes talgw
and make in manᵓ of a pleystir and lay ther on

214 ffor to sle the cancre   Stampe rede onyons and lay
þ⁹on and itt shall sle it

215 An othir for the same make watir of therfoill that is
the hony sowke off the hegge it sleth the cankyr in the
mouth and on the hand ꝛ in all othir places of the body

216 An othir ffor the cancre in þe mouth   Take powdre
of coperose and put it in a vessell with water and lat it stand
so a nyght and a day and than still itt in a stillatorye and
then kep it in a glasen vessell ffor it is goode

217 Also for noli me tangere¹ and in the visagge and [folio 20
recto] the webb in the eye and for dede flesshe in woundis
or oþ⁹ sores //

218 An oþ⁹ for the same Medle the powdir of celydoyne
rote with the powdir of dry rosis in vinegre and seth heme
till it thike as mustard ꝛ þen anoynt þe þ⁹ wᵗ

---

¹ In the MS. these words are underlined in red.
² Trefoil is the name usually applied to clover, a totally different
plant from honeysuckle.

210 [Another]. Stamp rue and mix it with fresh butter. and keep it so in a vessel nine days well covered; and then boil it and skim it well; and then put thereto, while is hot, powdered incense and stir it well; and make ointment to anoint therewith.

211 For canker in the mouth. Take alumglass (crystallized alum), two parts, and the third part of verdigris; powder them well and temper them well with honey in the manner of a plaster, and lay it to the sore.

212 Another. Take lovage and anise, and stamp them together; and seethe them well in wine, and give him to drink as hot as he may [suffer it]; and anon he shall cast [out] all the poison and the venom.

213 For canker in the paps. Take pigeon's dung, honey, virgin wax, flour of barley and of beans, and linseed; and seethe them in vinegar or wine, and put thereto ram's tallow; and make [it] in the manner of a plaster, and lay · thereon.

214 For to slay the canker. Stamp red onions and lay thereon, and it shall slay it.

215 Another for the same. Make water of trefoil, that is the honeysuckle of the hedge.[2] It slayeth the canker in the mouth, and on the hand, and in all other places of the body.

216 Another for the canker in the mouth. Take powder of copperas, and put it in a vessel with water; and let it stand so a night and a day, and then distill it in a stillatory (still); and then keep it in a glass vessel, for it is good.

217 Also for noli-me-tangere[3] in the visage, and the web in the eye, and for dead flesh in wounds or other sores.

218 Another for the same. Mix the powder of celandine root with the powder of dry roses in vinegar, and seethe them till it be thick as mustard; and then anoint thee therewith.

---

[3] " Touch-me-not," the name given to *lupus exedens*. *Cf.* §§ 630 and 943. Perhaps § 217 is really a continuation of § 216 ;· but it is divided by a paragraph-mark, and begins with a capital letter, and the first five words are underlined in red.

219 An othir take v⁹tgresse arnement brymstone and brandekele of ech lich moch and meng to gedir and make powdir and straw þ⁹on and iff it be a man than wasshe it wᵗ pisse of a man child that is a clene mayde and then strew the powdir on the cankyr and wasshe ech day the sore or thow do the powdir ther on till till (*sic*) the cankyr be dede and whan the wound is washe dry it with tow or do þ⁹on thi powdir and the cankyr shall dry

220 Take juyse of smalach and a littell hony and sayme and do itt togedir in a panne and do it to boyle a littyll with a littell fyre and do therto a littell whete mele till it be thike as grewell ꝺ then do itt fro the fire and then take clene flex wᵗ out schybes and hake it small and straw on þᵉ kankyre and then lay the pleystir þ⁹on and do so ech day to þou be hole

221 Anothir take arnement pep and brymston and stamp all to powdir and take of ech one lich moch be wyght and do þ⁹to aysell and make it hoote and do it in the cankyr

222 To kest out blode of a wond that bledith inward[1]   Take the juys of nept and drynke it and it shall kest owte the blode

223 ffor kestynge or brakynge that cometh of febilnes of the Stomake[1] · seth the ryndes of asshe in vynegre and wete a sponge ther in and lay on the stomake

224 ffor kestynge that comyth of colde   Ete myntis that be soden with [fo. 20 *verso*] wᵗ flesshe

225 An othir for kestynge or womet.   Take mowser ꝺ bray it wele with a littell Anneys and comyn pchid on the fire and wrynge oute þᵉ juse of this and seth it a littill with hony to make it swete and giff the syke a lyttill ther off aftyr hys mete

226 ffor the cardiacle   Take borage and still it and drynke it contynually ffor his vertu is to engendir good blode and to make a man lyght and mery and ruddy of

---

[1] In the MS. these words are underlined in red.
[2] From *atramentum*, the black powder used for making ink.
[3] That is to say, a boy who has not reached puberty.   A young boy played an important part in ancient Egyptian and other magical

219 Another. Take verdigris, arnement,[2] brimstone and cinders, of each equally much, and mix together, and make powder and strew thereon ; and if it be a man, then wash it with the urine of a man-child that is a pure maid ;[3] and then strew the powder on the canker, and wash each day the sore before thou put the powder thereon, till the canker be dead ; and when the wound is washed, dry it with tow, or put thereon thy powder, and the canker shall dry.

220 [Another]. Take juice of smallage and a little honey, and seam (lard), and put it together in a pan ; and let it boil a little with a gentle fire, and put thereto a little wheat meal, till it be thick as gruel ; and then take it from the fire, and then take clean flax without scutch,[4] and hack it small, and strew on the canker ; and then lay the plaster thereon. And do so each day till you be whole.

221 Another. Take arnement, pepper and brimstone, and stamp all to powder ; and take of each one a like quantity by weight, and put thereto vinegar ; and make it hot, and put it in the canker.

222 To cast out blood from a wound that bleeds inwardly. Take the juice of nept (catmint) and drink it, and it shall cast out the blood.

223 For casting or breaking (vomiting) that cometh of feebleness of the stomach. Seethe the rinds of ash-trees in vinegar ; and wet a sponge therein, and lay [it] on the stomach.

224 For casting (vomiting) that cometh of cold. Eat mint that is sodden (boiled) with flesh.

225 Another for casting or vomit. Take mouse-ear and bray it well with a little anise and cumin parched on the fire ; and wring out the juice of this, and seethe it a little with honey to make it sweet. And give the sick to drink a little thereof after his meat.

226 For the cardiacle (spasm of the heart). Take borage and distill it, and drink it continually ; for its virtue is to engender good blood, and to make a man light and merry,

---

ceremonies, and acted as medium. *See* G. Maspero, *Causeries d'Egypte*, Paris, 1907, p. 135. The implied alternative for a female patient is not stated.

⁴ *Schybes* ; scales or fibres.

chier and ther for it is good for heme that bene keuerynge
of siknes and for the cardiacle and for all maṅ of siknes
that cōmyth of malencoly · his rote is vsịd moost in
medecyns and sith the seede and sith þe levys whill thei
bene grene ffor when thai bene old and dry thai bene of
lyttell vertu borage is hote and moyst

227 An oþ⁹ ffor the cardiacle and gowtis and to kepe a
flemmatyke man and a malencolyke man in hele Stamp
an vnce or halue an vnce of pollipody and seth it with
plumbes and wᵗ violett and put þ⁹to fenell sede and comyne
as moch as of the othre and clene yᵗ and lett hym drynke
þᵃᵗ at morow and at eve

228 Also stampe the rote of pollipody all grene ꝫ þ⁹ wᵗ
floure and eyien and make small kakys and thei wīll make
a man làxatiffe / pollipody in þe hotter place it growith
þe bettir and it is hote and dry in the second degree

229 An oþ⁹ for the same take a gwine that is clepid
aȝafetịda and wynd it in rede leddyr and put it in the nose
thrịllis for it helpith moch agayne the cardiacle and dryueth
dōwn þe rysynge.

230 [fo. 21 recto] ffor costyffnes take þe rote of polipody
that growith on an hoke and wasshe it and stamp it ꝫ
temp it with wyne and lat it stand so all nyght ꝫ on morow
streyne itt and giff hym to drynke and he shall soone make
deliu⁹ance

231 An othir ffor costyfnes that comyth of drynes or som
coloryke humós that is in the gutts   Jff thou haue fresshe
plumbes lat hym ete heme and iff the plūmes be dry lay
heme in soke in waẗ and giff hym the plūmes to ete and the
watir to drinke

232 ffor colde humors that bene in the breste seth the rote
of mayden wede licores and barlich in watir and lett hyme
drynke the watir

233 Anothir iff a man be caldyd seth a chikkyn and make
itt in colys and then take psely and violett and carsen and
peletre ꝫ pound hem togedir ꝫ tak the juyse and seth it
with the colis and then latt hym soupe it

and ruddy of cheer ; and therefore it is good for him that is covering (recovering) of sickness, and for the cardiacle, and for all manner of sickness that cometh of melancholy. Its root is used most in medicines, and likewise the seed, and likewise the leaves while they are green, for when they be old and dry, they are of little virtue. Borage is hot and moist.

227 Another for the cardiacle and gouts, and to keep a phlegmatic man and a melancholic man in health. Stamp an ounce or half an ounce of polypody and seethe it with plums and with violet ; and put thereto fennel-seed and cumin as much as of the other ; and clean it and let him drink that at morn and at eve.

228 [Another]. Also stamp the root of polypody all green, and therewith [put] flour and eggs ; and make small cakes and they will make a man laxative. Polypody, in the hotter place it groweth the better, and it is hot and dry in the second degree.

229 Another for the same. Take a drug that is called asafetida, and wind it in red leather, and put it in the nostrils ; for it helpeth much against the cardiacle, and driveth down the rising.

230 For costiveness. Take the root of polypody that groweth on an oak, and wash it and stamp it, and temper it with wine, and let it stand all night ; and on the morrow strain it, and give him to drink, And he shall soon make deliverance.

231 Another for costiveness that cometh of dryness, or some choleric humor that is in the guts. If thou hast fresh plums, let him eat them ; and if the plums be dry, lay them in soak in water ; and give him the plums to eat and the water to drink.

232 For cold humors that are in the breast. Seethe the root of maidenweed (maidenhair), liquorice and barley in water, and let him drink the water.

233 Another, if a man hath a cold. Seethe a chicken and prepare it with cabbage ; and then take parsley and violet and cresses and pellitory ; and pound them together, and take the juice, and seethe it with the cabbage. And then let him sip it.

234 To make a woman to conceyue   Take a trowte and seth it in gotis mylke and giff it hir to drynke when she shall haue at do with hir husband

235 Also lekys oft etyne will help a woman to conceyue lyghtlj

236 how a man shuld kepe hym fro cold seth nettill sede and anoynt[1] oyle and enoynt thi fete and handis ꝫ it will do away the colde

237 Cake in womannes bely take pslye sawge ysopp wormode tansey and take a potell of stale ale writh the erbys ther in ꝫ seth hem fro a potell to a quart ꝫ giff to hir at morow hoote and at even cold.

238 An othir ffor the same   Take a catt and smyte of the hede take owt the bowelles and lay it to the syde

239 Chynes that bene soore of rankelynge take blakk sope white sope and vynegre and medle hem wele to [fo. 21 verso] gedir and make enoyntment þ⁹off and kepe it in a box and vse it //

240 An oþ⁹ for þe same   Take white wyne of gascoyne a pynt and a sponeful and an halue of hony and a sponefull and an halue of grete salt and stepe all togedir in an holow basynne wele hillyd ix dayes and ix nyghtes and eu̾y day stir it wele syns and then enoynt ther with the soore

241 Celidoyne is hote and dry and in þe iiij degre his vertu is to dissolue and to consume and draw out of a man wikkyd humós both colore and flemme and melencoly and eke roten blode   There beene two maners ther of on growith in ynd and that othir here emonge vs but that of ynd is moch more vertuose neu̾ the lesse that oþ⁹ is wondyr gode the erb is moch vertu the floure is of moch more and the rote althirmost conserue the floure in sugure ryght as thou wilt rosis and so vse it   Jt dried kyndely agayn the sonne may be kepid iij ꝫere

242 ffor the cough a þ⁹cious drynke and for the brest and is clepid mede eglyn and also wyne of tyrie of teibiañ and this is the pfite makynge   Take the rote of fenell pscly with þe rote tansay with the rote of Elenacampana radisshe rotis

---

[1] The dots indicate that the word is to be deleted. Cf. § 1005.

[2] Clotting, dysmenorrhœa. Most of the herbs named were commonly used as emenagoques.

234 To make a woman conceive. Take a trout and seethe it in goat's milk, and give it her to drink, when she shall have converse with her husband.

235 [Another]. Also leeks oft eaten will help a woman to conceive lightly (readily).

236 How a man should keep him[self] from cold. Seethe nettle-seed and oil and anoint thy feet and hands, and it will keep away the cold.

237 Cake[2] in a woman's belly. Take parsley, sage, hyssop, wormwood, tansey ; and take a pottle of stale ale, stir the herbs therein, and seethe them from a pottle to a quart ; and give her at morn hot and at even cold.

238 Another for the same. Take a cat and smite off the head, take out the bowels, and lay it to the side.

239 Chines that be sore from rankling. Take black soap, white soap and vinegar, and mix them well together and make an ointment thereof ; and keep it in a box and use it.

240 Another for the same. Take white wine of Gascony a pint, and a spoonful and a half of honey, and a spoonful and a half of great salt (rock-salt) ; and steep all together in a hollow basin well covered nine days and nine nights ; and every day stir it well. And then anoint therewith the sore.

241 Celandine is hot and dry in the fourth degree. Its virtue is to dissolve and consume and draw out of a man wicked humors, both choler, phlegm and melancholy, and also rotten blood. There be two kinds thereof : one groweth in India and the other here among us, but that of India has much more virtue ; nevertheless the other is wondrous good. The herb is of much virtue, the flour is of much more, and the root most of all. Conserve the flour in sugar just as thou wilt roses, and so use it. It, being dried gently in the sun, may be kept three years.

242 For the cough, a precious drink, and for the breast, and is called metheglin, and also wine of Tyre or Tiberias, and this is the perfect [method of] making. Take the root of fennel [and] parsley, with the root [of] tansey, with the

the rote of wormode valarian herb Robt mowser mynt with oute the rotis of ech of thies an handfull mugwort comfery borage levys or lorer mylfoyll camamyll violett waybrede hertistunge mede puliall mowntayn of ech of thies a culpon and sawge ysop saueray tyme lauandre rosemary calamynt margeron̄ scabiouse betayn eyrenioyn eufrace turmentill daysee auence of ech of thos ij culpons put all thies in a lede [fo. 22 *recto*] wyth as moch of clene ryver watir as they may easely be boyled in and boyll hem all togedir till the herbis go down to the botom̄ of the lede and that the rotis be ryght tendur ꝫ then lat hem kele and when thei are will warme than tho mayst handyll heme wᵗ owt skaldynge then clene and wrynge all thorowe a stronge canvas in to a clene vessell puttynge a way the drass of the erbis and make þen thi lede clene and put in thi watir whille it is warme and put þᵒto a pound of licoresse or ij afᵗ the quantitee of thi waᵗ that is to vj galons of the waᵗ a pound of licoresse or more small poundys to powd⟩ and seth it wele and oft clene it ꝫ then to ij galons of þis waᵗ one of hony for the fynyst or to iij galons of this waᵗ one of hony for the secunde   And wheþᵒ it be that on or the oþᵒ boyle heme togedr alway skymmynge with a skymmere till it be clene and aftyr that take it oute and put in to kevers þᵒ to stand opene iiij dayes and then try oute the clere and kest away the thyke but that shuld be or thow put in thyne hony but after þᵗ þou hast put in ym hony and it is cold after þe kelyng of iiij dayes then put ther on a potell of barme as brewers done apon ale fletynge it when it nedith iiij days or v ꝫ þen tune it in barell or pypis and kepe it as wyne and þen take clowes greynes galyngale peꝑ quybibbys maces nutmuges canell and gynger of ech of thies halue an vnce powdrede and put heme þᵒin ꝫ stopp it fast that noone eyer gos owte Jt shold at the lest lye halue a ꝫere or it were brochid Jtt [fo. 22 *verso*] may of

---

¹ From French *coupon*, a small part cut off, rather less than a handful.

² A *lead* was originally a pot or vessel made of lead, but afterwards came to be used for a large pot of iron or brass. A " copper " has changed its meaning in the same way.

root of elecampane, radish roots, the root of wormwood ;
valerian, herb-Robert, mouse-ear, mint, without the roots,
of each of these, a handful. Mugwort, comfrey, borage
leaves or laurel, milfoil, camomile, violet, waybread, hartstongue, mede (daisy), mountain-pileole (thyme), of each of
these a culpon.[1] And sage, hyssop, saverey, thyme,
lavender, rosemary, calamint, marjoram, scabious, betony,
eirenion, eufrasia (eyebright), tormentil, daisy, avens, of
each of those two culpons. Put all these in a cauldron,[2]
with as much of clean river-water as they may easily be
boiled in ; and boil them all together till the herbs go down
to the bottom of the cauldron and the roots be right tender.
And then let them cool, and when they are still as warm as
thou mayest handle them without being scalded, then clean
and wring all through a strong canvas into a clean vessel,
putting away the dross of the herbs. And make then thy
cauldron clean, and put in thy water while it is warm,
and put thereto a pound of liquorice, or two, according to
the quantity of thy water, that is, to six gallons of the water
a pound of liquorice, or smaller in proportion.[3] And seethe
it well and oft clean it, and then to two gallons of this
water, [put] one of honey of the finest [quality], or to three
gallons of this water, one of honey of the second [quality].
And whether it be the one or the other, boil them together,
always skimming with a skimmer till it be clean. And
after that, take it out and put it into covers,[4] there to stand
open four days. And then draw off the clear and cast away
the thick ; but that should be [done] before thou puttest in
thy honey. But after that thou hast put in thy honey, and
it is cold, after the cooling of four days, then put therein
a pottle of barm (yeast) as brewers do upon ale, skimming it
when it needeth, four days or five. Then turn it in a
barrel or pipes (casks) and keep it as wine. And then take
cloves, grains (kermes), galingale, pepper, cubebs,[5] mace,
nutmegs, canell (cinnamon), and ginger, of each of these half
an ounce powdered, and put them therein ; and stop it
fast that no air go out. It should at least lie half a year

---

[3] The text is here corrupt. This seems to be the meaning.
[4] Large shallow pans.
[5] Aromatic berries of *Piper cubeba* ; Arabic كبابة

hyme selue last vij ȝere and in the begynnynge when þou
puttist in hony in to the water it is myghty enough if it ber
an eye that þᵘ may see a peny brede of the ey aboue the
watere

243 TO make clarre or pyment   Take a galon of good
clene wyne that is swete and a pound of puryd
hony and menge heme wele togedir and put ther in halue
an vnce of canell a quart of an vnce of gyngᵒ ij peny wiȝt
of clows a peny wight of galyngale made all in to powders
and meng thies togedire and put it in to a bagg and let thi
licours ren thorow till the moost vertue be owte but put
þᵒto quybibbis and maces all so thou myght make also of
good ale

244 An othir gode drynke boile x galons of clere watir and
a galon of hony iij howres and skymme it wele and kest in
iiij galons of damysyns or of chires and boyle as longe and
then put þᵒto ij vnces of powdir of rosemary and as moch
powdyr off sawge and when itt is cold clene it and twne itt
in a barell opon a galon of good reede lyes that bene new
And þᵒin a small clout an vnce of powdyr of galyngalle and
half an vnce of powdir of canell and stop it fast þᵗ noon eyre
go owte and lett it stand so x wekes or xij and þan broch
it iff þᵘ wilt to ·2̲

245 Drynk for all manᵌ ffeuers or empostemys or for
what syknes that is in the wombe or in the
body that eủ shall be holpyne wᵗ eny medecyn   Take
eủy day of the powdyr a quantitee þᵗ spekyth of the
dropsy in the wombe here [fo. 23 recto] aftyr J write and
than take jsop rosemarye violet verneyne betayne erb John
mowser planteyn Auence sawge feþᵒfoyle of each an handfull
and wasshe hem clene and stamp heme a littell and do hem
in an erthen pott that was new occupied and do þᵒto a galon
of white wyne ꝸ so lat hym stand all nyght keủyd on þe
morowe seth hem till thei com till a potell ꝸ let it renne
thorow a clene here syve and keủ it in a fayre vessell and
lat the syke vs this drynke first and last ix dayes at evyne
hote at morow colde

before it is broached. It may of itself last seven years, and in the beginning when thou puttest honey into the water, it is mighty (strong) enough if it bear (*i.e.* float) an egg, so that you may see a penny's breadth of the egg above the water.

243 To make clary or pyment. Take a gallon of good clean wine that is sweet, and a pound of purified honey, and mix them well together ; and put therein half an ounce of canell, a quarter of an ounce of ginger, two penny-weight of cloves, a pennyweight of galingale, made all into powders ; and mix this together, and put it into a bag, and let thy licour then run through till the most virtue be out ; and put thereto cubebs and maces, all as thou mightest do in making good ale.

244 Another good drink. Boil ten gallons of clear water and a gallon of honey three hours, and skim it well ; and cast in four gallons of damsons or of cherries, and boil as long (*i.e.* three hours) ; and then put thereto two ounces of powder of rosemary, and as much powder of sage ; and when it is cold, clean it and tun it into a barrel, upon a gallon of good red lees that are new ; and [put] in a small cloth an ounce of powder of galingale and half an ounce of powder of canell ; and stop it fast, that no air go out ; and let it stand so ten weeks or twelve, and then broach it if thou wilt to.

245 Drink for all manner of fevers or imposthumes, or for that sickness which is in the womb or in the body, that ever shall be helped with any medicine. Take every day of the powder a quantity that speaketh of[1] the dropsy of the womb [of which] hereafter I write ; and then take hyssop, rosemary, violet, vervain, betony, herb-John, mouse-ear, plantain, avens, sage, feverfew, of each a hand-ful ; and wash them clean, and stamp them a little, and put them in an earthen pot that was new ocupied (used for the first time) ; and put thereto a gallon of white wine, and so let it stand all night covered. On the morrow seethe them till they come to [the measure of] a pottle, and let it run through a clean hair-seive, and cover it in a fair vessel. And let the sick use this drink, first and last, nine days ; at even hot, at morn, cold.

---

[1] Meaning : " that is specified in connection with."

246 An oþ⁹ drynke for the dropsy   Drynke the powd⁷⟩ of spykernell of spayne and he shall be hole

247 An oþ⁹   Take spigarnel of spayne and comyn and annyse and sauge bake it togedir in a pasty and breke it in a pott of good ale first and last

248 An othir Drynke þᵉ juys of the eldirbery tēpid with wyne foure days ꝯ all the evyll will pass thorow the foundement

249 An othir take walwort and make a bath and put þᵉ syke þ⁹in and hill hym wele with walwort and that shall draw oute the evyll and sporge hyme clene and when the wat⁹ is betwene the fell and the flesshe take þᵗ men shavyth off the shepis fellis and the netis fellys and seth þᵗ in wat̾ till it be thyke as glew and that do in a cloth and bynd it about thi̲ bodye ꝯ also about thi wombe

250 An othir   Take ruw ꝯ sawge and drynke itt with watir

251 An oþ⁹ for dropsy in the wombe and in the fete ꝯ for costyfnes and for glett [fo. 23 *verso*] and for wormes in the wombe and for badd stomake   Take iiij peny wyght of scamony and ij peny wight of rubarb and vj peny wyght of cene and iij halpeny wight of redewale and halfe a peny wight of spyknard iij peny wiȝt of powder watter a peny wiȝt of floure of canell and d̄j vnce of sugre of cipress and bray hem wele in a brasen mortare all to powdir and vse this medecyne fastynge ech day a sponefull iij dayes ꝯ he shall be hole and haue a good stomake

252 An oþ⁹ for the dropsy take sowthistilles that haue mylke with in heme and ote mele and watir and boyle hem togedir and make thicke wortis and giff hym ech day hys fyll fastynge þ⁹of till he be hole

253 An othir ffor al man̉⟩ of dropsyes.   Take sawge and beteyn cropp and roote even porcions and seid of alisaundre and seid of sowthistill and make hem in powdre of ech elich moch and powdre halue an vnce of Spyknard of Spayne do

246 Another drink for the dropsy. Drink the powder of spikenard of Spain, and he shall be whole.

247 Another. Take spikenard of Spain, and cumin and anise and sage ; bake it together in a pasty, and break it in a pot of good ale first and last.

248 Another. Drink the juice of the elderberry tempered with wine four days. And the evil will pass through the fundament.

249 Another. Take walwort, and make a bath and put the sick therein, and cover him well with walwort, and that shall draw out the evil ; and sperge (sprinkle) him and clean him ; and when the water is between the fell[1] and the flesh, take that which men shave off sheeps' skins and neats' skins, and seethe that in water till it be thick as glue. And put it in a cloth and bind it about thy body and also about thy womb.

250 Another. Take rue and sage and drink it with water.

251 Another for the dropsy in the womb and in the feet, and for costiveness and for gleet and for worms in the womb and for bad stomach. Take four pennyweight of scammony and two pennyweight of rhubarb, and six penny-weight of senna and three half pennyweights of red cole, and half a pennyweight of spikenard, three pennyweight of powder [of] woodruff,[2] a pennyweight of flour of canell, and half an ounce of sugar of cypress ; and bray them well in a brazen mortar all to powder, and use this medicine fasting each day a spoonful [for] three days. And he shall be whole and have a good stomach.

252 Another for the dropsy. Take sowthistles that have milk within them, and oatmeal and water and boil them together ; and make thick wort, and give him each day his fill, fasting, thereof ; till he be whole.

253 Another for all manner of dropsies. Take sage and betony, crop and root, even portions, and seed of alexanders (smyrnium), and seed of sowthistle, and make them into powder, of each equally much ; and powder half an ounce

---

[1] The tissues immediately under the skin.
[2] Also called herb-Walter, in honour of Walter of Elvesden. See note to § 654.

þᵘto and then do al thies togedir in a cake of white dawgh
and all hote put it in a steue full of goode ale and stop it
wele and giff it þᵉ syke to drynke all day   Also giff hym
the same powdre in his potage made of watir cressis and of
betayn both at eve and at morow or ellys ete wortis made
of planteyn and it will hele the dropsy iff it be oft eten

Also ruw sothen longe with fygges in wyn and than
dronken doth the same

254 An oþᵘ stampe the medle rynde and the leves and the
blossomes or the froite of eldren and take the juys of heme
and put þᵘto iij peny wyght of esula and mastyke ether
seth hem [fo. 24 recto] in watir and do sugure þᵘto and vse
it

255 Anoþᵘ take ruw Sawge ꝫ as moch as of hem both of
watir cressis and boyll hem in gode white wyne and then
clene and put it in A vessell wele hiled and drynke þᵘof
fyrst and last and that will dryve it downe ꝫ then make a
bath ꝫ (sic) heyhound broune fenell and walwort and lay
ij latthes on crosse oũ) þᵉ sethynge waᷤ and sett thi fete
ther on and wrapp thi feete with clothis and so make a
stew to thi legges but lat nat thi leggis com þᵘin

256 ffor Delyveraunce if a dede childe   Take leke blades
and skilde heme and bynd to the wombe abowt the navell
and itt shall kest owt the dede child ꝫ when she is delyveryd
do away the bladis or she shall kest owt all that is in hir

257 An othir   Gyff her detayne to drynke and she shall
haue childe with oute pill or ellis gyff hir to drynke ysop
with hote wattir and she shall be delyvered thowgh þᵉ
childe be dede or rotid and then giff for to drynke roses
soden [in] wyne at evyn and at morow that she be hole

258 An othir take the rotes of madir whil it is grene and
make heme clene and seth anoynt hem wᵗ hony ꝫ sprenge
powdre off madir on hem and make a suppository þᵘoff and
it shall make a woman haue hir termes and to be delyverid
of a dede childe ꝫ of the secundyne

259 An othir drynke sauᷤ)ay with with (sic) wyne ꝫ it will
delyuᷤ) a woman of a dede childe

of spikenard of Spain, put it thereto, and then put all these together in a cake of white dough and put it in a stewpan full of good ale, and stop it well ; and give it the sick to drink all day. Also give him the same powder in his pottage made of watercresses and of betony, both at eve and at morn, or else eat worts made of plantain, and it will heal the dropsy if it be oft eaten. Also rue seethed long with figs in wine and then drunken, doth the same.

254 Another. Stamp the middle rind and the leaves and the blossoms or the fruit of elders, and take the juice of them, and put thereto three pennyweight of esula (spurge) and mastic. Or seethe them in water and put sugar thereto and use it.

255 Another. Take rue, sage, and as much as of both of them of watercresses, and boil them in good white wine ; and then clean and put it in a vessel well covered, and drink thereof first and last, and that will drive it (the disease), down. And then make a bath of horehound, brown fennel and walwort, and lay two laths across over the boiling water, and set his feet thereon, and cover his feet with cloths and so make a stew (vapour-bath) to thy legs, but let not thy legs come therein.

256 For deliverance of a dead child. Take leek blades and scale them, and bind to the womb about the navel ; and it shall cast out the dead child ; and when she is delivered, take away the blades or she shall cast out all that is in her.

257 Another. Give her dittany to drink, and she shall have child without peril. Or else give her to drink hyssop with hot water, and she shall be delivered, [even] though the child be dead or rotted ; and then give for to drink roses sodden in wine at even and at morn, that she be whole.

258 Another. Take the roots of madder while it is green, and make them clean ; and then anoint them with honey, and sprinkle powder of madder on them, and make a suppository thereof ; and it shall make a woman have her terms, and to be delivered of a dead child and of the after-birth.

259 Another. Drink saverey with wine, and it will deliver a woman of a dead child.

G

260 ffor to make Dyaclū   Take botre oyle of olyfe and melt hem and put þˢto powdir of litarge and temp heme togedir and make rolles of heme in papyre when itt is kele and so of plumby wᵗ rede lede

261 [fo. 24 *verso*] ffor defnes   Take camamyll and seth it in a pot and put in the ere that is deffe and wasshe the ere and do so iiij days or v and he shall be hole

262 An othir for the same   Take jubarb and stāp it wele and take iiij culpons of an ele that is fat and do not salt þˢto and rost heme on a spytt and kepe the grese that droppith oute of it in a clene vessell and take gresse and the Juyse of jubarb and medle heme togedir and the first nyght put itt in þᵉ hole ere and þᵉ secund nyȝt put it in the sore ere and the iij nyght in the hoole ere and the iiij nyght in þᵉ sore ere as hote as the syke may suffrre it ꝑbatū est

263 An othir take the gall of ane hare with aqua vite and woman mylke euen porcions and wele medle togedir and put it in the ere

264 Anoþˢ   Take pisse of a ȝonge childe and put it to the ere when it is newe ꝑb est

265 An oþˢ for the same   Take powdir of comyn and brymstone and lay it on an hote tile stone till it be wele moltene and holde the ere ouꝫ the smoke þᵗ þᵉ smoke may go in to it and when þou gost to thi bedd than hill thy hede hote and do so ech nyght in the same ere till thou be hole ꝑb est

266 Anothir ffor them that haue euell heres.   Take the braunches of asshe when thei bene grene and lay hem on a brandiren in the fyre and gadyr the watir that cōmyth oute at the endys of heme an ey shell full of juys of the blades of lekys and an ey shel full of the juse of rubarbe and ey shell full of the droppynge off helys and medle all these togedir and seth hem a lyttill and [fo. 25 *recto*] clene ham than thorow a cloth and put it than in a glasen vessell and when thow hast nede put this in the hole ere and ly on the sore ere and with in littell tyme he shall be hole

---

¹ Diaculum is called Diaquilon in MS. *Harleian*, 2378.   The word evidently corrupted from the Greek διάχυλον.   Another recipe

260 For to make Diaculum.[1]   Take butter, oil of olive, and melt them and put thereto powder of litharge and temper them together ; and make rolls of them in paper when it is cool and so of plumby with red lead.

261 For deafness.   Take camomile and seethe it in a pot, and put in the ear that is deaf, and wash the ear ; and so do four days or five, and he shall be whole.

262 Another for the same.   Take jubarb (houseleek) and stamp it well, and take four culpons of an eel that is fat, and put no salt thereto ; and roast it on a spit, and keep the grease that droppeth out of it in a clean vessel ; and take [the] grease and the juice of jubarb, and mix them together ; and the first night put it in the whole ear, and the second night put it in the sore ear ; and the third night in the whole ear, and the fourth night in the sore ear, as hot as the sick may suffer it.   *Probatum est.*

263 Another.   Take the gall of a hare with aqua vitæ and woman's milk, equal portions, and well mix together and put it in the ear.

264 Another.   Take urine of a young child and put it to the ear when it is new.   *Probatum est.*

265 Another for the same.   Take powder of cumin and brimstone and lay it on a hot tile-stone till it be well molten ; and hold the ear over the smoke that the smoke may go into it ; and when thou goest to thy bed, then wrap thy head hot ; and so do each night in the same ear till he be whole.   *Probatum est.*

266 Another for them that have evil ears.[2]   Take branches of ash-trees when they are green and lay them on a grid-iron in the fire, and gather the water that cometh out at the ends of them ; an eggshell full of the juice of the blades of leeks ; an eggshell full of the juice of rhubarb ; an eggshell full of the dripping of eels ; and mix all these together and seethe them a little, and clean them then through a cloth ; and put it then in a glass vessel, and when thou hast need, put this in the whole ear and lie on the sore ear, and within a little time he shall be whole.   Then take the wool that is

---

for this, or a closely similar, preparation occurs in the damaged § 279.   *Emplastrum diachylum* occurs in later medicine.
    [2] This prescription is a duplicate of § 18.   *See* note thereon.

then take þe wol þat is vnder a blake shepis bely and lay it
wete in the same juyse and lay it on the ere for it restoreth
herynge and doth away akynge of eres þb est

267 An othir   Take the powd⁾ of clowes and the powdre
of seide of lilys and temp heme wele with juse of ruw and
wete a tent þ⁹in and put it in the ere but I warne the kepe
the fro thies thynges · that is garlyke ete but lyttill or
noon and kepe the fro the hete of the sonne and leve to
sowp late and kepe the fro cryynge for thies bene grevous
thynges for syknes

268 An othir ffor the same   Take the white that bene
emonge empt hillis that bene clepid empt hors and lat
hem dry that þᵂ powdre of heme and do it in white wyne
and do ij droppis þ⁹ of in his ere and vse this a good while

269 An oþ⁹ for the same   Take þe juys of levys of a bech
tre and good vynegre euen porcion and put ther to powdir
off whyk lyme and then clene it thoro a cloth and of this
when it is clensid put hote in to þe syke ere

269ᴀ Drynke wyne oft temped wᵗ the juys of sothernwode
for it doth gode agayne the cough and the chynk and agayn
all the grevance of wymmens pryuie membre

270 To voyd dronkennesse drynk the juse of lekys and it
will both void Dronkennesse and lechery.

271 Emerauntis or piles   Take a panne wᵗ coles and
     [fo. 25 *verso*] hete a littell stone glowynge and
put ther on the levys of an herb þᵗ is clepid moleyñ and put
it vnder a cheyre or vnder a stole wᵗ a segge that the smoke
þ⁹off may ascend to thi foundment as hoote as thou mayst
suffre

272 Anothir take the same erbe moleyn a handfull and
stamp it ī a mortᵉ and put it in a vessell and put þ⁹to oyle
off olyue and old bores gresse and boyle thies togedir and
stire heme wele and lay þ⁹of on a cloth to the foundement
as hoote as he may suffre and do this oft till thi be driede
jnne

---

¹ Ants' eggs are meant. They are called " emmets horses " in
the Anglo-Saxon MS. *Royal*, 12, D, xvii, fo. 15 verso (Cockayne,
Leechdoms, Vol. ii, p. 43). In the same MS. (fo. 15 recto) ants' eggs

under a black sheep's belly and lay it wet in the same juice ; and lay it on the ear for it restoreth hearing, and doth away aching of ears. *Probatum est.*

267 Another. Take the powder of cloves and the powder of seed of lilies, and temper them well with the juice of rue and wet a tent (pledget) therein and put it in the ear. But I warn thee keep thee from these things, that is [to say, of] garlic eat but little or none, and keep thee from the heat of the sun, and lief to sup late, and keep thee from crying, for these be grievous things for sickness.

268 Another for the same. Take the white that is amongst ant-hills that is called ant-horses,[1] and let them dry that you may powder them and put it in white wine and put two drops thereof in his ear, and use this a good while.

269 Another for the same. Take the juice of leaves of a beech tree and good vinegar, even portions, and put thereto powder of quicklime ; and then clean it through a cloth ; and of this, when it is cleansed, put hot into the sick ear.

269A Drink wine oft tempered with the juice of southern-wood, for it doth good against the cough and whooping-cough and against all the grievance of a woman's privy member.

270 To void drunkenness. Drink the juice of leeks and it will void both drunkenness and lechery.

271 Hæmorrhoids or piles. Take a pan with coals (charcoal) and heat a little stone glowing [-hot], and put thereon the leaves of a herb that is called mullein ; and put it under a chair or under a stool with a siege,[2] that the smoke thereof may ascend to thy fundament as hot as thou mayest suffer.

272 Another. Take the same herb mullein a handful, and stamp it in a mortar ; and put it in a vessel, and put thereto oil of olive and old boar's grease ; and boil these together, and stir them well ; and lay thereof on a cloth to the fundament as hot as he may suffer ; and do this off till they (the piles) be driven in.

---

are mentioned. In both cases they are used for the ears, and both are borrowed from Marcellus. *See also* § 443.

[2] A siege-stool, *i.e.,* a commode.

273 Anothir iff thei swell and flowen nat seth horhowne in salt watir and wyne and let hyme sytt þᵒ ou) that his nethir ptie may soke þᵒin and sith make hyme a suppository off the powdre of horhowne and of honye

274 Anothir   Take þᵉ holyhokke rote parid and pound small ꝗ rede rose levys and sywete of a dere or of a shepe and all wele stamped togedir and then lay it on a few hardis ꝗ warme it agayne the fire and put it in to the soore pbaȝ est

275 An oþᵒ take a rede onyone and do away the hert þᵒof and fill it full of the oyle of olyue and sett it in the hoote eymeres ꝗ lat hym boyle wele or rost in the cyniers and then lay it to the fundement as hoot as he may suffre it and be hoole

276 An othir take barly floure and oyle of olyue and fry hem togedꝰ and lay hem to þᵉ fundement and that pleyst will draw owt the piles pb e)

277 ffor eddir or snake ī a mannys body   Stamp ruw with a mannes awn vryn or womans or what best that that evell hath and giff hym to drynke [fo. 26 *recto*] either Stamp arneme[nt   .   .   .   .

[a large piece has been torn from fo. 26 carrying away most of the first 14 lines.]

278
Line 2. make it somdelle t[............................
   3. ffor cres that h[...............................
   4. floweth ow[t...................................
   5. and ther w[ith..................................
   6. dryeth a w[....................................
   7. of brente ysop[................................
   8. Servyth for medec[yne........................
   9. and namely the sed[e.. ....
279 10. fflewme pryncipally [To make Diaculū ....
   11. Take oyle of olyue ꝗ gal[lengale.................
   12. longe and put þᵒto a p̄ond[.....................
   13. it be strawede wele and [.......................
   14. dj pound of white lede and [...................

---

¹ *I.e.*, do not bleed.
² A.-S. *heordan*, the refuse or fibres of tow.

273 Another if they swell and flow not.[1]   Seethe horehound
in salt water and wine ; and let him sit therover, that his
nether part may soak therein ; and then make him a
suppository of the powder of horehound and honey.

274 Another. Take the hollyhock root, pared, and pound
[it] small, and red rose leaves and suet of a deer or of a
sheep, and all well stamped together ; and then lay it on a
few hards[2] and warm it by the fire, and put it into the sore.
Probatum est.

275 Another. Take a red onion and do away the heart
thereof, and fill it full of the oil of olive, and set it in the hot
embers ; and let it boil well or roast in the cinders, and then
lay it to the fundament as hot as he may suffer it, and be
whole.

276 Another. Take barley-flour and oil of olive, and fry
them together ; and lay them to the fundament, and that
plaster will draw out the piles.   *Probatum est.*

277 For adder or snake in a man's body. Stamp rue with
a man's own urine or woman's, or that of a beast which hath
that evil, and give him to drink ; and arneme[nt . .

278
Line 2. make it somewhat [............................
      3. for cress that h[as............................
      4. floweth ou[t ....
      5. and therew[ith ....
      6. dryeth a w[..................................
      7. of burnt hyssop [.............................
      8. serveth for medic[ine ....
      9. and especially the see[d ....

279 10. phlegm principally.[3] [To make Diaculum ....
    11. Take oil of olive and gal[engale ....
    12. long, and put thereto a pound [.................
    13. it be strewed well and [.......................
    14. half a pound of white lead and [................

---

   [3] This is the end of a recipe, and it is followed by a trace of a
blue paragraph-mark. The next is evidently for an ointment,
identical with, or closely resembling the Diaculum described in § 260.

then late it seth wele till it wax towgh and that it rope and
wax blake and then take it off the fyre and put þᵍin in
litarge d̄j pounde and a pound of rosyne and stire it wele
togedir till it be molten and lat it stand and colde Ꝫ put it
in a vessell and make þᵍof culpons and roll it in a papyre.

280 Empleyst̆ for gowte   Take ambros and wild nepe Ꝫ
seth it wele to gedir with olde grese and enoynt the gowt
þᵍwith

281 ffor festre an empleystir   Take waybrede white tansey
nosebled whit malow smalach and auance of ech elich moch
Ꝫ wrynge owt the juys of each by hem selue and take
walwort [fo. 26 *verso*] . . .

[Of the first 14 lines, only the end of each remains.]

Line 1. ....lev]ys of walwort as of
     2. ....] virgyn wax and
     3. ....swy]nes grese and
     4. ....an]d loke that
     5. ....] is as moch
     6. ....t]hies ī a pan
     7. ....] nat wrynge
     8. ....]ebe for it is so
     9. ....] thyes thynges the
    10. ....]en whete flowre Ꝫ
    11. ....an]d boyle it togedir thatt
    12. ....wa]sshe the wound with wyne
    13. ....] and lay than the pleist̆ þᵍto
    14. ....] be hole and eüˢy day drynke

282 auence and wormod fastynge   To make emplayst̆ de
ianna solempne this emplastir is but nw knawen emonge
cristyn men and helith fejre with owten any tent thogh þe
wound be thorow depe and one pleyst̆ will hill an hundreth
wounds and it be betwene thyn handis hote and so this
pleist̆ shall be sett on grete hempe kytt short nygh as longe
as þe wound and wasshe the wound with white wyne or rede
twyes a day at morow and at eve and eüˢy tym hete wele

---

¹ Of the first fourteen lines, only the last words remain. I have
restored the text approximately with the help of a very similar, but
not identical, recipe in H. (Henslow, *op. cit.*, p. 21). The restored
portions are printed in italics between square brackets.

then let it seethe till it wax tough, and that it thickens and waxeth black ; and then take it off the fire, and put therein litharge, half a pound, and a pound of rosin ; and stir it well together till it be molten ; and let it stand and cool, and put it in a vessel and make thereof culpons, and roll it in a paper.

280 Emplaster for gout. Take wood-sage and wild-nept (catmint) and seethe it well together with old grease and anoint the gout therewith.

281 For the fester, a plaster.[1] Take waybread, white tansey, nosebleed (yarrow or milfoil), white mallow, smallage and avens, of each equally much ; and wring out the juice of each by itself and take walwort [*a good quantity, as much of the leav*]es of walwort as of [*the other herbs, and wash it and seethe it ; and then take*] virgin wax and [*fresh sheep's tallow, and honey and may-butter*] and swine's grease, and [*mix them together and stamp them ; an*]d look that [*the quantity of all these things last named*] is as much [*as the juice of all the other herbs ; and take the walwort, and do*] all this in a pan, [*and boil them together, but the white mallow thou shalt boil all whole, for thou mayest*] not wring [*the juice out thereof as thou didst for the other herbs*] for it is so [*fat ; and when all that is boiled, wring*] these things [*through a cloth, and put it in a box ; take*] then wheat flour, and [*put a part of the ointment thereto,*] and boil it together that [*it be as thick as gruel ; and*] wash the wound with wine [*at morn and at eve, and*] lay the plaster thereto, [*and do so each day*] till he be whole ; and every day drink avens and wormwood, fasting.

282 To make emplastrum de ianna solempne.[2] This plaster is but newly known among christian men, and healeth fair without any tent,[3] though the wound be very deep ; and one plaster will [serve to] cover a hundred wounds, if it be between thy hands hot ; and so this plaster shall be set on great hemp cut short nearly as long as the wound ; and wash the wound with white wine or red, twice a day at morn and at eve ; and every time heat well the

---

[2] This name is so corrupt as to be unintelligible.
[3] A little roll of lint. A tent is used, however, in this recipe.

þe pleysȝ betwyn thyn handis thatt (*sic*) take clene soft
flex off hempe and make a tent nought the depnesse of the
wounde but to þe lenght of the wound and kest in to the
soor wyn ꝫ [fo. 27 *recto*] sett it in the wound by the mydle
of the pleistir and all the maȝ and þe filth of the wound
shall pass away thorow the medle of the tent and if the
wound greue hym moch kest þᵒon a littell oyle of olyue
and it shall greue hyme no more[1] Now the pleistir take
thies herbis apm̄ planteyn and betayn and first take juse of
euᴵy by hyme selue till thou haue of euᴵy a pound of the
juys ꝫ do it in a pott Take than a quarte of goode virgyn
wax and kytt it small and take ij vnces of clene pich rosen
and kest all thies in a pott wᵗ the juyse and lett heme seth
wele and þen sett down þe pott of the fire and streyne hem
thorow a cloth then take an vnce of turmentyne and kest
þᵒto and temp heme wele togedir and when it is colde
gedir it vp ffor it is a noble emplaystyr and a pᵒciouse
emonge all emplasters pþ êᴵ

284 Emplastrū bonū strutorm̄ Take planteyn grete morell
petymorell ribwort syngrene daysy smalach jusquinannis
groundswylly herba canep clote leves ellerue leves stamp
hem with rennynge waȝ and then clence it thorow a cloth
and þen do in that waȝ whete floure wex and rosen and
litarge of lede and shepis taligh or sywet and boyll it wele
and stire it wele till it be colde and make þᵒof a pleistre on
the sore take juyse of dayse and of Ribbwort and the whit
of eyien ꝫ bray hem togedir and clence thorow a cloth and
skymme itt and do it in a glasse or in an othir vessell then
take fayre lynet and wete it in that Juyse and ley on the
sore legg there þe sore is and lay the strutorye apon thi
sore ꝫ about the legge and than roll the legge and lat it
ligg a day and a nyght and than [fo. 27 *verso*] lay to an
oþᵒ

285 Her is a goode entrete for ach and brusid blode ffor
woundis and boyles or oþᵒ brusurs Take þe fat of bacon
and of old barows grese and melt it in a panne and lat it
stand till þe salt be fall to þe ground and take than halve

---

[1] A blue paragraph mark has been deleted here.
[2] A splint. *Cf.* M. E. *Strout.* " stiff," " rigid."
[3] Often written *trete*. *O.F. entrait*, a plaster.

plaster between thine hands, then take clean soft flax of hemp and make a tent, not of the deepness of the wound, but of the length of the wound ; and cast wine in the sore, and set it (the tent) in the wound by the middle of the plaster (*i.e.* fix the tent by means of the plaster), and all the matter and the filth of the wound will pass away through the middle of the tent ; and if the wound grieve him much, cast thereon a little oil of olive, and it shall grieve him no more. Now the plaster : take these herbs, apium, plantain and betony, and first take juice of each by itself, till thou hast of each a pound of the juice, and put it in a pot. Take then a quart of good virgin wax, and cut it small ; and take two ounces of clean pitch rosin, and cast all these in a pot with the juice ; and let them seethe well, and then set down the pot from the fire, and strain them through a cloth ; then take an ounce of turpentine and cast thereto, and temper them well together ; and when it is cold, gather it up, for it is a noble and a precious plaster, among all plasters. *Probatum est.*

284 Emplastrum bonum strutorium. Take plantain, greater morell (nightshade), lesser morell, ribwort, sengreen, daisy, smallage, jusquiamus (henbane), groundsel, herb-canep (cannabis, hemp), clove leaves, ellerue (sambucus) leaves ; stamp them well with running water, and then cleanse it through a cloth. And then put in that water wheat flour, wax and rosin and litharge of lead, and sheep's tallow or suet ; and boil it well, and stir it well till it be cold, and make thereof a plaster on the sore. Take juice of daisy and of ribwort and the white of eggs, and bray them together and cleanse through a cloth ; and skim it, and put it in a glass or in another vessel ; then take fair lint, and wet it in that juice and lay [it] on the sore leg where the sore is ; and lay the strutory[2] upon the sore and about the leg, and then bandage the leg, and let it lie a day and a night ; and then lay on another.

285 Here is a good entrete[3] for ache and for bruised blood, for wounds and boils or other bruises. Take the fat of bacon and of old barrow's grease, and melt it in a pan ; and let it stand till the salt be fallen to the bottom ; and

so moch virgyn wex as þ⁹ is of grese and take store and grynd
it small and do þ⁹to when the grete hete to ou⸍goo /
take powdre off mastlynge and styve it welle in a skellet
with a slyce till itt be also thike as hony and do itt in a box
and when thow haste nede þ⁹to take þ⁹off on a clene cloute
or on lethir and lay to the wound and it shall draw owt the
ach what ach so a man hath enoynt it twys on the day
þ⁹with and it shall distroy the evyll ꝫ do hyme goode

286 An othir take fat bacon of an old barowȝ and melt it
in a panne and lat it stand to þᵉ salt go to þᵉ botome and
take the clere aboue ꝫ do it in a panne and halue so moch
of wex and when it is molten do þ⁹to stoore and stir wele
togedir and when it is colde do it in a box and this is good
to draw owt ach of woundes or of boylys

287 Anoþ⁹ entrete   Take illegoñe that is smerwort centory
sigilla salamonis and pound all thre infere and dryve owt
the juyse in a vessell and take fresshe botre and the juys
ꝫ seth all in fere ꝫ when thei be a littell sothen take a lyttell
virgyn wex as moch as will pforme the threddendell and as
moch of raw code and viij peny wiȝt of turmentyn and
togedir seth the wax the code and the turmentyne ꝫ
wrynge itt throw a cloth in to the water for seide

288 To make an [fo. 28 *recto*] entrete þᵗ is Oxarecconū that
is a man⸍ of white entrete   Take Safron Dort of the best
and stamp it small wᵗ ȝolkys of egges ꝫ thanne take Sywet
of a dere or shepis talowe and melt it in a panne of erth and
than take a porcion of prosyn and do þ⁹to a littell rosen
and mastyke and a good quantitee of oyle debay and litarge
of golde and of Sylue⁹ and vyrgyn wex and a littell oyle
de olyue and seth heme wele togedir and then do hem fro
the fyre ꝫ lett it kele a littell and then do ther to thi Safron
and yolkes of eyēn and than styre it togedir wele and do it

---

¹ *Stor* is probably here storax or incense (A.S. *Stor*), as it is a
substance that requires grinding.
² *Maslin* is mixed grain, especially rye mixed with wheat.
³ *Stoore* is hardly storax here. It is the substance made of a
mixture of ale and oatmeal.

take then half so much virgin wax as there is of grease, and take storax[1] and grind it small, and put it thereto when the great heat is overgone, (*i.e.* when it is becoming cool); take powder of maslin,[2] and stew it well in a skillet with a slice till it be as thick as honey ; and put it in a box. And when thou hast need thereof, take thereof on a clean cloth or on leather, and lay to the wound ; and it shall draw out the ache. Whatsoever ache a man hath, anoint it twice a day therewith, and it shall destroy the evil and do him good.

286 Another. Take fat bacon of an old barrow-hog and melt it in a pan, and let it stand till the salt go to the bottom ; and take the clear [substance] above, and put it in a pan with half so much of wax ; and when it is molten, put thereto stoore,[3] and stir well together ; and when it is cold, put it in a box. And this is good to draw out ache of wounds or of boils.

287 Another entrete. Take illegonum, that is smearwort, centaury, Solomon's seal, and pound all three together and drive out the juice in a vessel ; and take fresh butter and the juice, and seethe all together ; and when a be a little seethed, take a little virgin wax, as much as will amount to one third part, and as much of raw code (cobbler's wax), and eight pennyweight of turpentine, and together seethe the wax, the code and the turpentine ; and wring it through a cloth into the water aforesaid.

288 To make an entrete that is Oxarecconum,[4] that is a kind of white entrete. Take saffron-darts[5] of the best, and stamp it small with yolks of eggs, and then take suet of a deer or sheep's tallow and melt it in a pan of earth[enware] ; and then take a portion of perosin and put thereto a little rosin and mastic and a good quantity of oil of bay and litharge of gold and of silver, and virgin wax, and a little oil of olive ; and seethe them well together, and then take them from the fire and let it cool a little ; and then put thereto thy saffron and yolks of eggs, and then stir it

---

[4] The name is corrupt. A very similar compound is described in MS. *Sloane* 521 under the name of *Occicrucyon*. The two recipes, both corrupt, are derived from the same source. The name should probably be *Oxycroceum*. *Cf.* § 173.

[5] Saffron-darts are the stigmata of the saffron-flower, so called from their shape.

in boxis this is the best trete of all both helynge and
drawynge

289 An othir entrete that is called apostolicon or entrete
of yne   Tak the iuse of smalach and the juse of betayn
and þe juse of weybrede of ech of hem a pound and put all
this to gedir in a pott and put to hem a quartion of goode
mede wex small mynsede ꝫ a ꝗrtron of perosyn powdred ꝫ
seth heme ꝫ styre hem allway wᵗ a slyce and looke that
thow haue by the a basyn that be dry and clene ꝫ if thou
will witt iff it be soden enough put a drop on a basyn and
when it is cold thrust thorow with thi fyngure and if þ⁹ com
any licó owt þ⁹of it is nat soden ynogh and then take it
out fro the fire and put þ⁹in an vnce of serpentyne and stire
it fast and medle heme wele togedir and then sett it oft on
the fire agayne and seth it till it be welle medled togedir
and stir itt alway with a sclyce and then pute a quart of
whit wyne and lett it kelle ꝫ when it is wele kelyd temp
it with thi handis wele ꝫ kepe it

290 ffor to make an entrete that is clepid popilion   Take
[fo. 28 *verso*] iiij pound of the ȝong buddis of poplers ꝫ iij
pound of erbe watir of hennebane pety morell orpyne
sengrene añ ℔ of weybrede endyne violett watir cresses
añ ℔ ℈ wasshe hem clene and stampe heme and do þ⁹to
barowes gresse ℔j ℈ molten and purid and when thai bene
wele medeled do ham in to a pot and close it and lat it
stand ix days and worch it vp and þen take it out of the
pott and do it in a panne and sett it on the fyre and fry it
wele and stir it wele wyt a slyce that it sytt nat to þe panne
botom and when it is enowȝ take it down and streyne it
in to a vessell and sett it oꞔ the fyre agayne and do ther to
a halue a quartion of wex small mynsede and a ꝗrtion of
wethers talow molton and puryd and boyle hem a lyttell
and þen do ther to a quartion of encence powdrede wele
and styre it wele togedir till it be melcyd and relentid ꝫ
then anon take it down and streyne itt and latt it kele and
kerue it and lat owt the watir and turne it and clence the

together well, and put it in boxes. This is the best entrete of all, both [for] healing and drawing.

289 Another entrete that is called apostolicon, or entrete of India. Take the juice of smallage, and the juice of betony, and the juice of waybread of each of them a pound; and put all these together in a pot, and put to them a quantity of good made (prepared) wax, minced small, and a quarter [of a pound] of perosin powdered; and seethe them and stir them always with a slice, and look that thou have by thee a basin that is dry and clean. And if thou wilt know if it be seethed enough, put a drop in a basin; and when it is cold, thrust through with thy finger, and if there come away licour out thereof, it is not seethed enough; and then take it from the fire, and put therein an ounce of turpentine; and stir it fast, and mix them well together; and then set it oft on the fire again, and seethe it till it be well mingled together, and stir it always with a slice; and then put a quart of white wine [to it], and let it cool, and when it is well cooled, temper it with thy hands well, and keep it.

290 For to make an entrete called popilion.[1] Take four pounds of the young buds of poplars, and three pounds of herb-water, of henbane, little morell, orpine, sengreen, of each one pound; of waybread, endive, violet, watercress, of each half a pound. Wash them clean and stamp them, and put thereto half a pound of barrow's grease, molten and purified; and when they are well mingled, put them into a pot and close it, and let it stand nine days; and work it up. And then take it out of the pot, and put it in a pan; and set it on the fire and fry it well, and stir it well with a slice that it stick not to the bottom of the pan; and when it is [cooked] enough, take it down and strain it into a vessell; and set it over the fire again, and put thereto half a quartern of wax, small minced, and a quartern of wether's tallow, molten and purified, and boil then a little. And then put thereto a quartern of incense powdered well, and stir it well together till it be softened and relented; and then anon take it down, and strain it, and let it cool; and cover it,

---

[1] There are similar recipes for popilion in H. and in *Harl.* 2378. (Henslow, *op. cit.*, pp. 52, 118). For somewhat similar preparations, *see* §§ 929–931.

nethir syde of the fylth and sett it oũ the fyre agayn till
it be moltyn and with a fethir skyme it and this is þe
makynge of popilion kyndely

291 To make anoþ⁹ goode entrete Take iij q̃rtrons of
spaynysshe code or of cleene rosen and a q̃rtron of prosyn
Ij ℔ of mede wex ꝛ a ℥j off galbanū ꝛ ℥ ℔ of mastyke ꝛ a
℥j of frannkencens sanb drigon ℥ ℔ small powdred luf hony
℥ ℔ bores greses iij ℥ ℔ haule a q̃rtron ꝛ a ℥ of vertgresse
small powdred [fo. 29 *recto*] let fry heme all togedir till þai
be relentid and wele medelyd ꝛ then streyn hem and do
þ⁹to a pound of turpentyne that is al redy powdred and lett
do hem to the fyre agayn till thai be relentid and medle
hem togedir with a slyce and then powre in to þe box this
is noble both drawynge and helynge

292 An othir entrete to lay on a wound or on a bocch or
on blake nayles to make hem to growe and itt may be kepid
xx wynter Take rosyne of the pyne tre and an vnce of
white wex and an vnce of othir rosen and an vnce of
turpentyne and sett all togedir on an easy fyre till thei be
molten and when it is molten kest it in a vessell with colde
watir and after take it owte and temper it betwene thyne
handis wᵗ oyle de bay and when it is temperid ynowȝ kepe
kepe it wele for it is a goode entrete

293 To make an entrete for bocches and bules to clence
heme and to gedir new flesshe Take rosen as moch as you
wilt and melt it in a pott [with] vynegre and wrynge thorow
a cloth in to a vessell with cold watir and temp it wᵗin thyn
handys as it were wex but loke thai bene enoyntyd with
oile or with grese

294 Anoþ⁹ for the same Take prosyn ꝛ encens that is
white and wethirs talowȝ of ech lich moch but loke the
talowȝ be molten fyrst and purid and than put al togedᵉ
in a pott ꝛ melt thaym at the fyre and styre fast wᵗ a slyce
till thei bene molten and wele medelyd togedir and than

and let out the water, and cleanse the under side of the filth (scum), and set it over the fire again, till it be molten, and with a feather skim it. And this is the making of popilion kindly (properly).

291 To make another good entrete. Take three quarterns of Spanish code (cobbler's wax) or of clean rosin, and a quatern of perosin ; half a pound of made wax, one ounce of galbanum, and half an ounce of mastic and one drachm of frankincense ; dragon's-blood half an ounce, small powdered ; loaf[1] honey one drachm, boar's grease three drachms and a half, half a quartern,[2] and a drachm of verdigris, small powdered. Let them fry all together till they be soft and well mingled, and then strain them ; and put thereto a pound of turpentine that is already powdered ; and let them be put on the fire again till they be soft ; and mix them together with a slice, and then pour into the box. This is noble both [for] drawing and healing.

292 Another entrete to lay on a wound or on a botch or on black nails to make them grow, and it may be kept twenty winters. Take rosin of the pine-tree and an ounce of white wax, and an ounce of other rosin, and an ounce of turpentine ; and set all together on an easy fire till they be molten ; and when it is molten, cast it in a vessel with cold water ; and afterwards take it out and temper it between thy hands with oil of bay ; and when it is tempered enough, keep it well for it is a good entrete.[3]

293 To make an entrete for botches and boils to cleanse them ; and to gather new flesh. Take rosin as much as thou wilt and melt it in a pot [with] vinegar ; and wring [it] through a cloth into a vessel with cold water, and temper it with thy hands as [if] it were wax, but look that they [first] be anointed with oil or with grease.

294 Another for the same. Take perosin and incense that is white, and wether's tallow, of each equally much ; but look that the tallow be molten first and purified. And then put all together in a pot and melt them at the fire, and stir fast with a slice till they be well molten and mingled

---

[1] Apparently honey dried and cut into loaves, or cubes.
[2] The name of some substance is here omitted in error.
[3] This recipe is a duplicate of § 633.

H

wrynge thorow a cloth in to a clene vessell and put þer to
as moch juyse of rotys of walwort as of any oþ⁹ [fo. 29
verso] thitt þ⁹ be off ech on lich moch ⅃ medle heme wele
to gedir//

295 To make ane entrete for festrynge Take hony and
vertgresse powdrede as moch as thou wilt and seth hem
togedir in an erthyn pott and stir it wele and iff thow wilt
wit when it is soden enogh put a drop on a cold yrene or
on a stoon and iff it be hard when it is colde it is wele
and than of thatt fyll the wound twyse on the day ⅃ he
shall hele

296 ffor to make a sanatise trete for to brynge rankeled
woundes brennyng ⅃ akynge to here own state Take þe
juse of smalach and of morell ⅃ the less waybrede ⅃ of the
more hony and the white of egges of ech lich moch and medle
all thies togedir and put to hem fayre floʳ of whete ⅃ stir
and medle hem togedir till thei be thyke and put hem nat
to the fyre but so raw lay it to the wounde and it shall do
away the akynge ⅃ it shall brynge it to good state and hele
it

297 To make an entrete sanatyse for broken tetys and open
Take an erb þat men call alla and lapp it in rede wort levys
and lay it vndir hote askes halue a mylway ⅃ then thies
erbes owt of þe fyre and stamp it as wele as þᵘ mayst wᵗ
goode hony and vynegre and medle it wele toged⁾ and put
hem in a box ⅃ lay it first to the papp a pleyst made of
ga (*sic*)¹ and of floure of whete sothen with vynegre and
lay this pleyst twyes on the soore and after lay þe trete
to (*sic*)

298 To make a gode blake entrete ffor woundis and
vnbicomes and brynnynges Take a quart of oyle of olyue
and boyle it wele And when it is boyled kest a [fo. 30
recto] quartron of reede lede and stir it wele wᵗ a slyce
and boyle it to it be blak and iff thow will witt when it
is enough drop a dropp on pchmyn and iff it be blake it
is enowȝ and then let it kele and than it is a good entrete
both drawynge and helynge

---

¹ Here a paragraph mark inserted in error.
² This is a duplicate of § 953.
³ *I.e.*, to a proper, or healthy, state.

together, and then wring through a cloth into a clean vessel ; and put thereto as much juice of roots of walwort as of any other that there be, of each one equally much, and mix them well together.

295 To make an entrete for festering.[2] Take honey and verdigris powdered as much as thou wilt, and seethe them in an earthen pot, and stir it well ; and if thou wilt know when it is seethed enough, put a drop on a cold iron or on a stone ; and if it be hard when it is cold, it is well ; and then of that fill the wound twice a day, and it shall heal.

296 For to make a healing entrete for to bring rankled wounds, burning and aching, to their own state.[3] Take the juice of smallage and of morell and the less of waybread and of the more of honey, and the white of eggs, of each equally much ; and mix all these together, and put to them fair flour of wheat ; and stir and mingle them together till they be thick, and put them not to the fire, and thus raw, lay it to the wound. And it shall do away the aching, and it shall bring it to a good state and heal it.

297 To make a healing entrete for broken and open teats. Take a herb that men call alla (wood-sorrel), and wrap it in red cabbage leaves ; and lay it under hot ashes half a mile-way,[4] and then [take] these herbs out of the fire ; and stamp it as well as thou mayest with good honey and vinegar, and mingle it well together, and put them in a box ; and lay first to the pap a plaster made of ga (sic) and of flour of wheat sodden with vinegar ; and lay this plaster twice on the sore, and afterwards lay the entrete [there]to.

298 To make a good black entrete for wounds and un-becomes[5] and burnings. Take a quart of oil of olive and boil it well. And when it is boiled, cast [in] a quartern of red lead, and stir it well with a slice, and boil it till it be black. And if thou wilt know when it is [boiled] enough, drop a drop on parchment ; and if it be black, it is enough ; and then let it cool, and then it is a good entrete, both drawing and healing.

---

[4] The time taken to walk a mile. The same expression is used in §§ 788, 1026, 1030.

[5] Papules or other disfigurements of the face.

299 To make an entrete that is called gracia dei   Take
verueyn and betayn and pympnell of ech an handfull with
the rotis and w^t the stalkes and wasshe thies herbes and
stampe in a morῖ small and after put hem in an erthyn
pott with a galon of good white wyne and if thou may
haue no white take rede and seth hem till the halue be soden
away of the wyne and then take it fro the fyre and lett it
kele a lyttell and wryng it thorow a cloth and than take
the licour and put in to the pot agayne and seth it on the
fyre and when it doth seth put in halue a pound of med wex
molten in womans mylk that hath a knaffe childe sowkynge
꓿ a pound of prosen powdrede and a pound of litarge and a
pound of galbanū and a pound of opopenalk ꓿. lj j of
astrologia rotunda and a ℥j of powdir of mastyke and stire
with a sclyce that the powders cleue nat by þᵉ pottis botom
and then put in a peny wight of bawm and a ferthyng wight
and lat it seth whil yow myght say thries this psalme
miserere mei deus ꓿ then take it fro the fyre and put þᶦᵗo
di quartron of turpentyne and alway stire it wele with a
sklyce till þat it be all wele medlede togedir and then take
it down ꓿ streyne [fo. 30 *verso*] it thorow a canvas in too a
clene vessell ꓿ w^t a fethir do away þᵉ fome ꓿ when it is cold
take owt the gobett owt of the licoure ꓿ temp it wele in
thyne handis ffor the more þat it is temped þᵉ bettyr itt is ·
the vertu of this is principally of woundes in hede by the
brayne and itt shall be layd on lynnen cloth or on a pece
of white lethir and it made with owten bawme but it is
betῖ with bawme and when þᵘ puttyst it in to any wound
chaunge it twyes on a day and is good fore new sores and
also for old

300 To make g̅r̅a̅ dei vpon anoþᶦ manῖ   Take beteyne
verueyn and pympnell of ech an handfull both the rotis and
the levys ꓿ wesshe hem wele ꓿ stamp hem in a morῖ and put
hem in to an new erthen pot ꓿ put þᶦᵗo a potell of good
whyte wyne and seth it on the fyre till þᵉ halue be soden
away and when it is sodyn soo do doune þᵉ pot of the fyre

---

¹ This confection was very popular in the Middle Ages and for long
after. Many MSS. contain variant recipes for its preparation. The
present Leechbook has three, there is one in H., two in *Harl.* 2378,
and another in *Sloane* 521. (Henslow, *op. cit.*, pp. 53, 86, 119, 143).

299 To make an entret ethat is called Gratia Dei.[1] Take vervain and betony and pimpernel, of each a handful, with the roots and with the stalks, and wash these herbs and stamp [them] small in a mortar ; and afterwards put them in an earthen pot with a gallon of good white wine, and if thou mayest have no white, take red ; and seethe them till the half be boiled away of the wine, and then take it from the fire and let it cool a little ; and wring it through a cloth, and then take the licour ; and put it into the pot again, and seethe it on the fire. And when it doth seethe (comes to the boil), put in half a pound of prepared wax molten in the milk of a woman who hath a male child sucking, and a pound of perosin powdered, and a pound of litharge, and a pound of galbanum, and a pound of opopanax and a pound of aristolochia rotunda (round birthwort), and one ounce of powder of mastic. And stir with a slice that the powders cleave not to the pot's bottom, and then put in a penny-weight of balm, and a farthing weight ;[2] and let it seethe while thou mightest say thrice this psalm *Miserere mei Deus*.[3] And then take it from the fire, and put thereto half a quartern of turpentine, and always stir it well with a slice till it be all well mingled together. And then take it down and strain it through a canvas into a clean vessel, and with a feather brush away the foam. And when it is cold, take the gobbet out of the licour, and temper it well in thy hands ; for the more it is tempered, the better it is. The virtue of this [preparation] is principally for wounds of the head near the brain, and it shall be laid on linen cloth or on a piece of white leather, and it [having been] made without balm, but it is better with balm. And when thou puttest it into any wound, change it twice a day, and it is good for new sores and also for old.

300 To make Gratia Dei upon another manner. Take betony, vervain and pimpernel, of each a handful, both the roots and the leaves, and wash them well and stamp them in a mortar, and put them into a new earthen pot, and put thereto a pottle of good white wine ; and seethe it on the fire till half be boiled away ; and when it is seethed, so take

---

   [2] There is either an omission here, or else we must read a penny-weight and a quarter of balm.
   [3] Psalm li.

and lat it stand hyllyd xij oures ⁊ þen streyn itt thorow
a canvas in to a clene vessell and wasshe the pot wᵗ white
wyne and put the licoure in to þᵉ pott ⁊ sett it agayn on
the fyre and lat it seth and than take d̄i a pound of mede
wex small mynsed and put in l̄i ℔ of prosyn ⊐ ℥ of galbanū
and a ℥ of powdre mastyke and l̄i ℔ of powdre encens ⊐
styr it alway with a sklyce that it sytt nat to þᵉ potts
botom and lat it seth while thou may say this psalme
miserere mei deus and till thai be medillyd and molten
togedyre and þen take it down and put in a quartron of
turpentyne and styr it wele till they be molten and wele
medled [fo. 31 *recto*] togedir and than anoon streyne hem
thorow a cansast in to a clene vessell and when it is welnygh
colde take a fethir and do away the foome ⊐ when the fome
is a way hill it and latt it stand to the morow and then
take an vnce of wymmans mylke of a knawe chylde and put
itt in a glass and stopp it wele till till (*sic*) the morowe as
thow didist that oþ⁹ and then put that licoure in to a pot
with the mylke and sett itt on the fire and het it wele but
looke that it seth nat and then take it down and lat it
stand to kele to thow may wele tempre itt bytwyx thy
hands and than take it owt of the licoure and temp it
bytwyx yʳ handys as thou didist that oþ⁹ bifore seide and
this good for the same that the oþ⁹ is

301 To make ḡra dei on the lyghttist manere Take
verveyn and betayn ⊐ pympnell of ech an handfull pound
hem and boyle hem in a galon of whit wyne to the thyrd
part than streyne hem thorow a lynnen cloth and then sett
it oū̃) the fyre and do ther to virgyn wex a pound of prosyn
a pound of mastyke poudrede iij ℥ seth all thies on an easy
fyre for it be desied and then sett it doune and do ther to
turmentyne x peny wight and stirre it till it be cold and wete
thyne handes in womans mylke and handle it wele and do
it in boxes and it will hele al mañ̃) off soores.

302 F̲Or the ffeuers A principall medecyn // Take ℥℔
    off pepyr and greynes ℥ ℔ and of gyng̃) ij or iij
gode Rasyns and make all this in powdyr and than take as
moch of senvoy sede as of all thies othiʳ and stamp it small
in a [fo. 31 *verso*] mortyre and then medle all thies with vj
sponefull of aysell and the threddendele of a quart of stale

down the pot from the fire, and let it stand covered for
twelve hours. And then strain it through a canvas into a
clean vessel, and wash the pot with white wine, and put the
licour into the pot ; and set it again on the fire and let it
seethe, and then take half a pound of prepared wax, small
minced, and put in half a pound of perosin, and an ounce of
galbanum and an ounce of powder-mastic, and half a pound
of powder-incense ; and stir it always with a slice that it
stick not to the pot's bottom ; and let it seethe while thou
mayest say this psalm, *Miserere mei Deus*, and till they be
mingled and molten together. And then take it down, and
put in a quartern of turpentine, and stir it well till they be
molten and well mingled together ; and then anon strain
them through a canvas into a clean vessel ; and when it is
wellnigh cold, take a feather, and brush away the foam ;
and when the foam is away, cover it and let it stand till the
morrow. And then take an ounce of the milk of a woman
who has a boy-child, and put it in a glass and stop it well
till the morrow, as thou didst that other ; and then put that
licour into a pot with the milk, and set it on the fire, and heat
it well, but look that it boil not. And then take it down,
and let it stand to cool till thou mayest well temper it between
thy hands. And then take it out of the licour and temper
it between thy hands as thou didst that other aforesaid.
And this is good for the same [purposes] that the other is.

301 To make Gratia Dei on the lightest (simplest) manner.
Take vervain and betony and pimpernel, of each a handful ;
pound them and boil them in a gallon of white wine to the
third part ; then strain them through a linen cloth, and
then set it over the fire ; and put thereto virgin wax, a
pound ; of perosin, a pound ; of mastic powdered, three
ounces. Seethe all these on an easy fire so that it be
dissolved, and then set it down, and put thereto turpentine
ten pennyweight, and stir it till it be cold. And wet thy
hands in woman's milk, and handle it well, and put it in
boxes. And it will heal all manner of sores.

302 **F**or the fevers. A principal medicine. Take half an
ounce of pepper, and grains (kermes) half an ounce,
and of ginger, two or three good raisins, and make all this in
powder ; and then take as much of senvey (mustard) seed
as of all these others, and stamp it small in a mortar ; and
then mingle all these with six spoonfuls of vinegar, and the

ale and seth it till it be all moost soden away vnto iij sopys
and then soup it vp and do so iij days durynge when the
colde begynneth to come and thow shall be hoole on
waranties for it hath bene p⁹vyed but when thow dost so
lat thi bedd be made with fresshe shetis and hill the warme
and stopp in thyne awn breth and if thow do so iij he will
shake no more pᵇ est

303 Also sothernwode when þᵉ disease comyth with watir
helpith the cold feuere and make an empleyster of sothernwode and medle it with fresshe gresse and it will draw owt
stubb or thorne that stykkyth in the fflesshe this erbe
cōfortith the stomake in what wyse some eũ) a man take
it and iff be sothen in reyn watir and drenken cold itt will
distroy wormes in the body and makyth lax ꝫ staunchith
ach of wombe and makyth to pysse

304 An othir take þᵉ rotis of turmentill and make in powdre
and medle it with clarified hony and vse a sponefull first
and last

305 ffor feũ) in the stomake   Take comyn annese fenell
seed rede rose levys wormode myntes vinegre soure brede
fried in a panne ꝫ mad in a pleystire and lay in a bagg to
the stomake lewke hote ꝫ new it oft with vinegre

306 ffallynge euell //   Take v̂)veyn and the clote and broune
ffenell and boyle hem in a galon of goode stale ale till the
halue and vse it

307 ffoundynge off hors   Take iiij egges and rost hem hard
and all hote put in euy⁹ off the hors fete on shell and all
and stop it fast about wᵗ [fo. 32 *recto*] hors dunge and so
latt hyme stand and he shall be hole

308 ffor the flix   Take the juyse of mylefoyll and temp it
with floure and make a cake and ete it all

309 Anoþ⁹ take a yonge chiken and dyght it and take owt
the bowelles and put wex in jt and rost itt and giff hym to
ete

310 ffor a felone to distroy hyme take hony and the yolke
of an ey and floure of whete and temp heme togedir and

third part of a quart of stale ale ; and seethe it till it be almost boiled away unto eight sups,[1] and then sip it up and do so three days during [the time] when the cold beginneth to come, and thou shalt be whole on warranty (certainly), for it hath been proved. But when thou dost so, let thy bed be made with fresh sheets, and cover thyself up warmly, and stop in thine own breath, and if thou do so three [days], he will shake (shiver, or tremble) no more.

303 [Another]. Also southernwood with water, when the disease cometh, helpeth the cold fever. And make a plaster of southernwood and mingle it with fresh grease, and it will draw out stub or thorn that sticketh in the flesh. ' This herb comforteth the stomach in whatever way soever a man take it ; and if it be seethed in rainwater and drank cold, it will destroy worms in the body ; and maketh lax, and stancheth ache of womb and maketh to urinate.

304 Another. Take roots of tormentil, and make [them] into powder, and mingle it with clarified honey, and use a spoonful first and last.

305 For fever in the stomach. Take cumin, anise, fennel-seed, red rose leaves, wormwood, mint, vinegar, sour bread, fried in a pan and made into a plaster, and lay [it] in a bag to the stomach lukewarm, and renew it often with vinegar.

306 Falling-evil (epilepsy). Take vervain and cloves and brown fennel, and boil them in a gallon of good stale ale to the half, and use it.

307 Founding (lameness) of horse. Take four eggs and roast them hard ; and, all hot, put in each of the horse's feet one, shell and all, and stop it fast about with horsedung ; and so let him stand, and he shall be whole.

308 For the flux. Take the juice of milfoil and temper it with flour, and eat it all.

309 Another. Take a young chicken and dress it, and take out the bowels, and put wax in it ; and roast it, and give it him to eat.

310 For a felon[2] to destroy it. Take honey and the yolk of an egg, and flour of wheat ; and temper them together,

---

[1] About a spoonful.
[2] A kind of whitlow, but used of any forms of inflammation, ulceration, or small boils.

lay it on the felone and as it dryeth lay on new and it shall sle hym v̄p̄p̄

311 ffor the foundment that goth owt Take apostolicon and hete it at the fyre and touch the foundment and it shall go in agayn and do so onys or twyes whē it gooth owt and after þat bath the foundement with waͭ that peritory is soden in and it shall be hole or vse to drynke antioch for the same Also wasshe the foundement that cōmyth owte with thyn awn vryn full oft and it will in agayne

312 ffor fantn̄s and dwelsynge make a garland of betayn and hange abowte thy neke when thou goost to bedd that you maist haue the savo̊ ther off all nyght and it will help the

313 ffor wymmen flo̊es Take the rotis of gladen and seth hem in wyn or vynegre and when it is wele soden sett it on the ground ꝺ·stryde she or stand she ther on that the fywme stye vp to hyre so that ther may noon eyre away but evyne vp but be she nat with child this medecyn faylid neuͬ

314 To draw down floures and dissolue heme take oyle of lylie and enoynt þᵉ pryue place at the fire and lay þer on a cloth and lay hyre abedd

315 ffor the same make powdere of frankencens and of gotis dunge and lay it on a few whik colis vndͬ ane [fo. 32 verso] holow stole or a cheyre and she sittynge þᵉon bare so þᵗ the fywme may go up to it

316 Anothir Take mugworte wormode camamell hayrisse hoorhound bayes fenell with wythien levys sothernwod alysaundre ysop camamell mauce and make þ⁹off a bath and take þᵉ rotis of ferne and levys of mogwort wasshen and branne and fresshe gresse of a shepe and boyle thies and make a pleystire and lay to her navell and so down ward

317 ffor to many floures Take a powder that is clepid antidotum ymagogū drynke þ⁹of wᵗ stale ale and itt shall ese heme and make hir hole

---

[1] See § 289.
[2] See note to § 161.

and lay it on the felon ; and as it dryeth, lay on anew, and it shall slay him up (destroy it).

311 For the fundament that goweth out (prolapse of the rectum). Take apostolicon[1] and heat it at the fire, and touch the fundament [therewith], and it shall go in again ; and do so once or twice when it goeth out, and after that bathe the fundament with water that pellitory is boiled in, and it shall be whole. Or use to drink Antioch[2] for the same. Also wash the fundament that cometh out with thine own urine, and it will [go] in again.

312 For phantasma and delusions. Make a garland of betony and hang about thy neck when thou goest to bed, that thou mayest have the savour thereof all night, and it will help thee.

313 For women's flowers. Take the roots of gladyne (iris), and seethe them in wine or vinegar ; and when it is well sodden, set in on the ground, and let her stride or stand thereover that the fumes may steam up to her, so that there may be no air but even up.[3] Unless she be with child, this medicine failed never.

314 To draw down flowers and dissolve them (*i.e.* promote the flow). Take oil of lily and anoint the privy place by the fire, and lay thereon a cloth, and put her to bed.

315 For the same. Make powder of frankincense and goat's dung, and lay it on a few quick (glowing) coals under a hollow stool or a chair, and she sitting thereon bare, so that the fumes may go up to it.

316 Another. Take mugwort, wormwood, camomile, sow-thistle, horehound, bay, fennel, with withy-leaves, southern-wood, alexanders, hyssop, camomile,[4] mace, and make thereof a bath ; and take the roots of fern and leaves of mugwort, washed, and bran and fresh grease of a sheep ; and boil these and make a plaster and lay to her navel, and so downward.

317 For too many flowers (flooding). Take a powder that is called antidotum emenagogum ; drink thereof with stale ale, and it shall ease them and make her whole.

---

[3] The meaning is, exclude all air, so that nothing but the steam of the decoction may reach the organ. *Cf.* § 321.

[4] Repeated in error ; it occurs earlier in the list.

318 Also make a pleistre of an hote turdyll of a horse dung
soden in vynegre and lay it to her navell as hote as she
may suffre it or ellis take whete flour and seth it in mylke
and hony and make a pleystre to hir navyll as hote as she
may suffre

319 An othir for to many floures for to cesse hem sone
Take an hare fote and brenne it to powdre and lat hir
drynke of that powder with stale ale first and last till she
be hole

320 Also Take comfery and wasshe it and stamp it and seth
it ī wyne and make a pleystir to her wombe and to the
navell ꝗ an oþᵒ to the reynes or take shepis tridellis and
stamp hem and medyll hem wᵗ ȝeltis grese and fry heme
to gedir and make a pleystre to the wombe and to the
reynes and that will help hir fayre and wele

321 ffor to make a woman haue her flõ red when thai
bene distroyed this medecyn faylith neũ but be ware that
she be nat with child Take þᵉ rote of gladen ꝗ seth hym
in vynegre or in wyne and when it is sothen set it [fo. 33
recto] on the ground ꝗ lett hir strid þᵒ oũ so that the eyre
may nat go away but euyn up in to þᵉ pryuytee

322 Another Take hony and sprynge powdre of madyr on
heme and make a suppository þᵒoff and it shall make a
woman to haue hyre termes

323 To dissolue flowynge flowres kytt madyr on small
gobettis and lay it in swete wyne fastynge / þᵉ juyse of the
same erbe doth the same if thou drynke it ix dayes

324 ffor the same put the juys of waybrede in the pryuytie
or drynke it and this is the best and none lyke it

325 Anoþᵒ ffor to brynge heme Take the juyse of m̃curye
hony floure and cockyll añ and make littell balles ther of
and giff hir one or twey or thre and that nyght shall she
haue hem and dispose hir to conceyfe

326 ffor the fire of hell that brynnyth in mannes flesshe
Take the dayse cropp and rote and bruse hyme and lay

318 [Another]. Also make a plaster of hot horsedung boiled in vinegar and lay it to her navel as hot as she may suffer it. Or else take wheat flour and seethe it in milk and honey, and make a plaster to her navel as hot as she may suffer [it].

319 Another for too many flowers, for to cease them soon. Take a hare's foot and burn it to powder; and let her drink of that powder with stale ale first and last, till she be whole.

320 [Another]. Also take comfrey and wash it, and stamp it and seethe it in wine; and make a plaster to her womb and to the navel; and another to the reins; or take sheep's droppings and stamp them, and mingle them with gelt's grease; and fry them together and make a plaster to the womb, and to the reins. And that will help her fair and well.

321 For to make a woman have her flowers red when they have ceased to flow. This medicine faileth never, but beware that she be not with child. Take the root of gladyne (iris), and seethe it in vinegar or in wine; and when it is sodden, set it on the ground; and let her stride thereover, so that the air (vapour) may not escape except up into the privity.[1]

322 Another. Take honey, and sprinkle powder of madder on it, and make a suppository thereof, and it shall make a woman to have her terms.

323 To dissolve flowing flowers (check flooding). Cut madder into small gobbets and lay it in sweet wine [and give it her to eat] fasting. The juice of the same herb doth the same if thou drink it nine days.

324 For the same. Put the juice of waybread in the privity, or drink it. And this is the best, and none like it.

325 Another for to bring them. Take the juice of mercury, honey, flour, and cockle (ergot), of each equal quantity; and make little balls thereof, and give her one or two or three; and that night she shall have them (the terms), and be disposed to conceive.

326 For the fire of hell[2] that burneth in a man's flesh. Take the daisy, crop and root, and bruise it, and lay thereto, and

---

[1] Cf. § 313.
[2] Also called wildfire and St. Anthony's fire (erysipelas).

þᵉto and chaunge it oft   And to preue iff it be that syknesse or nay take a lynnen cloth and wete it in vynegre and ley ther too and if it be that syknesse it will smoke anone and then lay ther to the juyse of planteyn ꝛ it will hele it

327 Also take broornaschen and mede þᵉwith the white on an ey and oyle of roses and drop it on the fyre till the smoke cesse than take an hare foote and bryn it to powdir and take hors dunge faire tirdelles and boyle hem togedire in vynegre ꝛ lay þᵉto

328 ffor the same   Take bene mele a goode quantitee of comyn brused and boyled wele in rede wyne of gascoyn and make a pleystir and ley þᵉtoo

329 a medecyne ffor þᵉ [fo. 33 *verso*] wyld fyre   Take old hard chees the eldyr the betᵗ and grate it small a good quantitee and medle it wele with hony by the more parte and enoynt the soore ther with till it be hoole this is pᵉvyd

330 ffor all maner of flix seth egges harde and stampe the yolkes with stronge vynegre and streyn itt and drynke it

331 An othir ffor the same take white brede and menge hard eyien and gratyd brede togedir and put þᵉto rede onyons mynsyd and poudre of pep and ete this twyes on the day till thou be hole

332 Anothir for ffor (*sic*) the fflyx   Take hertys horne in the shell if an oystere and brenne it and make powdyre þᵉoff and seth it with hony ꝛ pep ꝛ ix dayes ete þᵉoff erly and late

333 There bene iiij manᵉ of flix one is callid collides and that is a syknes of the stomake that comyth of kene coleryke humȯs and makyth a man to haue a stronge flix and a grete kestynge ꝛ it sleth a man wᵗin thre dayes but he haue hep the rather

334 The secund flix is clepid licentaria þat is when a mannys mete passyth from hyme vndefiede

335 Diarua is the thrid manᵉ of flix dirt medyled with blode

336 Dissincla is the iiij manᵉ of flix and that is when þᵉ comyth blode and the shavynge of guttis þᵉwith togedir

change it often.   And to prove if it be that sickness or not, take a linen cloth and wet it in vinegar, and lay thereto ; and if it be that sickness, it will smoke anon ; and then lay thereto the juice of plantain, and it will heal it.

327 [Another].   Also take brown ashes and mix therewith the white of an egg and oil of roses, and drop it on the fire till the smoke cease ; then take a hare's foot and burn it to powder and take horse-dung, fair portions, and burn them together in vinegar and lay thereto.

328 For the same.   Take bean-meal, a good quantity of cumin, bruised and boiled well in red wine of Gascony. And make a plaster, and lay thereto.

329 A medicine for the wildfire.   Take old hard cheese, the older the better, and grate it small ; [and take] a good quantity and mingle it well with a greater quantity of honey, and anoint the sore therewith till it be whole.   *This is proved*.

330 For all manner of flux.   Seethe eggs hard, and stamp the yolks with strong vinegar, and strain it and drink it.

331 Another for the same.   Take white bread, and mix hard [-boiled] eggs and grated bread together, and put thereto red onions minced, and powder of pepper, and eat this twice a day till thou be whole.

332 Another for the flux.   Take hartshorn in the shell of an oyster and burn it ; and make powder thereof, and seethe it with honey and pepper ; and nine days eat thereof early and late.

333 There be four kinds of flux.[1]   One is called collides, and that is a sickness of the stomach that cometh of keen choleric humors, and maketh a man to have a strong flux, and a great casting (vomiting), and it slayeth a man within three days, unless he hath help earlier.

334 The second flux is called licentaria ; that is, when a man's meat passeth from him undigested.

335 Diarrhœa is the third manner of flux : dirt mingled with blood.

336 Dysentery is the fourth manner of flux ; and that is when there cometh blood and the shaving of gutts (pieces of tissue) therewith together.

---

[1] This first paragraph of the gloss on flux is a duplicate of § 343.

337 To do away fraklyns in the face a quantitee of peletre
of spayn and seth it in wyne and when it is wele sothen let
it stand ꝛ when þᵂ gost to bedd wasshe thi face wyth that
wyne and then lay þʳ pleystre sothen and whan thou risist
on the morow wasshe þe with clere waᷘ

338 An othir for þᵉ same   Take hares blode ꝛ medle it wᵗ
swalows eyien ꝛ enoynt ye þᵒwith · but it must [fo. 34
recto] be doñe ech yer new this medecyn is good but the
oþᵒ is bettyr//

339 An othir ffor the same   Take boyles blode ꝛ enoynt
þᵒwith

340 ffor face þat semyth leprose   Take qwiksilvᵒ and grese
of a boor ꝛ blake pepyr and ensens ꝛ stamp it wele to
gedre and þᵒwᵗ anoynt thi face and kepe it fro the wynd
iij days and it shall be hoole

341 Many ar the syknes of the myddyll pty of a mannes
hede and it is to say madness or franesye and this syknes
comyth othir while of colory oþᵒ while of blode oþᵒ while of
malencoly   Jf it come of colory it makyth a man debatows
ꝛ harme full and iff it come of blode it makyth it makyth
(*sic*) a man playnge and synynge ꝛ noon harme doynge
Jff come of malencoly it makyth a man so leyn And
dredefull of all thynge

342 ffranesye is a postyme in the forthir ptie of the hede
and ppurely it comyth of colore that is to say of hete and
dremes neþeles othire while itt cōmyth vnpfitable oþᵒwhile
of hete and moystnes

343 Collides is a syknes of the stomake that cōmyth of
kene colleryk humós and makyth a man to haue stronge
flix and grete kestȳg and it sleth a man wᵗin iij days but iff
he haue the rathir helpe

344 ffor the frenesy a medecyn   Take an erbe that men clepe
shepardis ȝerde ꝛ stamp it and lay it on his hede when itt
is shaue

345 ffor the feuᷘ   Take an ℥ of planteyn wᵗ an ℥j of betayn
stampid togedire and drynke it wᵗ warme waᷘ or þᵉ colde

337 To do away freckles in the face.[1]   [Take] a quantity of pellitory of Spain and seethe it in wine; and when it is well sodden, let it stand.   And when thou goest to bed, wash thy face with that wine, and then lay there [the] plaster; and when thou risest on the morrow, wash thee with clear water.

338 Another for the same.   Take hare's blood and mix it with swallows' eyes and anoint thee therewith, but it must be done anew every year.   This medicine is good, but the other is better.

339 Another for the same.   Take bull's blood and anoint therewith.

340 For the face that seemeth leprous.[2]   Take quicksilver and grease of a boar, and black pepper and incense, and stamp it well together; and therewith anoint thy face and keep it from the wind three days and it shall be whole.

341 Many are the sicknesses of the middle part of a man's head; that is to say, madness or frenzy cometh sometimes of choler, sometimes of blood, sometimes of melancholy. If it come of choler, it maketh a man quarrelsome and harmful; and if it come of blood, it maketh a man playful and merry, and doing no harm.   If it come of melancholy, it maketh a man most timid and afraid of everything.

342 Frenzy is an aposteme in the further part of the head, and it cometh only of choler, that is to say, of heat, and dreams; nevertheless sometimes it cometh unprofitably; at other times of heat and moistness.

343 Collides (colic) is a sickness of the stomach that cometh of keen choleric humours, and maketh a man to have strong flux and great casting, and it slayeth a man within three days, unless he have help earlier.[3]

344 For the frenzy, a medicine.   Take a herb that men call shepherd's yard (wild-teazle), and stamp it and lay it on his head when it is shaven.

345 For the fever.   Take an ounce of plantain, with an ounce of betony, stamped together; and drink it with

---

[1] *Cf.* Henslow, *op. cit.*, p. 80.
[2] Duplicate in H. (*op. cit.*, p. 41, *cf.* p. 80), and below, § 791.
[3] Duplicate of § 333.

I

come and itt will distroy the cotidian feũer

346 An oþ⁹ for the same   Take the myddyll rynd of ellem and the blossoms ꝛ lay hem ij days or iij in watir and giff the pacient that [fo. 34 *verso*] watir to drynke

347 ffor the feuer tercian lat hym drynke the juse of the Swete pomegarnadis for to defy the mater the floures ther of bene clepid baulastica   Also iiij crabbes serue for hame that haue þᵉ feuers for to ete hem after mete both raw and sothen but thei bene bettir sothen or rostyde and it is good for heme that haue filthede stomake and coolde   Jn this wise kytt owt the core ꝛ fill the hoole wᵗ powd⁷ of nutmugs and of mastyke and of clows and with the powdire of pepyre and of comyn

348 ffor the feuer of A mannes hede that makyth the hede to Ake that he may nat slepe   Take euerferne that growith vpon an oke and seth the rote þ⁹of ꝛ mynt of ech lich moch and stampe hem and make a pleystir to thi forhede and oũ the eyen enoynt wᵗ piliall

349 An othir ffor the feũ quotidiañ   Take the seede of smalach and stamp it wele and temp it wele with iij sponefull of coold watyr and giff the syke to drynke whē thou supposist that the euyll will take hyme ffor the feũ tercian nyght or day when thow trowist that the euyll wele take the   Take ꝛ make a cake of barly mele and lat hyme þ⁹of as he may ꝛ then lat hyme drynke goode wyne good plentee or the syknes take hyme / than take thou iiij plantes of waybrede wᵗ the rote and all togedir and wasshe heme clene and stamp hem and tempre the Juse wᵗ wyne and lat hym drynke itt and latt hyme slepe and he shall fare wele

350 To breke a felone or A postyme with in or with owt Take agyst watches culid dunge Swynes grese and crommes of soure brede and grind hem small togedir and lay þ⁹to

350ᴀ take wormode smalach and as moch [fo. 35 *recto*] of swynes grese as erbis and bray heme togedir and do it in A cloth and lay it to þᵉ felon or postyme and it shall draw

warm water before the cold come out, and it will destroy quotidian fever.

346 Another for the same.   Take the middle rind of elms and the blossoms, and lay them two or three days in water ; and give the patient that water to drink.

347 For the tertian fever.   Let him drink the juice of sweet pomegranates ; for to define the matter, the flowers thereof are called balaustium.[1] Also three crabs (crab-apples) serve for them that have fevers for to eat them after meat, both raw and boiled or roasted ; and it is good for them that have a filthied stomach, and cold.   In this wise, cut out the core, and fill the hole with powder of nutmegs and of mastic and of cloves, with the powder of pepper and cumin.

348 For the fever of a man's head that maketh the head to ache, so that he cannot sleep.   Take everfern that groweth upon an oak, and seeth the root thereof, and mint, of each equally much ; and stamp them and make a plaster to thy forehead. and over the eyes anoint with wild thyme.

349 Another for the quotidian fever.   Take the seed of smallage and stamp it well, and temper it well with three spoonfuls of cold water, and give the sick to drink when thou supposest that the evil will take him for the tertian fever night or day.   When thou trowest that the evil will take thee, take and make a cake of barley-meal, and let him [eat] thereof as he may, then let him drink good wine [in] good plenty before the sickness take him.   Then take thou four plants of waybread, with the root and all together, and wash them clean and stamp them ; and temper the juice with wine, and let him drink it.   And let him sleep, and he shall fare well.

350 To break a felon or an imposthume within or without. Take earthworms,[2] pigeon's dung, swine's grease and crumbs of sour bread ; and grind them small together and lay thereto.

350A [Another].   Take wormwood, smallage and as much of swine's grease as of herbs, and bray them together ; and put it in a cloth, and lay it to the felon or imposthume ; and it

---

[1] βαλαύστιον. Dioscorides, *De Mat. Med.*, i, 154.
[2] A.S. *angeltwicce.*   *Cf.* §§ 463, 465.

out hem w^t owtyn any trete but lõke thou new it at morow
and at eve

351 ffor to make a felon com to what place so thow wilt
Take a not shell and fill it full of the Juys of tansay and
bynd it þ^2 as thou wilt haue it ꝫ then of the same Juys
make A strike fro the place wher thow wilt haue itt come
owt and it shall come thidir

352 ffor the felon þat makyth the hede to Swell   Take the
sywet of an hert hony barly and mele heyhoue and the
rede dok and pound hem all yfere and shaue the hede of
the syke and lay the pleystir all hote to the hede and lett
it be þ^2 forto it be sane

353 ffor a ffelon take solucle and the ȝolke of an ey salt
and blake sope and gresse of a bore and medle togedir and
lay on the soore ꝫ it shall hele it / Or seth in ale crommes
of soure brede and matfelon morell and auence ꝫ· stamp it
with hony and vse it

354 ffor festre and namely ī the mowth make stronge lye
w^t the asshes of vyne braunches and yonge asshe and
vynegre and then w^t that lyȝe medyll the powdir of celidony
rote and w^t a faiell do it in to þ^e mouth of the festire

355 Celidony is to say gift of hevyn

356 ffor festre in a wound and dede flesshe to distroy take
new wex and verdegrese code fraunkencens and pich and
tarre turmentyn shepis talowȝ w^t grese and fry that togedir
in a panne ꝫ when it is soden togedir cole it thorow a
colondre and do it in to boxis

357 An othir for to frete away the dede flesshe   Take
brent alom and [fo. 35 verso] copose and veredegresse and
sandeuere and grynd hem all togedire in to a powd⁀ and
straw þer on and it will frete it owt //   A festyr is A
stynkynge soore that is ill kept and stynkyth þ^{2}fore

358 ffor fleen and lyse to sle heme take hors mynt and
straw hem in thyn hows and it will sle heme

359 An othir take the juyse of rywe and enoynt thi body
þ^{2}with

---

¹ This is an interpolation, and has no relation to what precedes
or follows.   The etymology is false, for the word is derived from
χελιδών, " swallow," and not from coeli donum.

shall draw them out without any entrete, but look that thou renew it at morn and at eve.

351 For to make a felon come to whatsoever place thou wilt. Take a nutshell and fill it full of the juice of tansey and bind it thereto as thou wilt have it ; and then with the same juice make a streak where thou wilt have it, and it shall come thither.

352 For the felon that maketh the head to swell. Take the suet of a hart, honey, barley and meal, ground-ivy and the red dock, and pound them all together ; and shave the head of the sick, and lay the plaster all hot to the head and let it be there until it be sane (well).

353 For a felon. Take solsicle and the yolk of an egg, salt and black soap and grease of a boar ; and mingle together and lay on the sore and it shall heal it. Or seethe in ale crumbs of sour bread, and knapweed, morell and avens, and stamp it with honey and use it.

354 For fester, and especially in the mouth. Make strong lye with the ashes of vine-branches and young ash-trees and vinegar ; and then with that lye, mingle powder of celandine root, and with a file apply it to the mouth of the fester.

355 Celidony is to say, gift of heaven.[1]

356 For fester in a wound, and dead flesh to destroy. Take new wax, verdigris, code (cobbler's wax), frankincense, and pitch and tar, turpentine, sheep's tallow, with grease, and fry that together in a pan ; and when it is seethed together, cool it through a collander and put it in boxes.

357 Another for to fret away the dead flesh. Take burnt alum and copperas, and verdigris and sandiver,[2] and grind them all together in a powder, and strew thereon and it will fret it out. A fester is a stinking sore that is ill-kept, and stinketh therefore.

358 For fleas and lice to slay them. Take horsemint and strew it in thy house, and it will slay them.[3]

359 Another. Take the juice of rue and anoint thy body therewith.

---

[2] *See* note to § 205.
[3] *Cf. Ebers Papyrus,* 97, 16 (841).

360 Anoþ⁹ Take gorst and seþ it in watir and sprynge that waᵗ about the hous And þei will dye

361 ffor the ffallyng euell that is clepid the gowt cayne. Take ribwort polipody egrymoyn solsequy yarow and an vnce of pepir of all elich moch and stampe hem all togedir and giff the syke to drynke wᵗ waᵗ

362 There bene iij maners of fallyng euell wᵗ owt this before wrytyn ffor ther is one that is clepid epileusie the which is a syknes of the hyndyrparte of the hede þ⁹ as the nek and the hede bene joynyd togedire and is as moch to say as the fallynge euell that is epileusie is one that comyth of cold corrupt humors that bene behynd in the hede ther as the nek and the hede be joyned togedyrs and for the rote and bygynnynge of synows of a man is ther and by the synows all the body hath his mevynge nedely when the place is diseased by corupt humós that bene behynd in the hede a man is disposid to fall

363 Catalempsi is the secunde manᵈ of fallynge and it comyth of a corrupt stomake and it is knaw in þis wise before that a man fallith he shall fele a smoke ryse vp fro the stomake vnto the hede and his eyen shall wax dyrke and his forehede hote be fore his ffallynge

364 Analempsie is the thrid manᵈ of fallynge and it comyth of a smoke that risith vp in to þᵉ hede fro eny ptye [fo. 36 *recto*] of a mannes body that hath bene hurte and is nat wele helid as if a man haue had his legge or his arme or any othir partie of his body broken and hurt or a bocch þ⁹jnne and it be nat wele helide ther will gedir a corrupcion abowt it and of that corrupcion ther will oþ⁹while rise a smoke in to the hede that wil make a man to fall ⌁

365 GOwt ffestre Take the rote of radisshe and do it in hony iij dayes in somᵈ and in wynᵗ two days ꒋ after pound it in a mortar and make þ⁹ of powdre and dry itt wele in a new pot and enoynt the evell with hony and keste aboue þᵉ powdre

366 ffor the gowte Take ambrose ꒋ seth it wᵗ white wyne and drynke it oft and anoynt the gowte wᵗ hony þat is clene

---

¹ An unknown word. It occurs in a charm in *Harl.*, 2378. Henslow suggests that it may be intended for *sayne*, " healing," but

360 Another. Take gorse and seethe it in water, and sprinkle that water about the house, and they will die.

361 For the falling-evil that is called the gout cayne.[1] Take ribwort, polypody, agrimony, solsicle, yarrow, and an ounce of pepper, of all equally much, and stamp them all together, and give the sick to drink with water.

362 There be three kinds of falling evil, without this before written. For there is one that is called epilepsy which is a sickness of the hinder part of the head, where the neck and the head are joined together ; and this means that the falling-evil, that is epilepsy, is one that cometh of cold corrupt humors that are behind the head at the place where the neck and the head be joined, for the root and beginning of sinews of a man is there, and by the sinews all the body hath its movement ; necessarily, [therefore], when the place is diseased by corrupt humors that be behind the head, a man is disposed to fall.

363 Catalepsy is the second manner of falling [-evil], and it cometh of a corrupt stomach, and it is known in this wise : before that a man falleth, he shall feel a smoke rise up from the stomach unto the head, and his eyes shall wax dark (dim), and his forehead hot before his falling.

364 Analepsy is the third manner of falling [-evil], and it cometh of a smoke that riseth up into the head from every part of a man's body that hath been hurt and is not well healed ; as if a man had had his leg or his arm or any other part of his body broken and hurt, or a botch therein and it be not well healed, it will gather a corruption about it, and of that corruption there will sometime rise a smoke into the head that will make a man to fall.

365 Gout fester. Take the root of radish and put it in honey, three days in summer, and in winter two days ; and afterwards pound it in a mortar, and make thereof powder ; and dry it well in a new pot and anoint the evil with honey and cast above [it] the powder.

366 For the gout. Take wood-sage and seethe it with white wine, and drink it oft, and anoint the gout first with honey that is clean.

---

this does not suit the context here. It may be *capne*, and corrupted from the Greek κάθισις.

367 An oþᵉ ffor the gowte   Take pich and virgyn wex and frannke encens and shepis talwȝ euen pporcion and seth hem wele togedir and lay it on a lynnen cloth and lay it to þᵉ gowt and itt shall hele

368 An oþᵉ take mannes pisse and hold it in a vessell viij dayes or more till it be rotid and sethen seth it to haluendele and syyc cole it thorowe a cloth and aftyr take as moch of ᴦw and as moch of ȝuse of redenettill and do all togedir and take an handfull of comyn and a quantitee of virgyne wex and a quantitee of barowes grese and seth it wele togedir and wrynge it thorow a cloth and aftur take as moch of ᴦwe enoynt þᵉwith the soore

369 Anothir take the marye of hors bonys and garlyke and temp it wele togedyr and do it in a clowt and ley it on the sore agayn the fire but first seth barly in the watir [fo. 36 *verso*] and wasshe his feete oft

370 Anoþᵉ for þᵉ gout festir and canqe   Take may butter and erb watir vngle pigle syneclere Auance dayse egremoyn sporwort and buttur and make a playstire and lay þᵉto

371 An othir for the gowt in þᵉ monyth of may the fyrst thursday drynke a disshefull of the juse of betayn and that yere thou shall be saue of all maṅ of gowte

372 ffor all maṅ gowtes take walworte and bray itt in a mortar and take the Juyse and do it in a box and as moch of the blossoms of brome sotelly ground and stopp fast the box that noon eyre go in neþer go owt and then do so the box in a pot full of hote watir and seþe it so halue a day easlye vnto þᵉ ij parties of the watir be soden jnne and the thrid ptie be leue with owt the box ꝓ than take it vp and sett it in the sunne to dry and then opyn the box and it will seme with in an oyntement and than medle it with a littell may butture and claus ite on þᵉ fyre and enoynt þᵉwith the sore till itt be hole

373 Anothir for a goute festre that spryngith out hooles take alom and calamynt and make it on to powdre and medle it wᵗ hony and take floure of malt ꝓ temp itt þᵉwith till it be thike somdele as pleystre and lay it on a clowte to the sore as fere as it is rede or sore and lat it be þere ij days

367 Another for the gout.   Take pitch and virgin wax and frankincense and sheep's tallow, even proportions ; and seethe them well together, and lay it on a linen cloth ; and lay it to the gout and it shall heal.

368 Another.   Take a man's urine and hold it in a vessel eight days or more till it be rotted ; and then seethe it to its half measure, and filter it through a cloth ; and after, take as much of rue and as much of juice of red nettle, and put all together ; and take a handful of cumin and a quantity of virgin wax, and a quantity of barrow's grease, and seethe it well together, and wring it through a cloth ; and after, take as much of rue, [and] anoint therewith the sore.

369 Another.   Take the marrow of horse's bones and garlick, and temper it well together ; and put it in a cloth, and lay it to the sore by the fire ; but first seethe barley in the water, and wash his feet oft.

370 Another for the gout fester, and canker.   Take may butter and herb-Walter, ungle-pigle (stitchwort), sanicle, avens, daisy, agrimony, spearwort, and butter ; and make a plaster and lay thereto.

371 Another for the gout in the month of May.   The first Thursday drink a dishful of the juice of betony, and [all] that year thou shalt be safe from all manner of gout.

372 For all manner of gout.   Take walwort and bray it in a mortar, and take the juice and put it in a box, and as much of the blossoms of broom finely ground ; and stop fast the box that no air go in neither out ; and so put the box in a pot full of hot water, and seethe it so half a day easily (gently) until two parts of the water be boiled away, and the third part be left outside the box ; and then take it up and set it in the sun to dry, and then open the box and it will show within an ointment ; and then mingle it with a little may-butter, and close it on the fire, and anoint therewith the sore till it be whole.

373 Another for a gout fester that springeth out holes. Take alum and calamint and make it into a powder, and mingle it with honey ; and take flour of malt, and temper it therewith till it be about as thick as plaster ; and lay it on a cloth to the sore as far as it is red or sore ; and let it be there

or iij and then take it away and do so till itt be hole ꝑb e͡)

374 ffor gnawyng and fretyng in a mannys lymmes or bones
or syde   Take comyn camamyll and boyle hem togedir in
white wyne and lay it hoote to þe sore

375 ffor gryndynge in the wombe take rw and stampe wᵗ
stale ale or wᵗ watyr and wrynge owt and drynke it

376 Or take nept and stampe it and temp itt wᵗ hote wyne
and drynke it and the wormes will come owt

377 Garlyke is gode [fo. 37 recto] if a man enoynt þᵒwith
the bytynge of an hounde of eddir or of snake it will hele
it medle it with sond for houndis bytynge seth it in mulsa
꜀ put þᵒto a lyttell vynegre and drynk it for wormes anoynt
þe schare with mulsa and wᵗ vynegre for suellenge and ach
of the bladdere and the same will it do soden in wat͡ and leyd
þᵒto in a pleystre.

378 ffor gowt þat is colde take cowslop sawge lauandre rede
nettle and primerose and seth heme in wat͡ and wasshe þe
place wᵗ the watir it shall be holpen

379 ffor all man͡) of gowt   Take a pece of leþer or of lynen
cloþe and hete it wele at þe fyre and lay þer on the powdir
of aloes and lay on the gowte and it eu͡) he shall be hole
this medecyne shall hele hyme

380 An oþᵒ   Take þe mary of an hors and may butture
and medle heme wele to gedir and enoynt the gowt this is
pᵒvyd

381 ffor gowt festrede take auance archaungle the more
heyhown betayn verueyn of ech on lich moch sawe of the
heyhown ffor of hyme shall be as moch as of any of þe
oþᵒ be dowble and seþe wele in goode white wyne and lat
the syke drynke þᵒof first and last ꜀ sanabitʳ

382 An oþᵒ for þe same   Take a sawser full of þe Juys of
smalach and as moch of þe Juse of waybrede and of
wormod of hony and of salt and of vynegre of ech lich
moch and put þᵒto a quantitee of rye mele and medle it
wele togedir and make a pleystre of lynnen cloth and lay
on þe gowte and vse this pleystre and drynke þat drynke

two days or three, and then take it away, and do so till it be whole. *Probatum est.*

374 For gnawing and fretting in a man's limbs or bones or side. Take cumin [and] camomile and boil them together in white wine, and lay it hot to the sore.

375 For grinding in the womb. Take rue and stamp it with stale ale or with water, and wring out and drink it.

376 [Another]. Or take nept (catmint) and stamp it and temper it with hot wine, and drink it ; and the worms will come out.

377 Garlic is good if a man anoint therewith the biting of a dog or adder or of a snake, it will heal it. Mingle it with sand for dog's biting. Seethe it in mulsa[1] and put thereto a little vinegar and drink it for worms ; anoint the pubic region with mulsa and with vinegar for swelling and ache of the bladder, and the same will it do seethed in water and laid thereto in a plaster.

378 For gout that is cold. Take cowslip, sage, lavender, red nettle, and primrose, and seethe them in water and wash the place with the water, and it shall be helped.

379 For all manner of gout. Take a piece of leather or of linen cloth and heat it well at the fire, and lay thereon the powder of aloes, and lay on the gout ; and if ever he shall be whole, this medicine shall heal him.

380 Another. Take the marrow of a horse and may-butter, and mingle them well together and anoint the gout. *This is proved.*

381 For gout festered. Take avens, archangle, the greater ground-ivy, betony, vervain, of each one equally much, save of the ground-ivy, for of it shall be as much as double of any of the others ; and seethe well in good white wine, and let the sick drink thereof first and last. *Et sanabitur.*

382 Another for the same. Take a saucerful of the juice of smallage, and as much of the juice of waybread and of wormwood, of honey, and of salt and of vinegar, of each equally much ; and put thereto a quantity of rye-meal, and mingle it well together ; and make a plaster of linen cloth, and lay on the gout ; and use this plaster and drink

[1] Honey-sweet, or wine boiled with honey. *Cf.* §§ 691, 959.

that is in þat medecyne next before wreten and he shall be
hole þͮ est

383 ffor the hote gowte or colde gowte seth moleyn in wyne
꜏ it helpith the goute hote and seth it ī waͭ ꜏ it helpith þe
cold gout [fo. 37 *verso*]

384 An oþ⁹ for the colde goute   Take oyle de bay and hete
it oṷ þe fyre ꜏ put þer in woll and lay it hote on the goute
and it shall hele

385 A noble medecyne to cese a man of ach of cold goute
Take ripe eldrene beries ꜏ rype beries of walworte ꜏ take an
erthen pot and straw salt þ⁹in and than straw of aythire
beries iij handfull and lat it stand a day or ij and it will go
all to wattire and kepe that pott in the erth allway colde
that noone hete may come þer to and when thou hast ake
of gowte enoynt the ach agayn þe fyre ꜏ after shall the ach
sone slake and then take hors maryȝe and enoynt þ⁹with
þe sore place agayn the fyre and that will ease the moch ·
thies beries must be gadrid in harvyst betwene sent mary
days

386 Gederynge of sedes shuld be when thei bene full ripe ꜏
the moystnes be dryede somedele a way floures shuld be
takyne thei be somdele opyne or þai begynne to welow or
fade yerdis shuld gedryde when thei be full of moystnes or
thai begynne to schrynke Rotis shullen be gederyd when
the leves fallen ffroytis shullen be gedryd when thei bene
at theire full gretnesse or thei fall and the hevyare that the
froytes bene and the saddere the bettire thei bene and thos
that bene grete and lyght thow shalt nat chese   And tho
ben betͭ that bene gederyd in fayre weþ⁹ then tho that
bene gederid in rayne and tho erbis that bene gederid in
the felde bene betͭ then tho that groven in the town and in
gardyns ꜏ of tho that grow on þe felde tho þͭ groven on
hillis bene beste and comonly the felde erbis bene smallere
then the town erbis · many erbis þer bene [fo. 38 *recto*]
that haue speciall tyme to be gadryd and in that tyme thei
haue þ⁹ v⁹tu ꜏ if thei be gadrid in any oþ⁹ tyme thei haue
nat þ⁹ v⁹tue or ellis nat so gode some helpe when so eṷ

that drink, that is that medicine next before-written (§ 381), and he shall be whole. *Probatum est.*

383 For the hot gout or cold gout. Seethe mullein in wine, and it helpeth the hot gout ; and seethe it in water, and it helpeth the cold gout.

384 Another for the cold gout. Take oil of bay and heat it over the fire ; and put therein wool, and lay it hot on the gout, and it shall heal.

385 A noble medicine to cease a man of ache of cold gout. Take ripe elder-berries and ripe berries of walwort, and take an earthen pot, and strew salt therein ; and then strew of either berries three handfuls, and let it stand a day or two and it will go all to water ; and keep that pot in the earth always cold, that no heat may come thereto. And when thou hast ache of gout, anoint the ache by the fire ; and afterwards shall the ache soon slacken, and then take horse's marrow and anoint therewith the sore place by the fire, and that will ease thee much. These berries must be gathered in harvest between Saint Mary's days.[1]

386 Gathering of seeds should be when they be full ripe, and the moistness be dried somewhat away. Flowers should be taken [when] they be somewhat open, before they begin to wither or fade. Stems should be gathered when they be full of moistness before they begin to shrink. Roots should be gathered when the leaves have fallen. Fruits should be gathered when they be at their fullest size before they fall, and the heavier the fruits are and the sadder (denser), the better they be : and those that be large and light thou shalt not choose. And those be better that have been gathered in fair weather than those that have been gathered in rain ; and those herbs that have been gathered in the field be better than those that grow in the town and in gardens. And of those that grow in the field, those that grow on hills be best ; and commonly the field-herbs be smaller than the town-herbs. Many herbs there be that have a special time to be gathered, and in that time they have the virtue, and they be gathered in any other time, they have not the virtue, or else not so good. Some help[2] whensoever they

---

[1] The feasts of the Assumption (August 15th) and the Nativity (September 8th).

[2] *I.e.* are helpful as drugs.

thei be gadrid and some be noȝte iff thei be gadrid owt of tyme

387 Beteyn shall pryncipally be gadered in lammes monyth with þᵉ sede and with the rotes wᵗ owt reyne and itt shall and it shall (*sic*) be dryede in shadow for nede of medecyne Jt may be gadryd oþ⁹ tyme but eū it is the bett iff it be gedrede with owte rayne and itt shall be gederyd before þᵉ sonne rysynge

388 Swynes cressen shul be gaderyd when so eū a man nedþᵉ hem

399² Camamyll shall be gederid in aprile

400 Peritory shall be gadrede in June before þᵉ sone rysunge

401 The rede dok may be gadered ech tyme that þᵘnedist hyme

402 langedebefe shall be gaderid in June ꝛ in Jule

403 Penywort shall be gederid in the begynnynge of wynter

404 Germandre shall be gederid in lammes mone

405 Dragaunce shall be gadered in June and in Jule

406 Columbyne shall be gadered in lammes mone

407 Eddirtunge shall be gederid in the monyth of aprile

408 Pedelion shall be gaderyd aftir mydday when thou wilt haue it

409 Groundswilly shall be gadred after mydday

410 Walwort shall be gadered with owt reyne when thou wilt

411 Violet shall be gadred in þᵉ moneth of march ꝛ in this moneth shull sugre of violett be made and syrop

---

¹ Lit. "naughty."

² The numbers 389 to 398 were inadvertently omitted by me when numbering the sections of the MS., but as many cross-refer-

be gathered, and some be harmful[1] if they be gathered out of time.

387 Betony shall principally be gathered in Lammas month (August) with the seed and with the roots, without rain ; and it shall be dried in shadow (the shade) for need of (*i.e.* for use as) medicine. It may be gathered [at] other times, but it is ever the better if it be gathered without rain and it shall be gathered before the sunrise.

388 Swine's cresses should be gathered whensoever a man needeth them.

399[2] Camomile shall be gathered in April.

400 Pellitory shall be gathered in June before the sunrise.

401 The red dock may be gathered each time thou needest it.

402 Langdebeef (bugloss) shall be gathered in June and in July.

403 Pennywort shall be gathered in the beginning of winter.

404 Germander (speedwell) shall be gathered in Lammas month (August).

405 Dragance shall be gathered in June and July.

406 Columbine shall be gathered in Lammas month.

407 Adder's-tongue shall be gathered in the month of April.

408 Pedelion (pes leonis ; lady's mantle) shall be gathered after mid-day when thou wilt have it.

409 Groundsel shall be gathered after mid-day.

410 Walwort shall be gathered without rain, when [-ever] thou wilt.

411 Violet shall be gathered in the month of March, and in this month shall sugar of violet be made, and syrup.

---

ences had already been made before this error was discovered, the numbering has been retained unaltered.

144 A LEECHBOOK OR COLLECTION OF MEDICAL

412 Roses shuld be gadred in aprile and in may and off hem shuld be made sugure rosett and syrops of roses Jn this same monyth shuld oyle of camamyll be made ꝛ of lilye and opynere shold be made this monyth of thess hedis that men clepith popy

413 Rosemarye floures shuld [fo. 38 *verso*] be gadred in may

414 Centory shold be gadrede when he begynnyth to floure

415 Origanū shold be gederid in the moneth of Juyne

416 Solsecle shold be gaderid in the same monyth þe xvj day be fore the rysynge of the sunne wᵗ owte reyne

417 hertistunge shold be gederid in nouembre

418 Astrologia rotunda shold be gederid in hervyst and þe oþꝰ in the same tyme

419 Garlyke may be takyne when thou nedist hym to medecyn

420 Wild garlyke shuld be takyn when he flourith.

421 Agnus castus shuld be gaderyde when he flourith

422 Cowrdis shuld be gadered in the end of Septembre and octobre when þai bene rype thei shuld be dried in such a place that thai myght haue the sonne all day

423 Wild nepe beries shuld be gedrid when thei waxen ȝalowe

424 Cucumbre shuld be gederid when the froite is rype and the froyte shuld be layd vndꝛ vynes ther as the sonne may natt haue all his strenght to hym in a moyst place þᵗ it may roote for than þe seede shuld be goode and full of kernell

425 Citrull shuld be gedereid weh the froit is rype and it shuld be dried in a dry place in þe sunne

426 Watire calamynt shall be gedrede when it floureth and dried in þe shadow and he will last goode a ȝere and no lengare for no pfytt

427 Safron shuld be gederid erly before the sune rysynge

412 Roses should be gathered in April and in May, and of
them should be made sugar roset[1] and syrup of roses. In
this same month should oil of camomile be made, and [oil] of
lily, and opinere (opium) should be made this month of
those heads that men call poppy.

413. Rosemary flowers should be gathered in May.

414 Centaury should be gathered when it beginneth to
flower.

415 Origanum (pennyroyal) should be gathered in the month
of June.

416 Solsicle should be gathered in the same month, the 16th
day, before the rising of the sun, without rain.

417 Hartstongue should be gathered in November.

418 Aristolochia rotunda (round birthwort) should be
gathered in harvest, and the other (*A. longa*), at the same
time.

419 Garlic may be taken when thou needest it for medicine.

420 Wild garlic should be taken when it flowereth.

421 Agnus castus should be gathered when it flowereth.

422 Cowdris should be gathered at the end of September
and October when they be ripe, they should be dried in
such a place that they might have the sun all day.

423 Wild nepe (bryony) berries should be gathered when
they wax yellow.

424 Cucumber should be gathered when the fruit is ripe ;
and the fruit should be laid under vines, where the sun may
not give out all its strength to it, in a moist place, that it
may rot, for then the seed should be good and full of kernel.

425 Colocynth should be gathered when the fruit is ripe,
and it should be dried in a dry place in the sun.

426 Water calamint shall be gathered when it flowereth, and
dried in the shadow, and it will last good a year, and no
longer profitably.

427 Saffron should be gathered before the sunrise.

---

[1] Also called mel-roset. *See* § 532.

K

428 Dodure that growith amonge flax shuld be gederid in the somer when he begynnyth to floure ꝫ it may be kept ij ȝere

429 Drawk shuld be gederid when he floureth and in the shadow placys he shall be driede ꝫ a ȝere he will last

430 Elibure shold be gadrede in hervyste

431 ffenell sede shuld be gederid in hervyst in the begynnynge þᵒof and a ȝere it may be kept

432 The rotis of fenell shuld be gedereid in [fo. 39 *recto*] the begynnynge of the ȝere and a ȝere it is gode

433 Baldmoyn that som men clepe genciane shuld be gaderid in the last end of þe ȝere ꝫ iiij ȝere it may be kept / the rote of this is vsid and how þᵘshalt knaw it on þis manere þat it be ryȝt bytter for the lass bitt that it is the wors it is Also loke þᵗ he be hevy and with jn ȝelow and nat holough but sad ne brotell ne full of powdre

434 Galyngale that is clepid in fysike cipus it may be taken ech tyme of the ȝere best that is to take it in the end of veere iij days it most be layd in the sonne that the moystre þᵒof rote it nate to lyghtly and then kepe it in the shadow

435 ffloure delyse shuld be gadrid in the end of vere and dry itt in þe sone and it will last ij ȝere

436 Pilado is the rote of philipendula and that seruyth for medecyns and it is gederid out of the erth in the end of hervyst

437 Auence leues serue more for medecyns then the rote hys vertu is to dissolue and consume and to opyne and his vᵒtu is moost while he is grene

438 Take grapis or thei bene rype and wrynge owt þe moystnesse þᵗ is in heme and sith dry heme in the sonne and seþen make poudre of heme and that powdire is goode to vse in metys for kestynge þat cōmyth of coloryke humós and for the flux

439 ffor gnawynge in a joynt take herbe benett and shepis talowȝ oyle olyue ꝫ fry hem togedir and lay þᵒto

428 Dodder that groweth among flax should be gathered in the summer, when it beginneth to flower, and it may be kept two years.

429 Drauk (darnel) should be gathered when it flowereth, and in shady places shall it be dried, and a year it will last.

430 Hellebore should be gathered in harvest.

431 Fennel-seed should be gathered in harvest in the beginning thereof, and a year it may be kept.

432 The roots of fennel should be gathered at the beginning of the year, and a year it is good.

433 Baldemayne, that some men call gentian, should be gathered in the last end of the year, and four years it may be kept. The root of this is used, and how thou shalt know it is in this manner, that it be right better for the less bitter it is, the worse it is. Also look that it be heavy, and yellow within, and not hollow, but sad (tough) and not brittle, nor full of powder.

434 Galingale that is called in physic ciprus (cyperus); it may be taken each (any) time of the year ; best it is to take it in the end of spring ; three days it must be laid in the sun, that the moisture thereof rot it not too readily, and then keep it in the shadow (shade).

435 Fleurdelys (lily) should be gathered at the end of spring, and dry it in the sun and it will last two years.

436 Pilado is the root of philipendula (dropwort) and that serveth for medicines, and it is gathered out of the earth at the end of harvest.

437 Avens leaves serve more for medicines than the root. Its virtue is to dissolve and consume and to open, and its virtue is most while it is green.

438 Take grapes before they be ripe, and wring out the moisture that is in them, and then dry them in the sun, and afterwards make powder of them ; and that powder is good to use in meats for casting (vomiting) that cometh of choleric humors, and for the flux.

439 For gnawing in a joint. Take herb-benet (avens) and sheep's tallow, oil [of] olive, and fry them together ; and lay thereto.

к 2

440 ffor gryndynge in the belye samp ryw w^t stale ale or with watyr and wrynge itt and drynk it ⁊ it shall do goode sce⸺ [fo. 39 *verso*]

441 HEre   To make jit grow   Sethe leves of wythye with oyle and lay þ⁹ the here wantith

442 An oþ⁹ for the same   Take orpyment and seth it in watire or in all to the thriddendele and enoynt where þou wilt

443 Anothir take arnement and orpement and the Juyse of yuy and the white þat is emonge pissmyres of each lich moch and do all to gedir and enoynt where thow wilt

444 An oþ⁹ to kepe here fro fallynge wasshe thyne hede with lyȝhe þat is made of salueñ leues

445 Also to make here growe take rede onyons and grynd hem small ⁊ enoynt þ^e bare place þ⁹with

446 Anoþ⁹ to restore here þ⁹ if faylith · take cowe tordes and old soles of shone and bren hem to powdyr i an nw erthyn pott fast stoppid and than medle it w^t raw hony and make an oyntment þ⁹off and þ⁹of enoynt thi hede and close þ⁹ aboue a cappe of lethir ⁊ vse this ix days

447 Also an oþ⁹ shaue the hede and wasshe it in watir þat thies herbis bene sothen jnne þ^t is to say madyn here and okyn rynd ⁊ hoorhown and then enoynt the hede w^t raw hony ⁊ than straw aboue powdire þ^t is made of rattis tordes of gotis clawes brent ⁊ of ryndys of chestans and the shellis of nottis and (*sic*) the jyndys.   Stopp all thies in an nwe erthen pott and brenne hem on a brande yren ⁊ than make powdre ther of and straw on þ^e hony vse this ix days for it faylith nat pƀ ẻ

448 ffor to do away here for euere take iiij ℥ of slekkyd lyme and lat it stand all nyght in a quart of wat̃ and on the morow boyle it on þ^e fyre and put þ⁹to powdere of orpement ℥j ⁊ thus thou shalt wit when it is enough take a feþere and put it to þ^e pott and if þͧ may [fo. 40 *recto*] slipe the

---

¹ Ants' eggs.   *Cf.* § 268 and note thereon.   In the Syriac medical MS., published by Sir Ernest Budge, ants' eggs are used for the opposite purpose, *i.e.*, to prevent the hair from growing. (*Syrian Anatomy*, etc.   Oxford, 1913, Vol. ii, p. 691.)

440 For grinding in the belly.   Stamp rue with stale ale or with water ; and wring it and drink it, and it shall do good service.

441 Hair, to make it grow.   Sethe leaves of withy with oil and lay [it] where the hair is wanting.

442 Another for the same.   Take orpiment and seethe it in water or in ale to its third part, and anoint where thou wilt.

443 Another.   Take arnement and orpiment and the juice of ivy, and the white that is among pismires,[1] of each equally much ; and put all together, and anoint where thou wilt.

444 Another to keep hair from falling.   Wash thine head with the lye that is made of sallow leaves.

445 [Another].   Also to make hair grow, take red onions and grind them small, and anoint the bare place therewith.

446 Another to restore the hair where it faileth.   Take cow-dung and old soles of shoes and burn them to powder in a new earthen pot fast stopped ; and then mingle it with raw honey, and make an ointment thereof ; and therewith anoint thy head, and close thereabove a cap of leather, and use this nine days.

447 Also another.   Shave the head and wash it in water that these herbs have been seethed in. that is to say : maidenhair and oak-rind and horehound ; and then anoint the head with raw honey, and thew strew above powder that is made of rat's dung and goat's hoofs burnt, and of the rinds of chestnuts and the shells of nuts of the Indies.[2] Stop all these in a new earthen pot and burn them on a gridiron, and then make powder thereof, and strew [it] on the honey. Use this nine days for it faileth not. *Probatum est.*

448 For to do away hair for ever.[3]   Take four ounces of slaked lime and let it stand all night in a quart of water ; and on the morrow boil it on the fire and put thereto one ounce of powder of orpiment ; and thus shalt thou know when it is [boiled] enough : take a feather and put it into

[2] Perhaps pistacia nuts.
[3] A depilatory for superfluous hair.

feþers fro the stalke than it is enoughe ꝫ ellys nat and when thow shalt avoyd here þᵘ most be in an hote place and then enoynt the with the licoure and let rest awhile and after wasshe it in hote watir but loke at the formere licoure be nat to hote ne to colde for hildynge of the skynne ꝫ vse þis thries and it will voyde

449 ffor ech manere yuell in the hede   Take ryw and pound it and lay it in aysell ꝫ enoynt þᵉ⁹with thyn hede all abouue

450 Also take ryw and fenell and seth in watyr and wasshe thyne hede and take the Juyse of the blake bete and enoynt þᵉ⁹with thyne hede and thi tempulls

451 Anoþᵉ⁹ take þe juse of hertwort and medle it with oyle and with salt and brenne to poudre and enoynt þᵉ⁹with thyne hede

452 Anoþᵉ⁹ take verveyn betayn wormod and celidony waybrede and rwe walwort and rynd of eldren hony wᵗ pip cornes pound heme all in fere and seth heme wele in wyne and drynke þᵉ⁹of ech day fastynge at nyʒt last till thow be hole

453 A goode medecyn for the hede   Take betayn verveyne wormode and celidoyne weybrede and rw walwort and sawge and v cornes of pep stamp heme ꝫ sèth heme togedir in watir ꝫ drynke it fastynge

454 An oþᵉ⁹ for the hede ach take mustard and rwe and stamp hem togedre ꝫ temp hem toged⁹ with clene watir that it be thyke and ley it on thyne hede

455 ffor hurtynge of thyne hede˙   When suellyng with owt wound is ꝫ with owte brekynge of the brayne panne þat comyth of strokys by thies signes jt may be knawen wᵗ in the v or the seuenth day˙ as if he haue appetite to mete ꝫ drynke and if he haue goode digestions and goo wele to segge and wele to pisse and hath no feble hete than is þe brayne pann hoole And for this make a pleist [fo. 40 verso] such   Take wormode Artamasye rw comyn grese of porke and of moton añ and grynd alJ wele togedire wᵗ oyle of olyue and boyle all wele togedir in to thiknesse and lay

the pot, and if you may slip the feathers from the stalk,[1] then it is enough, otherwise not. And when thou shalt avoid (remove) hair, thou must be in a hot place, and then anoint thee with the licour, and let [it] rest awhile ; and afterwards wash it in hot water, but look that the former licour be not too hot nor too cold for [fear] of stripping the skin. And use this thrice, and it will void [the hair].

449 For each manner (every kind) of evil in the head. Take rue and pound it and lay it in vinegar, and anoint therewith thine head all above.

450 [Another]. Also take rue and fennel and seethe in water, and wash thine head ; and take the juice of the black beet and anoint therewith thine head and thy temples.

457 Another. Take the juice of heartwort (persicaria), and mingle it with oil and with salt, and burn [it] to powder, and anoint therewith thine head.

452 Another. Take vervain, betony, wormwood, and celandine, waybread, and rue, walwort and rind of elders, honey, with peppercorns ; pound them all together, and seethe them well in wine ; and drink thereof each day fasting, last thing at night, till thou be whole.

453 A good medicine for the head. Take betony, vervain, wormwood, and celandine, waybread and rue, walwort and sage, and five corns of pepper. Stamp them and seethe them together in water, and drink it fasting.

454 Another for the headache. Take mustard and rue and stamp them together ; and temper them together with clean water, that it be thick ; and lay it on thine head.

455 For hurting of thine head. When it is swollen without a wound and without breaking of the brain-pan that cometh of strokes (blows). By these signs it may be known within the fifth or seventh day : for if he have appetite for meat and drink, and if he have good digestion, and go well to stool and well to urinate, and hath no feeble heat (fever), then is the brain-pan whole. And for this make a plaster thus : take wormwood, artemisia (mugwort), rue, cumin, grease of pork and of mutton, of each equal parts ; and grind all well together with oil of olive, and boil all well

---

[1] *I.e.*, pull off the filaments from the shaft.

it on þe hede iiij fiches or v by a naturall day as hote as he
may easely suffre and wt enbroca þe mat̃ is nat fully put
away take wormode arthimasum comyn malow peritory
of ech on an handfull and grynd all thies in a mort̃ and
grynd to thies erbis iij dragmes of swynes grese and wele
encorpe hem togedir and do þ⁹to iij dragmes of whete mele
and be thei medyllyd togedir ꝫ iij vnces of hony and encorpe
wele toged⁀ with myghty wyne ꝫ it shall be set oũ þe
fyre and it shall boil till it be thyke eũ stirrynge with a
sklyce that it cleue nat to þe panne and than þis enbroca
shall be leid to þe swellynge hede in to þat it draw to mat̃/
then wt an Jnstrument Jt sall be opynyd in the part that
is moost dependannt and than þe matere shall be thrust
owte as easely as a man may and if it be nede put þ⁹in a
fyng⁹ to make it more clene

456 ffor to purge the hede   Take the juyse of yuye and
powdir of pep and medle hem togedir and drynke it

457 ffor the jawndes or þe ȝelowȝ euell take wild tansay
the roote and the herbe and stampe itt small and wrynge
owt the Juse and temp itt wt ale and drynke it and it hele
the and for a soferayn medecyn take it for itt is well
p⁹vyd

458 Anoþ⁹ for the same take the Juyse of mylfoil and
safron and seth hem in swete barly wort and giff it the syke
to drynke

459 Anoþ⁹ take puryd hony planteyn powdr of gyng⁹, tried
thies iij boylyd togedir and vse this medecyn iij [fo. 41
recto] morows and iij evennes ich tyme iij sponefull durynge
iij days

460 Anoþ⁹   Take celidony and seth it wele in wyne or in
ale and giff hyme to drynke eythir take the greene thistill
keue and endyve and lyverwort and the roote of yonge
fenell and the rote of yonge psely and do away that þt is
with in the rynde and seth heme wele togedir in stale secund
ale and gyf hym to drynk vij sponefull at evyn and vij at

---

¹ A fitch is a little brush.   Here it means that the medicament
must be applied with a brush four or five times in a day of twenty-
four hours.

together till it is thick, and lay it on the head, four fitches[1] or five per natural day, as hot as he may easily suffer. And [if] with embrocation the matter is not fully put away, take wormwood, artemisia, cumin, mallow, pellitory, of each a handful ; and grind all these in a mortar, and grind to these herbs three drachms of swine's grease ; and incorporate them well together, and put thereto three drachms of wheat meal, and let them be mingled together ; and three ounces of honey, and incorporate them well together with strong wine ; and it shall be set over the fire, and it shall boil till it be thick, ever stirring with a slice that it cleave not to the pan. And then this embrocation shall be laid to the swelling head, until it draw out the matter. Then with an instrument it shall be opened in the part that is most dependent,[2] and then the matter shall be thrust out as easily as a man may ; and if it be needful, put therein a finger to make it more clean.

456 To purge the head. Take the juice of ivy and powder of pepper, and mingle them together, and drink it.

457 For the jaundice or yellow evil. Take wild tansey, the root and the herb, and stamp it small ; and wring out the juice, and temper it with ale, and drink it, and it healeth thee. And for a sovereign medicine take it, for it is well proved.

458 Another for the same. Take the juice of milfoil and saffron, and seethe them in sweet barley wort ; and give it the sick to drink.

459 Another. Take purified honey, plantain, powder of tried ginger,[3] these three boiled together, and use this medicine three mornings and three evenings, each time three spoonfuls, during three days.

460 Another. Take celandine and seethe it well in wine or in ale, and give him to drink. Or take the green thistle, chives (?) and endive, and liverwort and the root of young fennel and the root of young parsley ; and take away that which is within the rind, and seethe them well together in stale second (mild) ale, and give him to drink seven spoonfuls

---

[2] Where the secretion of pus is greatest.
[3] " Tried " means tested, of good quality. *Cf.* § 481.

morowe till þat he be hole and vse sugre rosett wᵗ white
spyke and spody and wasshe oft the syde next the lyuᷗ
wᵗ watir of endyue and euwe rost

461 Anoþᵒ take the rote of the rede doke and the rote of
the clote and pound heme and temp hem with mannys
vryne and giff hyme to drynke ix days

462 Anoþᵒ take an appull that is clepid a rede steere or
Ricardon and take owt the core and fill the hole wᵗ safron
and euᷗy poudrede even porcion and ete such appulls first
and last

463 ffor the blake Jawndes take angylltwacches er þei go
in to the erth in the mornynge and fry hem and haue out
so þᵉ eyre of hem and fry hem till thei be dryed and then
grynd hem small in a mortare and temp hem vp wᵗ goode
alle and with a littell safrone and latt the syke drynke it
first and last et sanabitur

464 ffor the Jawndes take hard spaynysshe sope and a
littyll stale alle in a cup and rub þᵉ sope in a cuppe botom
till thyne alle be white and shaue in yuery and lat the syke
drynke þᵒof first ꝛ last and he shall be hoole

465 Anoþᵒ Dygge in the erth and take ix or x small
angyltwacches [fo. 41 *verso*] nat tho that bene blake knottis
or grey knottis but thos þᵗ haue ȝelow knottis and bray hem
in a disshe wᵗ somdele moore þan a ferþing wiȝt of safron
and giff the syke to drynke fastynge with stale ale and do
this iij tymes alway fastynge but loke þᵗ thei bene grounden
so small that þᵉ syke may nat se ne witt what it is for
lothynge

466 ffor yren thorne or stubb in a wound or what so it be ·
to draw it owt take egremoyne and ditayn and rotes of
roses of ech lich moch and stamp hem wele in a mortᷗ and
aftᷗ put in hony and the white of an egge and rye mele and
after medyll heme wele togedir and make a pleystre and lay
on the wounde and it shall open the wound and draw owt
all þᵉ corrupcion þᵒof and yren or thorn and hele it pᵬ eᷗ

---

¹ Sugar of roses, *cf.* § 412.
² Spodium, σπόδιον, a powder made of ashes.
³ An unknown substance, but apparently something derived

at even and seven at morn till he be whole. And use sugar-roset[1] with white spikenard and spody[2] and wash oft the side next the liver with water of endive and yew-rust.[3]

461 Another. Take the root of the red dock and the root of the clove and pound them with a man's urine, and give him to drink nine days.

462 Another. Take an apple that is called red steer or ricardon, and take out the core, and fill the hole with saffron and ivory powdered, even portions ; and eat such apples first and last.

463 For the black jaundice. Take earthworms before they go into the earth in the morning, and fry them, and so have the earth out of them ; and fry them till they be dried, and grind them small in a mortar ; and temper them up with good ale, and with a little saffron : and let the sick drink it first and last. *Et sanabitur.*

464 For the jaundice.[4] Take hard Spanish soap and a little stale ale in a cup ; and rub the soap in the bottom of the cup till thine ale be all white ; and shave therein ivory, and let the sick drink thereof first and last, and he shall be whole.

465 Another. Dig in the earth and take nine or ten earthworms, not those that have black knots or grey knots, but those that have yellow knots ; and bray them in a dish with somewhat more than a farthing weight of saffron, and give the sick to drink fasting, with stale ale. And do this three times, always fasting, but look that they be ground so small that the sick may not see nor know what it is for loathing.

466 For iron or thorn or stub in a wound, or whatso it be, to draw it out. Take agrimony and dittany and roots of roses, of each equally much ; and stamp them well in a mortar, and after put in honey and the white of an egg and rye-meal ; and after mingle them well together and make a plaster and lay on the wound and it shall open the wound and draw out all the corruption thereof and iron or thorn and heal it. *Probatum est.*

---

from the yew, unless *euwe* is an error for " iron."
    [4] There is a duplicate of this recipe in *Sloane*, 521. (Henslow, *op. cit.*, p. 137.)

467 Anoþ⁹ for the same stamp egremoyn in a morͭ wᵗ old
wyne a littell quantitee and lay to the wound and it shall
draw owt that that is in the wound pͭ eꝯ

468 ffor illica passio make a glisͭ of the powdre of philipendula and of salt watir and of oyle and of hony

469 ffor ey3en that bene rede and rynnynge take the rede
caule lefe and enoynt it wᵗ the glayre of an ey and lay it
to þyne ey3en when thou gost to bede

470 An othir for rede eyen take þᵉ rede snayle and do hyme
in a basyn ꓶ perce full of small holes ꓶ ech hole crame full
of salt and sett a glasse vndir the basyne and kepe the
watyre and do that to þᵉ rede ey3en and it shall hele

471 ffor to do away the web in the ey3e Take pympnell a
goode quantitee and stamp it and wrynge the juse thorow
a cloth and take swynes grese and as moch of goose grese
and as moch of hennes grese [fo. 42 recto] and melt all
togedir and do the juse þ⁹to and kepᵕ it in boxis and anoynt
the ey3en þ⁹with when thou gost to bedde

472 ffor eyen þᵗ ben sore Take arnement hony and þᵉ
white of an egge of ech lich moch and temp heme togedre
and then take hardis of tawe and wete it in watir and wrynge
it owte and do thies thre thynges on the hardys as a pleystre
and iff ther be euyll blode or whiͭ þ⁹in þat will brynge it
owt

473 Anoþ⁹ for webbe in the ey3en take stronge vynegre
or aysell and do in a vessell of brass and the blake flo of the
wode and wormode do þ⁹ with and lat stand longe keueryd
ꓶ when nede is do it in the ey3e and it will breke the webb
and do away the euyll

474 Anoþ⁹ for the webbe in the eyen Take a good porcione
of eufracie and breke it wele in A morͭ and take owte the
juse and put it in a panne and hete it and then put in the
juyse of rede fenell and seth hem togedꝯ and þan sett it
down and lett it colde and þ⁹ wt enoynt thyne ey3en when
thou gost to slepe

---

¹ A reddish-brown slug is evidently meant, *Arion hortensis* or
Agriolimax lævis. The " water " is the copious discharge of mucus
which the animal would exude under the irritation of the salt. *Cf.*
§ 476.

467 Another for the same. Stamp agrimony in a mortar with old wine, a little quantity, and lay to the wound and it shall draw out that which is in the wound. *Probatum est.*

468 For iliac passion. Make a clyster with the powder of philipendula (dropwort) and of salt water and of oil and of honey.

469 For eyes that be red and running. Take the red cabbage leaf and anoint it with the white of an egg and lay it to thine eyes when thou goest to bed.

470 Another for red eyes. Take the red snail and put it in a basin, and pierce it full of small holes, and each hole cram full of salt, and set a glass under the basin, and keep the water, and put that to the red eyes and it shall heal.[1]

471 For to do away the web[2] in the eyes. Take pimpernel a good quantity and stamp it, and wring the juice through a cloth ; and take swine's grease, and as much of goose-grease, and as much of hen's grease ; and melt altogether and put the juice thereto, and keep it in boxes and anoint the eyes therewith when thou goest to bed.

473 For eyes that be sore. Take arnement, honey and the white of an egg, of each equally much ; and temper them together and then take hards (fibres) of tow, and wet it in water, and wring it out ; and put these things on the hards as a plaster, and if there be evil blood or quittor (pus) therein, that will bring it out.

473 Another for web in the eyes. Take strong vinegar or aysel, and put it in a vessel of brass, and the black fluid of the woad and wormwood put therewith ; and let it stand long, covered ; and when need be, put it in the eye, and it will break the web and do away the evil.

474 Another for web in the eyes. Take a good portion of eufrasia (eyebright) and break it well in a mortar ; and take out the juice, and put it in a pan and heat it ; and then put in the juice of red fennel, and seethe them together ; and then set it down and let it cool, and therewith anoint thine eyes when thou goest to sleep.

---

[2] Usually *pin-and-web*, probably *pterygium* or *phlyctenular conjunctivitis.*

475 Also ete betayn and it will amend moch thi syght

476 ffor all man͡) of yuell in thyne ey3en sett þe rede snayll
in the watir and gadre the grese and anoynt ther with thy
ne3en

477 ffor ey3en that bene blew or blak off brusurs take white
of yren and stamp it w^t psely and make it thyke as oyntement with out fyre and lay it to þe lyddys

478 Also the juyse of wormod oft drynk with hony clerith
a mannes sigght and iff it be put in his ey3en it doth away
the redenes and the webbe that is in the ey3en

479 Also planteyn juse wile hele the swellynge and the hete
of the eyen if þei be enoynted þ⁹with

480 [fo. 42 verso] And þ⁹ is a syknes of the ey3en and is
when a man may bet͡t se a feire than ne3e and it is clepid
obcolmy

481 ffor to clence the eyen that haue nat clere syght take
ij ℥ of calamyn stoone powdrede lx fyne clowes and a few
greynes ꝯ 3j tried gyng⁹ wele puryd ꝯ ℥ ꝭue of anneys and
all thies powdred put in a quart of fyne oseþe or malnesyne
and set on the fyre when it begynneth to boyle set it in
fyre with a brynnynge styke and lett it bren so a lyttell
while and then whenche it with a wete lynen cloth and
hile it till it be colde at þe broth go nat owt þ⁹of and put ij
or iij droppes þ⁹off in þyn eyen qwen þᵘ wilt rest þe

482 ffor the perle in the eye and the webb · take þe lefe of
o̲c̲l̲s̲ ẋ pyllyd down ward and y̲s̲o̲p̲p̲ with a leff of sauge and
drynke the juyse of thies iij days first and last pb est

483 ffor the webbe in the ey3e take þe juse of daysie auence
sothernwode w^t wa͡t of fenell and put in the ey3e ꝯ sanabitur

484 Ther be dyuers manner of helpis for ey3en ffyrst is
the watir of mays͡t pe͡t off spayn þe which clarifieth and

---

¹ This is similar to § 470.
² The text has y̆ren, " iron," surely an error for eyien, " eggs."
³ The meaning of this phrase is obscure.
⁴ Probably an error for calcium or calomel. Calamint is a herb.
⁵ See note to § 459.

475 [Another]. Also eat betony and it will amend much thy sight.

476 For all manner of evil in thine eyes. Set the red snail in water and gather the grease (mucus) and anoint therewith thine eyes.[1]

477 For eyes that are blue or black with bruises. Take white of eggs[2] and stamp it with parsley, and make it thick as ointment, without fire (*i.e.* without heating it), and lay it to the lids.

478 [Another]. Also the juice of wormwood oft drunk with honey cleareth a man's sight, and if it be put in his eyes, it doth away the redness and the web that is in the eyes.

479 [Another]. Also plantain juice will heal the swelling and the heat of the eyes, if they be anointed therewith.

480 And there is a sickness of the eyes, and that is when a man may better see a fire than not,[3] and it is called ophthalmia.

481 For to cleanse the eyes that have not clear sight. Take two ounces of calc[4]-stone powdered, sixty fine cloves and a few kermes, and one drachm of tried ginger[5] well purified, and half a drachm of anise, and all these powdered ; put [them] in a quart of osey[6] or Malmsey and set on the fire ; when it beginneth to boil, set it on fire with a burning stick, and let it burn so a little while, and then quench it with a wet linen cloth, and cover it till it be cold so that the breath (steam) go not out thereof ; and put two or three drops thereof in thine eyes when thou wilt go to rest.

482 For the pearl in the eye,[7] and the web. Take the leaf of oculus christi (clary), peeled downward, and hyssop, with a leaf of sage ; and drink the juice of these three days first and last. *Probatum est.*

483 For the web in the eyes. Take the juice of daisy, avens, southernwood, with water of fennel, and put in the eyes. *Et sanabitur.*

484 There be divers manners of helps for eyes. First is the water of Master Peter of Spain,[8] the which clarifieth and

---

[6] A wine of Alsace.

[7] Probably cataract.

[8] Petrus Hispanicus, a thirteenth century Portuguese physician and philosopher who wrote the *Liber de Oculo*. This has been edited by A. M. Berger, Munich, 1899.

cōforteth the eȝen Take fenell rywe celydoyne eufrace clarre watir of roses of ech lich moch bruse heme ꝫ temp hem by a naturall day in white wyne and than put all togedir in alambeke and distill a waͭ

485 þᵉ secund is putt þᵉ white colre of akye of eyȝen ꝫ Galien techith it take ceruse wasshe viij dragmes sarcacole iij ȝ amydū ij ȝ of draganti ȝj apm̄ ꝓ poudre heme wele and make heme soft on a tyle stone with reyn waͭ and make small troaskes of hem and distemp hem vp wᵗ womans [fo. 43 *recto*] mylke or with watir of rosis and when it is nedefull mynystre

486 The iij is sett the colrye of tutye ꝫ they of monpellers vse it in the last ende obtalma for it resoluyth and dryeth stronge humyditees that fallith in the eyȝen · take tutye p̄perate calmyn ā Auence j xv clowes an ȝj of an hony combe with hony that shall be powderid sotelly and put hem all jnne ij ȝ of white wyne and a quartron ꝓ of watir of rosis of carifere an ȝj toile it sotilly and make a colrye þ⁹ of

487 Sett a colrye for reednesse of eyen and teteers take an ȝ of tutie p̄parate aloes acotryne d̄j an vnce of cammfere a dragme waͭ of roses and (*sic*) pound ꝫ an halue wyne of pomegarnett halue a pound þᵗ shall be powdred powdre it sotilly and medle it with oþ⁹ and chaufe vpon hoote coles wᵗ a lyttell boylynge and cole it and kepe it

488 Maysͭ petire bonant cōmendyd þis medecyne that folowith · for polupus ꝫ ꝛrase Make a tente of the rote of acharus tempid in oyle of jennype in the which oyle scamony is resoluyd in ffirst þᵂ must knawe or thou come to medecynes that þies thyngis bene euel for the syght in the eyȝen moch lechery for to loke moch on schynynge ymges and for to rede moch on small letͭ to slepe at noone after thi mete ꝫ he þat hat fawte in hys syght muste be ware that he ete nat ere þᵉ mete þᵗ he ete before be defiede and drunkonnes

---

[1] A gum from Persia, σαρκοκόλλα; Dioscorides, *De Mat. Med.*, iii, 99.

[2] A product obtained from smelting-furnaces. (*Cadmium*, oxide of zinc).

comforteth the eyes.   Take fennel, rue celandine, eyebright, clary, water of roses, of each equally much ; bruise them and temper them for a natural day (24 hours), in white wine, and then put all together into an alembic and distill a water.

485 The second is, make the white colyrium for aching of eyes, and Galen teacheth it.   Take ceruse, wash eight drachms of sarcocolla ;[1] amydum (starch) three drachms ; two drachms of dragance ; one and a half of apium (small-age) ; powder them well, and make them soft on a tile-stone with rainwater ; and make small trochisci of them, and distemper them up with woman's milk, or with water of roses.   And when it is needful, apply it.

486 The third is, make the collyrium of tutty,[2] and they of Montpellier use it in the last end (last stages) of ophthalmia, for it resolveth and drieth strong humidities that fall (befall) in the eyes.   Take prepared tutty, calamine,[3] equal parts ; avens one [ounce] ; fifteen cloves ; an ounce of honey-comb with honey, that shall be finely powdered ; and put them all in two ounces of white wine and a quartern and a half of water of roses [and] of carifere[4] an ounce ; work it finely and make a collyrium thereof.

487 To make a collyrium for redness of eyes and [for] tetters.   Take an ounce of prepared tutty, aloes, aconite (?) half an ounce, of camphor a drachm, water of roses a pound and a half, wine ; of pomegranates that shall be powdered half a pound.   Powder it finely and mingle with the other [drugs] and chafe upon hot coals with a little boiling, and cool it and keep it.

488 Master Peter Bonant commended this medicine that followeth.   For polypus and redness (?)   Make a tent of the root acorus (yellow flag) tempered in oil of juniper in the which oil of scammony has been first soaked.   Thou must know, before thou comest to medicines, that these things be evil for the sight of the eyes : much lechery, to look much on shining images (pictures) and to read much of small letters, to sleep at noon after thy meat, and he that hath fault in his sight must beware that he eat not until the meat he ate

---

[3] Hydrous silicate of zinc.
[4] I cannot identify this substance.

and for to brake before mete and to moch slepe and to
moch blode lattynge w^t cuppynge all man͡ of metys þ^t
bene salt and sharpe and stronge wyne [fo. 43 *verso*] that
is trubly and thyke lekès onyons rype olyues anete worts
of cole and fygges garlyke wyne benes smoke fyre fume
hoote blode grete travaylle lauʒhynge chese wepynge pep
strokys mustarde and moch wakynge All thies thyngis
bene euell for þe syght and after all medecynes that thou
receyvyst to thyne eyʒen washe heme nat but with wat͡
that fenell hath bene sodone jnne and looke that all
medecyns that thou receyvyst to thyne eyen be colde and
to all thies thynges take goode tente for it is pryncipally
p^9vyed

489 ffor akynge of the eyen take new fresshe chese and lay
vpone the eyʒen and it will voyde the akynge

490 ffor eyene þat bene rennynge blerid þoughe þe lyddis
be ouerturnyde byneth Take arnement ꝫ hony and the
white of an eye enculþe and temp heme to gedir wele and
take flex and wete it and wrynge it and do thou this bature
on the flex as it were a pleystre and ley this to þe eyʒen
and it shall draw owt watir and blode iff ther be any and do
good to the eyʒen pᵇ est

491 An oþer Take wormode ꝫ temp it with hony and
enoynt þ^9with the eyʒe and it helpith moch all man͡ of
akynge and many othre syknes of the eyʒe

492 ffor a stroke in a mannes eyʒe Take þe juse of
smalach and of fenell and þe white of an ey and medle
heme togedir and put in the eyʒen

493 Anoþ^9 iff there bee blode in the eyʒe þat is smyten
Take the v levyd grasse ꝫ stamp it w^t swynes grese and
w^t a lyttell salt and bynd it in the eyʒen

494 ffor dyrknes in a mannys eyʒe syght and [fo. 44 *recto*]
for akynge take may butt^r and hony by euén porcion and
seith hem togedir and after put the whit of an egge and cold
put þis in thyne eyhen All man͡ of thynge that shall be
puttid in the eyʒen shall be colde ꝫ that thou shallt put in
thyne eie shall be hote

before be digested, and [of] drunkenness, and to vomit before meat, and too much sleep, and too much blood-letting with cupping, all manner of meats that are salt and sharp, and strong wine that is turgid and thick, leeks, onions, ripe olives, anetum (dill), cole (cabbage) worts, and figs, garlic, wine, beans, smoke, fire, fume, hot blood, great travail, laughing, cheese, weeping, pepper, blows, mustard and much wakefulness. All these things are evil for the sight, and after all medicines that thou receivest for thine eyes, wash them not but with the water that fennel hath been sodden in ; and look that all water that thou receivest for thine eyes be cold. And to all these things pay good attention, for it is principally (authoritatively) proved.

489 For aching of the eyes, take new fresh cheese and lay [it] upon the eyes, and it will void the aching.

490 For eyes that be running [and] bleared, though the lids be overturned beneath.[1] Take arnement and honey and the white of an egg, mix and temper them together well ; and take flax and wet it, and wring it and put thou this paste on the flax as it were a plaster ; and lay this to his eyes and it shall draw out water and blood, if there be any, and do good to the eyes. *Probatum est.*

491 Another. Take wormwood and temper it with honey, and anoint therewith the eyes. And it helpeth much all manner of aching and many other sicknesses of the eyes.

492 For a stroke (blow) in a man's eyes. Take the juice of smallage and of fennel and the white of an egg, and mingle them together and put them in the eyes.

493 [Another]. And if there be blood in the eye that is smitten, take the five-leaved grass and stamp it with swine's grease and with a little salt, and bind it to the eyes.

494 For darkness in a man's eyesight, and for aching. Take may-butter and honey by even portions, and seethe them together ; and afterwards take the white of an egg, and put this cold into thine eyes. All manner of things that be put into the eyes shall be cold, and that which thou shalt put in thine eye shall [not] be hot.

---

[1] Probably *entropion, trychiasis* or some other affection involving the eyelids.

495 Anoþᵒ for the same take a quantitee of clyoyue and stamp it wele in a morᵗ and make þᵒ of a lyttill ball and lapp it in a littell hempe or in a littell flex and lay it in hote askys and aftere wrynge out the Juse in to a clene basyne or in to an oþer clene vessell and dry it in the sune and when it is driede temp it wᵗ a littell egre¹ of goode ale ꝯ put it in to the eyȝen þb est

496 ffor to clarifye the sight Take þe gall of a swyne and þe gall of an ele and the gall off a koke and temp thies togedir with hony and clere watire and kep it in a vessell of brasse and enoynt the eyn there with this is the medecyn þat ypocras vside²

497 Calamyn brent and qwenchid ix tymes in white wyne may longe be kept dry and when men nedyth take and grynd it on a stone or on a borde ꝯ temp it vpe wᵗ white wyne and this watir is ryght goode for gondye eyȝen and many euellis ꝯ many do þᵒto poudre of tutye for the brest and it is goode for worms in the eye lyddis

498 ffor webbe in mannys eyȝe iff it be old take the gall of an alle and dry it in the sun and make poudre and put in the eyen

499 Anoþᵒ for the same   Take the rede pympnell and stamp it in a morᵗ ꝯ afᵗ þat put it ī a panne with clene capons grese and sett it oũ þe fyre and fry itt to gedir and aftyr wrynge it thorowe a cloth in to A vessell of brasse ꝯ lat stand þᵒin iij days afᵗ þen put it in a box [fo. 44 verso] of horne or of cop ꝯ when you wilt · put a littell of this in the webbe in the eye ffor this is a soũyen medecyn ↗

500 Anoþᵒ take rede chesse that growith emonge corne and take away þe levys and the rote ꝯ than take the stalke and stamp itt and wrynge owt the Juyse and dry itt att the sune and make þᵒ of balles and when thou wilt take of hem temp hem wᵗ som waᵗ or licoʳ that is goode for the eyȝen and this is ryght gode

---

¹ Written egre. See note to § 25.
² It does not occur in any of the Hippocratic books.

495 Another for the same. Take a quantity of clover and stamp it well in a mortar, and thereof make a little ball, and wrap it in a little hemp or in a little flax, and lay it in hot ashes ; and afterwards wring out the juice into a clean basin, or to another clean vessel ; and dry it in the sun, and when it is dried temper it with a little aleger[1] of good ale and put it into the eyes. *Probatum est.*

496 For to clarify the sight. Take the gall of a swine and the gall of an eel, and the gall of a cock, and temper these together with honey and clear water, and keep it in a vessel of brass, and anoint thine eyes therewith. This is the medicine that Hippocrates used.[2]

497 [Another]. Calamint burnt and quenched nine times in white wine may long be kept dry, and when men need it, take and grind it on a stone or on a board ; and temper it up with white wine, and this water is right good for puffy eyes and many [other] evils. And many put thereto a powder of tutty (cadmium) for the breast,[3] and it is good for worms in the eyelids.

498 For web in a man's eyes. If it be old, take the gall of an eel and dry it in the sun, and make powder, and put it in the eyes.

499 Another for the same. Take the red pimpernel, and stamp it in a mortar ; and after that put it in a pan with clean capon's grease, and set it over the fire, and fry it together ; and afterwards wring it through a cloth into a vessel of brass, and let stand therein three days after, then put it in a box of horn or of copper ; and when thou wilt, put a little of this in the web in the eye, for this is a sovereign medicine.

500 Another. Take red chess[4] that groweth among corn, and take away the leaves and the root ; and then take the stalk and stamp it, and wring out the juice, and dry it in the sun ; and make thereof balls, and when thou wilt take of them, temper them with some water or licour that is good for the eyes. And this is right good.

---

[3] So written, but meaningless here.
[4] *Bromus secalinus.*

501 Anoþ⁹   Take a goode quantite of eufras and stamp it
and wrynge out the juse thorow and than take bores gresse
and capons grese and medle wele togedir in a panne of
brasse and stirre wele wᵗ a round staffe and seth heme wele
and lett hem kele and put in a box and when the syke goth
to slepe put a littell in the soore eyȝe pᵬ

502 Anoþ⁹ for the same   Take a gall of an hare and
clarified hony by euen porcion and medle hem togedire and
wᵗ a fether lay on the webbe and with in iij nyghtys itt
shall breke and saue the syght pᵬ est

503 Anothir ffor the webb or perle   Take stronge aysell
or vynegre and put it in a vessell of brasse ꝗ blakk slone
of the wodde and lede ꝗ wormode and lat thies stand longe
togedir well hillid and than put of that licoure in hys eyȝen
and itt shall breke the webb and do away the euell

504 ffor waterynge eyen take betayn and ete it raw and it
doth away the waterynge and maketh the syght clere

505 Or take þᵉ rote of betayn and drynke þᵉ Juyse þʳof
with clene wyne

506 ffor tendyr eyȝen that lyghtly ake   Take the Juyse of
planteyn with the white of an ey and wete þ⁹in a littell
smal flex [fo. 45 recto] and lay apon the eyen when þ~
goote to þ̷ bedd

507 ffor wormes that ete the liddes of eyȝen take salt and
brenne it in a lynnen cloth and after temp itt with hony
and with a feþ⁹ enoynt the lyddys off the eyȝen when thou
goost to bedde

508 ffor the white that ou͡lgoth the appull of the eyȝe
Take the juyse rotis and stamp hem wᵗ encence and do it
in the eyȝen

509 Anoþ⁹ for the same take floures of ȝarow and stamp
hem wᵗ womans mylke and put in the eyȝen and it shall
hele heme

510 ffor beryd eyȝen take levys of v⁹ueyn and stamp hem
and make balles of hem and so bynd on the blerid eyȝen
and thow shallt be hole þᵉ secund or the thrid day

511 Anoþ⁹ for the same   Take dragance and stamp it wᵗ
watir and enoynt þᵉ eyȝe þ⁹with

501 Another. Take a good quantity of eufrasia (eyebright) and stamp it, and wring out the juice through [a cloth]; and then take boar's grease and capon's grease and mingle well together in a pan of brass; and stir well with a round staff, and seethe them well; and let them cool, and put it in a box; and when the sick goeth to sleep, put a little in the sore eyes. *Probatum [est]*.

502 Another. Take the gall of a hare and clarified honey in even portions, and mingle them together; and with a feather lay on the web, and within three nights it shall break, and save the sight. *Probatum est*.

503 Another for the webb or pearl. Take strong aysel or vinegar and put it in a vessel of brass, and black sloes of the wood, and lead and wormwood, and let this stand long together, well covered; and then put of that licour in his eyes, and it shall break the webb and do away the evil.

504 For watering eyes. Take betony and eat it raw, and it doth away the watering and maketh the sight clear.

505 [Another]. Or take the root of betony and drink the juice thereof with clean wine.

506 For tender eyes that readily ache. Take the juice of plantain with the white of an egg, and wet therein a little small flax, and lay upon the eyes when thou goest to bed.

507 For worms that eat the lids of eyes. Take salt and burn it in a linen cloth, and afterwards temper it with honey; and with a feather, anoint the lids of the eyes when thou goest to bed.

508 For the white that overgroweth the apple of the eyes. Take the juice [and] roots of . . .[1] and stamp them with incense, and put it in the eyes.

509 Another for the same. Take flowers of yarrow and stamp them with woman's milk, and put in the eyes, and it shall heal them.

510 For blurred eyes. Take leaves of vervain and stamp them, and make balls of them, and so bind on the blurred eyes, and thou shalt be whole the second or the third day.

511 Another for the same. Take dragance and stamp it with water, and anoint the eyes therewith.

---

[1] The name of the herb is omitted.

512 ffor the webbe in the eyȝe or spottis in the eyȝe   Take
the juyse of the wild tasell and the juyse of wodebynd ꝛ
put hem in the eyen when thou gost to bedd and it shall
breke itt wele

513 ffor defaute of syght   Take eufras the juyse or the waͭ
for it is a pryncipall erbe ffor the eyen for what manꝫ sore
þat thai haue take it for it is previd

514 ffor to clence the eyȝen off eny filth take the gume that
cōmyth oute of pynapill tre draw itt by thyn eyȝen and
what syknes or soore be ther in it drawith out aftyr be it
festure or heere

515 ffor echynge and the webb in the eyȝe   Take the Juys
of fenell rotis and do it in the sun ī a brasyne vessell 12
dayes and sethen put it in his eyȝen in the manꝫ of colrye

516 Anoþ⁹ for echynge of eyȝen ꝛ it p⁹vyd soþe   Take
alittell of goode aloes and medle it with the juse of fenell
and do itt in a brasen vessell v days to þe sone and seþen
do þ⁹of in his eyen in the maner of a colrye

517 ffor ich take asshe off grene asshen ȝif [fo. 45 verso]
tide clene and medle it wᵗ clene waͭ and oft stirre itt be
halue a day then gadir the clere watir ther off and do ther
to a littell vynegre and a littell alom seth all thies togedire
and wasshe sores and swellyngs and for echynge and for
clousynge dyuerse sores/

518 Anoþ⁹ ffor icchynge and the webb in the eyȝe   Take
the Juys of fenell rotis and do itt in the sun and seþe put
it in his eyhen

519 Anoþ⁹ for ichynge wasshe clene thy handis and than
take a panne wᵗ fayre colis of fyre and kest on the colys a
gode quantitee of henbane sede and hold thyne handys a
good while ouꝫ þe smoke of þe sede as nygh as thow mayst
suffyre for hete and loke than thow haue a clene basyne
full of watir hote and put þ⁹in thyne handys and þou shalt
see that the worms shall crepe owte of thyne handis in to
þe basyn with þe watir

512 For the web in the eyes or spots in the eyes. Take the juice of wild teazle and the juice of woodbine (honeysuckle), and put them in the eyes when thou goest to bed. And it shall break it well.

513 For default of sight. Take eufrasia (eyebright), the juice or the water, for it is a principal herb for the eyes, for what[ever] manner of sore that they have. Take it, for it is proved.

514 For to cleanse the eyes of any filth. Take the gum that cometh out of the pineapple tree ; draw it by thine eyes, and what sickness or sore be therein it draweth out after [it], be it fester or a hair.

515 For itching and the web in the eye. Take the juice of fennel-roots, and put it in the sun in a brazen vessel twelve days ; and then put it in his eyes in the manner of a collyrium.

516 Another for itching of eyes, and it is proved true. Take a little of good aloes and mingle it with the juice of fennel ; and put it in a brazen vessel five days to the sun, and then put thereof in his eyes in the manner of a collyrium.

517 For itch. Take ash (cinders) of green ashes (trees),[1] clean and mingle it with clean water and oft stir it for half a day ; then gather the clear water thereof, and put thereto a little vinegar and a little alum. Seethe all these together, and wash sores and swellings, and for itching, and for closing divers sores.

518 Another for itching and the web in the eyes. Take the juice of fennel-roots and put it in the sun, and then put it in his eyes.

519 Another for itching. Wash clean thy hands, and then take a pan with fair coals of fire, and cast on the coals a good quantity of henbane seed ; and hold thy hands a good while over the smoke of the seed, as nigh as thou mayest suffer for heat ; and look then thou have a clean basin full of hot water, and put therein thine hands, and thou shalt see that the worms shall creep out of thine hands into the basin with the water.

---

[1] *Cf.* § 559.

520 An oþ⁹ ffor ychynge   Take henbane seede ꝫ bruse it a littill and than put it in stronge vynegre ꝫ let it ly þ⁹in a goode while and than wasshe hyme þ⁹with that hath the iche where so euer itt be

521 An oþ⁹ ffor the same stampe mustard seede wele and medle itt wᵗ hony and enoynt the place that ecchith

522 An oþ⁹ for ichynge of wormys where so itt be enoynt the place that echith wᵗ the juse of germandre or cormodrios or with the juyse of the beries of petymorell and itt sleth ꝫ doth away the echynge ꝛ—

    Capitulū xiii

523   **K**NOWinges the defaute of concepcion wheþ⁹ itt be longe of the mane or the woman   Take ij new erthyne potts ich by heme selue ꝫ lat the woman make waʒ in the on and the mane in the oþer and put in ech of hem a qntitee of whete [fo. 46 *recto*] branne ꝫ nat to moch þᵗ it be thik but at be liquyde or rennynge ꝫ marke wele þe pottis for forzetynge ꝫ lat hem stand x days and a nyghtis ꝫ þ˜ shall se in þe watir þᵗ is defaut in small qwyke worms and if þ⁹ apere no worms in neþ⁹ watir than bene thei lykly to haue children in pcess of tyme when god will

524 To knaw the lyue of a woundid man wheþ⁹ he shall leue or dye take þe rede pympnell and stamp it in a mortere ꝫ tamp it with watir or wyne and giffe it to þe woundid man to drynke fastynge ꝫ it (*sic*) iff it come out at þe wound he shall dye ꝫ iff it come nat owt at the wound he shall lyve pbat est

525 Anoþ⁹ take þe Juse of letuʒe and giff þe syke to drynke wᵗ watir ꝫ iff he kest it vpe anone he shall dye and iff he do nat he shall lyue and the juse of mowsere will þe same pb e̋

526 To knaw iff a worme be in a wounde or in an oþ⁹ sore where so it be take new clese (*sic*) þat no salt come jnne and enoynt the chese with hony and bynd it to þe sore all

520 Another for itching. Take henbane seed and bruise it a little, and then put it in strong vinegar; and let it lie therein a good while, and then wash him therewith that hath the itch, wheresoever it be.

521 Another for the same. Stamp mustard-seed well and mingle it with honey, and anoint the place that itcheth.

522 Another for itching of worms wheresoever it be. Anoint the place that itcheth with the juice of germander or cormodrios or with the juice of petymorell, and it slayeth and doth away the aching.

Chapter XIII.

523 Knowing the default of conception, whether it belong to the man or the woman. Take two new earthen pots, each by itself; and let the woman make water in the one, and the man in the other; and put in each of them a quantity of wheat-bran, and not too much, that it be not thick, but be liquid or running; and mark well the pots for identification, and let them stand ten days and ten nights, and thou shalt see in the water that is in default small live worms; and if there appear no worms in either water, then they be likely to have children in process of time when God will.[1]

524 To know the life of a wounded man, whether he shall live or die. Take the red pimpernel and stamp it in a mortar, and temper it with water or wine; and give it to the wounded man to drink, and if it come out at the wound he shall die; if it come not out of the wound he shall live. *Probatum est.*

525 Another. Take the juice of lettuce, and give the sick to drink with water; and if he cast it up anon, he shall die; and if he do not, he shall live. And the juice of mouse-ear will [do] the same. *Probatum est.*

526 To know if a worm be in a wound or in another sore, wheresoever it be. Take new cheese that there is no salt in, and anoint the cheese with honey; and bind it to the sore

---

[1] This and similar experiments are very ancient, and occur in Egyptian papyri. I have collected a number of them in my *Magician and Leech*, pp. 141–146.

nyght ꝫ on þe morow iff thow see the chese atamyd þꝰ is a
worme in the sore pɓ ẻ)

527 knaynge iff he þᵗ hath þe flux may lyue or nat take a
peny wiȝght of toun cresse seede and giff the sike to ete
and after giff drynke wyne or watir and do thus iij days ꝫ
iff he ceesse he shall lyue wᵗ help of medecyns and iffe he
ceese nat he shall dye ypꝰvyde

528 knowynge if gowte be hote or colde   Take vynegre
and white mele and medle hem togedir ꝫ lay on the gowte
and iff it be hote gowte it shall natt greue ꝫ iff it be þe
cold gout it shall greue hym moch [fo. 46 *verso*]

529 Cokyll hath vertu to dissolue and to consume the seed
is vsid in medecynis for stoppynge of the splene and of the
lyvere ꝫ of the reynes ꝫ for strangure and dissure and illica
passio ꝫ for ach of the stomake that cōmyth of wynde · vse
þe wyne that the seede of kokyll is soden jnne and ete þe
powdire with oþꝰ metis ffor wormes ete the powdir with
hony and make a pleystre wᵗ poudre ꝫ of the Juyse of
wormode and lay apon thy navell ffor worms in thyne eres
medle the poudre of (*sic*) the juse of wormode and do in
thyne erene

530 kyrnelles to distroy heme take planteyn and stamp it
with salt and lay þꝰto and itt will distroy heme

531 kyttyngs ꝫ sores in yontes a souꝰeyn medecyne þꝰfore
opene wele the wound and do there on oyle of roses boyled
scaldynge hote as he may suffre iij dayes or iiij first or last
and then when the soore is wele clensid make a pleysṫ ꝫ
mele rosett and hele it vp þꝰwith

532 Roses or the the (*sic*) leves bene fully sprongene oute
he shall be gaderid and of the rede levys shrede small and
of hony togedir is made mel rosett to a pound of roses thou
shalt viij pound of hony the roses shall be schrede small and
sothen with þe hony easely on an easey fyre of coles till the
hony haue both the sauoure and coloure of roses

533 knawynge if a kan�q̄ꝰ be in a soore or wōnd loke wher
a wound is v wyke olde or more and hys yuell helyde and
brokene and breke oute agayn after þᵗ it was onys closide

all night ; and on the morrow if thou seest the cheese broken up, there is a worm in the sore. *Probatum est.*

527 Knowing if he that hath the flux may live or not. Take a pennyweight of towncress seed, and give the sick to eat ; and after give [him to] drink wine or water, and do thus three days ; and if he cease he shall live, with help of medicines ; and if he cease not, he shall die. *Proved.*

528 Knowing if gout be hot or cold. Take vinegar and wheat-meal and mingle them together, and lay on the gout ; and if it be hot gout, it shall not grieve (pain) ; and if it be the cold gout, it shall grieve him much.

529 Cockle (ergot) hath virtue to dissolve and to consume. The seed is used in medicines for stopping of the spleen, and of the liver, and of the reins ; and for strangury, and dysuria, and iliac passion ; and for ache of the stomach that cometh of wind. Use the wine that the seed of cockle has been boiled in, and eat the powder with other meats ; for worms, eat the powder with honey ; and make a plaster with powder and of the juice of wormwood, and lay upon thy navel ; for worms in thine ears, mingle the powder with the juice of wormwood, and put [it] in thine ears.

530 Kernels[1] to destroy them. Take plantain and stamp it with salt, and lay thereto ; and it will destroy them.

531 Cuts (cracks) and sores in joints, a sovereign medicine therefor. Open well the wound, and put thereon oil of roses boiled, as scalding hot as he may suffer, three days or four, first and last ; and then when the sore is well cleansed, make a plaster of mel-roset and heal it up therewith.

532 Roses, before the leaves be fully sprung out, shall be gathered ; and of the red leaves, shredded small, and of honey is made mel-roset. To a pound of roses, thou shall [take] eight pounds of honey ; the roses shall be shredded small and seethed with the honey gently on an easy fire of coals (charcoal), till the honey have both the savour and colour of roses.[2]

533 Knowing if a canker be in a sore or wound. Look where a wound is five weeks old or more, and is ill-healed and broken, and break out again after that it was once closed ;

---

[1] Glandular swellings. Sometimes used of tonsilitis.
[2] This is a duplicate of § 619. *Cf.* also §§ 412, 460, 531.

and than loke iff þ⁹ come oute rotyn flesshe and thyke lyke
somdele roten blode than is the cancre ī the [fo. 47 *recto*]
flesshe ꝫ iff þ⁹ come owte as it were thyne lyʒe than is the
cankre in the synows and iff þ⁹ come oute as it were thike
blode thane he is in the bone

534 ffor to knaw a mesell kest salt in hys blode and it wile
fall to ground

535 knawynge the lyfe of a woundid mane take therfoile ꝫ
giff hyme to drynke and iff he kest itt oute he shall be dede

536 knawynge iff a sore come of hete he shall than fele
more sore and iff itt come of colde he shall fele lesse sore

537 knawynge iff morfyw be curable or nat pryke þᵉ place
ther the morfyw is jnne with a nedle so þat the nedle
poynte passe natt the thyknesse of the skynne with in the
flesshe and iff blode come oute þ⁹ off after þᵉ prykkynge itt
is curable

538 An oþ⁹ ffor the same   Rub the morfwe wᵗ a sharpe
cloth and if it be rede it may be helyde   Jff the morfyw be
brode and haue many spottis it is nat lykly to hele/

539 kepynge the hote of the sonne fro the hede in travayle
take erth yuye and stamp it wᵗ vynegre and anoynt þ⁹with
thi face and thi temples

540 kybes comyth of colde ꝫ in latyne it is seide pnio for
þough it noyeth ꝫ grevyth the hele ꝫ also it is clepid inula

541 ffor to hele it take þᵉ watir that dragaunce rotis bene
sodone jnne ꝫ bath wele thi kybe þ⁹in ꝫ itt will hele it

542 kynd of man to stopp itt   Take sadd blew cloth and
brenne itt in a rede pott or apone a rede tyle stone ꝫ make
powder ther of and take goode ale ꝫ bete it in the pott and
kest þ⁹in the poudre and giff hym to drynk iij dayes and
that is medecynable

543 ffor the cankre   Take vnslekkyd lyme and blake pep
and hors mynt ꝫ stronge aysell [fo. 47 *verso*] and hony and

---

¹ The salt will fall to the bottom of the vessel, the blood being
first obtained by cupping.
² A skin-disease like *Sceleroderma*.
³ An ulcerated chilblain, especially of the heel.

and then look if there come out rotten flesh and thick, like somewhat rotten blood; then is the canker in the flesh. And if there come out as it were thin lye (discharge), then is the canker in the sinews; and if there come out as it were thick blood, then it is in the bone.

534 To know a leper. Cast salt in his blood and it will fall to the ground.[1]

535 Knowing the life of a wounded man. Take trefoil and give him to drink; and if he cast it out, he shall be dead.

536 Knowing if a sore come of heat. He shall then feel more sore; and if it come of cold, he shall feel less sore.

537 Knowing if morphew[2] be curable or not. Prick the place where the morphew is in with a needle, so that the needle-point pass not the thickness of the skin within the flesh; and if blood come out thereof after the pricking, it is curable.

538 Another for the same. Rub the morphew with a sharp (rough) cloth; and if it be red, it may be healed. If the morphew be broad and have many spots, it is not likely to heal.

539 Keeping the heat of the sun from the head when working. Take ground-ivy and stamp it with vinegar, and anoint therewith thy face and thy temples.

540 Kibes[3] come of cold, and in Latin it is called *pernio*, because it annoyeth and grieveth the heel; and also it is called *inula*.[4]

541 For to heal it. Take the water that dragance roots have been seethed in, and bathe well thy kibe therein, and it will heal it.

542 Kynd[5] of man, to stop it. Take heavy blue cloth and burn it in a red pot or upon a red tile-stone; and make powder thereof, and take good ale; and beat it in the pot, and cast therein the powder and give him to drink three days; and that is medicinable (curable).

543 For the canker. Take unslaked lime, and black pepper, and horsemint, and strong vinegar, and honey, and barley-

---

[4] This is an error for some other word. *Inula* is a herb, elecampane.

[5] Venery, lechery.

barly mele of ech lich moch ꝛ seth hem wele in an newe
pott of erth till men may take powdre þᵒoff ꝛ do the powdir
ther to

544 knawynge iff a a sore be hote or colde take powdyre
of encence and straw on the sore and iff itt be molten sone
the sore is hote and iff it do nat it is cold

545 knawynge the festire ꝛ kankre / the festire ꝛ kankre
comyth of a wound or of a sore that is wronge hilled and
breckyth out afterward and iff it be in the flesshe þᵒ comyth
owte watir and iff it be in the synows þᵒ comyth out as it
were broune and iff it be in the bonys as it were blode and
a festire hath a narow thrile wᵗ owte ꝛ wydd wᵗ jnne the
cankyre festyre is selde þat it no hath moo holes thane one
the kankyre is euere more with on thrill

546 ffor knees swollen take rwe and loueach and stamp hem
togedire ꝛ temp with hony and ligge it apoñ the sore

547 Anoþᵒ for akynge of knees and swellynge take wormode
egrymoyne verveyne loueache erbe benett pety morell and
iff thow wilt take rwe of ech lich moch ꝛ stampe heme small
then fry heme wᵗ ij pties of fresshe butture and on pte of
white wyne and make a pleystre as hote as the syke may
suffre and lay itt to hys kne

548 L Ectuaries ffor dyuerse yuelles.¹ To make a lectuary
      for rysynge and ach at the hertt take hony þᵗ is
clarified and seþe itt and for to knaw when itt is sothen
enough take a dropp þᵒof and latt it fall in cold watir ꝛ iff
it be harde bytwen thy fyngurs than it is enouge and do
þᵒin þan powdꝛ of bayes a ꝗrtron of an vnꝯ gyngᵒ halue
an uncᵒ of longe pepyre [fo. 48 *recto*] and a littell canell
añ ꝛ coloure it wᵗ saunders ꝛ sill it forþe

549 A gode lectuarye for a spicer to gedir his sokne² to giffe
and to sell take hony and bakne floure gynger and powdere
of pepire and barly wort and seth heme to gedire till it be
standynge and then sell itt forth

---

¹ Many different complaints are comprehended in this term,
including dyspepsia, heartburn, flatulence, etc.
² The phrase is very obscure. *Sokne* seems to be derived from

meal, of each equally much ; and seethe them well in a new earthen pot, till men may take powder thereof, and put the powder thereto.

544 Knowing if a sore be hot or cold. Take powder of incense and strew it on the sore ; and if it melt, the sore is hot ; and if it do not, it is cold.

545 Knowing the fester and canker. The fester and canker come of a wound or of a sore that is wrongly (badly) healed and breaketh out afterwards. And if it be in the flesh, there cometh out water ; and if it be in the sinews, there cometh out as it were brown [fluid] ; and if it be in the bones, as it were blood. And a fester hath a hole narrow without and wide within the canker. Fester seldom hath more holes and one : the canker always has more than one hole.

546 For knees swollen. Take rue and lovage and stamp them together, and temper with honey, and lay it upon the sore.

547 Another for aching of knees and swelling. Take wormwood, agrimony, vervain, lovage, herb-benet, pettymorell ; and if thou wilt take rue, of each equally much, and stamp them small ; then fry them with two parts of fresh butter, and one part of white wine ; and make a plaster as hot as the sick may suffer, and lay it to his knee.

548 Electuaries for divers evils. To make an electuary for rising and ache at the heart.[1] Take honey that is clarified and seethe it ; and to know when it is seethed enough, take a drop thereof and let it fall in cold water : and if it be hard between thy fingers, then it is enough. And put therein then powder of bay, a quarter of an ounce of ginger, half an ounce of long pepper, and a little canell (cinnamon), same quantity, and colour it with alexanders (smyrnium), and sell it forth.

549 A good electuary for a spicer to gather for his trade[2] to give and to sell. Take honey and baking-flour, ginger, and powder of pepper, and barley-wort ; and seethe them together till it be standing (solid), and then sell it forth.

A.-S. *soken*, held by privilege or right of socage, and hence as a matter of custom or livelihood. But I make this suggestion with all reserve.

M

550 A lectuary for many yueles for the host for the brest for rotelynge in the throte for byles for sores in the side for the myst and for the stomake take horshowe and groundswylly jsop centory ach fenell rywe solsegwy puliall and nept of ich lich moch and grynd heme togedyre ⁊ do pep̄ þꝰto and hony ⁊ ete þꝰof at morow and at euen

551 ffor the same. Drynke the juse of sawge iij days wt goode hote watir

552 ffor the same Take puliall and comyn off ech lich moch and boyle heme in ale and drynke itt at evyn and at morow colde

553 To make a man laxatiffe take borage m̃cury ij levys or iij of laureall ⁊ make hyme potage and giff hyme to ete

554 Anoþꝰ laxatiffe take the juyse of violett eiþꝰ of the floures a goode quantitee of sugre ⁊ medle hem to gedir ⁊ put it than in a glasse ⁊ stopp itt and sett it in the sun and take the florey þꝰof and kep it wele in a box and vse it first and last

555 Anoþꝰ take hokkes and boyle hem wele and streyne heme thorow a cloth ⁊ medle it wt new ale ⁊ drynke

556 Also a glistre made of the Juyse of m̃cury or of the wat̃ þat m̃curye was soden jnne or of oyle ⁊ of hony ⁊ salt it makyth a man laxatife ⁊ purġyth his guttis

557 A gude laxatiffe [fo. 48 *verso*] Take a peny wyght of powdre of laureall and d̄j a peny wyght of powdir of comyne and drynke itt first and last with a littyll quantitee of ale

558 ffor peyne of hors legges take old vryne of a man and hene dirt ⁊ tamp̄ it togedyr and it shall hele hyme made in a pleyst̃

559 A gode medecyne for sores in legges in fete and also for swellynge and vnkynd hetis Take aschen of grene asshe and make lyȝe and when it is fyne take þe ixth dele of white

---

[1] *Myst* is debility. In the duplicate of this recipe in H. the reading is *mylte*, "spleen," which may be correct. (Henslow, *op. cit.*, p. 9.)

[2] The Henslow duplicate has "without water."

550 An electuary for many evils ; for the cough, for the breast, for rattling in the throat, for boils, for sores (pains) in the sides, for debility,[1] and for the stomach. Take horse-hoof (colt's-foot) and groundsel, hyssop, centaury, ache, fennel, rue, solsicle, pennyroyal and nept (catmint), of each equally much ; and grind them together, and put pepper thereto, and honey ; and eat thereof at morn and at even.

551 [Another] for the same. Drink the juice of sage three days with good hot water.[2]

552 [Another] for the same. Take pennyroyal and cumin, of each equally much ; and boil them in ale and drink it at even and at morn, cold.

553 To make a man laxative. Take borage, mercury, two leaves or three of laurel, and make him pottage and give him to eat.[3]

554 Another laxative. Take the juice of violet or of the flowers, a good quantity of sugar ; and mingle them together, and put it then in a glass, and stop (close) it ; and set it in the sun, and take the florey[4] thereof, and keep it well in a box and use it first and last.

555 Another. Take hocks (mallows) and boil them well, and strain through a cloth ; and mingle it with new ale, and drink.

556 [Another]. Also a clyster made of the juice of mercury, or of the water that mercury was boiled in ; or of oil and of honey and salt, maketh a man laxative and purgeth his guts.

557 A good laxative. Take a pennyweight of powder of laurel and half a pennyweight of powder of cumin, and drink it first and last with a little quantity of ale.

558 For pain of horse's legs. Take old urine of a man and hen's dung and temper it together and it shall heal him made in a plaster.

559 A good medicine for sores in legs and feet, and also for swelling and unkind heats (inflammation). Take ashes (cinders) of green ashes (trees),[5] and make lye ;. and when it is

---

[3] There is a duplicate of this recipe in H. (*op. cit.*, p. 36).
[4] Take the residue or sediment.
[5] *Cf.* § 517.

vynegre and do þᵒto a lyttell alome ꝗ seth itt togedir in to
the halue and put in to a vessell and her with washe the
soore and wete a lynnen cloth þᵒin and many fold lay itt
to the sore and chaunge it when itt is dry

560 ffor a mannes legge or arme þat is kytt off make oyle
seþinge and put the stump or the legge þᵒin all seþinge as
itt is

561 ffor sores off legges a pleystre genⁿall take the juyse of
erbe benett a q̅r̅t and a halue and a quart of tarre and d̅j̅
a quarte of swyns grese of a barowȝ and melt thies togedir
on the fire take than caluⁿ dunge and stire hem wele togedir
and then streyn heme wele hote and put þᵒto a sawser full
of powdir of alyme and stirre heme wele till thies bene colde
ꝗ putt itt in boxes

562 ffor legges swollen the law membres off a man haue
many syknesse dyuers and many dyuers helpis of the
which the first is to abate the inflaccion eiþᵒ þᵉ swellynge
of the legges theyes and fete stwe hem ꝗ fomete heme with
salt watir of the decoccion of walwort elleiū [fo. 49 *recto*]
tribulo⸝ marm⸗ a̅n̅ j pty of banne ꝗ of floure of benes o
pty of caluer dunge halue a pty powdre heme ꝗ with vynegre
and the decoccion of affodalis þat is ramson and the Juyse
of the rede cole encorpe hem upon the fyre and make an
enplastre and lay pᵒto

563 ffor the same take a peny worth of alom ꝗ a peny
worth of madere and a galon of tanwoos and boyle wele
togedⁿ ꝗ put þᵒin a lynnen cloth to roll the legge in and vse
this roll offt put in the foreside juys hoote and encresse it
till itt be hole

564 ffor a man that is benomyn on his legges or on his
arms or in any oþᵒ place of hyme //   Take a basyn full or ij
of withien levys and seth heme in clene watire till þai bene
alto soden and than take a porcion of vynegre and medle
wᵗ þᵉ levys ꝗ make a pleystre and lay itt to thi body þᵒ

---

¹ Folded many times.
² Until the beginning of the nineteenth century it was customary
to plunge the stump of an amputated limb into boiling pitch to stop
the bleeding.
³ Oil, from Greek ἔλαιον.

fine (clear), take the ninth part of white vinegar, and put thereto a little alum ; and boil it together to half, and put into a vessel, and therewith wash the sore ; and wet a linen cloth therein, and manifold,[1] lay it to the sore, and change it when it is dry.

560 For a man's leg or arm that is cut off. Make oil seething and put the stump of the leg therein, all seething as it is.[2]

561 For sores of the legs, a general plaster. Take the juice of herb-benet, a quart and a half, and half a quart of tar and half a quart of swine's grease of a barrow-hog ; and melt these together on the fire. Take then pigeon's dung and stir them well together, and then strain them well hot, and put thereto a saucerful of powder of alum, and stir them well till they be cold, and put it in boxes.

562 For legs swollen. The lower members of a man have many divers sicknesses, and many divers helps, of which the first is to abate the inflation or the swelling of the legs, thighs and feet. Steam them and foment them with salt water, and the decoction of walwort, *eleium*[3] *tribulorum marmoreum*, of each one part ; of bran and of flour of beans, one part ;[4] of pigeon's dung, half a part ; powder them with vinegar and the decoction of asphodel, that is ramson,[5] and the juice of the red cabbage ; incorporate them upon the fire, and make a plaster, and lay thereto.

563 For the same. Take a pennyworth of alum, and a pennyworth of madder, and a galon of tan-ooze ;[6] and boil them well together, and put therein a linen cloth to roll the leg in ; and use this roll oft put in the aforesaid juice hot, and increase (repeat) it till it be whole.

564 For a man that is benumbed in his legs or in his arms, or in any other place of him. Take a basinful or two of withy leaves, and seethe them in clean water till they be altogether sodden ; and then take a portion of vinegar and mingle with the leaves and make a plaster, and lay it to thy

---

[4] The text has *o*, the usual abbreviation for a pint, or some liquid measure, evidently wrong here, especially as it is followed by " part."

[5] A.-S. *hramsan*, a species of garlic, *Allium ursinum*.

[6] Licour from a tanner's vat.

þou art bynomyn ꝫ that will gedir the flesshe agayn and make þe blode whyke that was dede

565 ffor soore legges take tanwose a gallon ꝫ a qͬt of lyȝe of grene asshen wode and a quart of vynegre ꝫ kest all togedir and to þᵗ porcion a quartron of alom ꝫ a qͬtron of madre ꝫ mede hem wele togedir and seth hem on the fyre and stirre hem wele and boyle hem wele þe space of ij p̅r u̅r and kepe this wele to wasshe al fowle sores with

566 A medecyne that will help agayn the lepre take borage waͭ cressis grete nettellis langedebefe fenell marcury ꝫ waͭ mynt be gode in potage

567 Also Juys of fymͭ and of waͭ mynt medlid with raw ey bene gode to drynke fastynge ꝫ namely [fo. 49 verso] in apryle and in may and in octobₑ╱

568 Also blede wele on the ryght arme and ryghte fote in the wexynge of the mone of apryle and byfore the full mone of octobₑ and in the begynnynge of nouembₑ╱ on the left arme and on the left fote

569 Also ventosynge on the armes and garsynge of legges bene helpynge in wynͭ

570 Also it helpith moch in a monyth to drynke goode triacle with Juyse of fymͭ or of waͭ mynt the quantitee of triacle as a filberd not

571 Also drynke he fymͭ and scabiouse boylid in white wyne and lap hyme in a shete and hill hyme warme and lat hyme slepe and swete and bath hyme with a littell morell

572 Also mylk and flesshe acord nat togedir to ete at a mele elles congre houndsfisshe soles porpos gose malard and oþ⁹ waͭ fowles synow flesshe vnclene porke moch pepir garlyke bene pilous for thies

573 Also a pryncipall medecyne for lepre   Take a busshell of good barlych in the monyth of march and halue a busshell of todes and seþe heme togedir in a lede with rennynge watir till the bones of the todes bene alto shake than take out the barlich of the watir and dry in the sun or on a kylne till itt be ryght dry then take an henne þat hath chekyns new hawght þat neuere ete mete and put hem in

body where thou art benumbed ; and that will gather the flesh again, and make the blood quick that was dead.

565 For sore legs.   Take tan-ooze a gallon, and a quart of lye of green ash-wood, and a quart of vinegar ; and cast all together, and to that portion [add] a quartern of alum and a quartern of madder, and mingle them well together ; and seethe them on the fire, and stir them well, and boil them well for the space of two hours.   And keep this well to wash all foul sores with.

566 A medicine that will help against the leprosy.   Take borage, watercress, great nettles, bugloss, fennel, mercury and watermint.   [They] be good in pottage.

567 Also juice of fumitory and of watermint mingled with raw egg be good to drink fasting ; and especially in April, and in May, and in October.

568 Also to bleed well on the right arm and right foot in the waxing of the moon of April, and before the full moon of October ;   and the beginning of November on the left arm and on the left foot.

569 Also cupping of the arms and lancing of the legs be helpful in winter.

570 Also it helpeth much in a month to drink good treacle with juice of fumitory or of watermint ; the quantity of treacle [being] as much as a filbert nut.

571 Also let him drink fumitory and scabious boiled in white wine, and wrap him in a sheet, and cover him warmly, and let him sleep and sweat, and bathe him with a little morell.

572 Also milk and flesh accord not together to eat at a meal ; eels, congers, dogfish, soles, porpoise, goose, malard and other water-fowls, sinewy flesh, unclean pork, much pepper [and] garlic, are perilous for this (i.e. leprosy).

573 Also a principal medicine for leprosy.   Take a bushel of good barley in the month of March, and half a bushel of toads ; and seethe them well together in a lead (cauldron) with running water, till bones of the toads be altogether shaken out ; then take out the barley from the water, and dry [it] in the sun or in a kiln till it be right dry.   Then take a hen that hath chickens new-hatched, that have never eaten food ;

close hous clene swope and giff hem of the barly brokyn
in a mortirre and afterward hoole when thei bene eldire
than lat the lepre ete those chekyns both rostyd and sothen
and noon oþ⁹ mete and lat his brede be made of barlich and
drynk but sceld ꝛ euͤ emonge drynke watire ale and wyne
but scolde [fo. 50 *recto*] ne none hote drynke ne spiced and
euͤ emonge lat the blode till thou se thi blade clene and
governe the in all thyngys as hitt is be fore seyde and
þᵘ shalt be hole ꝕ est

575 ffor the lupe take an handfull of salt as moch of hony
as moch of barlich ꝛ medle heme togedir ꝛ put heme in an
erþen pott ꝛ brenne hem in an ovyn ꝛ make powdre þ⁹of
and strew on the sore

576 Also take the juyse of moleyn halue a pynt and halue
a pynte of hony and seth hem to the thyknes of hony and
medle thies to the powdre and lay to the sore

577 To avoyd lecherye take nettill sede and bray it in a
mortare with pep and temp it wᵗ hony or with wyne and
it shall distroy it and iff thow will preve it giff it to a dogge
that goþe assant and he will forsake the biche and she will
go wode

578 To make a laxatyfe Take v peny wyght of rubarbe
x peny wiȝt of powdre of sugure ij peny wiȝt of scamony
dj a quartron of sugure cassatyn ij peny wiȝt of powdre of
sene ꝛ j peny wiȝt of spyknard and temp hem togedire and
vse it

579 Anoþ⁹ laxatiffe Take the rote of affodyll iiij peny
wight o the white titemall añ of caturpuse añ ꝛ dry hem
ꝛ make powdre of heme and giff the syke to drynke with
warme ale and he shall be delyuͤed and hole

580 ffor the lyvre that is syke make a pleystre of barly
mele ꝛ syngrene morell and aysell and lay itt to the ryght
syde with puliall ꝛ iff he be costyfe make hyme on this manͤ
Take encence and floures of violett and seth hem in a

and put them in a close house (coop) clean swept, and give them of the barley broken in a mortar and afterwards whole when they are older ; then let the leper eat those chickens both roasted and boiled, and no other meat ; and let his bread be made of barley and [his] drink scalded, and ever-among (from time to time) drink water, ale, and wine, but scalded,[1] nor any hot nor spiced drink, and ever-among let the blood till thou seest thy blood clean. And govern thee in all things as it be aforesaid, and thou shalt be whole. *Probatum est.*

575 For the lupus. Take a handful of salt, as much of honey, as much of barley, and mingle them together ; and put them in an earthen pot, and burn them in an oven ; and make powder thereof, and strew on the sore.

576 [Another]. Also take the juice of mullein, half a pint, and half a pint of honey ; and seethe them to the thickness of honey, and mingle these with the powder, and lay to the sore.

577 To avoid lechery. Take nettle-seed and bray it in a mortar with pepper, and temper it with honey or with wine, and it shall destroy it.   And if thou wilt prove it, give it to a dog that goeth on the scent, and he will forsake the bitch, and she will go mad.

578 To make a laxative. Take five pennyweight of rhubarb, ten pennyweight of powder of sugar, two penny-weight of scammony, half a quartern of sugar-candy, two pennyweight of powder of senna and one pennyweight of spikenard ; and stamp them together, and use it.

579 Another laxative. Take the root of asphodel, four pennyweight ; of the white spurge (*titimallus*), the same ; of catapuce (another kind of spurge), the same ; and dry them and make powder of them, and give the sick to drink with warm ale. And he shall be delivered and whole.

580 For the liver that is sick. Make a plaster of barley-meal and sengreen, morell and vinegar, and lay it to the right side with pennyroyal ; and if he be costive make it in this manner. Take incense and flowers of violet, and seethe them

---

[1] Scalded here means having been scalded, but allowed to get cold.

galon of watir till þe one dele be soden jnne then clence it
thorow a cloth do than to þe Juyse [fo. 50 *verso*] a pound
of sugure till it be thikk ꝛ þᵒof giff hym drynke eũ emonge
ij sponefull as iij and take iij braunchis of sawge ꝛ barlich
ꝛ malews ꝛ henne bell ꝛ watir and seth togedir and wasshe
þe fete and lay the erbis to the skhankes and shaue þe
fete vndᵒneth and be hole

581 An oþᵒ ffor the lyvere take lyverworte wormode fenell
and psely rote mayden here hillwort piliall tonncresse soure
gall violett roses crop of the brere polipody licoresse a gode
quantitee ꝛ take iij galons of watyre and seth it to a galon
and drynke it erly and late

582 An oþᵒ for the lyver that is chawfid   Take puliall and
enoynt hyme þᵒwith and giff hyme to sugur rosett and lat
hyme blode off the vayn for the lyvere

583 ffor lendys that bene sore take a shelfull of juyse of
betayn and a shell full of wyn and a shell full of hony and
ix cornes of pep ꝛ stamp togedir and giff hem to drynke thre
dayes and he shall amend.

584 MOdir or cardiacle for collica passio   Take j peny
wiȝt of scamony and kest on to hote ale ꝛ
drynk it ꝛ seuen nyȝt after take cassefistula and ete ix
cornes þᵒ off wᵗ the mustarde and then take hempe sede
and wasshe itt and stamp itt and kest þᵒto goode ale and
draw it thorow a cloth and make mylk þᵒof ꝛ iij peny wiȝt
of powdre of rubarbe and kest in to the mylke and so vse
a sponefull at ons first and last

585 ffor bledders in the mowth take heyhound ꝛ make
þᵒof a powdre and do it in the mouth wᵗ a penne.

586 An oþᵒ for the soore in the mowth toth ach ꝛ oþᵒ sores
Take [fo. 51 *recto*] v yue levys and iff thow mayst some of
the beries ꝛ seth heme togedir wele and then hold thi
mowth oũ itt and lat þe breth go in after that soup of the
hote watir and hold it in þe mouth till it be colde and do
so oft and than ach shall away

in a gallon of water, till one half be absorbed ; then cleanse it
through a cloth ; put then to the juice a pound of sugar,
till it be thick ; and thereof give him to drink ever-among
(from time to time), two spoonfuls or three. And take
three branches of sage, and barly, and mallows, and henbane,
and water ; and seethe together, and wash the feet, and lay
the herbs to the shanks ; and shave the feet underneath.
And he shall be whole.

581 Another for the liver.   Take liverwort, wormwood and
parsley-root, maidenhair, hillwort, pennyroyal, towncress,
sour gall, violet, roses, crops of briar, polypody, liquorice a
good quantity ; and take three gallons of water and seethe
it to a gallon, and drink it early and late.

582 Another for the liver that is chafed.   Take pennyroyal
and anoint him therewith ; and give him sugar-roset, and
let blood of the vein for the liver.[1]

583 For loins that be sore.[2]   Take a shellful of juice of
betony and a shellful of wine, and a shellful of honey, and
nine corns of pepper ; and stamp together and give them to
drink three days, and he shall amend.

584 [For] **M**other or cardiacle [or] for collica passio.
Take one pennyweight of scammony, and
cast it into hot ale, and drink it ; and seven nights after take
cassifistula[3] and eat nine corns thereof ; and then take
hempseed and wash it, and stamp it, and cast thereto good
ale ; and draw it through a cloth, and make milk thereof ;
and [take] four pennyweight of powder of rhubarb, and cast
it into the milk, and so use a spoonful at once, first and last.

585 For bledders (blisters) in the mouth.   Take horehound
and make thereof a powder, and put it in the mouth with a
quill.

586 Another for the sore in the mouth, toothache and other
sores.   Take five ivy leaves, and if thou mayest, some of the
berries, and seethe them together well ; and then hold thy
mouth over it, and let the breath (steam) go in ; after that
sip the hot water, and hold it in the mouth till it be cold ;
and do so oft, and then [the] ache shall away.

---

[1] Meaning, the vein that communicates with the liver.
[2] This is a duplicate of § 765.
[3] Purging Cassia (*Cassia fistula*, L.).

587 Mogwort dronken with wyne oft will make men to pisse and distroy the stone and helpith hem þat haue the jaundis · stamp this erbe and medle it with hennes grese and lay it in a pleisͭ to a boche / take this erbe as it growith stamp it and put itt in must / and when itt is fynede drynke it as medecyn for wymmens floures and it cōfortith the stomake and helpith the entrylis abowte the hert the seede þ⁹off soþen and dronken helpith the brest and distroyeth the wormes in the bely it dissoluyth þᵉ festre and drunkyn it distroyeth venym of edders

588 ffor þᵉ modͬᷓ of the euyll cake take an onyon and kytt owt the myddyll and fill the hole full of powdre of anneyse and comyn and keuᷓ it wᵗ the ouᷓ pile and rost itt in the fire and ete it and vse it oft

589 ffor the suffocacion of the modir lat hir receyue þᵉ smoke of turpentyne laid upon the coles þorow hir mouth for p⁹apitacion of the modir lat hir receyue it beneyth forth

590 a suppositorye made of cotone and enoynted wᵗ turpentyne clensyth þᵉ modͬᷓ

591 The matrice to purge it of wikkyd humόs and to help to make more easye mala matricˢ. Take v⁹ueyn mogworte gladen rotes of ech lich moch and as moch as of all they of celidoyn rots and alto stamp hem ꝫ seth heme ī white wyne ꝫ wasshe wele þ⁹with the place ꝫ let þᵉ breth go wele [fo. 51 verso] jnne and then lay þ⁹to alhote a pleystre ther of

592 ffor to dry þᵉ supfluytees of the moder   Seth calamynt in waͭ and þ⁹with wasshe hym byneyth forth

593 ffor boyles in a mannes mowth take an erbe that men clepe nyght shade and brenne itt and make poudyre ther of and blaw it in the mouth

594 ffor fikes in a mans mouth as euyll end ete dry puliall royall at eue and at morow and wasshe thy mowth with vynegre

595 ffor vias in the mouth and throte take a goode quantitee of v levyd grasse ꝫ stampe it in a morͭ and after seith a

587 Mugwort drunken with wine oft, will make men to urinate, and destroy the stone, and helpeth them that have the jaundice. Stamp this herb and mingle it with hen's grease, and lay it in a plaster to a botch. Take this herb as it groweth, stamp it and put it in must ; and when it is refined, drink it as a medicine for women's flowers. And it comforteth the stomach, and helpeth the entrails about the heart. The seed thereof seethed and drunken helpeth the breast and destroyeth worms in the belly. It dissolveth the fester, and drunken, it destroyeth venom of adders.

588 For the mother, of the evil cake.[1] Take an onion and cut out the middle and fill the hole full of powder of anise and cumin ; and cover it with the outer skin, and roast it in the fire, and eat it, and use it oft.

589 For the suffocation of the mother. Let her receive the smoke of turpentine laid on the coals through her mouth. For palpitation of the mother let her receive it from beneath.

590 A suppository made of cotton and anointed with turpentine cleanseth the mother.

591 The matrix, to purge it of wicked humors and to help to make more easy *mala matricis*. Take vervain, mugwort, gladden-roots, of each equally much ; and as much of all these of celandine roots ; and stamp them all together, and seethe them in white wine ; and wash well therewith the place and let the breath (steam) go well in ; and then lay thereto all hot a plaster thereof.

592 For to dry the superfluities of the mother.[2] Seethe calamint in water, and therewith wash her from beneath.

593 For boils in a man's mouth. Take a herb that men call nightshade, and burn it and make powder thereof, and blow it in the mouth.

594 For fikes[3] in a man's mouth that end evilly. Eat dry pennyroyal at eve and at morn ; and wash thy mouth with vinegar.

595 For vice in the mouth and throat. Take a good quan- tity of five-leaved grass, and stamp it in a mortar ; and

---

[1] *Dysmenorrhœa*, clotting.

[2] *Leucorrhœa*.

[3] A.-S. fīc, a sore or scab.

gode while in fayre wat̾ ꝫ þen holde thi mouth oũ the wat̾
þᵗ þe smoke may go in to þe throte as hote as þᵘ may suffre
and after þat the syke hold of that watir in his mouth and
do so iij or iiij tymes and wᵗ in iiij dais he shall be hole

596 ffor the mouth that stynkyth   Take þe juyse of blake
mynt and the juyse of ruwe of ech lich moch. and put in to
þe nose thrilles

597 An oþꝰ for the stynkynge mowth · Seth mynt in goode
vynegre and wasshe thy mowth and thi gumes þꝰwᵗ and
after rub heme wele with dry mynt

598 ffor the rofe of þe mouth sillid wᵗ cold humós take
mynt and stamp it ryght wele and seth itt in white wyne
ꝫ than take wele þe smoke þꝰof at thi mouth ꝫ gargaraȝie
it than wele wᵗ the wyne and it will purge wondir wele

599 ffor the morfywe take horehowne and seth it in clene
rennynge watir a potell to a quart and kest þꝰto gode
white wyne or ellys stale ale and seth it vp and drynke þis
at morow hote and at eve also hote at ech tyme a sawserfull
at ones and the morfiw shall go away wᵗ [fo. 52 *recto*] Jnne
viij dayes //

600 An oþꝰ garse the place where as the morfyw is frote
with garlyke and lay a playstre of garlyke þꝰ apon

601 Anoþꝰ   Take xij egges and rost heme hard and kepe
heme fro breckynge þᵗ þe shelles crase natt and that thei be
ryght hard ꝫ then put hem in stronge vynegre all oũ wete
and lat hem stand so ij days and a nyght and then take
heme vp and pryk heme with a nedyll or a pynne all abowte
thorow þe shelles and lay heme in a clene platere ꝫ þꝰ will
com oyle of heme and þꝰ with anoynt hym at the hert pit
and also at the bake before the hert and he shall be hole
this is pꝰvyd and wasshe the spotts with þe forseid vynegre
and do so oft till he fynd hym easid this medecyne will hele
the morfiw faire and wele and dryue it away fro the hert

602 Also oyle of terre is good for the morfiwe to do itt
a way and all oþꝰ wennes þat comyth of malencoly

afterwards seethe [it] a good while in fair water, and then hold thy mouth over the water, that the smoke may go in to the throat as hot as thou mayest suffer [it] ; and after that [let] the sick hold of that water in his mouth, and do so three or four times. And within four days he shall be whole.

596 For the mouth that stinketh. Take the juice of black mint and the juice of rue, of each equally much, and put it into the nostrils.

597 Another for the stinking mouth. Seethe mint in good vinegar, and wash thy mouth and thy gums therewith ; and afterwards rub them well with dry mint.

598 For the roof of the mouth silted (encumbered) with cold humors. Take mint and stamp it right well, and seethe it in white wine ; and then take well the smoke thereof, and gargle it then well with the wine. And it will purge wonderfully well.

599 For the morphew. Take horehound and seethe it in clean running water, a pottle to a quart, and cast thereto good white wine or else stale ale ; and seethe it up and drink this at morn hot and at eve also hot, at each time a saucerful at once. And the morphew shall go away within eight days.

600 Another. Lance the place where the morphew is, rub with garlic, and lay a plaster of garlic thereupon.

601 Another. Take twelve eggs and roast them hard, and keep them from breaking that the shells crack not, and that they be right hard, and then put them in strong vinegar, all over wet,[1] and let them stand so two days and a night ; and then take them up, and prick them with a needle or a pin all about through the shells, and lay them in a clean platter, and there will come oil of them ; and therewith anoint him at the heart pit,[2] and also at the back before the heart,[3] and he shall be whole. This is proved. And wash the spots with the aforesaid vinegar, and do so oft till he find himself eased. This medicine will heal the morphew fair and well, and drive it away from the heart.

602 [Another]. Also oil of tar is good for the morphew to do it away, and all other wens that come of melancholy.

---

[1] Completely submerged.
[2] Pit of the stomach.
[3] The region of the back that lies opposite the stomach.

603 Anoþ⁹ take vitriall romayn and put it in the clene waꝷ and lat it stand a nyȝt or a day and afterward clence þe waꝷ and enoynt þe morfiwe wᵗ that waꝷ and itt shall be hole

604 ffor the blak morfiwe Take an vnc⁹ of verdegrasse anoþ⁹ of brymston ꝫ grynd hem small to powdre than take ij fat shepis hedys ꝫ hile heme and clene heme and take away the brayn and than wasshe ham faire and clene and seth hem togedre and lat kele ꝫ gedir the grese and temp þ⁹with þe powders and make enoyntment þ⁹of but lat it come neiȝe no fyre for it shold be wrought cold and enoynt the syke þ⁹with and he shall be hole

605 ffor [fo. 52 *verso*] the mygreyne Take peletre of spayn ꝫ stanescarre in a littell poke and hold longe bitwene thi teth on the sore syde and chew it ꝫ it will renne on watir ꝫ sanabitur

606 Anoþ⁹ for the mygreyne take stanescarre ꝫ stamp it in to powdre and the gall of an eece wele swongen and skymmed and layd thyk as a pleistre on the hede

607 An othir for the mygrayn in the hede ꝫ for þe postyme and for the dropsye in the hede þis medecyn is good take iiij peny wiȝt of rotis of peletre of spayn dj peny wiȝt of spyknarde and grynd hem and boyle hem in gode vynegre and take a sawserfull of hony and v sawserfull of mustard and the licoure is boiled and cold do þ⁹ to thyn hony and thi mustarde ꝫ medle heme togedir and vse þ⁹of halue a sponfull at onys ꝫ hold it in thy mowth as longe as þᵘ may say ij acdys and then spitt it owt in to a vessell and than take an oþ⁹ and do thus x tymes or xij a gode while after þᵗ þᵘ hast ete at none and a littell bifor euen eft sonys as oft ꝫ euꝝ spit it out ꝫ or þᵘ go to bedd drynke a draught iff thow wilt in goddis name but wasshe wele thi mouth and vse this iiij days and þᵘ shalt be hole on warantise

---

¹ Blue vitriol : copper sulphate.
² Duplicate in *Sloane* 2584. (Henslow, *op. cit.*, p. 130.)

603 Another. Take Roman vitriol[1] and put it in a clean water, and let it stand a night and a day ; and afterwards cleanse (strain) the water, and anoint the morphew with that water, and it shall be whole.

604 For the black morphew. Take an ounce of vlerdigris [and] another of brimstone, and grind them smal to a powder ; then take two fat sheep's heads, and skin them, and clean them and take away the brain ; and then wash them fair and clean, and seethe them together and let [them] cool ; and gather the grease, and temper therewith the powders ; and make ointment thereof, but let it come nigh no fire, for it should be wrought cold ; and anoint the sick therewith. And he shall be whole.

605 For the migraine.[2] Take pellitory of Spain and stone-scar (lichen) in a little pocket, and hold long between thy teeth on the sore side ; and chew it and it will run to water. *Et sanabitur*.

606 Another for the migraine. Take stonescar, and stamp it into powder ; and the gall of an ass well beaten-up and skimmed, and laid as thick as plaster on the head.

607 Another for the migraine in the head, and for impos-thumes, and for the dropsy in the head. This medicine is good. Take four pennyweight of roots of pellitory of Spain, half a pennyweight of spikenard, and grind them and boil them in good vinegar ; and take a saucerful of honey and five saucerfuls of mustard ; and [when] the licour is boiled and cold, put thereto thy honey and thy mustard, and mingle them together ; and use thereof half a spoonful at once, and hold it in thy mouth as long as thou mayest say two *Agnus Dei* ;[3] and then spit it out into a vessel. And then take another, and do thus ten times or twelve, a good while after thou hast eaten at noon, and a little before evening, and again as often, and ever spit it out. And before thou goest to bed, drink a draught if thou wilt in God's name, but wash well thy mouth. And use this four days, and thou shalt be whole, on warranty.

---

[3] The word *acdys* in the text seems to be a garbled and corrupt abbreviation of *Agnus Dei*. It may be, however, a corruption of the first words (in Latin) of one of the Psalms, such as xxv, xlix or cxxiii. *Cf.* § 299, where the title of Psalm li is used in the same way.

608 An oþᵍ for the same take ᴣ j of gyngere ꜓ ᴣ j ℔ oꞇ
nutmuge and a q̃rtron of ᴣ j of clawes ꜓ ꝯ j of floure or canell
꜓ ꝯ j of spiknard ꜓ j ℔ of anneys ꜓ a q̃rt ᴣ of elenacampana
ᴣ ℔ of licoresse ꜓ ᴣ j and of sugre and bete heme all in to
powdre and medle hem wele ꜓ vse þᵍ of first and last a
sponefull at ones ꜓ þʷ shal be hole wᵗ in iiij days [fo. 53
recto]

609 Anoþᵍ for þᵉ mygreyn Take d̄j a disshefull of barlye
and lat boile a gode while and put þᵍto when it is boyled
an ꝳ j of beteyn of verueyne añ and oþᵍ erbis that bene
good for the hede and when thei bene wele boylid togedir
take hem vp and lapp heme in a cloth and lay hem to þᵉ
syke hede ꜓ it shall be hole J þᵍvyd

610 ffor the menyson Take rwe and waybrede and stamp
hem togedir and take þᵉ juyse and whete floure and make
a cake þᵍoff and bake it and ete itt hote and þʷ shalt be
hole

611 Anoþᵍ Take yarow and waybrede ꜓ stamp heme and
take þᵉ juse ꜓ white floure ꜓ make a kake and vse it as
thow didst þᵉ oþᵍ afor seide

612 An oþᵍ Take a wardon and kytt out the myddyll of
þᵉ coore and fill it full of a dry hony combe wᵗ a littell pep
and keũ it agayn with the pill and sett it vp ryght in hote
eymers and rost it wele and ete it last at even

613 Anoþᵍ take psely sede ꜓ stamp it and temp it with
white wyne and drynke it

614 Anoþᵍ take boyle armonyake ij pties ꜓ rede corall on
ptie and rosen an oþᵍ ptie and make all thies to powdre ꜓
vse itt and seth cow mylke till halue be wastid or brenne it
with steele and put in to þᵉ poudre forseid and so ete it

615 ffor the mormall Take cow mylke and floure soden
togedir as papp and after put þᵍto rede cole stampid ꜓ make
a pleystre þᵍto and when it purgith to þᵉ rede flesshe make
salue of roses and fresshe shepis talwᴣ ꜓ lay þᵍto till it be
hole

616 [fo. 53 *verso*] Anoþᵍ Take sanycle bugle and erb rob̄t
and stamp hem ꜓ boile heme wele in stale ale and wasshe

608 Another for the same. Take one ounce of ginger and an ounce and a half of nutmeg, and a quarter of an ounce of cloves, and a scruple of flour of canell (cinnamon), and a scruple of spikenard, and one and a half [ounces] of anise, and a quarter of an ounce of elecampane, half an ounce of liquorice, and an ounce of sugar ; and beat them all into powder, and mingle them well ; and use thereof first and last a spoonful at once. And thou shalt be whole within four days.

609 Another for the migraine. Take half a dishful of barley, one handful each of betony, vervain, and other herbs that are good for the head ; and when they be well boiled together, take them up and wrap them in a cloth and lay them to the sick head, and it shall be whole. *I proved* [*it*].

610 For the menison (dysentery). Take rue and way-bread, and stamp them together ; and take the juice and wheat-flour, and make a cake thereof, and bake it ; and eat it hot, and thou shalt be whole.

611 Another. Take yarrow and waybread, and stamp them, and take the juice and wheat-flour, and make a cake ; and use it as thou didst the other aforesaid.

612 Another. Take a warden (pear) and cut out the middle of the core, and fill it full of dry honeycomb, with a little pepper, and cover it again with the peel ; and set it upright in hot embers, and roast it well, and eat it at last at even.

613 Another. Take parsley-seed and stamp it, and temper it with white wine, and drink it.

614 Another. Take bol-ammoniac, two parts, and red coral, one part, and rosin, another part ; and make all these to powder, and seethe cow's milk till half be wasted, or burn it with steel ; and put [it] into the powder aforesaid, and so eat it.

615 For the mormal. Take cow's milk and flour seethed together as pap, and afterwards put thereto red cabbage stamped, and make a plaster thereto ; and when it purgeth to the red flesh, make salve of roses and fresh sheep's tallow, and lay thereto till it be whole.

616 Another. Take sanicle, bugle and herb-Robert, and stamp them and boil them well in stale ale ; and wash

þᵍwith oft the sore and lay þᵉ erbys þᵍ on by maň of a pleystre ꓸ sanabitur //

617 A gode salue for the mormall take whete floure and mylke of a blake cow ꓸ make mylk mete and lat it stand till it be cold ꓸ than take rede caule wortes and grynd hem ꓸ wrynge out the juyse and take than a porcion of that mylke mete and a quantitee of that Juyse put þᵍto and bynd to þᵉ sore

618 A mormall is curable that is but the brede of a spone and where the flesshe and the bone bene clere and when the mormall passith the brede of iij fyngers he is vncurable or elles longe or he be hoole for it farith þᵍby as who so smytith a grete stroke with an ax on the rynde of a growynge tre itt will be longe or it grow togedir agayn

619 Roses or the leves bene fully sprongen owt thei shul be gederid and of the rede levys schred small ꓸ of hony togedꞓ is made mel rosett to a pound of roses thow shalt take viij pound of hony þᵉ roses shuld be schred small and seþen with the hony till the hony haue takyne both colő ꓸ sauő of roses

620 Mylk þᵗ is hardyd in wymmens tetis Seþe mynt in wyne and oyle and lay hem apon the tetys in a pleistre and when þʷ giffist any man medecyne for venym giff him ther with Juyse of mynt

621 Anoþᵍ for Womans mylke that faylith take crystall and pound it and giff hire [fo. 54 *recto*] to drynk with the mylke of an oþᵍ woman but lat hir nat witt [what][1] mylk it is

622 Anothir for the same Gyff hyre the Juyse of verueyne wᵗ white wyne made mylke warme and so do iij or iiij tymes and she shall haue mylke enough on warantie ⚹

623 **N**ose that stynkith Take the blak mynt and the Juyse of rwe ꓸ do of euꞓ ich lich moch and put it in hys nose thrilles or in a wound that stynkyth

624 ffor rennynge nose take the juyse of mynt ꓸ the juse of rw temped togedir and do it in his nose thrilles oft and it

---

[1] Added by a later hand.

[2] The meaning of this simile is, that a large mormal takes long to heal, just as a great gash in a growing tree is long in uniting again.

therewith the sore, and lay the herbs thereto in the manner of a plaster. *Et sanabitur.*

617 A good salve for the mormall. Take wheat flour and milk of a black cow; and make milk-meat (batter), and let it stand till it be cold; and then take red cabbage plants and grind them, and wring out the juice; and take then a portion of that milk-meat, and a quantity of that juice put thereto, and bind to the sore.

618 A mormal is curable that is but the breadth of a spoon, and where the flesh and the bone be clear. And when the mormal passeth the breadth of three fingers, it is incurable, or else long before he be whole, for it fareth thereby as whoso smiteth a great stroke with an axe on the rind of a growing tree, it will be long before it grow together again.[2]

619 Roses before the leaves be fully sprouted should be gathered, and of the red leaves shredded small and of honey together is made mel-roset. To a pound of roses thou shalt take eight pounds of honey. The roses should be shredded small and seethed with the honey, till the honey shall have taken both colour and savour of roses.[3]

620 Milk that has hardened in a woman's teats. Seethe mint in wine and oil, and lay them upon the teats in a plaster; and when thou givest any man medicine for venom, give him therewith the juice of mint.[4]

621 Another for woman's milk that faileth. Take crystal and pound it, and give it her to drink, with the milk of another woman; but let her not know what milk it is.

622 Another for the same. Give her the juice of vervain with white wine, made lukewarm; and do so three or four times, and she shall have milk enough, on warranty.

623 Nose that stinketh. Take the black mint and the juice of rue, and take of each equally much; and put it in his nostrils or in a wound that stinketh.

624 For running nose. Take the juice of mint and the juice of rue, tempered together; and put it in his nostrils oft,

---

[2] This is a duplicate of § 532.
[4] The latter part seems misplaced here.

will moch amend and kest owt þe fylþe of the brayn where
of it comyth   Also take ground yue or þe Juys of dragaunce
and do also in the nose thrill ꝺ temp wele þe rose and boyle
hyme in wyne wᵗ a littell hony and wrynge it thorow a cloth
and do in hys nose thrilles

625 Anoþꝰ stamp cokle wᵗ stronge vynegre ꝺ put into þe
nose thrilles

626 To staunch bledynge at the nose take betayn ꝺ stamp
itt with a littell salt and as moch as thou mayst tak wᵗ
iij fyngers put in thi nose threlles

627 Anoþꝰ take shell of egges when the chekyns bene
hawght and brenne hem and put the poudre in the nose
thrill

628 Anoþꝰ take þe seede of rwe and make powdre þꝰof and
pute in the nose or in the wound ꝺ it shall staunch

629 ffor nosebledynge þat comyth of the boylynge of þe
lyuͣ take þe sengrene medyllyd wᵗ waͭ of rosis ꝺ a cloth
wete þꝰjnne is gode leyd to his forhede and on his temples
ꝺ the blode shall staunch

630 ffor noli [fo. 54 *verso*] me tangere in the visage ꝺ for the
eyȝen ꝺ for the cankᵲe in a mans mowth a good watir
þꝰfor tak coprose ꝺ grynd it all to powdire and do a littell
watir þꝰto and lat it stand a day ꝺ a nyȝt and streyne it
thorow a cloth and enoynt it þꝰwith

631 also watire of cerfoyill doth þe same þe which is the
hony soke of the hegge

632 ffor narownes of the brest take ʒ j of powdre of licoresse
ʒ j of sugure candi and boile hem in a quart watir till it com
to the haluendele and þen stopp in a pynt pott alday and
ich nyght after drynke last v sponefull while it lastith

633 Nayles þᵗ bene blak to make heme growe and it may
be kept xx wyntere   The medecyn þꝰof   Take rosen of the
pynetre and an vncꝰ off white wex and an ʒ of resen ʒ j of
the turpentyne and set all togedire on an easy fyre till thei

and it will much amend, and cast out the filth of the brain whence it cometh. Also take ground-ivy or the juice of dragance, and put it also in the nostril; and temper well the rose and boil it in wine with a little honey, and wring it through a cloth, and put in his nostrils.

625 Another. Stamp cockle (ergot) with strong vinegar, and put into the nostrils.

626 To stanch bleeding at the nose. Take betony and stamp it, with a little salt; and as much as thou mayest take with three fingers put in thy nostrils.

627 Another. Take shells of eggs when the chickens be hatched, and burn them, and put the powder in the nostril.

628 Another. Take the seed of rue and make powder thereof, and put in the nose or in the wound, and it shall stanch.

629 For nose-bleeding that cometh of the swelling of the liver. Take the sengreen mingled with water of roses, and a cloth wetted therein is good laid to his forehead and or his temples; and the blood shall stanch.

630 For noli-me-tangere[1] in the visage, and for the eyes, and for the canker in a man's mouth: a good water therefor. Take copperas and grind it all to powder, and put a little water thereto; and let it stand a day and a night, and strain it through a cloth, and anoint it therewith.

631 [Another]. Also water of chervil doth the same, the which is the honeysuckle of the hedge.[2]

632 For narrowness of the breast. Bake one ounce of powder of liquorice, one ounce of sugar candy, and boil them in a quart of water till it come to half, and then stop it (cork it up) in a pint-pot all day; and each night after drink last (thing) five spoonfuls while it lasteth.

633 Nails that are black, to make them grow: and it (the medicine) may be kept twenty winters. The medicine thereof: take rosin of the pine-tree, and an ounce of white wax, and an ounce of rosin, an ounce of turpentine; and

---

[1] *See* note to § 217. *Cf.* also § 943.
[2] Chervil, *Anthriscus cerefolium*, Hoffm., is an umbelliferous plant, totally different from the honeysuckle (*Lonicera*).

bene molten when it is molten kest it in a vessell with cold
watir ꝫ aft͛ take it out ꝫ tēp it wᵗ thyne handis wᵗ oyle
debay and when it is temped enowȝ kepe it wele for it is
a trete

634 ffor nayle that is fallen take poudire of egromoyn and
lay þ⁹ the nayle was and it shall do away the akynge and
make the nayle growe

635 Anothir to mak a nayle grow sone take whete floure
and medyll it with hony ꝫ lay þ⁹to

636 ffor clensynge of nayles take virgyn wex and turpentyn
and medle hem togedir and lay on the nayl ꝫ as it waxit
kytt it and itt shall be hole

637 To make nayles to fall enoynt hem with poudre of
brymstone ꝫ arsnyk and vynegre

638 ffor nytts in the hedde make liȝe of wild nepe ꝫ þ⁹wᵗ
wasshe thyn [fo. 55 *recto*] hede and it will distroy hem

639 Anoþ⁹ ffor the same   Take whykklyme and orpement
ꝫ make powdire of heme and temp the powd⁾ with vynegre
ꝫ enoynt the hede þ⁹with and this distroyeth heme wᵗ
owt fallynge of here or any oþ⁹ harme

640 Anoþ⁹ for the same take see watir or ellis bryne and
wasshe thyne hede and that shall distroy heme

641 Anoþ⁹ take the Juyse of an erbe that is clepid blyte
and enoynt thi hede þ⁹with and both lyes and nittis shall
fall away p̄b est

642 Anoþ⁹ for the same and best of all / take a brode lyste
the lenght of a gyrdyll and enoynt the one side wᵗ fresshe
grese medilled with wkikk silu⁾ and straw thane þ⁹on þe
powd⁾ of stanysacre and bat it with thi fynger þat it cleue
fast þ⁹to and then fold it togedir and saw fast the sydys
and then wynd it in a lynnen cloth and sow it fast and
gird the þ⁹with and the lyse and the nyttis shall deye þis
hath bene wele p⁹vyd

643 The vertues of nept   Take nept and seith hyme in
rede wyne and lay itt to a womans navell when she is

set all together on an easy fire till they be molten. When it is molten, cast it in a vessel of cold water, and afterwards take it out, and temper it with thy hands with oil of bay; and when it is tempered enough, keep it well for it is a [good] entrete.[1]

634 For nail that is fallen. Take powder of agrimony and lay [it] where the nail was, and it shall do away the aching and make the nail grow.

635 Another to make a nail grow. Take wheat-flour and mingle it with honey, and lay thereto.

636 For cleansing of nails. Take virgin wax and turpentine, and mingle them together, and lay on the nail; and as it waxeth (grows), cut it; and it shall be whole.

637 To make nails to fall. Anoint them with powder of brimstone and arsenic and vinegar.

638 For nits in the head. Make lye of wild nept (bryony) and there with wash thine head, and it will destroy them.

639 Another for the same. Take quicklime and orpiment, and make powder of them; and temper the powder with vinegar, and anoint the head therewith. And this destroyeth them without falling of hair or any other harm.

640 Another for the same. Take seawater or else brine, and wash thy head, and that shall destroy them.

641 Another. Take the juice of a herb that is called blight, and anoint thy head therewith, and both lice and nits shall fall away. *Probatum est.*

642 Another for the same. Take a broad list[2] the length of a girdle, and anoint the one side with fresh grease mingled with quicksilver, and strew thereon the powder of lichen, and press it with thy finger that it cleave fast thereto; and then fold it together, and sew fast the sides; and then wind it in a linen cloth, and sew it fast, and gird thee therewith; and the lice and the nits shall die. *This hath been well proved.*

643 The virtues of nept (catmint). Take nept and seethe it in red wine and lay it to a woman's navel when she is

---

[1] Duplicate of § 292.
[2] The selvage of woollen cloth, also used of a bandage or strip of cloth generally.

ly3thed and þat shall brynge owte all mañ corrupcion and make hir small and do a way þe modire

644 Also for wormes in a mannes body drynk hym ꝗ thei shall deye or come owte

645 Also for akynge woundis seyth it in wyne and lay to hem and thai shall stynt the ach

646 Also if the woundid drynke hyme and he kest he shall be dede and if he do nat he may be holpe ꝗ moch folk clepyth it catts gresse ffor cattis will ete it when thei bene syk in here wombes it will do away the after throwes if wymmen drynk itt

CＡＰＪＴＶＬＶ Ｍ—xiiij   [fo. 55 vo]

647 Oyntement that is clepid Lac Virginis Take liatarge of lede and grynd it small and do it in whit vynegre and than take as moch of sandyuere and grynd small on a marbill stone and than do it in watire of roses and so lat hym stand a day and a ny3t and then do still hym by a filt and do euꝰy watir by hym selue in to clene vialles of glasse and stopp heme wele and when thow wilt vse itt do of euꝰyth lich moch as thow wilt occupy at onys and no more for fretynge of hem selue togedire ꝗ þe will be white as mylke this watir is gode for grete ladies to make hem faire and for the morfiw and sausfleme and for frakkens and pymples in a mannes face and it is goode to do away dede fleeshe in woundis

648 Oyntment for to hele woundis take oyle of olyue hony and may butture of euꝰ ich lich moch and Juyse of planteyn as moch as of all tho and seth hem all togedir till þt þei be soden to þe haluendelle and then take that oyntment and enoynt the wound þꝰwith and it shall hele it faire and clere or elles take lynet and wete þꝰin and lay it in the wound and it shall hele fayre

---

¹ The chapter-numbers wherever they occur are wrong. Cap. xiii is at the head of the letter K.

² Not to be confused with the *Lac Virginis* of Alchemy.

³ *See* note to § 205.

lying-in ; and that shall bring out all manner of corruption, and make her small, and do away (reduce) the mother (womb).

644 Also for worms in a man's body, drink it, and they shall die or come out.

645 Also for aching wounds, seethe it in wine and lay to them, and they shall stint the ache (reduce the pain).

646 Also if the wounded drink it, and he cast (vomit), he shall be dead ; and if he do not, he may be helped.   And many folks call it cat's-cress, for cats will eat it when they are sick in their wombs (bellies).   It will do away the after-throes if women drink it.

CHAPTER XIV.[1]

647 Ointment that is called Lac virginis.[2]   Take litharge of lead, and grind it small, and put it in white vinegar ; and then take as much of sandiver,[3] and grind small on a marble stone ; and then put it in water of roses, and so let it stand a day and a night ; and then still it by a filter, and put each water by itself into clean vials of glass, and stop them well.   And when thou wilt use it, take of each equally as much as thou wilt employ at once and no more, for fretting of themselves together,[4] and they will be white as milk.   This water is good for great ladies to make them fair (beautiful), and for the morphew and acne,[5] and for freckles and pimples on a man's face, and it is good to do away dead flesh in wounds.

648 Ointment to heal wounds.   Take oil of olive and honey and may-butter, of each equally much, and juice of plantain as much as of all those ; and seethe them together till they be boiled away to half ; and then take that ointment and anoint the wound therewith, and it shall heal it fair and clean.   Or else take lint and wet [it] therein, and lay it in the wound, and it shall heal fair.

---

[4] Meaning, " to avoid shaking them up too much."

[5] From *salsa phlegma*.   An affection of the face producing spots or pimples, probably *acne*.

649 Anoþᵍ oyntment for Woundis take the breyre cropp and the rede wortt cropp dayse rede nettle cropp ach bugle senecle and stamp heme and dyght hem with greese or buttre in the mañ) of an oyntment

650 Oyntment for gowtes take brokkes grese and swynes grese ꝛ hares grese cattes grese dogges grese capons grese and sywet of a deere and shepis talwȝ of ech lich ꝛ melt hem in a pan than take the Juys of erb roᵬt morell bismalue ꝛ comfery dayse and rwe planteyn and mayden here matfelon and dragonds [fo. 56 *recto*] of ech liche moch Juys and fry hem in a panne wᵗ the forseid greses and kepe it wele for the best oyntment for gowtes this is //

651 To make Vnguentū Album   Take nete oyle as moch as thow wilt and put in a clene basyne and stire it all way wᵗ a sklyce ꝛ strewe it with vynegre a littell till the oyle be fayre and cleere the iiijᵗʰ pte as moch of vynegre as of oyle than take litarge of lede and stamp itt small and bult it thorow a cloth vnto þᵉ oyle a littell quantitee and stirre it togedire take to galon of oyle almost a quartron of white lede put þᵍto and alway styre and take as moch of sueris ꝛ stamp it small and put þᵍto and Styrre it wele and take a cotill bone which goldsmythes vsys and put þᵍto and stire itt alway till it be white in the sune for euñ) the langer it is styrred þᵉ betᵗ̃ it is / But iff thow wilt haue it goode and fyne put þᵍto comfery litarge of syluñ) and of gold oyle of olyue of lynesede oyle of roses this oyntment is gode for all mañ) of sores scabbes and whitors festires and cankres and all mañ) of woundes to enoynt hem þᵍwith

652 A þᵍciose oyle for ach is made of lorer levys and sauge and lauandre white wyne an nw oyle or the best oyle of ech a pound and halue a pond of aqua vite and grynd thyne erbys togedyre and put hem in a erthen pott togedir to the wyne and oyle and a lyttell chaufe it and lat it stand a day

---

¹ Presumably some kind of *malva*, or mallow.
² The mixture of the grease of many different animals is, of course, purely magical, and it occurs in Egyptian medicine. *See* my *Magician and Leech*, pp. 65–6.
³ The calcareous shell of the cuttle-fish, which was ground for making plate-powder.

649 Another ointment for wounds. Take briar crop ; and the red wort crop, daisy, red nettle crop, ache, bugle, sanicle, and stamp them well and dress them with grease or butter in the manner of an ointment.

650 Ointment for gouts. Take badger's grease, and swine's grease, and hare's grease, cat's grease, dog's grease, capon's grease, and suet of a deer, and sheep's tallow, of each equally much, and melt them in a pan ; then take the juice of herb-robert, morell, bismalve,[1] and comfrey, and daisy, and rue, plantain, and maidenhair, matfelon (knapweed), and dragance, of each equally much juice ; and fry them in a pan with the aforesaid greases, and keep it well, for the best ointment for gouts this is.[2]

651 To make Unguentum Album. Take neat-oil as much as thou wilt and put [it] in a clean basin and stir it always (continually) with a slice, and sprinkle it with vinegar a little, till the oil be fair and clear, the fourth part as much of vinegar as of oil. Then take litharge of lead and stamp it small and squeeze it through a cloth into the oil, a little quantity, and stir it together. Take two gallons of oil [with] almost a quartern of white lead put thereto, and always stir ; and take as much of ceruse, and stamp it small, and put thereto, and stir it well ; and take a cuttle-bone[3] which goldsmiths use, and put thereto, and stir it always till it be white, in the sun ; for the longer it is stirred, the better it is. But if thou wilt have it good and fine, put thereto comfrey, litharge of silver and of gold,[4] oil of olive, oil of linseed, [and] oil of roses. This ointment is good for all manner of sores, scabs, whitlows, festers and cankers, and all manner of wounds, to anoint them therewith.[5]

652 A precious oil for aches is made of laurel leaves, and sage, and lavender, white wine, equal parts, and new oil. Or [take] the best oil of each a pound, and half a· pound of aqua vitæ ; and grind thy herbs together, and put them in an earthen pot, together with the wine and oil, and chafe it

---

[4] A yellowish-red substance obtained in hard, scaly, crystalline masses by calcination of lead nitrate and other lead salts.

[5] Most MSS. of this kind contain a recipe for *unguentum album*, but they differ very considerably in their ingredients.

or ij fast stoppid and then streyne it thorow a cloth and
lat hym sytt agayn the fyre and enoynt hym þ⁹with ther
the sore is

653 Oyntment for vanytee of the hede take the Juyse of
walwort and hony and boyle togedire and anoynt [fo. 56
verso] thyne here þ⁹with

654 A gode oyntment for all man̄ of sores take the Juyse
of walwort and auence bugle pigle sanycle ach erb roƀt
herbe John erb watire waybrede baynwort of caules the
crop of the brere holy hocke take and stamp eū ich by
hym selue ꝫ of eū ich lich moch and do it in a panne and
iff the holy hoke be so fatt that thou may haue no Juyse
there of and ther fore do the levys þ⁹to and then take
virgyns wex and fresshe shepis talwȝ hony and may butt̄
old swynes grese and wyne of ech lich moch   And do than
althies thynges in a panne and sethe hem and thou may
wit by the levys of the holy hoke when it is soden enowgh
and when it is nesshe do then on thyn nayle a dropp and
loke that it be chiriannt and iff it is soden enough do floure
þ⁹to and styre it wele and do it of the fyre and wrynge it
thorow a cloth in a basyn and when it is somdele cold do it
in boxis

655 A goode oyntment for the goute.   Take an owle and
pull hym clene and opyne hyme clene and salt hym ꝫ do
hym in an nw pott and hill it with a stone and do it in an
ovyn and lat it stand till it be brent and then stampit wᵗ
bores grese and enoynt the goute þ⁹with

656 An oyntment ffor Woundis   Tak an handfull of Savyn
and an handfull of Sauge and an handfull of rwe an handfull
of tansay   Stamp hem wele togedire and boyle heme wele
in oyle of olyue and do wex and Swyns grese fresshe and
powdre of mastyke and so make thyne oyntement þ⁹of

657 An oþ⁹ oyntement ffor Scabbes.   Take horehowne and
celidoyne wormode and sorell de voys and elenacampana
of ech lich moch and bruse heme wele in a mort̄ and stirre

---

¹ Cf. § 941.
² Herb-Walter is said to have been named after Walter de
Elvesdon, Bishop of Norwich (fourteenth century).   It is a synonym
of woodruff (Asperula odorata, L.).

a little, and let it stand a day or two fast stopped ; and then strain it through a cloth. And let him (the patient) sit by the fireside, and anoint him therewith where the sore is

653 Ointment for vanity (vacancy, light-headedness) of the head.[1] Take the juice of walwort and honey, and boil together, and anoint thy head therewith.

654 A good oil for all manner of sores. Take the juice of walwort, and avens, bugle, pigle, sanicle, ache, herb-robert, herb-John, herb-Walter,[2] waybread, banewort, cabbages, the crop of the briar, hollyhock ; take and stamp each by itself, and of each equally much, and put it in a pan. And if the hollyhock be so fat that thou mayest have no juice thereof, then therefore put the leaves thereto ; and then take virgin wax and fresh sheep's tallow, and honey, may-butter, old swine's grease and wine of each equally much. And then put all these things in a pan, and seethe them, and thou mayest know by the leaves of the hollyhock when it is seethed enough ; and when it is soft, put then on thy nail a drop, and look that it be cherry-coloured ; and if it is seethed enough, put flour thereto and stir it well, and take it off the fire, and wring it through a cloth into a basin. And when it is somewhat cold, put it in boxes.

655 A good ointment for the gout.[3] Take an owl, and pluck it clean; and open it clean, and salt it ; and put it in a new pot, and cover it with a stone ; and put it in an oven and let it stand till it be burnt ; and then stamp it with boar's grease, and anoint the gout therewith.

656 An ointment for wounds. Take a handful of savin, and a handful of sage, and a handful of rue, [and] a handful of tansey. Stamp them well together, and boil them well in oil of olive ; and take wax and fresh swine's grease, and powder of mastic, and so make thine ointment thereof.

657 An ointment for scabs. Take horehound, and celandine, wormwood, and wood-sorrel and elecampane, of each equally much ; and bruise them well in a mortar, and stir

---

[3] Duplicate in H. (Henslow, *op. cit.*, p. 19). This recipe was popular long after, and was strongly recommended by Nicholas Culpeper in his *Last Legacy* (London, 1671), p. 77.

hem wᵗ may butᵗ and put [fo. 57 *recto*] itt in a glasse ꜓
stop it wele and lat it stand so ix dayes and then take itt
owt and fry hitt softly agayn and iff it nede put þ⁹to a
littell more butture when it is wele friede take a lynnen
cloth ꜓ Juyse it owt and kep þat and þ⁹with enoynt thy
scabbys

658 An oþ⁹ oyntement for scabbis take iiij peny wight of
whiksiluᵓ and put it in a disshe and put þ⁹to d̄j a sausere
full of fastynge spatyll and swynge it wele with a slyce till
it turnyd all in to fome and than put þ⁹to an oyntment
þat men call dente þᵉ q̄ntitee of an ey and stirre it fast till
thou see nouȝt of the whiksiluᵓ and here wᵗ enoynt the
pawms of thyne handes and soles of thy fete //

659 Oyntement ffor woundes take the rede brer cropp and
the rede cole dayse smalach rede nettle cropp and bugle
pygale and sanycle and stamp to gedᵓ and do þ⁹to grese
or botre and boyle heme and do heme thorow a cloth and
lett hem stand ꜓ kele

660 An oyntement to dissolue Wymmen floures iff thei bene
enoyntyd þ⁹with fro the navell downward and it is gode for
sore tetys and itt is clepid vnguentū liliū. Take oyle of
olyue and stop it full of lylye floures and late it stand opyne
in the sune ix days and than streyne itt thorow a cloth and
lat it stand eft to clere oþ⁹ ix dayes and then put itt in a
glasse or in A Joyne pot and let stand longe in the sune and
kepe it

661 Oyntment for festre in wound take hony and verede-
grasse and seþe togedir in an erthen pot ꜓ iff thou will witt
when itt is soden enouȝe take wᵗ the sklyce a drope nad put
itt on an yren or on a cold [fo. 57 *verso*] stone and iff the
dropp be hard when it is cold þᵗ oyle is gude for festre iff
thow fill itt twyes on the day

662 To make oyle of violett take violett and seth itt in
comyn oyle and drynke and drynke (*sic*) this oyle and
enoynt þ⁹with thi wombe and it will sle all the wormes
þ⁹in it colyth it easely the bodye and resoluyth it of
slomberynge but thou must clence that oyle soden and iff

---

[1] Presumably the spittle of a fasting man. The expression
"manys fastyng pisse" occurs in Henslow's MS. (*op. cit.*, p. 18).

them with may-butter. And put it in a glass and stop it well, and let it stand so nine days ; and then take it out, and fry it softly again ; and if need be, put thereto a little more butter. When it is well fried, take a linen cloth, and juice it out (wipe up the juice) and keep that, and therewith anoint thy scabs.

658 An ointment for scabs. Take four pennyweight of quicksilver, and put it in a dish, and put thereto half a saucerful of fasting spittle,[1] and stir it well with a slice till it be turned all to foam ; and then put thereto an ointment that men call dent[2] the quantity of an egg, and stir it fast till thou see nought of the quicksilver ; and therewith anoint the palms of thy hands and the soles of thy feet.

659 Ointment for wounds. Take the red briar crop, and the red cabbage, daisy, smallage, red nettle crop, and bugle, pigle and sanicle, and stamp all together ; and put thereto grease or butter, and boil them ; and put them through a cloth, and let them stand and cool.

660 An ointment to dissolve women's flowers, if she be anointed therewith from the navel downwards ; and it is good for sore teats, and it is called Unguentum Lilium. Take oil of olive and stop it full of lily flowers, and let it stand open in the sun nine days ; and then strain it through a cloth, and let it stand again to clear another nine days, and then put it in a glass or in a join-pot[3] and let [it] stand long in the sun, and keep it.

661 Ointment for fester in a wound. Take honey and verdigris, and seethe [them] together in an earthen pot ; and if thou wilt know when it is seethed enough, take with a slice a drop, and put it on an iron or on a cold stone, and if the drop be hard when it is cold, that oil is good for fester, if thou fill it (the wound) twice a day.

662 To make oil of violet. Take violet and seethe it in cumin [and] oil, and drink this oil and anoint therewith thy womb, and it shall slay all the worms therein. It cooleth easily the body, and resolveth it of slumbering (? sluggish humors). But thou must cleanse that oil by boiling ; and

---

[2] *Dent* may mean either " dainty," or it may refer to hardness, *dent* being also a tough kind of clay. *Cf.* § 783.

[3] A jar with a lid or stopper.

o

thou wilt haue itt ryght fyne do grene violet þᵉto ꝫ lat it
lygge ther in xv days in the sune and seþen kest thyke
leves and do in fresshe new levys as thow didst rathere and
that will be fyne oyle and all thynges that bene made of
violett bene gode for the feuers and for distempaunce of
hete it will distroy ach of the eres and þᵉ swonnynge þᵉin iff
it be poured in heme the oyle oyle (*sic*) is gode to be
enoynted with oute forth for clensynge of the lyu̅ and it
helpith for the hede ach

663 An oyntement for hede ach medle the Juyse of ꝛwe wᵗ
oyle of rosis and vynegre and enoynt ther with thi templese
ꝫ and Juyse of ꝛwe droppid in the nose threlles will staunch
bledynge

664 Oyntment for hete Take vynegre and old swynes
grese and canile stampid togedir and kest þᵉto oyle of
roses and this decoccion distroyeth the grete hete of fyre
if thou anoynt þᵉwᵗ thi stomake in the membres that bene
hote.

665 Take hole alome and sharpe vynegre and canile and
stamp all thies wele togedire and with oyntment thow may
hele the lepre and oþᵉ many spottis iff thow enoynt hyme
þᵉ with ꝫ it will kepe fro fallynge and this oyntment helpith
balokkys that bene swollen ꝫ oþᵉ diseases in the membres
[fo. 58 *recto*] ꝫ put þᵉto namely soden benes the askes of
canile wele gronden with old swynes grese ꝫ enpleystred
ꝫ it wil help hugely the cold ach both of the side and of the
teth ꝛ

666 An oþᵉ oyntement for brennynge take old wyne ꝫ ole
of olyue and swenge hem wele togedir till the wyne by nat
sene and than put in litarge of silu̅ and of gold or of lede
and medle wele togedir and ley þᵉof on the shaldynge and
lay lylye leves or some oþᵉ þᵉon and do thus till it be hole
and it shall hele p̅b̅ est

667 Anoþᵉ Take pure henne muk and fresshe grese of a
swyne and fry heme togedire or well hem and draw thies
thorow a cloth and enoynt the sore

668 All man̅ of floures ꝫ erbes that bene cold shuld be
leyd in oyle of olyues ꝫ þᵉin shuld rype iiij days or v and
then thow shalt boyle heme ꝫ set hem agayn the sune

if thou wilt have it right fine, put green violet thereto, and let it lie therein fifteen days in the sun ; and then cast [out the] thick leaves, and put fresh new fresh leaves as thou didst before, and that will be fine oil. For all things that be made of violet be good for the fevers, and for distempers of heat. It will destroy ache of the ears and singing therein, if it be poured in them. The oil is good to be anointed without for cleansing of the liver, and it helpeth for the headache.

663 An ointment for headache. Mingle the juice of rue with oil of 'roses and vinegar, and anoint therewith thy temples. And the juice of rue dropped in the nostrils will stanch bleeding.

664 Ointment for heat. Take vinegar and old swine's grease and canell (cinnamon), stamped together, and cast thereto oil of roses ; and this decoction destroyeth the great heat of fire, if thou anointest therewith the stomach and the members that be hot.

665 [Another]. Take whole alum and sharp vinegar and canell, and stamp all these well together, and with [this] ointment thou mayest heal the leprosy, and many other [kinds of] spots, if thou anoint him therewith. And it will keep [thee free] from falling [-evil]. And this ointment helpeth testicles that be swollen, and other diseases in the members. And by putting thereto especially boiled beans [and] the ashes of canell, well ground with old swine's grease, and used as a plaster, it will help hugely the cold ache both of the side and of the teeth.

666 Another ointment for burning. Take old wine and oil of olive and stir them well together till the wine be not seen ; and then put in litharge of silver and of gold or of lead, and mingle well together, and lay thereof on the scalding (scald), and lay lily leaves or some other thereon, and do thus till it be whole, and it shall heal. *Probatum est*

667 Another. Take pure hen's dung and fresh grease of a swine, and fry them together, or press them and draw these through a cloth, and anoint the sore.

668 All manner of herbs that be cold should be laid in oil of olive, and therein should ripen (mature) four days or five, and then thou shalt boil them, and set then in the sun.

669 Oyle of almondys put hem in hote waȝ and blanch hem and stamp hem and do hem in A pot and set þᵗ pot on an oþᵒ sethynge pot and þᵉ breth of the sethynge pot shall rise and entre in to the kyrnellys or in to the almodes and that will become oyle when it wrongon thorow a cloth // Also thou may do in the same wyse of the kernels of filberd nottis and walnottis

670 ffor to make oyle of sauge ꝛ of psely · seth hem in oyle of olyfe till it be thike and grene and this is gode for guwynge in Joynts and akynge

671 To make oyle of hilwort take hilwort in tyme of þe the (sic) croppes wᵗ þe flowres ꝛ braunches ꝛ make [fo. 58 verso] oyle in the manꝰ for seid þᵗ oyle is goode for to enoynt about þe lyuꝰ ꝛ about the navell and about the wombe pece of a womman þat is syke in the modir and þat will cōforth hyre and make hire Jseyue is (sic) she be distrobled

672 To make oyle of henbane at mydsomꝰ take þe croppes of henbane ꝛ fill a new pott þᵒoff ꝛ make an hole in the erth þat may stand in and make þe potts botom full of small holes ꝛ do an oþᵒ pot þat is empty vnder neth þe thrilled pott and close þe ouꝰ pot boþom to þe oþᵒ mowth and buy hem bote in the erth and close hem fast þᵗ noone eyre go owt and at the ȝeris end remeue the pot and thow shall fynd a clere oyle in the pott ꝛ þᵗ is clepid oleū jas'qamis

673 To make oyle of lorer tak þe bayes of lorere and g̅ynd hem and seth hem wᵗ oyle and cole it or streyne it and this is clepid oleum laureū þis oile is gude for male deflannke and all so when a man felith nat his awn lymmes þᵗ bene coldid for the pallisy and oþᵒ mortificacions

674 Oyle for the gout arcetik tak a pott ꝛ thrill þe boþom and do þᵒ in yuy berys and the braunches ꝛ as thou made oyle of henbane so make þis ꝛ þis before all oþᵒ manꝰ medecyns helyth þe gout arcetik þat comyth of cold. Also in the same manꝰ þʷ myȝt make oyle of the bowes of þe gorse þᵗ is gode for þe feuꝰ quarteyne who so enoyntith

669 Oil of almonds. Put them in hot water and blanch them, and stamp them, and put them in a pot ; and set that pot on another seething pot, and the breath (steam) of the seething pot shall rise and enter into the kernels or into the almonds. And that will become oil when it is wrung through a cloth. Also thou may do in the same wise, of the kernels of filbert-nuts and walnuts.

670 For to make oil of sage and of parsley. Seethe them in oil of olive till it be thick and green. And this is good for sharp pains in joints, and aching.

671 To make oil of hillwort. Take hillwort at the time when the flowers are on the crops and branches, and make oil in the manner aforesaid. That oil is good to anoint about the liver, and about the navel, and about the womb-piece of a woman that is sick in the mother. And that will comfort her and make her easy if she be troubled.

672 To make oil of henbane. At midsummer take the crops of henbane and fill a new pot thereof. And make a hole in the earth that [it] may stand in. And make the pot's bottom full of small holes. And put another pot that is empty underneath the pierced pot, and set the upper pot's bottom to the mouth of the other pot. And bury them both in the earth, and close them fast that no air go out. And at the year's end, remove the pot, and thou shalt find a clear oil that is called *oleum jusquiami*.

673 To make oil of laurel. Take the bays of laurel and grind them with oil, and cool it or strain it. And this is called *oleum laureum*. This oil is good for pain in the sides,[1] and also when a man feeleth not his own limbs when they be chilled, for the palsy, and other mortifications.

674 Oil for the sharp gout.[2] Take a pot, and bore the bottom, and put therein ivy-berries and the branches. And as thou made oil of henbane, so make this. And this before (more than) all other manner of medicines healeth the sharp gout that cometh of cold. Also in the same manner thou mightest make oil of the boughs of the gorse. That is good for quartan fever, for whoso anointeth therewith

---

[1] *Mal de flanc.*

[2] *Arcetic = acetic*, sharp, acid ; unless it be a corruption of *arthritic.*

þ⁹ wᵗ fro þe navyll downward and also fro chynne ꝫ þe
rygge ꝫ in the same mañ thow mayst make oyle of all mañ
of treese

675 Oyl of castor tak iij ℥ of castor ꝫ l̄j j of oyle ꝫ Seth
hem to the thrid pt ꝫ that oyl is gode for þe fallyng euell
if a mannes [fo. 59 *recto*] be enoynted þ⁹with also it is good
for the litarge

676 Oyle of tartary þat is wyne drestyn   Take argoyle and
poudre itt small and do þ⁹to vynegre and do it in a poket
as thou wold make liȝe or in an other clout ꝫ take hemp
and wete it wele in watir ꝫ fold þ⁹in thyne argoyle in thi
clout and rake itt wele in hote eymers after that do it in
an erthen pot and lat it stand iij days ꝫ iij nyghtes in a
moyst stede and you shall fynd an oyle that men clepith
oleum tartary þat oyle is good to do away the morfiw and
all oþ⁹ wemmes that comyth of malencoly also it clensith
moch a mannes face

677 A reule to make oyles that bene made of tre or of
braunches · thei shul be hewen in to pecis and put in to a
pot þᵗ þe boþom is thrillid full of small holes and an oþ⁹
pot þat is wele glasid sal be do in the erth vp to þe brynkes
Joynynge than shall þe hilled pot be sett a boue þat oþ⁹
pot and cleme it wele so þᵗ the eres of the oþ⁹ [*sic*] pot
bethipp þe oþ⁹ pot and cleme it wele a boute with clay and
make an easy fyre aboute þe oũ pot and then thorow
strenght of the fyre þ⁹ will fall an oyle owt of þe holid pot
in to þe pot þat standith in the erth and þᵗ is gode for many
mañ of syknes and namely for the pallesy

678 Oyle of roses is made of oyle of olyue and of roses
hangynge togedir in a glasen vessell xxx days or xl in the sune
but it is bettir to seþe þe roses ꝫ the oyle togedir oũ þe fire
and clence it and kepe it

679 Oyle of nettilles is thus made seth nettill sede in oyle
longe and the croppis and this will be a gode oyntment for
handes ꝫ fete þᵗ bene acoldyd

---

[1] Not *castor-oil* as understood to-day. Castor-oil made from
Ricinus was not introduced until the eighteenth century.

[2] The place where the rim or lip joins the body of the vessel.

from the navel downwards, and also from the chine and [from] the back. And in the same manner thou mayest make oil of all manner of trees.

675 Oil of castor.[1] Take three ounces of castor (castoreum) and one pound of oil, and seethe them to one third part. And that oil is good for the falling-evil if a man be anointed therewith, also it is good for lethargy.

676 Oil of tartary, that is wine-lees. Take argol (crude tartar) and powder it small, and put thereto vinegar ; and place it in a pocket as thou wouldst make lye, or in any other cloth. And take hemp and wet it well in water, and fold therein thine argol in thy cloth, and rake it well in hot embers. After that put it in an earthen pot, and let stand three days and three nights in a moist place, and you shall find an oil that men call *oleum tartari*. That oil is good to do away the morphew and all other wems (spots) that come of melancholy ; also it cleanseth much a man's face.

677 A rule to make oils that be made of trees or of branches. They should be hewn into pieces, and put into a pot of which the bottom is drilled full of small holes ; and another pot that is well glazed shall be put in the earth up to the rim-joint.[2] Then shall the drilled pot be set above the other pot. And daub it well so that the ears[3] of the one pot overlap the other pot. And daub it well about with clay. And make an easy fire about the upper pot, and then through the strength of the fire there will fall an oil out of the drilled pot into the pot that standeth in the earth. And that [oil] is good for many manner of sicknesses, and especially for the palsy.

678 Oil of roses is made of oil of olive and of roses hanging together in a glass vessel thirty days or forty, in the sun. But it is better to seethe the roses and the oil together over the fire, and cleanse it and keep it.

679 Oil of nettles is thus made. Seethe nettle-seed in oil long, and the crops. And this will be a good ointment for hands and feet that be chilled.[4]

---

[3] Handles.
[4] Probably chilblains are meant.

680 [fo. 59 *verso*] To make oyntement genest take floures
of brome ꝛ flowres of (*sic*) levys of wodwise lich moch ꝛ
stamp hem with may butture and lat it stand so togedire
alnyght ꝛ on the morow melt it in a panne ou͡ the fire and
skyme itt wele þis medecyn is gode for all cold yuellis ꝛ
for slepynge of hand or fote ꝛ for fleynge goute

681 To make an oyntement good and grene take a pound
of swyns grese ℥ of verdegrese ℥ ẞ of sall gemme þis oyntement may be kept xl wyn͡t and it is gode for the cankre ꝛ
for the rennynge holes and for to hele old woundes and it
fretith away dede flesshe ꝛ bryngith nw and put it wᵗ in
the wound þᵗ it festre nat.   This oyntement is gode for þᵉ
mormall and þ⁹ is none oyntment þat worchys so strongly
as it doth and put to the same oyntment pich rosen and
wex and it will be a fyne trete for old brusures and swellyngs
ꝛ mormals

682 To make a rede oyntement take a pynt of hony and d̄j
a pynt of vynegre and a porcion of verdegresse and boyle
hem to gedire ꝛ þis is gode for all man͡ of sores

683 A gode oyntment for woundes ꝛ for tentis of woundes
take a pynt of juyse of rybwort ꝛ a pynt of vynegre and a
pynt of hony and boyle hem to gedire to þᵉ thyknesse of
the hony ꝛ kep it for it is full p⁹ciose

684 Anoynt thi hede with onyons gronden small ꝛ temped
with hony ꝛ it will restore here on þᵉ hede onyons ben gode
for flemmatik men but nat for malencolyose men but þei
bene gode to the stomake onysede helpith hem þat bene
tisik

685 An oyntment to woundes take a pound of virgyn wex
l̄i j of lard 1. j [fo. 60 *recto*] of pich rosen lj ẞ of olibanū li j
of deteyn lj j of planteyn lj of rubarb l̄i j of littell cōsona
lj j of mylfoile lj j of watire cressis take thies erbes ꝛ stamp
ech on by hym selue and temp hem with wyne ꝛ lat hem
rest a nyȝt and the morow do hem in a pot ou͡ the fire and
let hem seth and boyle with wyne afterward take heme
down and dryue hem thorow a cloth

---

¹ Duplicate in Henslow, *op. cit.*, p. 66, but with variations.
Another duplicate, § 854, but with different title.
² Dyer's greenweed, *Genista tinctoria*. L.
³ *Sal gemme* is Lat. *sal gemmæ*.

680 To make ointment-geneste (broom).[1] Take flowers of broom and flowers and leaves of woadwaxen,[2] equally much, and stamp them with may-butter, and let it stand so together all night : and on the morrow melt it in a pan over the fire, and skim it well. This medicine is good for all cold evils, and for sleeping hand or foot, and for cold gout.

681 To make an ointment good and green. Take a pound of swine's grease, an ounce of verdigris, half an ounce of rock-salt.[3] This ointment may be kept forty winters, and it is good for the canker and the running holes (sinuses) and for to heal old wounds. And it fretteth away dead flesh and bringeth new. And put it within the wound that it fester not. This ointment is good for the mormal, and there is no ointment that works so strongly as it doth. And put to the same ointment pitch resin and wax, and it will be a fine entrete for old bruises and swellings and mormals.

682 To make a red ointment. Take a pint of honey, and half a pint of vinegar, and a portion of verdigris, and boil them together. And this is good for all manner of sores.[4]

683 A good ointment for wounds and for tents for wounds. Take a pint of juice of ribwort, and a pint of vinegar, and a pint of honey, and boil them together to the thickness of the honey, and keep it, for it is full precious.

684 Anoint thy head with onions ground small and tempered with honey, and it will restore hair on the head. Onions be good for phlegmatic men, but not for melancholic men, but they be good for the stomach. Onion-seed helpeth them that be phthisic.

685 An ointment for wounds. Take a pound of virgin wax, a pound of lard, a pound of pitch rosin, half a pound of olibanum, a pound of dittany, a pound of plantain, a pound of rhubarb, a pound of little consolida,[5] a pound of milfoil, a pound of watercress. Take these herbs and stamp each one by itself, and temper them with wine ; and let them rest a night, and on the morrow put them in a pot over the fire, and let them seethe and boil with wine ; afterwards take them down, and dry them through a cloth.

---

[4] There is no red colouring matter in this recipe, in spite of its title.

[5] Written in error *consona*. *Consolida minor*, frequently mentioned in the MSS., is identified with the common daisy, *Bellis perennis*, L.

686 An oþ⁹ enoyn to wound.   Tak erb John erb ro͠bt bugill
pigle mylfoil plantayn auence of all this erbs tak þᵉ juse
wex and pich and a littell grese make this enoyn to all
kyles and to all woundes

687 Oxmell which is goode to distroy glad to make it gedir
rotes of smalach louach elenacāpana fenell psely and wasshe
thies rotis and pike out the hard wᵗ in and bruse hem in a
morͭ and lay hem in vynegre al ou͠ a day ꝛ a nyꝫt cloose
and after þat boyle hem togedir till halue a quart be wastid
and do it þan in glassis ꝛ drynke þ⁹of erly ꝛ late wᵗ the
same ꝗntite of warme waͭ and this purgith right wele

688 **P**urgacion for to delyu͠ a man of flewme   Take iij
      peny wight of white copose iij sponefull of waͭ ꝛ.
chaufe it a littell and lat hym drynk it a littell warme ꝛ
coloure it with safron ꝛ gif hym afterward when his stomake
to worch ij sponfull of aqua vite ꝛ þ⁹in a littell triacle ꝛ he
shall kest vp ward at is vpward ꝛ then will it frete downward
and then take an hote tyle and lay to hys womb ꝛ if an
corrupcion be þ⁹in it shall delyu͠ hym

689 Anoþ⁹ gode [fo. 60 *verso*] purgacion   Tak lawriall and
make powd⁹ꞈ þ⁹of ꝛ dry it in þᵉ sun ꝛ temp it with as moch
hony

690 A gode purgacion for the hede take plelstre of spayne
and chew it wele a gode quantitee of the rote iij days and
that will purge the hede ad make þᵉ teth stand fast pᵬ est

691 An oþ⁹ purgacion for flewm take iiij ꝫ of betayn rotes
and giff hem to drynke in mulso or in vino passo for this
wil parge flewm by vomet.

692 pep is gode to purge a man of flewme if þᵉ poudre þ⁹of
be blowen in his nose and namely þᵉ flewme in the hede

686 Another ointment for wounds. Take herb-John, herb-Robert, bugle, pigle, milfoil, plantain, avens. Of all these herbs take the juice, wax and pitch and a little grease. Make this ointment for all kyles[1] and for all wounds.

687 Oxymel, which is good to destroy gleet. To make it, gather roots of smallage, lovage, elecampane, fennel, parsley, and wash these roots, and pick out the hard (fibre) within, and bruise them in a mortar, and lay them in vinegar, all one day and a night, close (*i.e.* corked-up). And after that, boil them together, till half a quart be wasted, and put it then in glasses. And drink thereof early and late, with the same quantity of warm water, and this purgeth right well.[2]

688 Purgation to deliver a man of phlegm. Take three pennyweight of white copperas, three spoonfuls of water, and chafe it a little. And let him drink it a little warm, and colour it with saffron ; and give him afterwards when his stomach works, two spoonfuls of aqua vitæ, and therein a little treacle. And he shall cast upward what is uppermost, and then it will fret downwards. And then take a hot tile and lay it to his womb, and if any corruption be therein, it shall deliver him.

689 Another good purgation. Take spurge (laureola) and make powder thereof, and dry it in the sun, and temper it with as much honey.

690 A good purgation for the head. Take pellitory of Spain, and chew well a good quantity of the root three days ; and that will purge the head, and make the teeth stand fast. *Probatum est.*

691 Another purgation for phlegm. Take four ounces of betony roots and give them to drink in mulsa[3] or in vinum passum ; for this will purge phlegm by vomit.

692 [Another]. Pepper is good to purge a man of phlegm if the powder thereof be blown in his nose, and especially the phlegm in the head.

---

[1] Old Norse *kýli*, " boil " or " abscess."
[2] The most essential element in oxymel, the honey, is not mentioned.
[3] *See* note to § 377.

693 Also the wyne that pep ꝫ dry fygges bene soden in
clensith þe brest and glett the powdre of pep etyn with oþ⁹
metis makyth good digestion but longe pep is more cõfort-
able

694 ffor þ⁹ is iij man͠ of pepir ther is blak pep þat is clepid
melan pepyre ꝫ þ⁹ is white pep and longe pep when the tre
þat berith pep blossometh the blossoms renne togedire ꝫ
when it is waxen harde þen it is clepid longe pepir and
within þat a littel white sede that is clepid white pep but
the blake pep is most of vertu ꝫ most vsid · but pep is
nat gode for coleryke men for sangwyn men but it be þe
lesse

695 Her begynneth þe makynge of good poudresse for dyu͠s
syknes A poudre for the goute festre Take arnment ꝫ brenne
hem to poudre ꝫ then take v⁹degrasse and pepire white
glasse and mustard sede and make poudere of hem and do
the powdre togedir ꝫ lay it on þe soore

695A A powdre for the palsye is made of mustard seede
and off [fo. 61 *recto*] sawge togedir and ich day vse it
fastynge and drynke in thi potage and ete barly brede and
thou shalt be hole

696 Agode poudre for all man͠ of syknesse in a mannes body
and iff a man be ou͠comon by þe way and it shall distroy
all man͠ of poyson ꝫ venym and dropsy and the ȝelow
yuell and for walmynge abowt a mannes hert take smalach
sede bayes and anneys the rote of turmentyne þe rote of
whyntfoyle þe rote of filipendula the sede of gromell the
rote of saxfrage and the seede of stanmarch sowtistill sedre
poudre of licoresse floure of canell and of galyngale ꝫ of
gyngere bray all thies in a mortare and put it togedir and
vse it oft

697 powdre for the brayn Tak centory of spayn ℥ j
nutmuge ℥ j of licores ℨ ẞ and make poudre of hem ꝫ ete it
first and last in mete ꝫ drynk ꝫ it shall help the brayn

698 Anoþ⁹ poudre for the brayn to clence it and to do away
hede ach and to clarify þe siȝt and to make gode digestion

693 [Another]. Also the wine that pepper and dry figs have been seethed in cleanseth the breast and gleet. The powder of pepper eaten with other meats maketh good digestion, but long pepper is more comfortable.

694 For there are three kinds of pepper. There is black pepper that is called melan pepper;[1] and there is white pepper and long pepper. When the tree that beareth pepper blossometh, the blossoms run together; and when it hath waxed hard, then it is called long pepper; and within that [is] a little white seed that is called white pepper. But the black pepper is of most virtue and most used. But pepper is not good for choleric men; for sanguine (full-blooded) men it be [even] less [good].

695 Here beginneth the making of good powders for divers sicknesses. A powder for the gout fester. Take arnement and burn it to powder, and pepper, white glass, and mustard-seed, and make powder of them; and mix the powder together, and lay it to the sore.

695A A powder for the palsy is made of mustard-seed and of sage together, and each day use it fasting and drink it in thy pottage, and eat barley bread, and thou shalt be whole.

696 A good powder for all manner of sickness in a man's body, and if a man be overcome by the way[side]; it shall destroy all manner of poison and venom, and dropsy and the yellow-evil (jaundice), and for warming about a man's heart. Take smallage-seed, bays and anise, the root of tormentil, the root of cinqfoil, the root of philipendula (dropwort), the seed of gromwell, the root of saxifrage, and the seed of stanmarch, sowthistle-seed, powder of liquorice, flour of canell (cinnamon), and of galingale and of ginger. Bray all these in a mortar, and put it together, and use it oft.

697 Powder for the brain. Take centaury of Spain, one ounce; nutmeg, one ounce; liquorice half a drachm. Make powder of them and eat it first and last in meat and drink, and it shall help the brain.

698 Another powder for the brain to cleanse it, and to do away headache, and to clarify the sight, and to make good

---

[1] From the Greek πέπερι μέλαν

and to distroy wynd.   Take anneise loueach and smalach
canell cardmamū origanū mele caraway fenell surmownteyn
sawge comyn calamynt tyme blake pep isop psely of ech
halue a dragme licoresse gyng⁹ pelettre of spayne of ech a
dragme amōn iij dragms clawes galyngall and safron of ech
dj dragme and sugure as moch as of the oþ⁹ by wyȝt

699 Powdre for akynge of the hede þat comyth of cold.
Take calamynt origanū sawge beteyn and floures of
rosemarye of ech ʒj of surmounteyn ij ʒ gyng⁹ ʒ ꝭ salgēme
ij ʒ of sugre ʒ j mak it in a powdre

700 ffor to make a poudre for the quarteyn and for yuell
in the splene   Tak coly-andre caruy brent silk of ech iij
dragmes and make powdre

701 [fo. 61 verso]   To mak a powdre for mygrayn and the
passio   Take p̶merose Solsecle auence sauge betayn rwe
of each   a dragme of rose mary flós iij dragms cardimony
sede cresses sirmounteyn of ech ij dragmes and a ʒ j of
kernellis of piony of tartre ʒ ꝭ of gyng⁹ galyngall canell
nutmuge clowes of the tre of aloes and casia lignea of ech
of hem iij ʒ of sugre ʒ j and make poudre of al thies and ete

702 fforto make a poudre for the palasye of the tunge and
wryinge of the mowth of cold humós   Take pep and pletre
of spayn and rw of ich a ʒ of salgene ij dragmes ꝛ make a
poud⁹)

703 poudre for dede flesshe and proude flesshe in a wound
and for vnd⁹) brusid nayles take allia ij parties and rw the
thrid pte and wasshe wele thies erbys and after stamp
heme wele in a mor̶t and put þ⁹to a gode quantitee of whik
lyme and medle togedire and dry it wele and when thei
bene dry make poudre of thies and when thou leist this
poudre on the sore ptyng þe yuell flesshe fro the gode wᵗ owt
any diseas pb e̶)

704 A poudre for the stomake ꝛ for venym þat is clepid
triacle de boyre tak l̄j j of the rotis of turmentill and the rotis

digestion, and to destroy wind. Take anise, lovage, and smallage, canell, cardamum, origanum, meal, carraway fennel, surmonteyn (siler montanum), sage, cumin, calamint, thyme, black pepper, hyssop, parsley, of each half a drachm ; liquorice, ginger, pellitory of Spain, of each a drachm ; ammoniac (marubium), three drachms ; cloves, galingale and saffron, of each half a drachm ; and sugar as much as of the other by weight.

699 Powder for aching of the head that cometh of cold. Take calamint, origanum, sage, betony, and flowers of rosemary, or each one ounce ; of surmonteyn, two ounces ; ginger, half an ounce ; rocksalt, two ounces ; of sugar, one ounce. Make it into a powder.

700 For to make a powder for the quartan [fever], and for evil in the spleen. Take coriander, carroway, burnt silk, of each three drachms, and make power.

701 To make a powder for mygraine and the passio. Take primrose, solsicle, avens, sage, betony, rue, of each a drachm ; of rosemary flowers, three drachms, cardomum seed, cress, surmonteyn, of each two drachms ; and one ounce of kernels of peony ; of tartar, half an ounce ; of ginger, galingale, canell, nutmeg, cloves of the tree, of aloes and cassia lignea, of each of them three ounces ; of sugar, one ounce. And make powder of all these and eat [it].

702 For to make a powder for the palsy of the tongue, and wrying of the mouth[1] from cold humors. Take pepper and pellitory of Spain and rue, of each an ounce ; rocksalt, two drachms. And make a powder.

703 Powder for dead flesh and proud flesh in a wound, and for under-bruised nails. Take allea (garlic), two parts, and rue the third part. And wash well these herbs, and afterwards stamp them well in a mortar ; and put a good quantity of quicklime, and mingle together, and dry it well ; and when they be dry, make powder of these. And when thou layest this powder on the sore, parting the evil flesh from the good, without any disease (discomfort). *Probatum est.*

704 A powder for the stomach and for venom that is called triacle-de-boire. Take one pound of the roots of tormentil

---

[1] Perhaps facial paralysis.

of filipendula of anneys poudred ꝫ of bays not old of
smalach of gromell of carm̃l of gyng⁹ poudred of saxfrage
of the hill of beteyn of canell of ich a quartron j of licoress
ij quartron clensid and poudred ₴ of þᵉ kernell of cheri
stones ₴ ſ of gromell sede and this is gode for venym in the
stomak and for raw flesshe eten and also it is gode for the
[fo. 62 recto] stone ꝫ it distroyeth euell humõs wᵗ in the
bodye ꝫ many oþ⁹ yuellis

705 Anothir poudre for the stomac Tak poudre of gyng⁹
galyngale and myntis of all lich moch and vse hem with a
q̃tite of wyne or ale at morow and in sauge at euen

706 Powdre to do oute dede flesshe out of a wound Take
sawndeũl vertegresse and copose Also take poudre of the
raven þat is to say of the hede and of the fete and of the
bowelles brent in an new pot

707 Also take vnquenched lyme blake peper orpement
· stronge aysell hony and barly mele euen porcions and
buyle hem in an nu pot to powdre this poudre is gode to
sle the cancre

708 Also poudre of brent bakon or of salt befe is gode for
ill sauoure of a festre do þ⁹on sope and copose and white
lyme mengid togedir

709 Also powdre for cankre and festre ryght gode Take
a tode and an eddire and a wesell or a moldwarpe ꝫ buke
rafen and brenne hem in a pot þat is new alto powdre ꝫ do
itt in the festre

710 Poudre to gedir flesshe take powdre of mastyke and
frankencens canell and corall of ech lich moch ꝫ make
poudre þ⁹of

711 ffor wound þᵗ is opyn ꝫ will nat hele take frankencens
ꝫ arnment ꝫ salt of ech lich moch ꝫ do hem all in an nw
pott of erþe and brenne it to þou may make poudre of hem
ꝫ bult it thorow a sarce ꝫ take a scele of an oke ꝫ like þat
it be welkyd ꝫ touge and wete it and do it in the poudre

---

¹ I cannot identify this word as it is written. It might be a
corruption of carmine, carmot (a word used in alchemy), or carmele
(Gaelic cairmeal), a wild pea.

and the roots of philipendula (dropwort), of anise powdered and of bays not old, of smallage, of gromwell, of carmer,[1] of ginger powdered, of saxifrage of the hill, of betony, of canell, of each one quarter [of a pound] ; of liquorice, two quarters, cleansed and powdered ; one ounce of kernels of cherry-stones ; half an ounce of gromwell-seed. And this is good for venom in the stomach and for raw flesh [when] eaten, and also it is good for the stone, and it destroyeth evil humors within the body, and many other evils.

705 Another powder for the stomach. Take powder of ginger, galingale, and mint, of each equally much ; and use them with a quantity of wine or ale at morn. and in sage at even.

706 Powder to take dead flesh out of a wound. Take saunders,[2] verdigris and copperas. Also take powder of raven, that is to say of the head and feet and of the bowels [of a raven] burnt in a new pot.

707 [Another]. Also take unquenched (unslaked) lime, black pepper, orpiment, strong vinegar, honey, and barley-meal, even portions, and boil them in a new pot to powder. This powder is good to slay the canker.

708 [Another]. Also powder of burnt bacon or of salt beef is good for ill savour of a fester. Put thereon soap, and copperas and white lime mingled together.

709 [Another]. Also powder for canker and fester right good. Take a toad or an adder, and a weasel or a mole, and [a] buck (cock) raven, and burn them in a pot that is new, all to powder, and put it in the fester.

710 Powder to gather flesh. Take powder of mastic, and frankincense, canell, and coral, of each equally much, and make powder thereof.

711 For wound that is open and will not heal. Take frankincense, and arnement, and salt, of each equally much ; and put them in a new pot of earth[enware], and burn it. Thou mayest make powder of them and sift it through a strainer. And take a scale of an oak (oak-parasite), and look

---

[1] This word is often used for the herb *alexanders*, but here it is more probably derived from *cendres bleues*, ultramarine, or a blue substance made from carbonate of copper. It might also be meant for *sandiver*.

þᵗ is (*sic*) cleue þᵒon all about ꝫ put in to þe þrilles down
to þe grownd ꝫ [fo. 62 *verso*] lay þe pleystre þᵒon þⁱˢ powdre
will sle the festre ꝫ do þe schele wiþ tre (*sic*) powdre þᵒin
v days or viij and afterward you may do a tent þᵒin of lynnen
cloth euⁿ as it begynnyth to hele make thi tent shorᵗ and
ech day wasshe thi thi (*sic*) wound twyse

712 ffor to breke a postyme wᵗin iiij oures in a man or
woman   Take a peny wiȝt of rubarb of cassia fistula aⁿ of
turbit aⁿ of cene aⁿ of scamony of the sede ꝫ of þe rote of
alisaundre ij peny wiȝt of sugure and make al thies to
poudre and seth laureall levys in stale ale ꝫ temp þies
powdres togedir þᵒwith and gif it to þe sike to drynke and
he be delyuerid wᵗ in iiij oures of the postyme

713 And make þan a restauratife in this manere take an
ʒ ℈ of clows of greyns aⁿ ʒ ℈ of mead iiij peny wiȝt of
safron of quybibbis ʒ ℈ and make al thies poudre and then
seth it in vynegre ꝫ tak it fro þe fire and lat it kele ꝫ þen
take þᵒto ij ʒ of powdre of canell ꝫ ʒ j of gyngeuⁿ ꝫ gif the
syke to drynk ij sponefull at morow and at eve

714 ffor a postyme in a wound gedre mayyen wede when
þei be sedyd ꝫ dry hem ꝫ make poudre of hem and gif the
sike to drynk wᵗ stale ale and white wyne so serue hym
iij days fastynge

715 ffor to breke a postyme in a best (sic)   Take erbe waᵗ and
egremoyn ꝫ mylfoyle ꝫ take þe juyse þᵒof and gif the syke
to drynke

716 ffor hote postyms and sodeyn swellynges a gode pleystre
þᵒ fore þᵗ is   Take þe [fo. 63 *recto*] Jnner rynd of ȝonge
Elme ꝫ peritory ꝫ moch alym ꝫ seth hem in white wyne till
thei be soft and put þᵒin iij vncᵒ of branne and seth heme
to the thyknes of a pleistre and lay it þᵒto to hote

that it be whelked[1] and tough, and wet it, and put it in the powder that it cleave thereon all about, and put it into the holes down to the ground (*i.e.* put it into the deepest part of the wound), and lay the plaster thereon. This powder will slay the fester. And put the [oak-]scale with the powder therein five days or eight ; and afterwards you mayest put a tent of linen cloth therein, and as soon as it beginneth to heal, make thy tent shorter, and each day wash thy wound twice.

712 For to break an imposthume (abscess) within four hours in a man or a woman. Take a pennyweight of rhubarb, of cassia fistula the same, of turpeth[2] the same, of senna the same, of scammony, of the seed and of the root of alexanders, two pennyweight of sugar ; and make all these to powder, and seethe laurel leaves in stale ale, and temper these powders together therewith. And give to the sick to drink, and he will be delivered within four hours of the imposthume.

713 And make then a restorative in this manner. Take half an ounce of cloves, of kermes the same, half an ounce of mead, four pennyweight of saffron, of cubebs[3] half an ounce. And make all these [into] powder, and then seethe it in vinegar ; and take it from the fire, and let it cool ; and then take thereto two ounces of powder of canell and one ounce of ginger. And give the sick to drink at morn and at eve.

714 For an imposthume in a wound. Gather mayweeds when they have seeded, and dry them and make powder of them. And give the sick to drink with stale ale and white wine, [and] so serve him four days fasting.

715 For to break an imposthume in the breast. Take herb-Walter, and agrimony, and milfoil, and take the juice thereof, and give the sick to drink.

716 For hot imposthumes and sudden swellings : a good plaster it is therefor. Take the inner rind of young elm, and pellitory, and much alum ; and seethe them in white wine till they be soft, and put therein three ounces of bran ; and seethe them to the thickness of a plaster, and lay it thereto, hot.

---

[1] Having whelks or rugosities.
[2] Mercuric sulphate.
[3] *See* note on § 242.

717 ffor the postym of a woman tetis tak þe Juse of morell
and the white of egges ꝛ floure of benes ꝛ and (sic) medle
hem wele togedir and lay it cold to þe tetis

718 Apenplesis is a postyme on þe side   Also þᵒis a syknes
þat is clepid tesyk þat comyth ppurly of þe distrucion of
radigal moystire of a mans body and it cōmyth when a
mannes longes beþe to replete of flewme

719 ffor the postym take march radisshe rw wormode
centory and saveyn and stamp hem fastynge or þᵒ handes
be wasshen and þu shalt be hole

720 ffor the postyme in the side.   Take a stamp wormod
mynt and calamynt erbe benett malows-chervyle roos
flours ꝛ sauge and do comyn þᵒto and crommes of brede
and boyle in wyn eythire in piss and make a pleistre and
lay to þe side

721 prikkynge of a nedle or thorne and the hoole be stoppede
tak faire bultid floure of whete and temp in wyne and boyll
togedir till it be thik ꝛ mak a pleistre þᵒof and lay it to þe
sore as hote as he may suffre ꝛ þat shall cese þe ach and
hele vp and faire opyn þe hole and close it agayn

722 ffor prykkyng in synow with nedle or with knyfe or
þorne   Take oyle of roses and hete it wele and lay it apon
[fo. 63 verso] the prykkynge as hote as he may suffre it and
bynd above blak woll and it shall hele wele

723 Pissynge of blode a medecyn þᵒfore drynk sangdragon
and borage in rede wyne or gote turdels in rede wyne þat
he wit nat off

724 ffor hym þat may nat hold his waẛ   Take hertis horne
and brenne it ꝛ shaue it and make poudre þᵒof and drynke
it last or take þe helys of swyne fete and do on þe same
maṇ as is before seid

725 Anoþᵒ for the same   Gyf the syke to drinke iiij ℥ of
encens ꝛ he sal be hole

---

¹ Probably an error for πλευρῖτις, pleurisy.   It can scarcely be
derived from ἀποπλήσσω.
ˢ Sanguis draconis, *Calamus draco,* Willd.   The Dragon's Blood
of modern commerce is the resinous exudation from the red sandal-

717 For an imposthume in a woman's teats. Take the juice of morell, and take the white of eggs, and flour of beans; and mingle them together, and lay it cold to the teats.

718 Apenplesis[1] is an imposthume on the side. Also there is a sickness that is called phthisis, that cometh purely of the destruction of radical moisture of a man's body, and it cometh when a man's lungs be too replete with phlegm.

719 For the imposthume. Take March radish, rue, wormwood, centaury, and savin and stamp them. [And take them] fasting before the hands be washed, and thou shalt be whole.

720 For the imposthume of the side. Take and stamp wormwood, mint, and calamint, herb-benet, mallows, chervil, rose flowers, and sage; and put cumin thereto, and crumbs of bread. And boil them in wine or in urine, and make a plaster and lay to the side.

721 Pricking of a needle or thorn, and the hole be stopped. Take fair sifted flour of wheat, and temper [it] in wine, and boil together till it be thick. And make a plaster thereof, and lay it to the sore as hot as he may suffer; and that shall cease the ache, and heal up and fair open the hole and close it again.

722 For pricking in [a] sinew with needle, or with knife or thorn. Take oil of roses and heat it well, and lay it upon the pricking as hot as he may suffer it; and bind above black wool, and it shall heal well.

723 Hæmaturia, a medicine therefor. Drink dragon's blood[2] and borage in red wine; or goat's droppings in red wine that he wit not of.[3]

724 For him that cannot hold his water. Take hartshorn and burn it and shave it, and make powder thereof, and drink it last; or take the heels (hoofs) of swine's feet and do in the same manner as aforesaid.[4]

725 Another for the same. Give the sick to drink four ounces of incense, and he shall be whole.

---

tree of the East Indies and from the *Pterocarpus draco* of South America.

   [3] *I.e.* the patient is not to know what the draught is made of.

   [4] Cf. § 731.

726 Anoþ⁹   Tak ambrose an ꝳ j of ꝑsely riw and gromell stampe hem with gots mylk or wyne thys medecyn is pissynge blode

727 ffor bestis that piss blode   Tak malt dust when it is ground þᵗ hangith on the myll and and tempᵽ it with watire and opyn þᵉ bests mowth ꞃ put itt in

728 Anoþ⁹ for prikkynge in joynt wᵗ nedill or thorne   Tak eġmoyne gandir muke and the rose of the rosere stampid togedir with virgyn wex hare grese hors grese ꞃ leyd in to a playsᵗ will draw out thorne or stub wheþ⁹ itt be in the flesshe or eū emonge. Drynke the juyse of egremoyn for ach

729 Ther be certayn placys in a man þat if it be ꝓkkyd into a synow þ⁹ but iff he haue help wᵗin vij days aftere he shall be dede þ⁹ on for þ⁹ will come a crampe for þᵉ place þat he was hurt in vp in to þᵉ nek ꞃ draw his chaules togedir þat he may nat opyn hys mowth ꞃ is callid þᵉ spasme ꞃ þ⁹fore if a man be ꝓkkyd in to a synow [fo. 64 *recto*] þat is a cord take gude oyle rosett and chaufe it as warme as the sik may suffre and poure into þᵉ place that is prykkyd and lay wole aboue and so bynd it vp and vse this medecyne till he be hole and none oþ⁹ for it is the best.

730 Anoþ⁹ for hym þat pissith blode   Take an handfull of ambrose and a ꝳ j of sangwynary and ꝳ j of ꝑsely seede and stampe heme togedir and tempᵽ heme with gotis mylk and streyn hem thorow a cloth and drynk it

731 ffor hym þᵗ may nat hold hys waᵗ   Take þᵉ clawes of a gote ꞃ brenne hem to poudre and do þᵉ poudere in thi potage ꞃ vse it

732 Palasy who so haue itt here is a soueren medecyne for to take a lofe of dough and take an ꝳ j of sauge and mold þᵉ sauge in myddyll of þᵉ douȝe and lat bake and than draw it forth and than take þᵉ hote lofe and breke it alto morsellys in to an erþen pott and menge þᵉ dauge emonge þᵉ brede and take a galon of white wyne with þᵉ brede and

726 Another. Take wood-sage, a handful of parsley, rue, and gromwell; stamp them with goat's milk or wine. This medicine is [for] hæmaturia.

727 For beasts that have hæmaturia. Take malt dust when it is ground that hangeth on the mill,[1] and temper it with water. And open the beast's mouth and put it in.

728 Another for pricking in [a] joint with needle or thorn. Take agrimony, gander's dung, and the rose of the rose-bush, stamped together with virgin wax, hare's grease [and] horse's grease. And laid into a plaster, [it] will draw out thorn or stub whether it be in the flesh or elsewhere. Drink the juice of agrimony for [the] ache [thereof].

729 There be certain places in a man where if he be pricked in a sinew; unless he have help within seven days after, he shall be dead thereof. For there will come a cramp in the place where he was hurt, passing up into the neck, and draw his jowls together so that he cannot open his mouth, and it is called the spasm (tetanus). And therefore if a man be pricked in a sinew accordingly, take good oil-roset, and chafe if as warm as the sick may suffer, and pour it on to the place that is pricked, and lay wool above, and so bind it up. And use this medicine till he be whole, and none other, for it is the best.[2]

730 Another for hæmaturia. Take a handful of wood-sage and a handful of sanguinaria (shepherd's-purse), and a handful of parsley-seed, and stamp them together and temper them with goat's milk. And strain them through a cloth and drink it.

731 For him that cannot hold his water. Take the claws (hoofs) of a goat, and burn them to powder in thy pottage and use it.[3]

732 Palsy, whoso have it, here is a sovereign medicine for it. Take a loaf of dough, and take a handful of sage, and mix the sage in the midst of the dough, and let bake; and then draw it forth, and then take the hot loaf and break it all in morsels into an earthen pot; and mingle the dough among the bread, and take a gallon of white wine with the

---

[1] Adheres to the millstone.
[2] It has been necessary to paraphrase this passage somewhat.
[3] Duplicate, D. § 16. Cf. § 724.

sauge ꝫ stop fast þe pott with a lid and stop þe chynes fast
a bout wᵗ dawȝ þat the breth pass nat oute and hete þe
ovyne agayne somewhat hote and put in þat pot and let
it bake wele ꝫ than draw forth þe pott and lat it kele ꝫ
than take euʒy day at morow fastynge þ⁹of ij sponefull or
iij and if þᵘ haue nat þat yuell þᵘ schalt neuʒ haue it and
if þᵘ haue it this medecyn shall souerenly help þe and vse to
ete moch mustard and take aqua vite ꝫ enoynt thi temples
ꝫ vndʒ thi mouth and take sauge waᵗ and [fo. 64 verso]
enoynt thi pawms of thyn hands ꝫ also wasshe þⁱ ponnce
ꝫ lay þ⁹to sauge ypoundid and bynd þ⁹to nyȝt and day

733 Also for the same take a porcion of lerere levys and as
many of sauge leves and as mych of senvoy sede ꝫ stamp
hem in may butture made of raw creme ꝫ nat soden and
stamp all togedʒ and sett it vp and lat it stand a vessell
of erth eyþ⁹ of tre stoppid fast þat noone eyre com þ⁹to
for to it be hore than fri it in a panne and than streyn it
thorow a cloth and then put it in a box this is a souʒeyn
medecyn for the palsie

734 ffor the palasy and epulensie giff hyme the wyne to
drynk that sauge is soden in and make a pleisᵗ of the erbe
and lay it to his pounce eythir wrist and lat hym vse the
powdre of sauge both in metis and drynkes | make sauce
both both (sic) of psely ꝫ of sauge and temp it wᵗ vynegre
and kest a littell powdir of pepire and it shall make a man
haue gode appetite to mete and clence þe stomake

735 An oyntment for the for (sic) palasie Take p̄merose
leues with the rote and sulvoye sede sauge and lorere leves
of ech lich moch and grid heme togedir and medle heme wᵗ
may butᵗ and lat it stand v days or vj and after fry hem
and make oyntment and wᵗ that oyntment enoynt thi nek
and the synows and the joyntis of tyne handis

736 Who so dredith the palasie or the fallynge euell let
hym drynk ix days his own pisse ꝫ he shall neuʒ haue it

737 ffor the palasy þat comyth to a man when he slepith
of coldnes of the ground tak watir cressis ꝫ let hem seth
in wyne till the haluendele be soden a way ꝫ make þ⁹of a
pleistre and lay it hote þ⁹on

bread and sage, and stop the pot fast with a lid and stop the chinks fast about with dough that the breath (vapour) pass not out. And heat the oven again somewhat hot, and put in that pot, and let it bake well ; and then draw forth the pot, and let it cool. And then take every day at morn, fasting, two spoonfuls thereof or three. And if thou hast not that evil (palsy), thou shalt never have it. And if thou hast it, this medicine shall sovereignly help thee. And use to eat much mustard, and take aqua vitæ, and anoint thy temples and under thy mouth. And take sage-water and anoint the palms of thy hands, and also wash thy pulse and lay thereto pounded sage and bind thereto night and day.

733 [Another]. Also for the same. Take a portion of laurel leaves and as many of sage leaves, and as much of senvey seed, and stamp them in may-butter made of raw cream not boiled. And stamp all together and set it up, and let it stand in a vessel of earth[enware], or of tree (wood), stopped fast that no air come thereto before it be stale ; and then fry it in a pan, and then strain it through a cloth, and then put it in a box. This is a sovereign medicine for the palsy.

734 For the palsy and epilepsy. Give him the wine to drink that sage is boiled in, and make a plaster of the herb, and lay it to his pulse or wrist ; and let him use the powder of sage both in meats and drinks. Make sauce both of parsley and of sage, and temper it with vinegar, and cast [in] a little powder of pepper, and it shall make a man have good appetite for meat, and cleanse the stomach.

735 An ointment for the palsy. Take primrose leaves with the root, and senvey-seed, sage, and laurel leaves, of each equally much ; and grind them together, and mingle them with may-butter ; and let it stand five days or six, and afterwards fry them, and make ointment. And with that ointment anoint his neck and the sinews and joints of thy hands.

736 Whoso dreadeth the palsy or the falling-evil, let him drink nine days his own urine, and he shall never have it.

737 For the palsy that cometh to a man when he sleepeth, from coldness of the ground. Take watercresses and let them seethe in wine till half be boiled away, and make thereof a plaster, and lay it hot thereon.

7.38 ffor the palasie of þᵉ tunge [fo. 65 *recto*] put the powdre
of castorye vnd⁹⟩ the tunge and lat it be there till it be
molten and wastid and it shall help hyme

739 Anoþ⁹ for the same take powdre of pepire and poudre
of pelettre of spayn and poudre of riw of ech ℥ j of poudre
of sauge ij ℥ and vse thies poudres in thi potage for this is a
goode poudre and helpith wele

740 Anoþ⁹ for the same take wodbynd pympnell and filago
and put hem in a sallatorye and make watir of heme this
watir is goode for the palasie of the tunge and of the spech
þat is sodenly lost

741 ffor the palasie in a mannes pyntell Seth castor in
wyne and wasshe hyme þ⁹wᵗ about þᵉ share and wete þᵉ
cloth þ⁹in and apon þᵉ pyntell in man⟩ of a pleisᵗ pᵬ e⟩

742 An oþ⁹ for hym þᵗ is scaldide þᵉ which man clepith
the appigale take lynsede or cloth ꝫ brenne it and tak þᵉ
poudre and do in a clowt ꝫ lay þ⁹too

743 An oþ⁹ for scaldynge Tak molowes and seth hem in
watir ꝫ þen take hem doun and grynd hem in a morᵗ ꝫ
tak may butture and fry hem in a panne and take a rede
cole leffe ꝫ lay þ⁹on and wrap þ⁹in þᵉ sore ꝫ make an hole
in the lefe þᵗ he may piss out at ꝫ he sall be hole

744 Anoþ⁹ boylynge of the same / shere clote levys small
and p⁹merose leves fry hem in saym and lay it about þᵉ
pyntell

745 who so suellyth in þᵉ same Take mele of bere corne
and set with hony and stamp comyn ꝫ menge þ⁹with and
do it in a cloute

746 To make pelettis of antioch take halue an hand full of
mowsere and ꝳ j of auence ꝫ a handfull of mader and stamp
hem togedir and do þ⁹to hony ꝫ [fo. 65 *verso*] make þ⁹ of
balles and dry heme and drynke it in stale ale or in whit
wyne ꝫ if þies erbis be styllyd it is clepid drynk of antioch

---

¹ Perhaps corrupted from ἀπογλυφή, a place scraped bare, or
flayed. The subject of this recipe and the next is scalding or
acrimony of urine, usually through excoriation or inflammation of
the meatus.

738 For the palsy of the tongue. Put the powder of castoreum under the tongue, and let it be there till it be melted and wasted away, and it shall help him.

739 Another for the same. Take powder of pepper, and powder of pellitory of Spain, and powder of rue, of each one ounce, of powder of sage two ounces. And use these powders in thy pottage, for this is a good powder, and helpeth well.

740 Another for the same. Take woodbine, pimpernel and filago (cudweed), and put them in a still and make water of them. This water is good for the palsy of the tongue, and of the speech that is suddenly lost.

741 For the palsy in a man's privy member. Seethe castoreum in wine, and wash him therewith about the pubic region, and wet the cloth there in and [lay it] upon the organ in the manner of a plaster. *Probatum est.*

742 Another for him that is scalded, the which men call appigale.[1] Take linseed or cloth and burn it, and take the powder, and put [it] in a cloth and lay thereto.

743 Another for scalding. Take mallows and seethe them in water ; and then take them down, and grind them in a mortar ; and take may-butter and fry them in a pan, and take a red cabbage leaf and lay thereon and wrap therein the sore, and make a hole in the leaf that he may pass water through, and he shall be whole.

744 Another [for] swelling of the same. Shred clove leaves small, and primrose leaves, and fry them in seam (lard) and lay it about the organ.

745 [Another for] whoso swelleth in the same. Take meal of brewer's grains and seethe with honey, and stamp cumin and mingle therewith, and put it in a cloth.

746 To make Pelotus of Antioch.[2] Take half a handful of mouse-ear and one handful of avens, and a handful of madder and stamp them together ; and put thereto honey, and make thereof balls ; and dry them and drink it in stale ale or in white wine, and if these herbs be distilled, it is called drink of Antioch.

---

² *Cf.* §§ 161, 893. Pelotus of Antioch or Syrup of Antioch occurs in *Harl.* 2378 and *Sloane* 2584 (Henslow, *op. cit.*, pp. 77, 128), but they all differ widely.

747 ffor pyn or webb in a mannes eygh   Take þe juys of
erth yuye and womans mylk and drop in his eyȝe and gif
hym to drynke lobchestres and trefoyle

748 ffor hym þat hath dronken poyson   Tak dragaunce
and gladyn and mynt of ech lich moch and stamp hem and
temp hem wᵗ wyne and drynk it warme

749 ffor pilis or fiches in þe fundement   Tak þe rotis of leke
and stamp and fry hem with shepis talwȝ and as hote as
he may suffre bynd to the fundement oft and he shall be
hole

750 ffor the pokkes tak moch fenell and make juyse þᵒoff
and hete it lew warme and wete a lynnen cloth þer in and
wynd the syk þᵒin iij ours at dyủ)s tymes and this is a
souͪen medecyn

751 Anoþᵒ tak a quantite of ficches and seth hem longe in
watir and then wete þᵒin a cloth louke warme and wynd
the syke þᵒin

752 ffor the poost take small nottis and rost the kernellis
and ete hem with poudre of pep when thou gost to bedde

753 Anoþᵒ put sauge and mustard in to þe nose þrilles

754 Purgynge of soore and al oþᵒ wonds ꝛ sores take a red
herynge nek or ij ꝛ stamp it and temp it with ale and streyne
it and wasshe the soore þᵒ with   Also it is good to drynke
for venym.

755 Quarteyn feủ)   Take iij leves of sauge iij leues off
mynt iij corns of pep droken in ale doth a way
the feủ) quarteyn

756 Anoþᵒ for the same take þe juyse of [fo. 66 *recto*] an
erbe þᵗ men clepe peny grasse and drynk it wᵗ stale ale or
venegre   .

757 Anoþᵒ for the same take iiij rotis of planteyn ꝛ stamp
hem and medle hem with wyne and with as moch waᵗ and
drynk it for the feuer quarteyn afore þe quakynge come

747 For pin or web in a man's eyes. Take the juice of ground-ivy and woman's milk, and drop it in his eyes. And give him to drink [water of] locust-beans and milfoil.

748 For him that hath drunken poison. Take dragance, and gladden (iris), and mint, of each equally much, and stamp them and temper them with wine, and drink it warm.

749 For piles or fikes[1] in the fundament. Take the roots of leek and stamp and fry them with sheep's tallow, and as hot as he may suffer it, bind to the fundament oft. and he shall be whole.

750 For the pox.[2] Take much fennel and make juice thereof, and heat it lukewarm. And wet a linen cloth therein and wind the sick therein three hours at divers times. And this is a sovereign medicine.

751 Another. Take a quantity of vetches and seethe them long in water, and then wet therein a cloth lukewarm and wind the sick therein.

752 For the poost (cold). Take small nuts and roast the kernels, and eat them with powder of pepper when thou goest to bed.

753 Another. Put sage and mustard into the nostrils.

754 Purging of sores and all other wounds and sores. Take a red herring's neck or two, and stamp it and temper it with ale, and strain it, and wash the sore therewith. Also it is good to drink for venom.

755 Quartan fever. Take three leaves of sage, and three leaves of mint, three corns of pepper. Drunken in ale it doth away the quartan fever.

756 Another for the same. Take the juice of a herb that men call pennycress, and drink it with stale ale or vinegar.

757 Another for the same. Take four roots of plantain, and stamp them and mingle them with wine, and with as much water. And drink it for the quartan fever before the quaking (trembling or shivering) come.

---

[1] *See* note to § 594.
[2] Not syphilis, but one of the eruptive diseases such as chicken-pox or smallpox.

758 Anoþ⁹ for the same tak an erbe þat is clepid azarabacca
and seth it in wyn and giff it hym to drynk and iff the
waᵗ be in the stomak it delyuerith it oute by brakynge
and iff it be in oþ⁹ pties of the body it wasshit it by pcesse

759 An oþ⁹ Tak an handfull of pselye and an oþ⁹ of comyn
and v q̃rts of wyne and seth togedir till halue be soden
Jnne and gif the syke to drynke at morow cold at euen
hote

760 ffor the qwynsy take cresse sede and dry figges in
vynegre in man̄) of gargasyn

761 ffor quynturynge eres put þ⁹in þe juyse of coste and it
dryeth the humors that floweth of the eren   And also stamp
itt with bulles gall and ther with enoynt þⁱ eren for it
cofortith heme and dryueth away þe wynd and the sowue
of the cres and the smoke and brent ysop doth þe same

762 An oþ⁹ put þe Juys of elderne in to his eres ꝫ it doth
away þe whitó þat is in heme ⸲

763 R Eynes that bene sore Take vnguentū alabastri
        vnguentū auriū of ech q̃rt j ꝫ medle hem toged⁹)
ꝫ enoynt þ⁹wᵗ thi bak þ⁹ it is sore and it shall be hole

764 ffor the same ꝫ for þe side Tak sauge ryall ꝫ alisaundre
and the rede nettle wormode and rede fenell rotes and all
of ∞ ꝫeris growynge and then on the ground make a grete
fire till the ground be hote a fote depe and then [fo. 66
verso] lay þe erbis on the ground and lay a cloth þ⁹on and
lay the sore sid þ⁹on while þe hete durith and hill hem wele
aboute ꝫ vse þis ꝫ þᵘ shalt be hole

765 Anoþ⁹ for þe reyns take a shell full of woos of betayn
and a shell full of wyn and a shell full of hony and ix corns
of pep ꝫ stamp togedir ꝫ giff hym to drynke iij days and he
shall amend

766 Anoþ⁹ for ach of reyns þᵗ cõmyth of hete anoynt thy
reyns wᵗ cold oyle and with some cold oyntment and perce

---

¹ This name is used both of Avens (*Geum urbanum*, L.) and of
Asarum europæum, L.
² *Auklandia costus*, Falc.   *Cf.* § 874.

758 Another for the same. Take a herb that is called asarabacca[1] and seethe it in wine, and give it him to drink. And if the water be in the stomach, it delivereth it out by breaking (vomiting), and if it be in other parts of the body, it washeth it [out] by process (*i.e.* by natural avoiding).

759 Another. Take a handful of parsley and another of cumin, and five quarts of wine, and seethe together till half be sodden in ; and give it the sick to drink at morn cold, at even hot.

760 For the quinsy. Take cress seed and dry figs in vinegar, in the manner of a gargle.

761 For curing ears. Put therein the juice of cost[2] and it dryeth the humors that flow from the ears. And also stamp it with bull's gall, and therewith anoint thine ears, for it comforteth them and draweth away the wind. And the savour of cress and smoke [thereof] and burnt hyssop doth the same.

762 Another. Put the juice of elders into his ears, and it doth away the pus that is in them.

763 R eins that be sore. Take *unguentum alabastri* [and] *unguentum aureum*, of each one quarter, and mingle them together, and anoint therewith thy back where it is sore, and it shall be whole.

764 [Another] for the same, and for the side. Take sage, [penny-]royal, and alexanders, and the red nettle, wormwood and red fennel roots and all of eight years growth. And then on the ground make a great fire, till the ground be hot a foot deep ; and then lay the herbs on the ground, and lay a cloth thereon. And lay the sore side thereon while the heat lasteth, and cover him well about. And use this, and thou shalt be whole.

765 Another for the reins.[3] Take a shellful of juice of betony and a shellful of wine, and a shellful of honey, and nine corns of pepper, and stamp together. And give him to drink three days, and he shall amend.

766 Another for ache of reins that cometh of heat.[4] Anoint thy reins with cold oil, and with some cold ointment. And

---

[3] This is a duplicate of § 583.
[4] This is a duplicate of § 65.

a plate of lede and lay on his reyns ꝫ the poudre of lede is
pfitable ffor swellynge þᵗ swellyth with oute forth take
arnment and white of an egge ꝫ medle hem wele togedir
and make an empleyst͛ of flex and lay þᵒto

767 ffor ranklynge wᵗin forþe drynke loueach with wyne
first and last and oþᵒ while drynke wormod a littell and
when þ͌ suellist.þ͌ helyst

768 ffor reume in mannes hede to breke it kyt a rede onyon
i small gobettis and seth it well in a littell vynegre and put
in a littell hony and whan thei be wele soden togedir put in
a sponefull of mustarde ꝫ eft seth it wele ꝫ make the syke
to lye on his bak a put a littell of this in his nose ꝫ lat hym
stirt vp anone þᵗ he may snese ꝫ do so iij days ech day ij

769 ffor rewm þᵗ comyth of cold ꝫ for to coforth the brayn
tak comyn ꝫ lorere bayes and stamp hem toged͛ ꝫ hete
hem in a vessell ou͛ þᵉ fire and put hem in a bagge and lay
to þᵉ sike hede

770 ffor a rennynge hole wasshe þᵉ hole wᵗ the Juys of
oculus x̌ ꝫ drynk it and it shall hele [fo. 67 recto] it

771 To rype bocches stamp the lelye wᵗ fresshe grese or
seth it in oyle and lay it apon the boch   And hocke leues
stampid and fried with fresshe grese doth þᵉ same

772 Reysyns etyn and also the wyne that thei bene soden
in is gode for the colde cogh

773 A pleystre made of raysyns þat bene soden in wyne is
goode for cold bocches ꝫ postyms ꝫ ach þat comyth of cold.

774 To restreyn the wombe þat is solible take an handfull
of encressen and an oythir of waybrede and grynd hem in a
mortar ꝫ þen fix hem wele togedir with shepis taluȝ and
wᵗ frank encence ꝫ make a pleistre and lay to the navyll
as hote as he may suffre.

pierce of plate of lead, and lay on his reins. And the powder of lead is profitable for swelling that swelleth outwards. Take arnement and white of an egg and mingle them well together, and make a plaster of flax and lay thereto.

767 For inward rankling. Drink lovage with wine first and last ; and between times drink wormwood a little, and when thou swillest, thou healest.

768 For rheum in a man's head, to break it. Cut an onion in small gobbets, and seethe it well with a little vinegar, and put in a little honey. And when they be well seethed together, put in a spoonful of mustard, and again seethe it well. And make the sick to lie on his back, and put a little of this in his nose ; and let him start up anon that he may sneeze. And do so four days, and each day twice.

769 For rheum that cometh of cold, and to comfort the brain. Take cumin and laurel-bays, and stamp them together ; and heat them in a vessel over the fire, and put them in a bag, and lay to the sick head.

770 For a running hole.[1] Wash the hole with the juice of oculus Christi (clary), and drink it, and it shall heal.

771 To ripen botches.[2] Stamp the lily with fresh grease, or seethe it in oil, and lay it upon the botch. And hock (mallow) leaves stamped and fried with fresh grease do the same.

772 Raisins eaten, and also the wine that they have been boiled in, is good for the cold cough.

773 A plaster made of raisins that have been seethed in wine is good for cold botches and imposthumes, and ache that cometh of cold.

774 To restrain the womb that is soluble.[3] Take a handful of cresses and another of waybread, and grind them in a mortar. Then fix them well together with sheep's tallow and with frankincense, and make a plaster and lay to the navel as hot as he may suffer.

---

[1] Suppurating sinus.
[2] To bring them to a head.
[3] To stop diarrhœa.

775 Scalled hedis tak popy iiij pound of þe buddis iiij pound of barows grese for a knawe child and as moch for a mayden of ȝiltis grese ꝫ a pynt of waᵗ of a grene hasell that droppith oute at the hasell when it in the fyre // Also take a pynt of creme and d̄j a pynt of oyle of eyien made thynne take the popy and grynd it small and sett it ouᵉ the fyre in a pot of erth and do þe grese þᵉto and boyle it wele till it be gyn to wast and then streyn it thorow a cloth then tak all that oþᵉ and kest þᵉto ꝫ mak a pleisᵗ and lay þᵉto and it shall be hole but first tak a pynt of tarre and clarifye it ouᵉ þe fire and menge it þᵉwᵗ

776 Also gordianus techith a souᵉeyne medecyne for scalles Tak litarge sulphure vyne calce bybe attrament vitriall orpment soote verdegresse elibere white and blak alom galles of ech halfe an vnce Wex pich and oyle of nottis of ech a pound ꝑ [fo. 67 *verso*] the Juyse of hokkes the Juys of fymᵗ scabiose borage of ech a quartron boyle the wex and the pich and the oyle wᵗ the Juyses till þat the Juyses be consumyd and then encorpe the oþᵉ thynges þᵉwith and make an oyntement diligently

777 Anoþᵉ for scalles take oute shelles and bren heme and grynd hem to small poudre and take henne yoost and capons grese and medle heme togedir and make a pleystre þᵉof but first shaue the hede clene ꝫ þen enoynt it with watir that is made of clotis and of salt stilled togedir in may and then lay þat playsᵗ þᵉto a lat it lye þᵉto v days and v nyghts and then do away that pleystre and wasshe eft the hede with waᵗ of clote leves and then eft lay a playstre þᵉto of the same a day ꝫ a nyȝt and then wasshe it the thrid tyme wᵗ waᵗ of clote leves and enoynt it with may buttre or ellis wᵗ bores grese

778 Anoþᵉ for the same take virgyn wex and pich of ech lich moch and boyle hem togedire and then sprede a lynnen

¹ Corruption of *scaled-head*, a general term used for several different diseases of the scalp, characterized by pustules, the dried secretion of which forms a scaly scurf, usually accompanied by falling-out of the hair.
² A spayed sow.

775 S cald-head.[1] Take poppies, four pounds of the buds,
four pounds of barrow's grease for a boy-child, and
as much for a girl-child of gilt's[2] grease, and a pint of water
of green hazel that droppeth out from the hazel [-twigs]
when they [are laid] on the fire.   Also take a pint of cream
and half a pint of oil of eggs made thin.   Take the poppy
and grind it small, and set it over the fire in a pot of
earth[enware], and put the grease thereto, and boil it well
till it begin to waste (evaporate), and then strain it through
a cloth.   Then take all that other[3] and cast [it] thereto, and
make a plaster and lay thereto, and it shall be whole.   But
first take a pint of tar, and clarify it over the fire and mingle
it therewith.

776 Also Gordianus[4] teecheth a sovereign medicine for scales.
Take litharge, sulphur, wine, chalk, bibbey,[5] arnement,
vitriol, orpiment, soot, verdigris, hellebore white and black,
alum, [and] galls, of each half an ounce ; wax, pitch, and
oil of nuts (almond-oil), of each half a pound ; the juice
of hocks (mallows), the juice of fumitory, scabious, borage,
of each a quarter [of a pound].   Boil the wax and pitch and
the oil with the juices, till the juices be consumed, and then
incorporate the other things therewith, and make an
ointment diligently.

777 Another for scales.   Take shells and burn them and
grind them to small powder, and take hen-yeast (broth)
and capon's grease, and mingle them together and make a
plaster thereof.   But first shave the head clean, and then
anoint it with the water that is made of cloves and of salt
distilled together in May ; and then lay that plaster thereto
and let it lie thereto five days and five nights.   And then
take away that plaster and wash again the head with water
of clove-leaves.   And then again lay a plaster thereto of
the same, a day and a night, and then wash it the third time
with water of clove-leaves, and anoint it with may-butter
or else with boar's grease.

778 Another for the same.   Take virgin wax and pitch, of
each equally much, and boil them together ; and then

---

[3] The cream, etc.
[4] Bernard Gordon, one of the earliest teachers of the medical
school of Montpellier, where he began to teach in 1285.   In 1305 he
issued his *Lilium Medicinæ*, which was printed in Naples in 1480.
[5] An unknown drug.   Halliwell quotes *Chester Plays*, i, 119.

cloth on a bord ꝺ enbawme it þᵒwith in mañ of a pleystre
and loke at it be layd thyn wᵗ a sklyce and þen do on the
hede hote so þᵗ it may hill all the skalles and do it nat
away ix days aftᵗ and ich day enoynt the hede aboue with
hony and it will hele fayre and wele //

779 ffor the scabb tak powdre of qwyk brymston and medil
itt with swyns grese and enoynt the scabb and it helith
wondᵒ͗ sone

780 Anoþᵒ for þe Scabb where so eũ it be   Tak þe [fo. 68
recto] Juys of the rote of walwort and tak iij pties of the
juyse and the iiij pty of barowȝ grese and make enoyntment
and enoynt the scabb at the sune

781 Anoþᵒ for the same   Take the rotis of elena campana
and seyth hem in watir till thei be nesshe and tak old
swyns grese or shepis taluȝe þat is cold ꝺ medle heme togedir
in a mortar and put all that in a lynnen cloth and enoynt
þe scabb agayns the fyre wheþᵒ it be man or best

782 Anoþᵒ for þe same stampe the rede dokk rote and
seith it with may buttʳ ꝺ clence heme thorow a cloth in to
a clene basyne wᵗ waᵗ and so lat it stand till it be cold and
than kepe it in a box and enoynt the scabb agayn the fire
pƀ.

783 A pᵒciose oyntment is mad for dry scabbes of quyksilũ
ꝺ of dence þe which makynge thou may fynde bifore in the
lettᵗ of O emonge þe oyntements

784 Anoþᵒ for the scabb seth a gode quantite of mele of
cokkyll sede in stronge vynegre ꝺ seth it till it be thik and
then kest þᵒto oyle and make an oyntement ꝺ þat is gode
for scabbes and it doth a way pickyls in a mannys face

785 Anoþᵒ for scabbes melt pich in watir oũ the fire and
than clence it thorow a cloth ꝺ medle þᵒwith the poudre of
glas and make oyntement and enoynt þᵒwith the scabbes

786 Anoþᵒ for dry scab. Medle the poudre of litarge wᵗ
vynegre ꝺ lett hem stand all nyght ꝺ at morow sett it oũ

spread a linen cloth on a board and embalm it therewith in the manner of a plaster. And look that it be laid thin with a slice. And then put [it] on the head hot so that it may cover over all the scales, and take it not away [till] nine days after. And each day anoint the head above with honey, and it will heal fair and well.

779 For the scab. Take powder of quick (melted) brimstone and mingle it with swine's grease, and anoint the scab, and it healeth wonderfully soon.

780 Another for the scab, wheresoever it be. Take the juice of the root of walwort, and take three parts of the juice, and the fourth part of barrow's grease, and make ointment, and anoint the scab in the sun.

781 Another for the same. Take the roots of elecampane and seethe them in water till they be soft, and take old swine's grease or sheep's tallow that is cold, and mingle them together in a mortar ; and put all that in a linen cloth, and anoint the scab by the fire, whether it be man or beast.

782 Another for the same. Stamp the red dock root and seethe it with may-butter, and cleanse them through a cloth into a clean basin of water, and so let it stand till it be cold. And then keep it in a box, and anoint the scab by the fire. *Probatum* [*est*].

783 A precious ointment is made for dry scabs of quicksilver and of dents, the which making thou mayest find before in the letter O, among the ointments.[1]

784 Another for the scab. Seethe a good quantity of meal of cockle-seed (ergot) in strong vinegar, and seethe it till it be thick ; and then cast thereto oil, and make an ointment that is good for scabs, and it doth away pimples in a man's face.

785 Another for scabs. Melt pitch in water over the fire, and then cleanse it through a cloth, and mingle therewith the powder of glass. And make ointment, and anoint therewith the scabs.

786 Another for dry scab. Mingle the powder of litharge with vinegar, and let them stand all night. And on the

---

[1] The quicksilver ointment for scabs is § 658 ; *Dent* is there mentioned, but its nature is not defined. *See* note thereon.

the fire ꝫ medle þᵒwᵗ oyle of nottis ꝫ kest þᵒto poudre of
tartre double [fo. 68 *verso*] so moch as of all the oþᵒ and anone
take it down of the fyre and enoynt the pacient þᵒwith

787 Anoþᵒ for the scabb þat is dry   Tak an vncᵒ of quyksilũ and ij ʒ of oyle de bay and medle hem wele togedir
and enoynt the handis with in the panne ꝫ no where ellis
saue in the sole of the fete and breke wele the whiksilũ and
thou shalt be sane

788 A surope for scabbe lepre and ich.   Take fymᵗ and
scabiose the double of fymᵗ and bray hem ich by hem selue
and take a potell of the juse of fymᵗ and a quart of the juse
of scabiose and boyle hem togedir in a panne with easy
fyre a (*sic*) let hem boile togedir the space of a halue a
quarᵗ of a myle away and then set it down of the fyre and
set þe pan heldynge and lat stand without mevynge till it
gedre to a crudd and do þen away the crudde and aftᵗ þan
take the Juyse and the white of iij egges and boyle hem a
littell while togedir to clarifye itt and then lat it renne
thorow a streyneoure and tak sugre as moch as of the
Juyse þᵒwᵗ þat it be liquid to make it clene fro heres ꝫ than
take the sugre and do it in to þis Juyse and boyll hem
togedᵒ till it be thik and when thou vsist the oyntment
forseid take a sponefull of þe surop and ij sponefull of waᵗ
of fymᵗ and vj sponefull of waᵗ of borage ꝫ littell wermyd
on the fyre and drynk it fastynge.

789 ffor handis þat ben scabbid of clawynge take the rote
of the dok ꝫ stamp [fo. 69 *recto*] it wele and seth it in may
buttʳ and clence þorow a cloth and do in a basyn full of
watir and do it in boxis and enoynt þᵒ with agayns the fire

790 ffor sausfleme take the rote of the doke and pound it
wele and take barowes grese and fry it in a panne and with
that enoynt thi face

791 ffor face þat semyth leprose   Take quyksilũ and bores
grese blak pep and encens ꝫ stamp hem well togedir and

---

¹ *See* note to § 297.

² The meaning seems to be that the sugar also is to be sifted to
free it from hairs or other impurities. " Liquid " here means no
more than clean, or mobile.

morrow set it over the fire, and mingle therewith oil of nuts, and cast thereto powder of tartar, double as much as of all the other ; and anon take it down from the fire, and anoint the patient therewith.

787 Another for the scab that is dry.   Take an ounce of quicksilver and two ounces of oil of bay, and mingle them well together, and anoint the hands within the palm, and nowhere else save in the soles of the feet ; and break well the quicksilver, and thou shalt be sane (cured).

788 A syrup for scab. leprosy and itch.   Take fumitory and scabious, double as much fumitory, and bray them each by itself.   And take a pottle (two quarts) of the juice of fumitory, and a quart of the juice of scabious, and boil them together in a pan with an easy fire, and let them boil together for the space of half a quarter of a mileway.[1]   And then set it down from the fire, and set the pan covered, and let [it] stand without moving till it gather to a curd ; and take then away the curd, and then afterwards take the juice and the white of three eggs, and boil them a little while together, to clarify it.   And then let it run through a strainer, and take sugar as much as of the juice therewith, that it be liquid and clean from hairs.[2]   And then take the sugar and put it into this juice, and boil them together till it be thick.   And when thou usest the ointment aforesaid, take a spoonful of the syrup and two spoonfuls of water of fumitory, and six spoonfuls of water of borage, a little warmed on the fire, and drink it fasting.

789 For hands that be scabbed through clawing (scratching). Take the root of the dock and stamp it well, and seethe it in may-butter ;   and cleanse through a cloth, and put [it] in a basin full of water, and put it in boxes and anoint therewith by the fire.

790 For sausfleme (acne).[3]   Take the root of the dock and pound it well, and take barrow's grease, and fry it in a pan, and with that anoint thy face.

791 For a face that seemeth leprous.[4]   Take quicksilver and boar's grease, and black pepper, and incense ; and stamp

---

[3] *See* note to § 647.
[4] Duplicate of § 340. and *see* note thereon.

ther with enoynt thi face and kepe it fro the wynd iij days
and it shall be hole

792 Anoþ⁹ for the sauffleme to do it a way fro the face
Take stronge vynegre made of white wyne ꝫ enoynt iij
tymes or iiij where the sore is and it will breke out as it
were a mesell ꝫ aftᵉ it is out enoynt it as is before seid vj
days þᵗ þᵉ filth may renne out but loke as oft as thou
enoyntist the face enoynt the hede and the noddill bihynd
with hote watyre and when it hath renne tak and breke
almondis and mak oyle of hem and enoynt it þ⁹with and it
will hele heme vp anone so þat þe sike com nut in þᵉ wynd
in al þat tyme that hys cure is in doynge till he be hole

793 Anoþ⁹ for the sausfleme and for the tetire Take the
poudre of brymstone and barowȝ grese and grynd hem
togedir ꝫ sall armonyak and whik siluᵉ and grynd hem al
togedire and make þ⁹of an nesshe oyntement and enoynt
the syke þ⁹wᵗ at euen on his face on the tetir and on morow
wasshe it away and enoynt hym agayn at euen ꝫ so serue
hym til he be hole

794 Anoþ⁹ tak sauge and swyns mylt and grese [fo. 69
verso] neuᵉ towchid waᵗ and whikk Siluᵉ and grynd wele
togedire and when he goth to bedd enoynt the face and at
morow wipe it away with a cloth or wasshe it and serue
hym so oft and he shall be hole

795 Now begynnyth the medecyns for al manᵉ of suellynge
Tak watir cressis and crmmes of brede and boyle hem wele
in fayre watir and then take hem vp and stamp hem vp
togedire and take þe white of ij eggis or iij ꝫ put þ⁹ to and
make a pleistre þ⁹off all hote and lay to þe sore and a pleistre
layd of rye mele and of shepis taluȝ doth the same

796 Also for the same drynke warme ground swylly and
matfelon

797 ffor swellynge eyȝen stamp violet with myrre and
safron and make a pleystre and lay þ⁹to and the Juyse of
planteyn doth þe same if thou enoynt þ⁹with thyne eyhen

798 ffor all manᵉ of suellyngs of the bodye or of the reyns
or of the buttoks or of þe sidis or of the armes or of the

them well together, and therewith anoint thy face, and keep it from the wind three days, and it shall be whole.

792 Another for the sausfleme (acne), to do it away from the face. Take strong vinegar made of white wine, and anoint three times or four where the sore is. And it will break out as [if] it were leprosy ; and after it is out, anoint it as aforesaid six days, that the filth may run out. But look (take care) as oft as thou anointest the face, to anoint the head and the noddle (nape) behind with hot water. And when it hath run, take and break almonds, and make oil of them, and anoint it therewith, and it will heal him up anon, so [long] as the sick come not in the wind all the time that is cure is being done, till he be whole.

793 Another for the sausfleme (acne) and for the tetter. Take the powder of brimstone and barrow's grease, and grind them together ; and sal-ammoniac and quicksilver, and grind them all together. And make thereof a soft ointment, and anoint the sick therewith at even on his face [or] on the tetter ; and on the morrow wash it away, and anoint him again at even. And so serve him till he be whole.

794 Another. Take sage and swine's mylt (spleen) and grease [that has] never touched water, and quicksilver, and grind well together. And when he goeth to bed, anoint the face, and at morrow wipe it away with a cloth, or wash it. And serve him so oft, and he shall be whole.

795 Now beginneth the medicines for all manner of swelling. Take watercresses and crumbs of bread, and boil them well in fair water ; and then take them up, and stamp them up together. And take the white of two eggs or three, and put thereto ; and make a plaster thereof all hot, and lay to the sore. And a plaster made of rye meal and of sheep's tallow doth the same.

796 [Another] Also for the same, drink warm groundsel and matfelon (knapweed).

797 For swelling eyes. Stamp violet with myrrh and saffron, and make a plaster and lay thereto. And the juice of plantain doth the same, if thou anointest therewith thine eyes.

798 For all manner of swellings of the body, or of the reins, or of the buttocks, or of the sides, or of the arms, or of the

dropsye and for the waȝ bytwene the skyn and the flesshe
seth in watir the shauynge of glouꝰs leþer till it be thik as
glyw and lay it on a clout to þe suellynge

799 An oþꝰ for the same lay to þe suellynge smalach with
the cromes of brede

800 Anoþꝰ for suellynge of arms tak archaungle ꝛ seth it
wele in watir and put þꝰto ij sponefull of hony and seth it
to þe haluendele and wasshe the sore with the waȝ þꝰof and
lay the erbis to þe sore and it will draw wele and hele fayre

801 Anoþꝰ to cōsume Swellynge   Tak cow dunge strong
drestis of ale waȝ crassis stampid ꝛ boyl hem togedir till
thei be thyk ꝛ also hote lay to þe [fo. 70 *recto*] swellynge pḃ eꝰ

802 To dystroy Swellynge or rankyllynge where it be   Take
malows and stamp hem and oten mele and seth hem in
mylk and good stale ale to it þik and all hote lay it to the
swellyngs pḃ est

803 Anoþꝰ ffor swellynge coughe and wynd vndꝰ the sydes.
Take wormod horsmynt ꝛ soþerne wod and stamp hem and
seth hem in iij pties of watire and the iiij pte of vynegre to
it be tendre and þan take it vp and medle it with soure
douȝe and all hote pleistre it to þe side ꝛ þan behovyth a
suppository or a laxatife on þe morow after þe pleistre

804 ffor swellynge of a soore tak þe Juyse of smalach and
the poudre if lynesede mylk of a cow floure of otemele ꝛ
mak a pleisȝ pḃ eꝰ

805 ffor to make a swellynge breke   Take pisse and vynegre
and a handfull of sauge stampid ꝛ floure boyle hem togedir
till thei be thik and all hote ley to þe soore and hete agayne
as oft as it nedith

806 ffor swellynge in the stomake take þe rote of fenell and
the rote of smalach and stamp hem and temp hem with
wyne and giff þe syk to drynk

807 To hele þe soore and abate þe swellynge   Take þe rede
cole sauge and smalach well stampid and medle wᵗ soure
douȝ ꝛ hony and lay to þe soore

dropsy, and for the water between the skin and the flesh. Seethe in water the shavings of glover's leather till it be thick as glue, and lay it on a cloth to the swelling.

799 Another for the same. Lay to the swelling smallage with the crumbs of bread.

800 Another for swelling of arms. Take archangel and seethe it well in water, and put thereto two spoonfuls of honey, and seethe it to half measure. And wash the sore with the water thereof, and lay the herbs to the sore, and it will draw well and heal fair.

801 Another to consume swelling. Take cow-dung, strong dregs of ale, [and] watercresses stamped, and boil them together till they be thick. And all hot, lay to the swelling. *Probatum est.*

802 To destroy swelling or rankling where[soever] it be. Take mallows and stamp them, and oatmeal, and seethe them in milk and good stale ale till it [be] thick, and all hot lay it to the swellings. *Probatum est.*

803 Another for swelling, cough, and wind under the sides. Take wormwood, horsemint and southernwood, and stamp them and seethe them in three parts of water and the fourth part of vinegar, till it be tender ; and then take it up, and mingle it with sour dough ; and all hot plaster it to the side. And then behoveth a suppository or laxative on the morrow after the plaster.

804 For swelling of a sore. Take the juice of smallage and the powder of linseed, milk of a cow. flour of oatmeal, and make a plaster. *Probatum est.*

805 For to make a swelling break. Take urine and vinegar, and a handful of stamped sage, and flour, and boil them together till they be thick ; and all hot, lay to the sore, and heat again as oft as it needeth.

806 For swelling in the stomach. Take the root of fennel and the root of smallage ; and stamp them, and temper them with wine, and give the sick to drink.

807 To heal a sore and abate the swelling. Take red cabbage and smallage well stamped ; and mingle with sour dough and honey, and lay to the sore.

808 Swellynge of a mannes codd is amendid with a pleistre made of malows ꝰ flo of benes ꝰ comyn boylid with watir

809 ffor swelt in the stomake   Take þe rote of fenell and þe rote of ach and temp wᵗ wyne and gif the sik to drynke

810 Who so hath suellynge i his knees   Take rw ꝰ loueach ꝰ stamp togedre ꝰ do þ⁹to hony ꝰ [fo. 70 verso] lay to þe sore

811 who so haue suellynge in his fete or in his toon take the rote of walwort and seith it in watir and do away the ou)most of the rote and take þe myddist of the rote and stamp it wᵗ barowȝ grese and do it in a clowt and bynd to þe soore

812 ffor swelt of womb pound ruw wᵗ wyne eyther with ale and drynke it oft or ellis drynk weybrede and ruw soden in wyne

813 ffor suellynge of reyns or of knees tak ruw ꝰ poñd it with salt and hony ꝰ þ⁹of make a pleistre and lay þ⁹on

814 ffor the swelt of nayles   Take soure ale and mylk and do togedir and ete (sic) it and take the cridde and lay to þe nayles to they be hole

815 ffor swellynge of body take lard old grese shepis taluȝ of ech lich moch and take encence psen wex of ech lich moch oyle the thrid dele þe rote of holy hokke rostid and wele pound yfere with þe grese and lat it softly seth and kele it and do it in boxes and do it a clowt and lay to the wound

816 Anoþ⁹ for knees swollen take hakkyehay and grese and vryne and seþe heme togedir and lay þ⁹to

817 ffor al mañ of suellynge   Tak groundswylly ꝰ broklemke ꝰ chikenmete dayseeyȝen pety morell and erb benett ꝰ stamp hem togedir small and boyl hem and fry hem wᵗ ij pts of buttʳ and j pte of white wyne and lay it to his bake as hote as he may suffre

808 Swelling of a man's cod (scrotum) is amended with a plaster made of mallows, and flour of beans and cumin boiled with water.

809 For swelling in the stomach. Take the root of fennel and the root of ache, and temper with wine, and give the sick to drink.

810 Whoso hath a swelling in his knees. Take rue and lovage, and stamp together; and put thereto honey, and lay to the sore.

811 Whoso hath swelling in his feet or in his toes. Take root of walwort and seethe it in water; and do away the outermost [part] of the root, and take the middle [-part] of the root, and stamp it with barrow's grease; and put it in a cloth, and bind to the sore.

812 For swelling of womb. Pound rue with wine or with ale, and drink it oft. Or else drink waybread and rue seethed in wine.

813 For swelling of reins or of knees. Take rue, and pound it with salt and honey; and thereof make a plaster, and lay thereon.

814 For the swelling of nails. Take sour ale and milk and put them together; and drink it and take the scum and lay to the nails till they be whole.

815 For swelling of the body. Take lard, old grease [and] sheep's tallow, of each equally much, and take incense, perosin [and] wax, of each equally much; [and] oil, the third part. [And take] the root of hollyhock roasted and well pounded together with the grease, and let it softly seethe, and cool it, and put it in boxes, and put it [on] a cloth and lay to the wound.

816 Another for knees swollen. Take mallow-crops[1] and grease and urine, and seethe them together and lay thereto.

817 For all manner of swellings. Take groundsel and brooklime, and chickweed, daisies, little morell, and herb-benet, and stamp them together small, and boil them; and fry them with two parts of butter and one part of white wine, and lay it to his back as hot as he may suffer.

---

[1] I take *hakkehay* to be "hock-heads," *i.e.* mallow-crops.

818 ffor the stone take an ℥ j of saxfrage seed of gromell
seed añ philipendula añ of geet añ of psely seed añ of kyddis-
blode bakyn in an ovyn añ of lanniḃ añ of anneys of longe
pep añ of fyne [fo. 71 *recto*] canell añ of cheristone kyrnell
añ of rede filbert shellis añ and ℥ ℔ of poudre of glasse ℥ j
of date stones of the poudre of gray flynt añ and giff the
syk to drynk a sponefull here of with wat̃ of perspere or
with white wyne and so serue hym at morow and at eve
till he be hole pḃ ẽ

819 Anoþ⁹ for the stone   Take a march hare and put hym
in a pott altogedre saue the guttis ꝫ brenne hym to poudre
ꝫ vse it in his mete
820 Also take the rote of philipendula and the rote of
saxfragge and the rote of turmentyne and the kernellis of
chery stones and the seede of gromell and þe pile þᵗ is in
þe stomake of douse byrdis and make poudre þ⁹ of ꝫ vse
it
821 An oþ⁹ for the stone and for the soornes of the sides
and reyns take the Juyse of rede fenell and wat̃ of fenell
añ and good white wyne and medle all thies togedir and
drynk þ⁹of first ꝫ last pḃ est

822 Anoþ⁹ for the stone   Take þe watir of saxfrage watir
of beteyn watir of ramson wat̃ of cowslop euen porcionyd
and drynke hem first and last and thow shall fare wele

823 ffor the stone strangury and dissure Drynk wyne that
the rote of philipendula is soden in and for the same make a
pleystre of ij pties of philipendula powdrede and of saxfragge
iij ptie and lay on the share wᵗ wyne

824 An oþ⁹ for þe strangurye and dissure make small bundels
of origanū and seþe hem in wyne and lay hem alhote on his
reyns
825 fforto staunch blode when a maystire vayn is corven
and will nat be staunchid gladly Jf th wounde [fo. 71

818 For the stone. Take an ounce of saxifrage seed, of gromwell seed the same, philipendula (dropwort) the same, of jet the same, of parsley seed the same, of kid's blood baked in an oven the same, of nibwort the same, of anise, of long pepper the same, of fine canell the same, of cherry-stone kernels the same, of red filbert shells the same ; and half an ounce of powder of glass ; one ounce of date stones, of the powder of grey flint the same. And give the sick to drink a spoonful thereof with water of knotgrass or with white wine, and so serve him at morn and at eve till he be whole. *Probatum est.*

819 Another for the stone.[1] Take a March hare and put him in a pot altogether save the guts, and burn him to powder, and use it in his (the patient's) meat.

820 [Another]. Also take the root of philipendula (dropwort), and the root of saxifrage, and the root of tormentil, and the kernels of cherry-stones, and the seed of gromwell, and the stone that is in the stomach (crop or gizzard) of duck-birds, and make powder thereof, and use it.

821 Another for the stone and for the soreness of the sides and reins. Take the juice of red fennel and water of fennel, equal quantities, and good white wine. And mingle all these together, and drink thereof first and last. *Probatum est.*

822 Another for the stone. Take the water of saxifrage, water of betony, water of ramson (asphodel), water of cowslip, even portions ; and drink them first and last, and thou shalt fare well.

823 For the stone, strangury and dysuria. Drink wine that the root of philipendula (dropwort) is boiled in, and for the same make a plaster of two parts of philipendula powdered and of saxifrage the third part, and lay on the pubic region with wine.

824 Another from strangury and dysuria. Make small bundles of origanum (pennyroyal), and seethe them in wine, and lay them all hot on his reins.

825 To stanch blood when a master vein[2] is severed, and will not be stanched gladly (readily), if the wound be large.

---

[1] There is a more elaborated form of this March-hare recipe in H. (Henslow, *op. cit.*, p. 42). *Cf.* § 890.

[2] A large vein (or artery).

verso] be large Take a pece of salt befe þe lene and nat the fat that thou chopist will in the wound and lay it in the fyre and rost it till it thorow hote and all hote thrust it in the wound and bynd it fast and it shall staunch anone

826 Anoþ⁹ for to stanch blode Tak copose and sandeủ of eythir lich moch by wiȝt and bete heme small to poudre and lay hem on the wound ꝫ take þe croppis of rede nettels and stamp hem small and do þ⁹to luf hony and medle heme wele togedir and lay on þe wound and fayre bynd it vp

827 Also take the woll of a fullynge myll that goth fro the cloth with walkynge and flieth about on the walles Make poudre þ⁹ of in a brasen mort̃ and take a poudre of the white of the buttid floure and tempre toged⁀] and lay on the cloth or elles on fayre flex and lay it on

828 An oþ⁹ take encens and aloes and the tere of whete and an ey and grynd hem togedir þat it be thyk and lay this pleistre to the veyn that is kyt and do it nat away till thow trow that the kerfe be closid togedir and if it be nede lay þis medecyne apone raþ⁹ till þ⁹ be a sadd seine on the place þᵗ was soore ꝫ put to his forseid medecyne flex of (*sic*) an hare small kitt or spiþere webb þis is a p⁹vyd medecyne

829 ffor to staunch blode of woundis take lyme and make powdre and tak poudre of the white of egges ꝫ stamp togedire and menge togedir wele ꝫ flasshe it on the wound abouen the flesshe and lay flex to þe wound and flasshe it oft on the flax till it staunch and do it nat away to the thrid day and when thow remeuyst it wasshe it with mannes pisse tille þe [fol 72 *recto*] pleystre renne by hyme selue for it (*sic*) thou draw it away þe wound will blede eft sonys

830 Anoþ⁹ Take brome and do away þe rynd with a knyfe and make balles þ⁹ of and do on the wound

831 Anoþ⁹ Take grene mathen̄ and tendre leves of the blossoms and stamp hem small with yonge mogwort and rede nettil croppis and temp þ⁹with the poudre of brent

---

¹ These words seem to be intrusive here, and stultify the sense. Probably the scribe lost his place when copying from the original.

Take a piece of salt beef, the lean and not the fat, [that thou choppest well in the wound][1] and lay it on the fire and roast it till it be thoroughly hot, and all hot thrust it in the wound, and bind it fast and it shall stanch anon.

826 Another to stanch blood. Take copperas and sandiver,[2] of each equally much by weight, and beat them small to powder, and lay them on the wound. And take the crops of red nettles, and stamp them small, and put thereto loaf honey, and mingle them well together, and lay to the wound, and fair bind it up.

827 [Another]. Also take the wool (fluff) from a fulling-mill that goeth from the cloth with working, and flieth about on the walls. Make powder thereof in a brazen mortar, and take powder of the white of sifted flour, and temper together and lay on a cloth, or else on fair flax, and lay it on [the wound].

828 Another. Take incense and aloes and the fine flour of wheat and an egg, and grind them together that it be thick, and lay this plaster to the vein that is cut, and do not [take] it away till thou knowest that the gash be closed together. And if need be, lay this medicine [there]upon till there be a solid seam (union) on the place that was sore. And put to this aforesaid medicine flax or a hair cut small, or a spider's web. This is a proved medicine.

829 For to stanch blood of wounds. Take lime and make powder, and take powder of the white of eggs, and stamp together and mingle together well, and sprinkle it upon the wound above the flesh, and lay flax to the wound, and sprinkle it (the powder) oft on the flax till it stanch ; and take it not away till the third day. And when thou removest it, wash it with man's urine till the plaster run (comes away) of itself, for if thou pullest it away, the wound will bleed again immediately.

830 Another.[3] Take broom, and take away the rind with a knife, and make balls thereof, and put [them] on the wound.

831 Another. Take green mayweed, and tender leaves (petals) of the blossoms, and stamp them small with young mugwort and red nettle crops, and temper therewith the

---

[2] *See* note to § 205.
[3] There is a duplicate of this recipe in H. (Henslow, *op. cit.*, p. 29).

salt and lay to the wound and it shall staunch anone on
warantise and an hote houndis torde will do the same

832 To staunch blode of veyns kitt a two take a croppe of
sauge and greyns of lecke and stamp hem togedir and make
tondre of lynnen cloth brent and stamp þᵒwith and lay
þᵒto alday and nyght at the lest and thou may haue
maddokkys take þᵉ knotts that growith abouth the worme
⁊ stamp wᵗ oþᵒ thynges and this is a soůeyn stoppynge
so þat it ligge longe enouȝ þᵒto and nw it if it nede be at
morow and that þᵉ lyme be holden vp mych in tyme of
staunchynge
833 To staunch blode at the nose enoynt þᵉ nose wᵗ the
juyse of lekys wᵗ in forþe ⁊ if thou drynke the Juyse of
lekys it will staunch hem þat kestith oute blode at here
mouth and the juyse of planteyn doth the same and helpith
hem þat haue þᵉ thesyk
834 Also dentdelyon will staunch blode at þᵉ nose if thou will
breke it and hold it to þᵉ nose þᵗ þᵉ sauó may go in to it

835 ffor hem þat spitt or kest blode at þᵒ mowth Take
þᵉ rote of elenacampana and rost in in (sic) hote asshes and
then make it clene ⁊ lay it in hony ⁊ ete it fastynge
836 [fo. 72 verso] Ffor spittinge blode of a fall take beteyne
verveyn ȝarow and v levyd grasse of ech lich moch and
stamp heme togedir in A mortare and wrynge owte the
juyse and put to þᵉ juyse as moch of gotis mylk and lett it
seth to gedir and lat hym that is hurt drynke this drynke
iij days in the waxynge of the mone hoote and vij dayes in
the waynynge of the mone and also lat hyme drynke
osmund and comferye ix dayes with stale ale ⁊ he shall be
hoole
837 Anoþᵒ for hem þat spave blode Take smalach rw
mynt and boyle heme wele in gotis mylke and drynk it and
take piliall and beteyn and make poudre þᵒoff and do it in
an eyȝe and ete it and do this iij days or take horshelme
with the rote of nosebledd and grynd it and temp it with
watir and drynk it
838 he þᵗ for spwynge may not hold mete ne drynke take
mylfoyle and pound it and temp it wᵗ wyne þat is warme
and temp it also with juyse of betayn and drynke it

powder of burnt salt ; and lay to the wound and it shall stanch anon, on warranty.   And hot dog's dung will do the same.

832 To stanch blood of veins cut in two.   Take a crop of sage and greens (leaves) of leek, and stamp them together. And make tinder of burnt linen cloth, and stamp therewith, and lay thereto all day and night at the least ; and thou mayest take maggots, and take the knots that groweth about the worm and stamp it with [the] other things.   And this is a sovereign stopping (styptic) if it lie long enough thereto, and renew it if need be on the morrow, and [if] the limb be held up much at the time of the stanching.

833 To stanch blood at the nose.   Anoint the nose with the juice of leeks within.   And if thou drinkest the juice of leeks, it will stanch them that cast out blood at the mouth. And the juice of plantain doth the same, and helpeth them that have phthisis.

834 [Another].   Also dandelion will stanch blood at the nose, if thou wilt break it, and hold it to the nose that the savour may go into it.

835 For them that spit or cast blood at the mouth.   Take the root of elecampane, and roast it in hot ashes, and make it clean, and lay it in honey and eat it fasting.

836 For spitting blood after a fall,   Take betony, vervain, yarrow, and five-leaved grass, of each equally much, and stamp them together in a mortar, and wring out the juice ; and put to the juice as much goat's milk, and seethe it together.   And let him that is hurt drink this drink three days at the waxing of the moon hot, and seven days at the waning of the moon ; and also let him drink [the juice of] osmund (fern) and comfrey nine days with stale ale, and he shall be whole.

837 Another for them that spew blood.   Take smallage, rue, mint, and boil them well in goat's milk, and drink it. And take pennyroyal and betony and make powder thereof, and put it in an egg and eat it, and do this three days.   Or take coltsfoot with the root of nosebleed (yarrow), and grind it and temper it with water, and drink it.

838 He that for spewing may not hold meat nor drink. Take milfoil and pound it, and temper it with wine that is warm, and temper it also with juice of betony, and drink it.

839 ffor spech that is lost in syknesse   Take wormod and
temp it in watir and do it in his mowth and sone shall he
speke

840 Also take take (*sic*) garlyk and temp it with watir and
do it in his mowth and he shall speke

841 Also temp savyne and the leves of pionre and pep
and menge hem togedir and make a drynke and gif hyme

842 Also take Ruw and garlyk and stamp hem togedir
and temp hem with vynegre or with eysell and streyne
hem thorow a cloth ꝫ put in his mowth and the juyse of
houndistunge doth þe same

843 Jff the scull of the breyn panne be broken or bowed
so þat þe [fo. 73 *recto*] pacient may nat speke   Stamp violet
and gif hym to drynk first in wyne and if the right side of
the hede be hurt stampe violett and bynd it to the sole of
the left fote   And if it be þe left syde of the hede lay it to
þe right fote and the bone wile ryse vp and the pacient shall
now speke

844 fforto make childrene forto speke sone rubb hertis
tunge with salgeme medyllyd with hony and it shall make
heme to speke

845 ffor hem that speke in slepe   Take sothernwode and
stamp itt ꝫ medle the juyse with white wyne or wᵗ vynegre
and gif the syk to drynk when he goth to his bedd and it
shall lett hyme to speke in his slepe

846 An oþ⁹ for the same   Take the croppis of rwe and of
verueyn of ech lich moch ꝫ stamp hem in a mort and temp
hem with vynegre and gif the syke to drynke last when he
goth to bedde and lat hyme vse this medecyne ix days and
with in the x day he shall be hole

847 ffor hym þat may nat slepe take letuȝ sede and smalach
seede and stamp hem in a mort and temp hem with the
white of an ey and bynd hem to þe forehede and he shal
slepe

848 An oþ⁹ for the same   Tak cresse seede ꝫ stamp it and
medle it with wyne and giff hym to drynk

839 For speech that is lost in sickness. Take wormwood and temper it in water, and put it in his mouth, and soon he shall speak.

840 [Another]. Also take garlic and temper it with water, and put it in his mouth, and he shall speak.

841 [Another]. Also temper savin and the leaves of peony, and pepper, and mingle them together, and make a drink and give him.

842 [Another]. Also take rue and garlic, and stamp them together, and temper them with vinegar or with aysell, and strain them through a cloth, and put in his mouth. And the juice of houndstongue doth the same.

843 If the skull of the brain-pan be broken or bowed (crushed), so that the patient may not speak. Stamp violet and give him to drink first in wine. And if the right side of the head be hurt, stamp violet and bind it to the sole of the left foot. And if the left side of the head, lay it to the right foot. And the bone shall rise up, and the patient shall speak again.[1]

844 For to make children speak soon. Rub hartstongue with rocksalt mingled with honey, and it shall make him to speak.

845 For those who speak in sleep. Take southernwood and stamp it, and mingle the juice with white wine or with vinegar, and give the sick to drink when he goeth to his bed, and it shall let (hinder) him from speaking in his sleep.

846 Another for the same. Take the crops of rue and of vervain, of each equally much, and stamp them in a mortar, and temper them with vinegar, and give the sick to drink last when he goeth to bed. And let him use this medicine nine days, and within the tenth day, he shall be whole.

847 For him that may not sleep. Take lettuce seed and smallage seed and stamp them in a mortar; and temper them with the white of an egg, and bind them to the forehead. And he shall sleep.

848 Another for the same. Take cress-seed and stamp it, and mingle it with wine, and give him to drink.

---

[1] This observation of the effects of brain-injury on the opposite side of that injured is both correct and interesting. *See* Introduction, § III.

849 An othir take the powdre of smalach and of henbanne and mynt powdred and temp hem with oyle or w^t grese and enoynt þe forehede and the temples

850 Anoþ⁹ Take poudre of mastyk and medle w^t vynegre and oyle and [fo. 73 verso] enoynt the ponns box of the hede and of the handis ⁊ of the fete and he shall slepe with out dowte

851 Anoþ⁹ take leke sede and stamp it and temp it with womans mylk ⁊ the white of an eye and bynd to the temples and he shal slepe

852 To do a man slepe to he be shorue or kerven take the gall of a swyne iij sponefull and take juyse of hemblok rote iij sponefull of aysell iij sponefull and menge all toged⁽ and pan do hem in a vessell of glass to hold to þe syke man that thow will shere eythire kerue and take þ⁹on a sponefull and do to a galon of wyne or of ale and if þᵘ wilt make it stronge do ij sponefull þ⁹of and giff hyme to drynke and he shall slepe sone. shere hym and kerue hym than as thow wilt

853 Anoþ⁹ To make a man slepe all a day Take the wild nepe and þe grete morell and pety morell letuȝ and white popy and bray hem in a mort and take the juyse ther of and tempre it [with] ale and giff hyme to drynke

854 ffor slepynge hand or fote take flours of brome and flours of leues of wodwyse of ech lich moch and stamp hem with may butture and let hem stand togedre all nyȝt and on the morow melt it in a panne oul the fyre and skym it wele this medecyn is good for all· cold yuelles and also for the fleynge goute

855 ffor the stomak þt is encõbred w^t fleume or malencoly Tak ij dragmes of aloes ⁊ a dragme [fo. 74 recto] of mastik it clensith the stomak and confortith hyme if he be acoldid eythiȝ feble or faynt And for colry in the stomak take a greyne of aloes with hony it clensith the stomak and makyth hyme wele to diffye but aloes and mastijk shuld be

---

¹ The temporal region, where pulsation can be felt.
² Shorven = shered, treated or remedied, referring to surigcal or manipulative treatment.

849 Another. Take the powder of smallage and of henbane and mint powdered, and temper them with oil or with grease, and anoint the forehead and the temples.

850 Another. Take powder of mastic and mingle with vinegar and oil, and anoint the pulse-box[1] of the head, and of the hands and feet. And he shall sleep without doubt.

851 Another. Take leek-seed and stamp it and temper it with woman's milk and the white of an egg; and bind to the temples. And he shall sleep.

852 To put a man to sleep, that he may be treated[2] or cut (operated upon).[3] Take the gall of a swine three spoonfuls, and take the juice of hemlock-root three spoonfuls, of vinegar three spoonfuls, and mingle all together; and then put them in a vessel of glass to hold to the sick man that thou wilt treat or cut; and take thereof a spoonful, and put [it] to a gallon of wine or ale. And if thou wilt make it strong, put two spoonfuls thereof, and give him to drink, and he shall sleep soon. [Then mayest thou] treat or cut him as thou wilt.

853 Another to make a man sleep all day. Take the wild nept (ground-ivy) and the great morell (nightshade) and petty morell, lettuce and white poppy, and bray them in a mortar; and take the juice thereof, and temper it [with] ale, and give him to drink.

854 For sleeping hand or foot.[4] Take flours of broom and leaves of woadwaxen, of each equally much, and stamp them with may-butter, and let them stand together all night; and on the morrow melt it in a pan over the fire, and skim it well. This medicine is good for all cold evils, and also for the cold gout.

855 For the stomach that is encumbered with phlegm or melancholy. Take two drachms of aloes and a drachm of mastic. It cleanseth the stomach and comforteth him if it be cold or feeble or faint. And for choler in the stomach, take a grain of aloes with honey. It cleanseth the stomach and maketh it well to digest. But aloes and mastic should

---

[3] This anæsthetic draught resembles that in *Harl.* 2378 (Henslow, *op. cit.*, p. 90).
[4] This is a duplicate of § 680, but with a different title. *See* note thereon.

stampid and soden w^t white wyne and so giffen to the sik
to drynk

856 ffor stomak that is bolnyd tak þe rote of fenell and the
rote of ach and stamp hem and temp hem with white wyne
and gife the syke to drynke

857 ffor stomak þat englymed   Take fenell and stamp it
in a mortare and take the juyse of it and drynk a sope with
a littell wyne or ale and thou shalt delyuꝰ both aboue and
byneth and do the moch gode

858 ffor filthied stomakys   Tak iiij apples or crabbes for
the serven to medecyns and kytt out þe cores and fill the
hole with poudre of nutmugys and of mastyk and of clowes
or with poudre of pep and of comyn

859 ffor stynkynge breth þat cōmyth of the stomake   Take
ij handfull of comyn and bete it in a morꞇ to poudre and
seth it in good wyne fro a potell to a quart and lat þe syk
drynk þꝰof first and last as hote as he may suffre goodely
and he shall be hole with in xv days on warantise and ech
day drynk a pynt

860 An oþꝰ   Take piliall mounteyn a goode handfull and
wasshe it clene and shred it small and grynd it in a mortare
and do ther to halue an vnce of poudre of comyn ꝫ medle
hem in a potell of rede wyne and seth hem to haluendele
ꝫ vse þis afꞇ mete ꝫ ones at even last [fo. 74 *verso*] and alway
hote and he shall be hole

861 Anoþꝰ gode helpe for the stomak   Tak an handfull of
camamill and a handful of psely rotis and stamp hem and
boyle hem in vynegre and then all hote mak it with soure
(*sic*) and lay þ^t pleisꞇ all hote to thi stomak and when it is
cold hete it in the same vynegre and eft lay it to thi
stomak and þᵘ shalt be hole

862 Anoþꝰ for the stomak   Tak mynt sauge camamyll and
most of wormod brayed and soure brede sowed in a cloth
and boylid in vynegre and warme layd on the stomake

863 ffor byndynge in the stomak   Take a gude ptie of saue
and as moch of comyn and almost as moch of turmentill
ꝫ grynd hem togedre in a morꞇ of brasse and do sugur in a

be stamped and seethed with white wine, and so given to the sick to drink.

856 For stomach that is bulged. Take the root of fennel and the root of ache, and stamp them and temper them with white wine, and give the sick to drink.

857 For stomach that [is] engleimed. Take fennel and stamp it in a mortar ; and take the juice of it, and drink a sip with a little wine or ale. And thou shalt be delivered both above and beneath,[1] and do thee much good.

858 For filthied stomach. Take four apples or crab [-apples] suitable for medicine, and cut out the cores, and fill the hole with powder of nutmegs and of mastic and of cloves, or with powder of pepper and of cumin.

859 For stinking breath that cometh of the stomach. Take two handfuls of cumin, and beat it in a mortar to powder ; and seethe it in good wine from a pottle to a quart, and let the sick drink thereof first and last as hot as he may well suffer. And he shall be whole within fifteen days on warranty ; and each day drink a pint.

860 Another. Take thyme a good handful, and wash it clean, and shred it small, and grind it in a mortar ; and put thereto half an ounce of powder of cumin, and mingle them in a pottle of red wine ; and seethe them to half : and use this after meat, and once at even, last, and always hot. And he shall be whole.

861 Another good help for the stomach. Take a handful of camomile and a handful of parsley roots, and stamp them, and boil them in vinegar. And then all hot, make it with sour [bread into a plaster], and lay the plaster all hot to thy stomach. And when it is cold, heat it in the same vinegar, and again lay it to thy stomach, and thou shalt be whole.

862 Another for the stomach. Take mint, sage, camomile, and most of wormwood, brayed, and sour bread, sewn in a cloth and boiled in vinegar, and laid on the stomach warm.

863 For binding in the stomach. Take a good part of savin, and as much of cumin, and almost as much of tormentil ; and grind them together in a mortar of brass. And put sugar

---

[1] *I.e.* the glutinous matter encumbering the stomach will be voided both by vomit and by stool. *Cf.* § 864.

clene scourid panne and diȝt it as it were a lectuary. And
when it is diȝt stir it at the botome of the panne and lat
sprede a brode in the pan as it were a cake and when it is
cold breke it in small mosselles as a bene and giff the syk
at morow and at eve and lat hym vse þe colys made of
hennys and drynk diteyn

864 ffor engleymynge stomak Tak a saucerfull of aysell
and clene whete brede and do it in the aysell and take a
sponefull poudre of pepire and do it in the saucer and ete
fastynge ⁊ walk after

865 ffor synews hurt Tak pich and wex and grese and
menge togedir and hete it and lay it þᵖon

866 To leuȝt synows and abate suellis Tak a shepis hede and
clefe it in vj quarters and sett it to seth oṷ the fyre till þe
bones shak [fo. 75 recto] owt and that the flesshe be tendyr
and then pyke out þe bons and the gristels and the rofe of
the tunge than stamp it wele in a mortar as smeþe as a
pleystre and temp it with þe watir þat is soden in and then
sett it oṷ the fyre till it be ryȝt hote and all warme lay it
to þe soore pties and vse it till itt be hoole

867 A pleystre for synews and veyns kytt Take ij knyues
in somer when thow fyndist ij wormes knytt togedir and kytt
of the knottis and lay hem to dry agayns the sonne and make
þᵖoſ poudre and that poudre will knytt synows or veyne
that is kyt or broken

868 Anoþᵖ Tak worms þat men clepith agilpercy and seth
hem in a littell oyle with a littell ypoquissidos þat poticaris
haue and lay to þe wound and tak it nat A way in the
somó to the iiij day and in wynͭ to þe ix day and this
byndith sinowes and veyns where so eṷ thei be

869 ffor swellynge to moch. Take lynsede and letuȝ and
bynd to þe stomake

870 Also take (sic) and salt and stamp hem togedir and
temp hem with wyne and drynk it

---

¹ Cf. § 857.
² Six parts, of course, should be understood.
³ Perhaps the hyoid bones are meant.
⁴ This is a survival of a magical rite. Why two knives are
required is not clear. The worms are to be taken in copula, and
presumably the " knots " are the parts so distended. The union of

in a clean-scoured pan, and dress it as [if] it were an electuary. And when it is dressed, stir it at the bottom of the pan, and let it spread abroad in the pan, as [if] it were a cake. And when it is cold, break it into morsels as small as a bean, and give the sick at morn and at eve. And let his use cullis made of hens (chicken-broth), and drink dittany.

864 For engleiming [of the] stomach.[1] Take a saucerful of vinegar, and clean wheat bread, and put it in the vinegar. And take a spoonful of powder of pepper, and put it in the saucer, and eat fasting, and walk after [eating].

865 For sinews hurt. Take pitch and wax and grease, and mingle them together ; and heat it, and lay it thereon.

866 To ease sinews and abate swellings. Take a sheep's head and cleave it in six quarters,[2] and set it to seethe over the fire till the bones shake out, and the flesh be tender. And then pick out the bones and gristle, and the roof of the tongue,[3] then stamp it well in a mortar as smooth as a plaster. And temper it with the water it was boiled in, and then set it over the fire till it be right hot. And, all warm, lay it to the sore parts, and use it till (the swelling) it be whole.

867 A plaster for sinews and veins cut. Take two knives in summer when thou findest two worms knit together, and cut off the knots, and lay them to dry in the sun, and make thereof powder. And that powder will knit (unite) sinews or vein that is cut or broken.[4]

868 Another. Take worms that men call grubs,[5] and seethe them in a little oil, with a little hypocistis[6] that apothecaries have, and lay to the wound. And take it not away in the summer till the fourth day, and in winter till the ninth day. And this bindeth sinews and veins wheresoever they be.

869 For swelling too much. Take linseed and lettuce, and bind to the stomach.

870 [Another]. Also take . . .[7] and salt, and stamp them together, and temper them with wine, and drink it.

the two worms on the principle of sympathetic magic cause a union of the severed vein.

[5] The word *agilpercy* seems to be a corruption of *anguille perçant*. a boring worm. The word I have used, " grub," is quite conjectural.

[6] A preparation made from *Cytinus hypocistis*, a parasitic plant of South Europe. *Cf.* Cassius Felix, *De Medicina*, lxxxii, *ad fin.*

[7] The name of the drug is omitted.

871 To mak a man to swete take dry comyn and bete it to poudre and medle it with oyle and enoynt wele vnd⁀ the fete and hill hyme hote   And nettyl seyd in oyle doth the same

872 To make saue   Tak burnet drauk turmentill mayden here bugle piggle sancle erb John erb roƀt erb walter the grete confond þat is comferye þe mene confonde þat is daysie hemp cropp the rede cole cropp the rede brere crop madere calů⁀fote souþistill groundswylly violett willd tasel mod⁀wort egromoyn wodbynd rybwort mowsere mousepose flours of brome diteyne verueyn croppis of white thorn so [fo. 75 verso] thernwod sauge the crop of the rede nettill osmond quyntfoyl scabiose strayberye wyse pympnall selsehell and as moch of auence os of all the oþ⁹ erbis and of the oþ⁹ erbis euen porcion and shall be gadered in may before seynt John day and bray hem in a mortar and medle hem with may butt⁀ fresshe and clene made as the mylk cōmyth fro þe cow and if thow haue no may butt⁀ take oþ⁹ butt⁀ purge it clene and lat it kele and medle it in a vessell and keů⁀ it vj days or vij forto it bygynne to hore and after fry it in a panne and clense it thorow a cloth and lat it stand in a vessell till þat it be cold and sithen kerfe it and lat the ground go owt and seþen do it and oů⁀ the fire and clere it and lat it kele and do it in boxes and the woundid man shall drynk þ⁹of with alle as moch as ones as a barly corne first and last ech day tyll þat he be hole and keuere that wound wᵗ a lefe of rede cole ℞ if thou may nat fynd all those erƀis tak xxxij of the first and the auence peywith as moch as all the oþer erbs with mader for it nedith none oþ⁹ saue the entrete and that is the pfite makynge

873 ffor the schyngles which is an euell þat will sprynge owt of a man as it were fyre but it is grett⁀ and redd⁀ and it will sprynge eů⁀ a raw and iff begird a man happely he

---

¹ See the similar preparations in H. and in Sloane 2584 (Henslow, op. cit., pp. 55, 126).   " Save " is mentioned by Chaucer in The Knightes Tale, line 1855.
² Woodruff.   See note to § 654.

871 To make a man to sweat. Take dry cumin and beat it to powder, and mingle it with oil and anoint well under the feet, and wrap him up warmly. And nettle seed in oil doth the same.

872 To make save.[1] Take burnet, drauk (darnel), tormentil, maidenhair, bugle, pigle, sanicle, herb-John, herb-Robert, herb-Walter,[2] the great confond that is comfrey, the little confond that is daisy, hemp-crop, red cabbage-crop, the red briar-crop, madder, culverfoot (dove's-foot cranesbill), sowthistle, groundsel, violet, wild teazle, mugwort, agrimony, woodbine, ribwort, mouse-ear, mouse-foot (pea), flowers of broom, dittany, vervain, crops of white-thorn, southernwood, sage, the crop of the red nettle, osmund (fern), cinqfoil, scabious, strawberry-shoots, pimpernel, solsicle, and as much of avens as of all the other herbs, and of the other herbs, even portions. And [they] shall be gathered in May before St. John's day.[3] And bray them in a mortar, and mingle them with may-butter fresh and clean made, as the milk cometh from the cow. And if thou hast no may-butter, take other butter, purge it clean and let it cool, and mingle it in a vessel, and cover it six days or seven till it begin to thicken, and afterwards fry it in a pan, and cleanse it through a cloth, and let it stand in a vessel till it be cold ; and then cut it up, and let the sediment go out, and then put it over the fire, and clear it, and let it cool, and put it in boxes. And the wounded man shall drink thereof with ale as much at once as a barley-corn, first and last each day till he be whole. And cover the wound with a leaf of red cabbage. And if thou mayest not find all those herbs, take thirty-two of the first, and the avens availeth as much as all the other herbs, with madder, for it needeth none other, save the entrete. And that is the perfect [manner of] making.

873 For the shingles which is an evil that will spring out of a man as it were fire,[4] but it is greater and redder. And it will spring a-row,[5] and if it begird a man, haply he shall

---

[3] St. John the Evangelist, 6th May.
[4] *I.e.*, St. Anthony's fire, or erysipelas.
[5] In a row, or a straight line.

shall neũ be hole ther fore tak calid dunge and barly mele
and stamp hem togedir ꝛ tēp hem wᵗ aysell ꝛ do þᵒto tyll
he be hole and the juys of mynt doth þᵉ same

874 ffor stoppynge of the splene giff hym þᵉ poudre of
coost wᵗ þᵉ juyse [fo. 76 *recto*] wormod

875 ffor stoppynge of the lyũ of the splene ꝛ of þᵉ reyns
ꝛ for strangury and dissure and illica passio ꝛ for ach of
the stomak þat cōmyth of wynd vse the wyne that the
seede of cokkell is soden jnne and ete þᵉ poudre with oþᵒ
metis

876 Anoþᵒ for the same Drynk þᵉ wyne þat þᵉ seede of
hony souk is soke is soden in (*sic*) for it makyth good
digestione and wastith wyndis and opynneth þᵉ stoppynge
of the splene and of the reyns and of the bleddyre and if
the seede be soden with flesshe it makyth þᵉ broth haue
gode sauó and to smell soote

877 To make a serid cloth take iiij pound of swyns grese
clene molten and when it is hote do þerto iij quartrons of
clene rosen rosen (*sic*) and when it is molten do þᵒto iij
quartrons of ȝelow wex small mynsed and when it is molten
sett it fro the fire and put þᵒto a quartron of turpentyn and
staire it wele till it be almost cold then take the glayre of
xij egges wele swongen togedir stirryng it littell and littell
till it be cold and when this oyntment shall be vsid tak a
faire lynnen clothe of flex and melt this oyntment and ther
in wete thi cloth and all hote lay it on the brusure in
wynᵗ ꝛ in somͅ cold till þᵘ be hole

878 Anoþr serid cloth for the gout and for ach þᵗ cōmyth
of cold   Tak a gum þᵗ is clepid golsony a pound and as moch
of rosyn wex halue a pound and halue a pound of shepis
talwȝ a q̊rtron of encens and iij sponeful of tarre then first
take þᵉ golsony and rosyn and thi tarre ꝛ meet hem togedͅ
in a panne and then kest it in a vessell [fo. 76 *verso*] wᵗ
watir and then melt it agayn and kest þᵒto shepis taluȝ in
thi wex and mak poudir of thyn encens and as [it] frieth
throw it þer in strawyng it and stire it fast and than throw

never be whole.[1] Therefore take pigeon's dung and barley-meal, and stamp them together, and temper them with vinegar, and put it thereto till he be whole. And the juice of mint doth the same.

874 For stopping of the spleen. Give him the powder of cost[2] with the juice of wormwood.

875 For stopping of the liver, of the spleen, and of the reins, and for strangury and dysuria, and iliac passion, and for ache of the stomach that cometh of wind. Use the wine that the seed of cockle (ergot) is boiled in, and eat the powder with other meats.

876 Another for the same. Drink the wine that the seed of honeysuckle is sodden in, for it maketh good digestion, and wasteth (disperseth) winds, and openeth the stopping of the spleen and of the reins, and of the bladder. And if the seed be seethed with flesh, it maketh the breath have good savour and to smell sweet.

877 To make a cerecloth. Take four pounds of swine's grease clean melted, and when it is hot put thereto three quarterns of clean rosin ; and when it is melted, put thereto three quarterns of yellow wax small minced ; and when it is melted, take it from the fire, and put thereto a quartern of turpentine ; and stir it well till it be almost cold. Then take the white of twelve eggs, well beaten together, stirring it little by little till it be cold. And when this ointment shall be used, take a fair linen cloth of flax, and melt this ointment, and therein wet the cloth. And, all hot, lay it on the bruise in winter and in summer till thou be whole.

878 Another cerecloth for the gout, and for ache that cometh of cold. Take a gum that is called golsony (galbanum) a pound, and as much of rosin, wax half a pound, and half a pound of sheep's tallow, and a quartern of incense, and three spoonfuls of tar. Then take first the golsony and rosin and tar, and melt them together in a pan, and cast it into a vessel of water ; and then melt it again, and cast thereto [the] sheep's tallow in thy wax ; and make powder of thy incense, and as [it] fryeth, throw it therein [by]

---

[1] *Shingles* is derived from the O.F. *cengle*, " a girdle," because the eruption, *herpes zoster*, often spreads till it completely encircles the body.

[2] *See* note to § 761.

it in watir and wesshe it vp and mak it togedir os gobet of
wex and when þou wilt ocupie it melt it in a panne and put
thi cloth þ⁹in and thorow wete it and hete it agayn the
fyre and lay it þ⁹ it akyth

879 To hele a sore schynne   Take osmund bugle planteyn
and betayn riȝt small stampid ꝛ medle þ⁹with bene mele
hony and oyle and boyle heme wele togedir and vse þ⁹of
till he be hole

880 ffor the sifrak   Tak þe seede of stanmarch at mydsom̅¹
a gode porcion of auence and erb yve ꝛ som smalach and þe
myddyll bark of eldyr tre of oo ȝere spryngynge and let
this be dryed in the sonne and be made in to poudre and
of this poudre vse first and last nat etynge ne drynkyng aftere
þe space of an oure and vse it also in potage and make
juyse of smalach and wasshe the place and wete a cloute
þer in and lay þ⁹to and thou shalt be hoole

881 ffor a man þᵗ is smyten on the hede and þe hedde to
swoll   Take a sowkynge whelpe and clene it and lay it to
the hedd a nyȝt and that will draw owt þe bolnynge and make
the wound clere to the leche

882 ffor a sore þat is bolnyd and nat open ne roued breke
egges ꝛ put all in a disshe but þe shelles and put þ⁹to ij
sponefull of clene flour and ij sponefull of teere of hony
[fo. 77 recto] ꝛ ij sponefull of mete oyle and swynge altogedir
with a spone ꝛ enoynt the sore þ⁹wᵗ when þᵘ gost to bed
bynd it wᵗ a lynnen cloth and do it away on þe morow ꝛ
lay nw þ⁹to and wasshe þe cloth fro filth þat it hath draw
out byfore and do so eu)y day at morow ꝛ at eue till
thow be hole and this will distroy kankre felon or poyson
or venym pᵬ est

883 ffor styngynge of an eddir stamp planteyn and make a
pleistre and lay þ⁹to and it shall be hole

---

¹ Perhaps corrupted from σύμφραξις " obstruction."

sprinkling it ; and stir it fast, and then throw it in water, and work it up, and make it together as a gobbet of wax. And when thou wilt use it, melt it in a pan, and put thy cloth therein, and thoroughly wet it.   And heat it by the fire, and lay it [on] where it acheth.

879 To heal a sore shin.   Take osmund (fern), bugle, plantain and betony, right small stamped, and mingle therewith bean-meal, honey and oil ; and boil them well together, and use thereof till he be whole.

880 For the sifrak.[1]   Take the seed of stanmarch at mid-summer, a good portion of avens, and ground-ivy,[2] and some smallage, and the middle bark of [an] elder-tree of eight years growth.   And let this be dried in the sun and made into powder ; and of this powder use first and last, not eating nor drinking after [for] the space of an hour, and use it also in pottage.   And make juice of smallage and wash the place, and wet a cloth therein, and lay it thereto, and thou shalt be whole.

881 For a man that is smitten on the head, and the head [thus made] to swell.   Take a sucking-whelp, and cleave it [open], and lay it to the head for a night, and that will draw out the swelling and make the wound clean for the leech (*i.e.* for treatment).

882 For a sore that is swollen and not open nor reddened (inflamed).   Break eggs and put all but the shells in a dish ; and put thereto two spoonfuls of clean flour and two spoonfuls of tar [and] of honey and two spoonfuls of mete-oil ;[3] and stir all together with a spoon, and anoint the sore therewith.   When thou goest to bed, bind it with a linen cloth, and take it away on the morrow, and lay [a] new [one] thereto ; and wash the cloth from the filth it hath drawn out before.   And do so every day at morn and at eve, till thou be whole, and this will destroy the canker [or] felon or poison or venom.   *Probatum est.*

883 For stinging of an adder.   Stamp plantain and make a plaster, and lay thereto, and it shall be whole.

---

[2] The text has *erb yve*, an error for *erþ yve*, " earth-ivy."
[3] Measured oil, or refined oil.

884 Also the juyse of smerwort will hele the bytynge of venymo⁹ bestis iff it be dronken with wyne and also distroy venym that man hath eten and dronken

885 ffor þe strangulū   Take iiij hedis of seynt mary garlyk and radish as moch of the rotis ⁊ grynd hem small and put it ī a grete disshe and take ij sponefull of vynegre and halue a pynt of white wyne in the quantite of ale and seth hem toged⁊ and kest in to the garlyk and radisshe a saucerfull of hony ⁊ put to þe floure of whete and put it togedir and take a styk and clene it and put a cloþe in the end ⁊ tak ech morow and each eue and put it þ⁹in ⁊ put it on his tunge

886 ffor strokes þat ar blo ⁊ nat brokyn   Take þe juyse of wormode hony and medwex and barowȝ grese and poudre of comyn of ech lich moch by wight and lat fry hem all togedir and make a pleistre and lay to the sore and that shall haue away the blaknes

887 ffor sore about amannys hert or vnd⁊ his syde   Take a spice þat men call saundresse ⁊ mak to poudre [fo. 77 *verso*] and tak an obley and lay it in wyne ot in ale Till it be thorow moyst and tak of the foreseid poudre when þᵘ haste layd the obley on a day trenchoure as moch as will be lappid þ⁹in and put it in the sykkys mowth and lat him swalo it down all hole

888 Anoþ⁹ for hym þᵗ hath grete sorowes in his sides   Tak hilwort that is clepid piliall mounteyn ⁊ alisaundre psely louach rede fenell burnet gromell añ and seth hem in white wyne till the halue be wastid and þan streyn it and lat þe syk drynk þ⁹of first and last at euen hote at morow cold till he be hole

889 A gode salue to a wound tak ȝeltis grese hony oyle of nottis ⁊ do þ⁹to oyle of chesboll knappis grene with all the juyse and the sede and juyse of ruw and waybrede and seth wele al þies Jusys togedir ⁊ mak þi salue wele þ⁹of ⁊ do it in boxis

---

¹ By ale-measure, or else read " and a quantity," etc.

² Usually ultramarine (carbonate of copper), but here more probably sandalwood is meant, as the copper-salt is poisonous. It

884 [Another]. Also the juice of smearwort will heal the biting of venomous beasts if it be drunken with wine : and also destroy venom that a man hath eaten or drunken.

885 For the strangulum (choking). Take four heads of Saint-Mary (costmary), garlic and radish as much of the roots, and grind them small ; and put it in a great dish, and take two spoonfuls of vinegar, and half a pint of white wine in the quantity of ale,[1] and seethe them together. And cast into the garlic and radish a saucerful of honey, and put [it] to the flour of wheat, and put it [all] together. And take a stick and clean it, and put a cloth on the end [of the stick], and take each morn and each eve and put (dip) it therein, and put it on his tongue.

886 For strokes (blows) that are blue and not broken. Take the juice of wormwood, honey, and prepared wax, and barrow's grease, and powder of cumin, of each equally much by weight. And let them fry all together, and make a plaster and lay to the sore. And that shall take away the blackness.

887 For sore about a man's heart and under his side. Take a spice that men call saunders[2] and make to powder, and take an obley (wafer) and lay it in wine or in ale till it be thoroughly moist. And take of the aforesaid powder, when thou hast laid the obley on a dry trencher, as much as will be lapped therein (absorbed thereby), and put it in the sick man's mouth, and let him swallow it down whole.

888 Another for him that hath great sorrows (soreness) in his sides. Take hillwort that is called piliole-monteyn (wild thyme), and alexanders, parsely, lovage, red fennel, burnet, gromwell, equal parts ; and seethe them in white wine till half be wasted, and then strain it ; and let the sick drink thereof first and last, at even hot at morn cold, till he be whole.

889 A good salve for a wound. Take gelt's grease, honey, oil of nuts ; and put thereto oil of green buds of chess-apple[3] with all the juice and the seed, and juice of rue and way-bread ; and seethe well all these juices together, and make thy salve well thereof, and put it in boxes.

---

may, however, be a corruption of " alexanders," a well-known herb.
    [3] *Pyrus aria.*

890 ffor the Scores   Tak a quyk haare ꝭ hete hote an oven hett̃ þen þan (sic) for to make brede and put þe hare in the oven all whyk and stopp fast the ouen and lat hym bake alday and all ny3t and þen draw forth the hare and all hote stamp hym to poudre and ete and drynk þ⁹of first and last

891 To mak a suppositorye tak purid hony and salt it and boyl it wele and then take fresshe grese in a disshe and enbawm all the dysshe þ⁹with and then take a drop on the disshe and iff it wax hard then it is enough and þan make round wekys as a mannes littel fyng⁹ sharp at on end and temp it in the hony and a threde [fo. 78 recto] on the grete end ꝭ put in the fundement vp all in ꝭ let þe threde hange with oute and he shall haue a segge sone ⸲—

892 ffore sore pyntell chaufed   Tak þe juyse of morell brusid lynsede and barow3 grese and boyle togedir and lay þ⁹on hote

893 Sirup of antioche   Take an handfull of dayse3e and an handfull of bugle and an handfull of rede cole of strawbery withis of sanyele hemp auence tansay erb roƀt mad'[1] of ech an handfull of comfery iiij braunches or orpyn vj tendrons of rede brere vj croppis of nettils put al thies in a galon off wyne v⁹nage or oþ⁹ gode wyne and let heme seth to a potel and than put þ⁹to as moch of clarified hony as þ~ gessyst þe juys cōmyth to ꝭ medle hem wele togedir and boyle it and eft skymme it and boyle it but a littell and kepe itt wele for it is full p⁹ciose and in this man͡ shall it be vsid to iij sponefull of syirip vj sponefull of watir and first ꝭ last vse it for all yuellis in the body ⸲⁄

894 TO mak termentyne · Tak rosen ꝭ melt it and than tak oyle and held it þ⁹to littill and littill and Stire it wele till it wex thyk and then set it down and kepe it as the thynke gode

---

[1] Cf. § 819.
[2] See note on § 746.
[3] Young shoots are here meant, not the organs of a climbing plant.

890 For the scores (scurvy).   Take a live hare,[1] and heat
an oven hot, hotter than for making bread, and put the
hare in the oven all alive.   And close the oven fast and let
him bake all day and all night.   And then draw forth the
hare, and all hot stamp it to powder, and eat and drink
thereof first and last.

891 To make a suppository.   Take purified honey and salt
it, and boil it well ; and then take fresh grease in a dish, and
embalm all the dish therewith ; and then take a drop on the
dish, and if it wax hard, then it is [boiled] enough.   And
then make round wicks as [big] as a man's little finger, sharp
(tapering) at one end, and temper it in the honey.   And [tie]
a thread on the great end, and put it well up into the fundament, and let the thread hang out, and he shall have a
motion soon.

892 For a sore privy member that is chafed (excoricated).
Take the juice of morell (nightshade), bruised linseed, and
barrow's grease ; and boil together, and lay thereon hot.

893 Syrup of Antioch.[2]   Take a handful of daisies, and a
handful of bugle and a handful of red cabbage, of strawberry-
shoots (runners), of sanicle, hemp, avens, tansey, herb-
Robert, madder, of each a handful, of comfrey four branches
or orpine, six tendrils[3] of red briar, six crops of nettles ;
put all these in a gallon of wine-vernage[4] or other good
wine, and let them seethe to a pottle (two quarts).   And
then put thereto as much of clarified honey as thou guessest
the juice cometh to, and mingle them well together, and boil
it, and again skim it, and boil it but a little.   And keep it
well for it is full precious and in this manner shall it be used.
To three spoonfuls of syrup [put] six spoonfuls of water,
and [drink it] first and last.   Use it for all evils of the body.

894 To make turpentine.[5]   Take rosin and melt it, and
then take oil and add it thereto little by little ;
and stir it well till it wax thick, and then set it down, and
keep it as thou thinkest good.

---

[4] *Vernaccia,* an Italian wine.
[5] *Termentyne* is the usual form of *tormentil,* a herb.   Turpentine
was a compound made of various resinous and oily substances, not
the fluid that is expressed by the present-day use of the word.

895 Anoþ⁹ turpentine þat is bettir   Tak a quartron of
clene rosyn and a quartron of prosyn ꝫ halue a pound of
oyle of olyue that is gode and grene if thou may fynd such
and temp the rosen and the prosen togedir made in poudre
ꝫ put the oyle with thies poudres and medle hē wele togedir
in a panne ꝫ set it in a charcole fire þᵗ is easye [fo. 78 verso]
and let it seth softly ꝫ also sone as the poudres bene molten
and wele medled with the oyle take it down and lat it kele
till þᵉ grete hete be oulpassid ꝫ þen wrynge it thorow a
cloth and kep it in a box

896 fforto make turmentyne for flees   Tak a pound of
rosen þat is purid and halue a pound of gode oyle of olyue
and powdre of rosen ꝫ put the rosen in a panne oul þᵉ fire
ꝫ melt þᵉ rosen or þʷ put in the oyle and seþe it a littell for
if it seth moch it is þᵉ wors

897 Anoþ⁹ maň of turpentyn   Take rosen poudred ꝫ put
a littell oyle þ⁹to and medle hem togedir and put hem in a
brasen panne oul the fire and melt the rosen or þʷ put in
the oyle and then put in and seth it a littell with a littell
swyns grese put þ⁹to and stire it till it be molten ꝫ þen
streyn it thorow a cloth ꝫ kepe it in som clene vessell

898 ffor wymmen tetis þat bene swollen take lynesede and
þᵉ white of an egge oþ⁹ þᵉ juyse of smalach and lay þ⁹to
ꝫ iff she lese hir mylk giff hir to drynk þᵉ juys of verueyn
ꝫ she shall haue enough

899 ffor tetys þat akyn   Tak mynt and wyne ꝫ oyle of
olyue and seþe togedir ꝫ bynd to þᵗ tetys and it shall do
away þᵉ akynge

900 ffor ranklyng tetys · þᵗ cōmyth of to moch mylk make
poudre of hempsede and gif it hir in all hir metis and
drynkys

901 ffor to make tetis small stamp þᵉ sede of hembloke
with vynegre and þ⁹ with enoynt hem oft

902 Anoþ⁹ medle þᵉ poudre off [fo. 79 recto] encens wᵗ
vynegre and enoynt hem þ⁹ with ꝫ þei shall wax small

903 ffor the cankre in the tetis   Tak goose dunge and
juyse of celidoyne ꝫ stamp hem and lay on the sore tete
and it shall sle þᵉ cankyr and hele it

895 Another turpentine that is better. Take a quartern of clean rosin and a quartern of perosin, and half a pound of oil of olive that is good and green, if thou mayest find such ; and temper the rosin and the perosin together made into powder, and put the oil with these powders, and mingle them well together in a pan, and set it on a charcoal fire that is easy. And let it seethe softly, and as soon as the powders be melted and well mingled with the oil, take it down, and let it cool, till the great heat be overpast. And then wring it through a cloth, and keep it in a box.

896 To make turpentine for fleas. Take a pound of rosin that is purified, and half a pound of good oil of olive and powder the rosin ; and put the rosin in a pan over the fire, and melt the rosin before thou puttest in the oil. And seethe it a little, for if it seethe much it is the worse.

897 Another manner of turpentine. Take rosin powdered, and put a little oil thereto, and mingle them together ; and put them in a brazen pan over the fire, and melt the rosin before thou puttest in the oil. And then put in [the oil] and seethe it a little with a little swine's grease put thereto. And stir it till it be melted, and then strain it through a cloth, and keep it in some clean vessel.

898 For women's teats that be swollen. Take linseed and the white of an egg or else the juice of smallage, and lay thereto. And if she lose her milk, give her to drink the juice of vervain, and she shall have enough.

899 For teats that ache. Take mint and wine, and oil of olive, and seethe together ; and bind to thy teats, and it shall do away the aching.

900 For rankling teats that come of too much milk. Make powder of hempseed and give it her in all her meats and drinks.

901 To make teats small. Stamp the seed of hemlock with vinegar, and therewith anoint them oft.

902 Another. Mingle the powder of incense with vinegar, and anoint them therewith, and they shall become small.

903 For the canker in the teats. Take goose-dung and juice of celandine, and stamp them, and lay on the sore teat ; and it shall slay the canker, and heal it.

904 Anoþᵒ for the same   Tak dowkes dunge hony wyrgyn wex floure of barly ꝫ of benes and lynesede and seth heme in vynegre or wyne and put þᵒto rammes talwӡ and make in man͡ of a pleistre and lay þᵒon and it will sle the cankyre in tetis

905 A pouder to confirme teth that bene lose   Tak white corall and rede corall of ech an vnce poudre hem and lay this poudre on thi teth þat bene loose and it festynneth hem anoon

906 ffor toth ach þᵉ galles þat men make ynk wᵗ qwich haue none holes and alym and leves of sauge made in to poudir and than kest þᵒto mustard and vynegre and temp hem togedir than in a fryynge panne chaufe heme all toged͡ and lay it in a clene cloute and as hote as you may suffre lay it bytwix the toth and the cheke

907 ffor to clence and make hem white   Take þᵉ rote of malews ꝫ rub thi teth and thi gūmes þᵒwith ꝫ after þat tak a greyned cloth and rub thi teth þᵒwith   Jff thou wasshe thi mouth onys in the monyth with watir or with wyne þt titemall þᵗ spurge is soden in the teth shull neu͡ fall ꝑsepire gnoddid and layd to the teth is a gode medecyne

908 ffor teth þat bene ӡelow or blak to mak white [fo. 79 *verso*]   Tak ry mele and salt ꝫ hony by euen porcion and medle heme wele togedir and þᵒ with rub wele thi teth ij or iij on a day and after wasshe hem wele with waᵗ and it shall do away þᵉ blaknesse ꝑƀ

909 Anothir for ӡelow teth roten ꝫ stynkynge   Take sauge and stamp it in a morᵗ and put þᵒto as moch salt and mak littell pasties and put hem into an oven till þei be blak and brent and with þᵗ rub wele thi teth and it shall do away the corrupcion and make faire teth and gode

910 ffor heth þᵗ worms beth in   Take cokkell floure and temp it with hony and with vynegre and lay to the toth and it sleith the worms in [*sic*] a game þat is clepid asa-

904 Another for the same. Take duck's dung, honey, virgin wax, flour of barley and of beans, and linseed, and stamp them in vinegar or wine ; and put thereto ram's tallow, and make in the manner of a plaster, and lay thereon. And it will slay the canker in [the] teats.

905 A powder to confirm (fix) teeth that be loose. Take white coral and red coral, of each an ounce ; powder them and lay this powder on thy teeth that be loose, and it fasteneth them anon.

906 For toothache. The galls that men make ink with which have no holes, and alum, and leaves of sage, made into powder ; and then cast thereto mustard and vinegar, and temper them together. Then in a frying-pan chafe them all together, and lay it on a clean cloth, and as hot as you may suffer, lay it between the tooth and the cheek.

907 To cleanse [teeth] and make them white. Take the root of mallows and rub thy teeth and thy gums therewith. And after that take a rough cloth, and rub thy teeth therewith. If thou washest thy mouth once a month with water or with wine that titemall, that is spurge, is seethed in, the teeth shall never fall. Knotgrass kneaded and laid to the teeth is a good medicine.

908 For teeth that be yellow or black, to make [them] white. Take rye-meal, and salt, and honey, by even portions ; and mingle them well together, and therewith rub well thy teeth twice or thrice a day ; and afterwards wash them well with water, and it shall do away the blackness. *Probatum* [*est*].

909 Another for yellow teeth, rotten and stinking. Take sage and stamp it in a mortar, and put thereto as much salt, and make little pastilles, and put them into an oven till they be black and burnt. And with that rub well thy teeth, and it shall do away the corruption and make them fair teeth and good.

910 For teeth that worms be in.[1] Take cockle (ergot) flower and temper it with honey and with vinegar, and lay to the tooth, and it slayeth the worms. And a gum that is

---

[1] The belief that dental disease is due to worms is very ancient. *See* my *Magician and Leech*, p. 147.

fetida doth þe same iff the hole of the toth be stopped full

911 Anoþ⁹ take poudre of longe fengete and longe pep and lay it oft to þe soore toth//

912 Anoþ⁹ take the sede of henbane and leke sede and encens by euen porcion and lay hem on an hote glowynge tile stone and loke thow haue a pipe of laton that the neþ⁹ end be so brode þat it may keu⸿ all the sede and poudre and than open thi mowth that þe smoke may come to þe toth and do away the akynge þis is p⁹vyde

913 To make the teth of children to grow hastely seith hares brayn and enoynt ther with the gumes

914 An oþ⁹ for the same   Take the brayn of an henne and run þe gumes þ⁹with ⁊ it sal mak hem togrow wᵗ owt any sorow or diseases or akynge

915 Anothir ffor Wormes in the teth   Tak þe poudre [fo. 80 recto] of peletre and temp it with hony and mak a littell ball ⁊ put in the toth and it shall sle the worms and sothernwod sethen in vynegre will do the same

916 ffor bulis on womans tetis   Tak the Juyse of morell with oyl of an egge and bene mele ⁊ mak a pleystre þ⁹of and lay it all cold to the sore

917 Anoþ⁹ for akyng of tetis   Tak myntis and stamp hem and lay hem þ⁹to in man⸿ of a pleistre all hote

918 ffor toth ach a fyne medecyn   Take longe pep peletre of spayn notgall stanesacre and seþe hem in wyneacre fro a quart in to a pint and put þ⁹in a pot of triakyll of a peny and then tak drestis of ale in a viall ⁊ þen take onys a weke and fresshe thi gommes þ⁹with

919 ffor trembelynge hand and handis a slepe Take lauandre and p⁹merose and seth hem in alle and drynk it

920 Anoþ⁹ Tak leues of loueach and seth in watir of a well and wasshe thyn handis when thou gost to bedd as hote as thou may suffre//

called asafetida doth the same, if the hole in the tooth be stopped full [of it].

911 Another. Take the powder of long fenugreek and long pepper, and lay it oft to the sore tooth.

912 Another.[1] Take the seed of henbane, and leed-seed, and incense, by even portions, and lay them on a hot glowing tile-stone. And look thou have a pipe of latten of which the nether end be so broad that it cover all the seed and powder. And then open thy mouth, that the smoke may come to the tooth [through the pipe], and do away the aching. *This is proved.*

913 To make teeth of children grow hastily (quickly). Seethe hare's brain, and anoint therewith the gums.

914 Another for the same. Take the brain of a hen, and rub the gums therewith. And it shall make them grow without any sorrow or diseases or aching.

915 Another for worms in the teeth. Take the powder of pellitory and temper it with honey, and make a little ball and put in the tooth, and it shall slay the worms. And southernwood seethed in vinegar will do the same.

916 For boils on women's teats. Take the juice of morell, with oil of an egg, and bean-meal ; and make a plaster thereof, and lay it all cold to the sore.

917 Another for aching teats. Take mint and stamp it, and lay thereto in the manner of a plaster, all hot.

918 For toothache, a fine medicine. Take long pepper, pellitory of Spain, nutgalls, lichen, and seethe them in vinegar from a quart to a pint ; and put therein a pot of treacle of a penny[worth], and then take dregs of ale in a vial. And then take [it] once a week, and refresh thy gums therewith.

919 For trembling hands, and hands asleep. Take lavender and primrose, and seethe them in ale, and drink it.

920 Another. Take leaves of lovage and seethe in wellwater, and wash thy hands when thou goest to bed, as hot as thou mayest suffer.

---

[1] Duplicates of this remedy are numerous, *e.g.*, H. ; ·*Harl.* 2378 (three times) ; *Sloane* 521 ; (Henslow, *op. cit.*, pp. 8, 95, 111, 112, 139) ; D., § 9 ; and *cf.* above, § 33.

921 ffor yuell at þe hert þitt a way þe talent of mete   Take
centory and seth it wele in stale ale and wrynge it thorow
a cloth and tak ij pties þ⁹of and the thrid of hony˙ that is
soden and skommed and lat thies ij seth togedir that thei
be all harde and do it in a box and lat the syk ete itt and
he shall haue talent to mete and void the glet fro the hert

922 Anoþ⁹ To make a man haue good appetite make
sawes of mynt and vynegre and kest þ⁹to a littel poudre
of comyn and pep and wasshe thi mowth wᵗ vynegre and wᵗ
waꝼ þat mynt hat bene soden Jnne And þe (sic) [fo. 80
verso] shal do away stynkynge of the mouth that cõmyth
of rotenes of þe gomes

923 A gode sauce to make a man to mak a man (sic) to
haue to haue (sic) talent to mete is made of pep and of
sauge and mynt ꞃ pselye ꞃ crõmes of brede rostid ꞃ syth
tempid with vynegre

924 ffor tesik or defaute of wynd and oþ⁹ syknes tak
elenacampana the rote and þe hert m j and dry it and
payre it and kyt it small and put it in vynegre till it be
soft and then dry itt and tak pured hony and kest both in
a chaufere and buyle heme togedir and put it in a box

925 ffor teters scabbes or cankres take pympnell rede
nettill croppis and blak sope ꞃ sulphur viuū and mak an
oyntment ꞃ put oũ þe fire and enoynt þe soore

926 ffor tremblynge hand that is a spice of þe palasy seþe
sauge wele and wasshe thyn hand oft wele in that watir

927 ffor tynglynge in a mannys ere Take þe juyse of
sothernwodd and do it in the ere and stopp the ere with
leves of the same erb and drynk þe juyse at euen ꞃ at
morow and it shall hele þe tynglynge and the juys of wormod
doth the same

928 Anoþ⁹ for tynglynge and defnes of eres Take anneys
fenell seede and bayes of lorer by euen porcions and seth
hem in wyn and put in to the ere ꞃ it sal be hole fro þat
siknes

929 To make entrete for cankres festers for bocches and
for old soores and nw Tak a pound of med wex and a pound
of barowȝ grese molten and purid and Ꝉj j of frankencens

921 For evil at the heart that [taketh] away the talent (appetite) for meat. Take centaury and seethe it well in stale ale, and wring it through a cloth ; and take two parts thereof, and the third of honey that is boiled and skimmed. And let these two seethe together till they be all hard ; and put it in a box, and let the sick eat it, and he shall have talent (appetite) to meat, and void the gleet from the heart.

922 Another, to make a man have good appetite. Make sauce of mint and vinegar, and cast thereto a little powder of cumin and pepper. And wash thy mouth with vinegar and with water that mint hath been boiled in. And it shall do away stinking of the mouth that cometh of rottenness of the gums.

923 [Another]. A good sauce to make a man have talent (appetite) to meat is made of pepper, and of sage and mint and parsley, and crumbs of bread, roasted, and then tempered with vinegar.

924 For phthisis or default of wind, and other sicknesses. Take elecampane, the root and the heart, one handful, and dry it and pare it, and cut it small and put it in vinegar till it be soft. And then dry it, and take purified honey and cast both in a chafing-dish, and boil them together, and put it in a box.

925 For tetters, scabs or cankers. Take pimpernel, red nettle crops, and black soap ; and sulphur vivum, and make an ointment ; and put over the fire, and anoint the sore.

926 For trembling hand that is a species of palsy. Seethe sage well and wash thy hand oft well in that water.

927 For tingling in a man's ear. Take the juice of southern-wood, and put it in the ear ; and stop the ear with leaves of the same herb, and drink the juice at even and at morn, and it shall heal the tingling. And the juice of wormwood doth the same.

928 Another for tingling and deafness of ears. Take anise, fennel-seed and bays of laurel, by even portions, and seethe them in wine ; and put into the ear, and it shall be whole from that sickness.

929 To make an entrete for cankers, festers, for botches and for old sores and new. Take a pound of prepared wax, and a pound of barrow's grease melted and purified, and a pound

˥ ℈ j of maskyk ˥ l̄j ℔ of [fo. 81 *recto*] prosyn and l̄j ℔ of
spanynyshe code and l̄i of stone pich ˥ iiij of verdegrasse
and take all thies thynges and breke heme small and set
hem oũ þe fyre in a panne and mele hem to gedir and when
thei bene molten then poudre þe verdegrasse and do it in
þ⁹to and algat stire it fast for clevynge to the panne and
then take it down and lat it kele till þᵘ mayst streyne it
˥ when thou streynyst it lat wete thi panne botome þat it
shall jnne with watir for it will lose þe botre when it is colde
and with a fethir scome away the fome aboue

930 To make a trete of erbis Tak a pound of betayn
an oþ⁹ of verueyn an oþ⁹ of egremoyn an oþer of
pympnoll an oþ⁹ of bugle an oþ⁹ of erbe watir an
oþ⁹ of ribwort of daysyen þⁱ men clepe breswort an
oþ⁹ of ȝarow an oþ⁹ of erb robt and wasshe hem clene
and do hem in an new erthen pot and do þ⁹to a galon
of white wyne and lat hem stand so all anyȝt and on
the morow set the pot oũ þe fyre and make it forto seth
and take a pound of medwex and breke it on small pecis
and kest in to the pot and take halue a pound of frankencens
an oþ⁹ of prosyn togedir in a brasen mort and kest þ⁹to a
pound of shepis talwȝ and halfe a pound of bores grese and
do it in to a pot and algate stire it fast with a sklyce and let
hem seth as thou woldist seth a pece of befe and than tak
down the pot and lat the grete hete oũgoo till thou may
streyn it and then thou hast streynd it lat it stand till a
morow and than do away [fo. 81 *verso*] the sounders vnd⁀-
neþe and take a fayre panne and do it jnne and take a pound
of spanysshe code and breke it small and do þ⁹to vj peny
wiȝth of verdegrasse and streyne hem and than do hem in
to the panne to þe od⁀ thynges and than set hem oũ the
fire and let hem melt togedir and when thei be wele molten
take hem doun and do away the skome with a feþ⁹ and lat
it stand till it be cold and þis is a gode trete

931 Anoþ⁹ gode trete Take iij quartrons of spanysshe
code or of clene rosen and a quartron of prosyn halue a
pound of medwex ℈ of mastyk ℈ of galbanū ℈ of encens
℈ ℔ of sangdragon small powdred ℈ ℔ of lufe hony iij ℈ of

of frankincense, one ounce of mastic, and half a pound of perosin, and half a pound of Spanish code (cobbler's wax), and a pound of stone pitch, and four [ounces] of verdigris. And take all these things and break them small, and set them over the fire in a pan, and melt them together. And when they be melted, then powder the verdigris, and put in thereto, and always stir it fast for [to prevent it from] cleaving to the pan. And then take it down and let it cool till thou mayest strain it. And when thou strainest it, let thy pan-bottom be wetted with water that it [go] in [to the strainer] with water, for it will lose the butter when it is cold, and with a feather, skim away the foam above.

930 To make an entrete of herbs. Take a pound of betony, another of vervain, another of agrimony, another of pimpernel, another of bugle, another of herb-Walter, another of ribwort, [another] of daisies that men call bruise-wort, another of yarrow, another of herb-Robert ; and wash them clean, and put them in a new earthen[ware] pot, and put thereto a gallon of white wine. And let them stand so all one night, and on the morrow set the pot over the fire, and make it to seethe And take a pound of prepared wax and break it in small pieces, and cast it into the pot. And take half a pound of frankincense, [and] another of perosin, together in a brazen mortar ; and cast thereto a pound of sheep's tallow and half a pound of boar's grease, and always stir it fast with a slice. And let them seethe as thou wouldst seethe a piece of beef, and then take down the pot, and let the great heat pass off till thou mayest strain it. And when thou hast strained it, let it stand till the morrow, and then take away the cinders underneath, and take a fair pan and put it therein. And take a pound of Spanish code and break it small, and put thereto six pennyweight of verdigris, and strain them. And then put them into the pan with the other things and then set them over the fire, and let them melt together. And when they be well melted, take them down, and brush away the scum with a feather, and let it stand till it be cold. And this is a good entrete.

931 Another good entrete. Take three quartrons of Spanish code (cobbler's wax) or of clean rosin, and a quartern of perosin, half a pound of prepared wax, an ounce of mastic, an ounce of galbanum, an ounce of incense, half an ounce of dragon's blood small powdered, half an ounce of loaf honey,

bores grese halue a quartrone of an vnce of verdegresse
small poudred and lat fry hem all to gedir till þei be relentid
and wele medelede and streyne hem and do þ⁹to a pound
of turmentyne that is all redy purid and lat do hem in to
the fire agayn till þei be relentid wele togedir and eu͡r stire
it wele wᵗ a slyce and pour it in to thi box.

932 VEnymynge of a sore shall thus be helid.   Tak
lauandre and gowldes syngrene and betayn and
stamp hem toged͡r and lay hem to the soore

933 ffor veyns kyt of blode lattynge seth ryw in watir and
enoynt þ⁹with the arme and in the same watere seth lambes
woll and lay to the arme and to the veynes ꝫ þei shull hele

934 fforto make vynegre   Take a quantitee of bene floure
and knede it with vynegre and bak it and twies or iij take
it out of the oven and enoynt it wele wᵗ vynegre till it haue
wele dronken and put it in a gayn and it shall turne [fo. 82
recto] in to vynegre and so in the same man͡r mak aysell or
alcegre

936 ffor to kepe the fro venym tak þᵉ rots of yarow and
stamp heme and lay hem in wyne or mylk till thei be nesshe
and than seth hem   A littell and at mydday let hym take
ther of fastynge and that þere shall he drede no veynm
but it is bettir to take the erb wᵗ the rote and dry it and make
þ⁹of poudre and vse it in wyne or mylk

937 ffor veyns that bene yvell smyten take benes and pyk
þᵉ bark and seth hem in vynegre and lay apon the stroke
hote in the manere of a pleistre

938 ffor a veyn þat is korven wᵗ blode lattynge and
rankyllyth   Tak rye floure the juyse of lylie ꝫ make past
þ⁹off and mak ij small cakes and bake hem in the eymers
and take þᵉ one and lay to þᵉ arme as hote as he may suffre
it and when it is colde take þᵉ oþ⁹ and do ryȝt so and he
shall be sane

three ounces of boar's grease, half a quarter of an ounce of verdigris small powdered. And let them fry all together till they be softened and well mingled, and strain them, and put thereto a pound of turpentine that is already purified. And let them [stand] on the fire again till they be run well together, and ever stir it well with a slice, and pour it into thy box.

932 Venoming of a sore shall thus be healed. Take lavender and marigolds, sengreen and betony, and stamp them together, and lay them to the sore.

933 For veins cut when blood-letting. Seethe rue in water and anoint therewith the arm. And in the same water seethe lamb's wool and lay to the arm and to the veins, and they shall heal.

934 To make[1] vinegar. Take a quantity of bean-flour and knead it with vinegar, and bake it. And twice or thrice take it out of the oven and anoint it well with vinegar till it hath well absorbed it ; and put it in again, and it shall turn into vinegar. And so in the same manner make aysell or alsegar.

936 For to keep thee [free] from venom. Take the roots of yarrow and stamp them, and lay them in wine or milk till they be soft, and then seethe them a little. And at mid-day let him take thereof fasting, and accordingly shall he dread no venom. But it is better to take the herb with the root and dry it, and make thereof powder, and use it in wine or milk.

937 For veins that have been evilly smitten. Take beans and pick [off] the bark (skins), and seethe them in vinegar, and lay upon the stroke (bruise) hot in the manner of a plaster.

938 For a vein that is cut with blood-letting, and rankleth. Take rye-flour and the juice of lily, and make paste thereof. And make two small cakes and bake them in the embers ; and take the one and lay it to the arm as hot as he may suffer it, and when it is cold take the other and do right so, and he shall be sane.

---

[1] " Make " here means to prepare or medicate vinegar.

T

939 ffor vnbicome on legge   Take erbe Robt and seth it tendre in stale ale ê) (*sic*)

940 To void glett a soû]eyne medecyn   Take a pynt of vynegre and a pynt of clarified hony and iij vnc⁹ of poudre of licoresse and seth hem a littell togedir and take þ⁹of iij sponefull by the morow

941 ffor vanyte of the hede   Take the juyse of walwort salt and hony wex and encens and boile hem wele togedir and enoynt the hede þ⁹with and iff he fall in frenesye lat shaue his hede and take a whelpe or a ȝonge catt and cleffe in two on the bak and all hote with the blode and the guttis lay on the hede but enoynt it first wᵗ popilion

942 ffor a webb in a hors eyȝe   Tak celidon ꝛ salt ꝛ stamp hem togedir and put hem into þᵉ eyȝe the juyse of coliandre medilled with bene mele and pleystrid wil distroy [fo. 82 *verso*] wormes and kyrnels and feruent whelkes

943 Waȓ of copose grynd copose all to poudre and do a littell waȓ to þat poudre and lat it stand a day and a nyȝt and streyn it thorow a cloth this watir is gode for eyȝen and for kankre in a mannes mouth and for noli me tangê) in the visage

944 ffor a wound that is curable giff the syk to drynk þᵉ juyse of this erbis pympnoll bugle sanycle thies erbis shull go out by the wound and clensse the wound of roten blode but be ware the wound be nat in the hede by the breyn for than may nat sanycle be dronken ne be in no drynk þᵗ a man shall drynk if the wound be in the hede by the brayn this is p⁹vyd

945 Anoþ⁹ to hele a wound with in ix dayes   Take comfery and stamp it with barowȝ grese ꝛ put it in to þᵉ wound this is p⁹vyd

946 Anoþ⁹ to hele woundes full of blode stampe the rede nettell in a mortare wᵗ rede vynegre and lay on the wound and it shall do away the blode ꝛ clence the wound

939 For unbecomes on the leg. Take herb-Robert and seethe it [until] tender in stale ale. [*Probatum*] *est*.

940 To void gleet. A sovereign medicine. Take a pint of vinegar and a pint of clarified honey, and three ounces of powder of liquorice, and seethe them a little together and take thereof three spoonfuls each morning.

941 For vanity of the head.[1] Take the juice of walwort, salt and honey, wax and incense, and boil them well together, and anoint the head therewith. And if he fall into frenzy, let his head be shaved, and take a whelp or a young cat and cleave it in two on the back, and all hot with the blood and the guts lay on the head, but anoint it first with popilion.

942 For a web in a horse's eye. Take celandine and salt, and stamp them together, and put them into the eye. The juice of coriander mingled with bean-meal, and plastered, will destroy worms, and kernels, and fervent whelks (pustules).

943 Water of copperas. Grind copperas all to powder, and put a little water to that powder, and let it stand a day and a night, and strain it through a cloth. This water is good for eyes and for canker in a man's mouth, and for noli-me-tangere in the visage.

944 For a wound that is curable. Give the sick to drink the juice of these herbs : pimpernel, bugle, sanicle. These herbs shall go out by the wound, and cleanse the wound of rotten blood, but beware the wound be not in the head near the brain, for then may sanicle not be drunken, nor be in any drink that a man shall drink if the wound be in the head by the brain.[2] *This is proved*.

945 Another to heal a wound within nine days. Take comfrey and stamp it with barrow's grease, and put it into the wound. *This is proved*.

946 Another to heal wounds full of blood. Stamp red nettle in a mortar with red vinegar, and lay on the wound ; and it shall do away the blood and cleanse the wound.

---

[1] The first part of this recipe is the same as § 653.
[2] *Cf.* § 961.

947 ffor rankelynge woundis take leke hedys with the rotis ⁊ stamp hem in a mort̃ and put þ'to faire whete floure and hony of ech lich moch and fry hē togedir and make a pleistre and lay apon the wound and it shall away the suellynge and the akynge

948 ffor wound helid aboue and nat with jnne seth gotis dunge ī vynegre ⁊ aft̃ stamp it in a mort̃ and put þ'to hony and prosyn and encens poudrdre ⁊ medle hem togedir and fry hem [fo. 83 *recto*] wt barowȝ grese and make a pleistre and lay somdele hote to the wound and it wil draw out roten fith (*sic*) þ'in what thynge that þ'in be wheþ' it be thorne or yren or any oþ' thynge ⁊ after that it shall wele hele with out dout pƀ est

949 Anoþ' to open a wound that is euell helid seth wele the cropps off groundeswilly in swyns grese and make a pleistre and lay it a littell apon the wound and it shall hele it

950 Anoþ' Tak hony and the white of an ege of ech lich moch and this two and barly mele make þe man̄ of an oyntment and þ'with twyes or iij on the day enoynt the wound and it shall open as it shold be opynyd

951 ffor swellynge of woundes stampe malows with shepis taluȝ and hote lay to the wound //

952 ffor the same stamp malows wt hony and womans mylk or gotis mylk ⁊ make in man̄ of a paast and bynd vpon the wound

953 ffor wound þat it festrid Take hony and verdegrese and seth togedir in an erthen pot and if thou wilt wit when it is sothen enough tak wt thy slyce a drop and put it on yren or on a cold stone and iff the drop be hard when it is cold it is enouȝ and then enoynt al the wound wt þis oyntement twies or iij on the day and this oyntement shall wele hele the festre pƀ est

954 fforto sle worme in a wound or in any oþ' place Take the white cluber and stamp it and medle it with wyne and lay on the sore and it shall hele þe wound pƀ e̅

947 For rankling wounds. Take leek heads with the roots and stamp them in a mortar, and put thereto fair wheat-flour and honey, of each equally much ; and fry them together and make a plaster, and lay upon the wound. And it shall [take] away the swelling and the aching.

948 For wound healed above and not within. Seethe goat's dung in vinegar, and afterwards stamp it in a mortar ; and put thereto honey and perosin and incense powdered, and mingle them together and fry them with barrow's grease and make a plaster, and lay [it] somewhat hot to the wound. And it will draw out the rotten filth therein, whatever thing there be therein, whether it be thorn or iron or any other thing. And after that it shall well heal without doubt. *Probatum est.*

949 Another to open a wound that is ill-healed. Seethe well the crops of groundsel in swine's grease, and make a plaster, and lay it a little [while] upon the wound, and it shall heal it.

950 Another. Take honey and the white of an egg, of each equally much, and these two and barley-meal make [in] the manner of an ointment. And therewith twice or three [times] a day anoint the wound, and it shall open as it should be opened.

951 For swelling of wounds. Stamp mallows with sheep's tallow ; and, hot, lay [it] to the wound.

952 For the same. Stamp mallows with honey and woman's milk or goat's milk, and make [it] in the manner of a paste, and bind upon the wound.

953 For wound that is festered.[1] Take honey and verdigris and seethe together in an earthen pot. And if thou wilt know when it is seethed enough, take with thy slice a drop and put it on iron or a cold stone, and if the drop be hard when it is cold, it is enough. And then anoint all the wound with this ointment twice or three [times] a day, and this ointment shall well heal the fester. *Probatum est.*

954 For to slay a worm in a wound or in any other place. Take the white clover, and stamp it, and mingle it with wine ; and lay on the sore, and it shall heal the wound. *Probatum est.*

---

[1] This is a duplicate of § 295.

955 ffor wertis take egromoyn and stamp itt with salt and temp it with vynegre and lay on the wert [fo. 83 *verso*] and w^t in iiij days it will do away the wert pb est

956 The man͡ of wrytynge of billes for receytis   A pound is writ on this l̄j j / halue a pound thus l̄j ƒ or þus l̄j dj. a quartron þus q̃rt̃ j. halue a q̃rtron þus q̃rt̃ ƒ or dj. an vnc⁹ thus ʒ j halue an vnc⁹ thus ʒ ƒ or dj   A dragme thus ʒ j halue a dragme thus ʒ ƒ or ʒ dj   A scripell thus Ꝫ ƒ or dj A scripall weith a peny | iiij scripels makyth a dragme viij dragme makyth an vnc⁹ and xvj vnc⁹ makyth a pound .// And an handfull is written þus ɱ j. or dj   Take xx whete corns and thei make a scripell

957 ffor to make wex rede to sele with melt a pound of wex with an vnce of turmentyne and streyn it to voyd the filth and put þ⁹to when it is don of the fire an vnce of vermylon while it is lowke and stire it wele in the kelynge and ʒet it in to cakes and so do w^t vertegresse for grene wex

958 ffor worms in þe wombe ʒif hym the poudre of cappres to ete with hony when cappres is sett in medecyns by hym selue take þe rynd þ⁹of

959 Anoþ⁹ for the same make a sauce of garlyke and pep and a littell psely and of the juyse of mynt and temp it with vynegre ꝫ with mulsa and lat hem ete his mete þ⁹with and also to put it in his mowth is gode for the moder

960 To cesse wepynge make a pleistre of small poudre of henbanne seede and of glayre and of eggis of vynegre and of womans mylk ꝫ of a littell encens and lay to þe hede and to þe stomake

961 To make a drynke that helith [fo. 84 *recto*] woundes w^t oute any pleistre or oyntement and wyth outen any tent most pfitly   Take sanycle mylfoyle and bugle of ech lich moch ꝫ stamp hem in a mortar and temp hem w^t wyne and giff the sike to drynk that is woundid twyes or thries the day till he be hole   This is the vertu of this drynke bugle holdith the wound open mylfoyle clensith the wound sanycle

955 For warts. Take agrimony and stamp it with salt, and temper it with vinegar, and lay on the wart, and within three days it will do away the wart. *Probatum est.*

956 A manner of writing bills for receipts. A pound is written like this, $\overline{\text{li}}$ j ; half a pound thus, $\overline{\text{li}}$ ß, or thus $\overline{\text{li}}$ $\overline{\text{di}}$; a quartern thus, q̄rt̃ j ; half a quartron thus, q̄rt̃ ß or $\overline{\text{di}}$; an ounce thus ℥ j ; half an ounce thus, ℥ ß or $\overline{\text{di}}$; a drachm thus ʒ j ; half a drachm thus ʒ ß or $\overline{\text{di}}$; a scruple thus ℈ ß[1] or $\overline{\text{di}}$. A scruple weigheth a penny ; three scruples maketh a drachm ; eight drachms maketh an ounce, and sixteen ounces make a pound. And a handful is written thus ꝳ ; j or $\overline{\text{di}}$. Take twenty wheat corns, and they make a scruple.

957 For to make red wax to seal with. Melt a pound of wax with an ounce of turpentine, and strain it to void the filth (scum), and put thereto when it is down from the fire, an ounce of vermillion while it is luke[warm], and stir it well as it cools, and set it into cakes. And so do with verdigris for green wax.

958 For worms in the womb. Give him the powder of capers to eat with honey. When capers are used in medicines by themselves, take the rind off them.

959 Another for the same. Make a sauce of garlic and pepper and a little parsley and the juice of mint, and temper it with vinegar and with mulsa,[2] and let him eat his meat therewith and also put it in his mouth. [It] is good for the mother.

960 To cease weeping. Make a little plaster of small powder of henbane seed, and of the whites of eggs, of vinegar. and of woman's milk, and of a little incense, and lay it to the head and to the stomach.

961 To make a drink that healeth wounds, without any plaster or ointment and without any tent, most perfectly. Take sanicle, milfoil and bugle, of each equally much, and stamp them in a mortar, and temper them with wine, and give to the sick that is wounded to drink twice or thrice a day till he be whole. This is the virtue of this drink : bugle holdeth the wound open ; milfoil cleanseth the wound ;

---

[1] This is the abbreviation for half a scruple.
[2] *See* note to § 377.

helith it but sanycle may nat be giffen to hyme þat his
hurt in the hede. Jff the panne off the brayne be broken
for it will sle hyme and þerfore it is better in any oþ⁹ place
this drynke is gode and wele p⁹vyde

962 Water for eyen suollen   Take egremoyne the leues of
verueyn of fenell of rw of roses and do in a sallatorye and
sprenge aboue gode white wyne and distill it þis water is
goode for suellynge of a mannes eȝen that cōmyth of cold
and also for blereeyȝed eyȝen ꝛ for the pynne in the eyȝen
and it clerith moch a mannes sight and iff thou will haue
this watir streng⁹ do þ⁹to leues of gallict⁹ū and an oþ⁹ erbe
þat is callid morsus galline þᵗ is the kynmete þat berith the
rede flours

963 Jff ther be wound apone the nose or on the lypp or in
any othir place or nobyll membre of the bodye that shall
be sewid ffirst þat one pt shall be joynyd to þe oþ⁹ ryghtly
and than þat ou) pties of the skynne as delicatly and easely
as it may be shall be sowed so as it may dure with a subtile
quarell and sylk threde eu)y stich by hym selue ech A
[fo. 84 verso] littell fro oþ⁹

964 And be it knawen that in all such thynges þe nether
part shall be left open for thei bene purgynge hem selue as
in nose or eres that shall be curid with rede poudir in to
xx days and after with apostolicon and vnguentu fustum or
with oþ⁹ oyntmentis and drynke loueach with wyne first
and last for rankylynge wᵗ in forþe and oþ⁹ while emonge
drynke wormod a littell and when thoir suellist þᵘ helist

965 ffor wynd in the sides   Tak an handfull of camamyll
anoþ⁹ of wormod ij of grene brome ꝛ stamp ꝛ tak a bagge
þᵗ will go fro the navell to þe reyns and thies maters couchid
abrode and brochid in the bagge somewhat brode þᵗ will
ligge abrode on þe wombe and than take a gode porcion of
malews and boyle hem in a pot full of clene reyn wat⁹ or
rennynge watir and when thei be all for soden plunge þe

---

¹ Cf. § 944.
² Morsus gallinæ is rightly identified with chickweed, but the
flowers are not red. Gallitricum, mentioned just before, is Salvia
verbenacæ, L.

sanicle healeth it.   But sanicle may not be given to him that is hurt in the head, if the pan of the brain (skull) be broken, for it will slay him, and therefore it is better in any other place.[1]   This drink is good and well proved.

962 Water for eyes swollen.   Take agrimony and leaves of vervain, of fennel, of rue, of roses, and put in a still, and sprinkle above good white wine, and distill it.   This water is good for swelling of a man's eyes that cometh of cold, and also for bleary eyes, and for the pin in the eyes, and it cleareth much a man's sight.   And if thou wilt have this water stronger, put thereto leaves of gallitricum (clary) and another herb that is called morsus gallinae, that is chickmeat (chickweed) that beareth the red flowers.[2]

963 If there be a wound upon the nose or on the lip or in any other place or noble member (principal part) of the body that shall be sewed (stitched), first the one part shall be joined to the other rightly ; and then that other part of the skin, as delicately and easily as it may be, shall be sewed, so as it may dure (hold together), with a fine needle and silk thread, every stitch by itself a little from the other.

964 And be it known that in all such things (sutures), the nether part shall be left open so that [the wound] may drain itself.   As to [sutures] in the nose or ears, they shall be cured with red powder up to twenty days and afterwards with apostolicon and unguentum fustum,[3] or with other ointments.   And drink lovage with wine first and last for inward rankling, and between whiles drink wormwood a little.   And when thou swellest, thou healest.

965 For wind in the sides.[4]   Take a handful of camomile, another of wormwood, two of green broom, and stamp [them] ; and take a bag that will go from the navel to the reins, and with these matters (herbs) laid flat and spread out in the bag somewhat widely that will lie across the womb. And then take a good portion of mallows, and boil them in a pot full of clean rainwater or running water ; and when they

---

[3] *Unguentum fustum*, ointment for blows, is not described in the MS., but directions for making Apostolicon are given in § 289.

[4] Duplicate of § 1070.

bagg in þe watir till it be thorow hote and then quese out
the watir   And all hote lay itt ou⁾ þe wombe till it com to
þe reyns and when it is cold hete it eft in þe same watir

966 ffor a wen take blak sope and vnslekkyd lyme made in
to poudre and temp hem togedir ꝫ mak a kake of wex and
make an hoole in the myddell ꝫ put þe salue of sope þᵉⁱn
and lay it on the wenne viij ours and then take it away and
lay þᵉon a colop [fo. 85 *recto*] of fat bacon for it ryse and
when þe core is owt hele it with helynge salue

967 ffor watir þat is fallen in to a mannes ere and doth
hym disease þᵉⁱn   Tak þe Juys of coliandre and do it in the
ere and it shall hele

968 ffor worms in amannes ere take the Juyse of mynt þat
growith by waᵗ sides and also in gardyns and put it with
old wyne hote in a mannes ere and it shall sle hem and þe
Juys of ersesmert doþe þe same

Waters

969 Thies bene pᵒciose waters and vertuose for dyuers
yuelles

970 Watir of wormod is gode for the stomake for the lyu⁾
and for the splene ffor worms in the wombe and for the
maras

971 Waᵗ of centory is gode for appetite for the lyu⁾ for the
myst ffor worms and saucefleme

972 Waᵗ of mogwort is a chefe thynge for the maras

973 Water of deteyn is gode for poyson ꝫ for pestulence

974 Waᵗ of fymᵗ is gode for morfywe for lepre for scabb
and for þe dropsie

975 Waᵗ of ysopp is gode ffore the cough and for the lungis

976 Watir of bawme is goode to clence the modre and for
the maras

977 A pᵒciose waᵗ emonge all waters is made of turmentill
scabiose deteyn pympnoll of ech lich moch and done

be all sodden, plunge the bag in the water till it be thoroughly hot, and then squeeze out the water. And, all hot, lay it over the womb till it come to the reins. And when it is cold, heat it again in the same water.

966 For a wen. Take black soap and unslaked lime made into powder, and temper them together. And make a cake of wax and make a hole in the middle, and put the salve of soap therein, and lay it on the wen eight hours. And then take it away and lay thereon a collop (rasher) of fat bacon, lest it rise. And when the core is out, heal it with healing salve.

967 For water that is fallen into a man's ear and doth him disease therein. Take the juice of coriander, and put it in the ear, and shall heal.

968 For worms in a man's ear. Take the juice of mint that groweth by the waterside and also in gardens, and put it with old wine hot in a man's ear, and it shall slay him (the worm). And the juice of horsemint doth the same.

Waters.[1]

969 These be precious waters, and virtuous for divers evils.

970 Water of wormwood is good for the stomach, for the liver, and for the spleen, for worms in the womb, and for the marasmus.

971 Water of centaury is good for appetite, for the liver, for debility,[2] for worms, and for acne.[3]

972 Water of mugwort is a chief thing for marasmus.

973 Water of dittany is good for poison and for pestilence.

974 Water of fumitory is good for morphew, for leprosy, for scab, and for the dropsy.

975 Water of hyssop is good for the cough and for the lungs.

976 Water of balm is good to cleanse the mother, and for marasmus.

977 A precious water among all others is made of tormentil, scabious, dittany, pimpernel, of each equally much, and put

[1] Distilled waters are here meant.
[2] *Myst. Cf.* § 196.
[3] *See* note to § 647.

togedir ꝛ stillid togedir for it is a and a pᵒciose watir for all
manꝺ of poyson and namely for pestulence for as philosophers
seyne it is impossibill that any man shuld dey of poyson
and of pestulence who so vsith [fo. 85 *verso*] to drynk of
that waꝛ next hys hert and it clepid waꝛ emperiall ffor all
emperoures and grote lordis emonge the sarsyns vse to
drynke it

978 A preciose watir for eyꝫen þat iff a man hadd lost his
sight x ꝫere iff it were possible he shall rekeuꝺ it agayn with in
xl days   Take smalach ruw fenell egremoyne betayn scabiose
auence houndstunge eufrace pympnoll and sauge and still
thies togedir with a littell vryne of a knave childe and v
greyns of frank encens and drop that watir ech nyꝫt in the
sore eyꝫen   Also celidoyn ruw filago eufrace ruddis wodbynd
still all thies togedire

979 Water of cherfoile is gode for a sore mouth //

980 Water of calamynt is gode fore the stomake

981 Waꝛ of planteyn is gode for the flux and the hote
dropsy

982 Waꝛ of fenell is gode to make a grete body small

983 Water of violet is good to hele a man that is thrustyd
and for the lyuꝺ

984 Waꝛ off endiue is gode for the dropsie and the Jawndisse

985 Waꝛ of borage is gode and a cheffe watir for the
stomake ffor collica passio and many oþᵒ syknes in the
bodye

986 Waꝛ of both sawgis is goode for the palasye

987 To make Aqua Vite   Tak quyte wyne of osay and
gyngᵒ and clowes maces greyns canell a littell pep galyngale
a littell sugre Juybibbes beteyne a littell turmentill smalach
apm̄ mousere scabiose bugle and violet take and [fo. 86
recto] grynd hem in a morꝛ the spicery in an opᵒ then take
and seth hem in a faire vessell in wyne that þai buyle ones
than still hem in A stillatorye and still hem iiij tymes or

together and distilled together for it is a [good] and a precious water for all manner of poison, and especially for pestilence. For, as philosophers say, it is impossible that any man should die of poison and of pestilence who useth to drink of that water [and putteth it] next his heart. And it [is] called Imperial, because all emperors and great lords among the Saracens[1] use to drink it.

978 A precious water for eyes, that if a man had lost his sight ten years, if it were possible he shall recover it again within forty days. Take smallage, rue, fennel, agrimony, betony, scabious, avens, houndstongue, eufrasia (eyebright), pimpernel and sage, and distill these together with a little urine of a boy-child, and five grains of frankincense. And drop that water each night in the sore eyes. Also celandine, rue, filago, eufrasia (eyebright), reeds, woodbine ; distill all these together.

979 Water of chervil is good for a sore mouth.

980 Water of calamint is good for the stomach.

981 Water of plantain is good for the flux and the hot dropsy.

982 Water of fennel is good to make a great body small.

983 Water of violet is good to heal a man that is thirsty (dipsomania) and for the liver.

984 Water of endive is good for the dropsy and the jaundice.

985 Water of borage is good, and a chief water for the stomach, for collica passio, and many other sicknesses of the body.

986 Water of both sages[2] is good for the palsy.

987 To make Aqua Vitæ. Take white wine of Orsay, and ginger, and cloves, maces, kermes, canell, a little pepper, galingale, a little sugar, cubebs,[3] betony, a little tormentil, smallage, apium, mouse-ear, scabious, bugle and violet. Take and grind them (the herbs) in a mortar, the spicery in another, and then take and seethe them in a fair vessel in wine, till they boil once. Then distill them in a still, and

---

[1] Meaning Arabs and Mohammedans generally.
[2] Common sage and wood-sage.
[3] See note to § 242.

v vnto the tyme it will brenne on a lynnen cloth with out
any wemme þᵒof than take it and do it in a glasse

988 A pᵒciose watir to clere a mannes eyȝen and to distroy
the pynne in a mannes eyȝe   Take the rede rose and
capillus veni⁹s that is clepid mayden here ffenell rywe
verueyn eufrace endyue beteyn of ech lich moch do þat
thou haue vnder all vj handfull and let hem rest in white
[wyne] a day and a nyght and the secund day distill hem in
a stillatorye the first watir will seme watir coloure of gold
the secund waᵗ̃ sylũ the thrid bawme this watir is pᵒciose
to gentill ladies in stede of bawme

989 A pᵒciose waᵗ̃ for al maͦ of ach   Take and fill a pot
of the drestis of good [ale] to the threddendele off the pot
be full and put þᵒto ij handfull of comyn and salt ꝛ put hem
in the lembek and stopp it wele all aboute wᵗ past and distill
a pᵒciose waᵗ̃

990 To make waᵗ̃ ardannt that is clepid brennynge waᵗ̃
tak argoile and grynd it wele alto powdre and do it in a
stillatory and distill it and that is clepid oleū tartary that
oyle is gode to spirtts sadd ꝛ hoole   Take þᵉ first watir of
this argoile and a pound of wyne þᵗ be distilled and distill
this togedir ꝛ that shall be waᵗ̃ brennynge

991 To brynge out brusid blode out of the wound   Tak
vnguentū fustū and vnguentū narbale ꝛ medle hē ꝛ þan fill
þe wound þᵒof ꝛ þen lay a lynnen cloþe aboue [fo. 86 verso]
on þᵉ oyntement and lay þan lynet on the cloth euen apon
the wound and bynd ꝛ so serue it ij on day till the brusid
blode fall oute of the wound and than hele vp the sore wᵗ
trete or wᵗ ḡra dei or with oþ⁹ salue

992 ffor to make aqua salutis or rubia aqua   Tak a galon
of tanne wose and d̄j a pound of crop madͦ of alym als
mych in small poudre as thou myght make it but first sethe

---

¹ The text has *brenne*, " burn," evidently in error.
² Duplicate in *Harl.* 2378 (Henslow, *op. cit.*, p. 117).
³ Crude tartar.
⁴ *See* § 676, in which another method of preparing this oil is given.

distill them four or five times until it will wet[1] a linen cloth without any stain.   Then take it and put it in a glass.

988 A precious water to clear a man's eyes, and to destroy the pin in a man's eye.   Take the red rose and capillus veneris that is called maidenhair, fennel, rue, vervain, eufrasia (eyebright), endive, betony, of each equally much ; take [so much] that thou hast under six handfuls in all, and let them rest in white [wine] a day and a night.   And the second day distill them in a still : the first water will appear as water the colour of gold, the second water silver, the third balm.   This water is precious to gentle ladies instead of balm.[2]

989 A precious water for all manner of aches.   Take and fill a pot with dregs of good [ale] till one third part of the pot be full, and put thereto two handfuls of cumin and salt ; and put them in the alembic and stop it well all about with paste, and distill a precious water.

990 To make ardent water that is called burning water. Take argol[3] and grind it well all to powder, and put it in a still and distill it, and that is called Oleum tartari.[4]   That oil is good for spirits, [both] sad and whole.[5]   Take the first water of this argol and a pound of wine that has been distilled, and distill these together, and that shall be burning-water.

991 To bring bruised blood out of a wound.   Take unguentum fustum[6] and unguentum narbale (nervale), and mingle them, and then fill the wound therewith.   And then lay a linen cloth above on the ointment, and lay then lint on the cloth evenly upon the wound, and bind it.   And so serve it twice a day till the bruised blood fall out of the wound.   And then heal up the sore with entrete or with Gratia Dei[7] or with some other salve.

992 For to make aqua salutis, or rubea aqua.   Take a gallon of tan-ooze,[8] and half a pound of madder-crops, of alum as much, in powder as small as thou canst make it.   But first

---

[5] Meaning, it is good for persons who are either low- or high-spirited.
[6] See note to § 964.
[7] See § 299.
[8] Licour from a tanner's vat.

thi tanwose and skymme it wele and than do þ⁹to thi madir
and thyne alym and seth hem togedir till thyn alym be
molten and with watir wesshe wele thi morole and wete
wele iiij fold lynen cloth in that watir and lay it on the sore
and roll wele thi legge ꝫ if þ⁹ be dede flesshe þ⁹in tak þe
poudre saluy tre and sawnders and do þ⁹on and iff the
sore be oul moyst take the floure of benes and temp it
with rede water and make þ⁹off a pleistre and lay it on the
sore and it will dry it wele and so will pleistre of paris
temperid with the same water

993 ffor a wenne   Take sall armoniak and alym ꝫ resalg⁹
ꝫ make the skynne raw aboute with sciseskyn or vnqueynt
lyme or with a rasor and þen lay to (sic) poudre and gife
hyme to drynke triacle and when the wenne is away hele
it vp wᵗ bawme

994 ffor worms in a mannys here take hony þat is in a hony
comb and do it in his ere þen ly doun on thylk syd and he
will com oute   Or tak hawȝthorn bowes and brenne hem
and kep þat watir þat cōmyth out at the end and menge it
wᵗ [fo. 87 recto] oyle and held it in the hole in the ere and lay
apon þe oþ⁹ side

995 ffor webb n the eyȝe take stronge vynegre or eysell and
do it in a vessell of brasse and the blak slo of the wodd ꝫ
wormod þ⁹with and lat stand keuered and when nede do it
in the eye it will breke the webb ꝫ do away all þe yuell

996 YVell in the stomak   Take ach sede lynsede ꝫ
comyn ꝫ stamp hem ꝫ giff to the sik to drynke
with hote waᵗ ꝫ sanabitʳ

997 ffor yuell in the womb or hardnesse or bolnynge take
ȝarow and stamp it and take ij sponefull of the juyse ꝫ
drynk it

998 ffor yuell in the bak   Take ach and egremoyne and
mousere both þe leves and the rotis ꝫ stamp hem with bores
grese ꝫ eysell and do it to thi bake

seethe thy tan-ooze and skim it well, and then put thereto thy madder and thine alum. And seethe them together till thine alum be molten. And with water wash well thy moralis,[1] and wet well a four-fold linen cloth in that water, and lay it on the sore, and roll well thy leg. And if there be dead flesh therein, take the powder-salutory and saunders,[2] and put thereon. And if the sore be very moist, take the flour of beans and temper it with red water, and make thereof a plaster, and lay it on the sore, and it will dry it well, and so will plaster of Paris tempered with the same water.

993 For a wen. Take sal-ammoniac and alum and realgar, and make the skin raw about with cut-skin (a corrosive) or unslaked lime, or with a razor ; and then lay on the powder, and give him to drink treacle. And when the wen is away, heal it up with balm.

994 For worms in a man's ear. Take the honey that is in a honeycomb and put it in his ear. Then lie down on thy side and he (the worm) will come out. Or take hawthorn boughs and burn them, and keep the water that cometh out at the end, and mingle it with oil, and hold it in the whole ear and lie upon the other side.

995 For web in the eye. Take strong vinegar or aysell and put it in a vessel of brass ; and the black sloe of the wood, and wormwood therewith, and let [it] stand covered. And when need [be], put it in the eye, and it will break the web and do away all the evil.

996 Evil in the stomach. Take ache-seed and linseed and cumin, and stamp them, and give to the sick to drink with hot water. *Et sanabitur.*

997 For evil in the womb or hardness or swelling. Take yarrow and stamp it, and take two spoonfuls of the juice and drink it.

998 For evil in the back.[3] Take ache and agrimony and mouse-ear, both the leaves and the roots, and stamp them with boar's grease and vinegar, and put it to thy back.

---

[1] *Moralis*, from Lat. *morum* (mulberry), Old French *morale*, properly a kind of skin-disease.
[2] Copper carbonate.
[3] Duplicate, D, § 13.

999 ffor yren or stele lopen into a mannys body take egmoyne ꝗ pound it with old grese and lay þᵒon eythir take deteyne and ete it and drynk it or rake the rote of rosere and put it wele in hony and do it in a cloute and lay it on the sore

1000 ffor yuell in þe wrest on the schynnes take mogwort and old grese of a swyne and stamp togedir and aysel þᵒto and bynd to the sore ꝗ if a mannys fote be wreȝt al medecyns that be goode for wrenchynges after þᵗ a mannys hand or fote be drawn in to his ryght stede

1001 ffor yuell at the hert take centorye seþe it wele in stale ale or with wyne and than stamp it wele than do it in the same broth and seth wele agayn then clence it thorow a cloth þan tak ij pties [fo. 87 *verso*] of the juys and the thrid of hony boylid and skymmid and seth wele togedir and ech day gif the sik iij sponefull fastynge

1002 ffor yuell in the stomake   Take the rote of fenell and the rote off ach stamp hem togedir and temp hem with white wyne and giff the syke to drynk

1003 ffor yuell at the brest   Take ambrose and horehowne of ech lich moch   Stamp hem ꝗ temp hem with wyne and drynk it iij days fastynge //

1004 Ysope is a mylde grasse and helith the brest if it be stampid and temp it with stale ale or with watir and dronken fastynge

1005 A gode drynke for all woundis   Take a porcion of rede cole and the rede nettle crop and the brede brere dayseȝe and the crop of hemp of all lich moch when it is stampid and (*sic*) the rede may and as moch of the may as of all þe oþᵍ erbis and stamp ech on by hym selue ꝗ make hem than on small pelettis and dry hem and let hem nat come to the sonne ne to the wynde and giff the syke to drynke on morow iij sponefull and at morow[1] euen ij sponefull and he shall be hole ⚼

1006 Thyes that aken or Synows þᵗ bene Stiffe of goynge Take brokelemk horehound and erb John and diȝt hem in man̉ of a pleystre with shepis talwȝ and swyns grese and hors dunge and lay þᵒto all hote

999 For iron or steel penetrated into a man's body. Take agrimony and pound it with old grease and lay thereon. Or take dittany and eat it, and drink it. Or take the root of rose and put it well in honey, and put it on a cloth and lay it on the sore.

1000 For evil in the wrist [or] in the shins. Take mugwort and old grease of a swine, and stamp together ; and [put] vinegar thereto, and bind to the sore. And if a man's foot be sprained, [use] all medicines that be good for wrenchings, after a man's hand or foot to drawn to its proper place.[2]

1001 For evil at the heart. Take centaury and seethe it well in stale ale or with wine, and then stamp it well. Then put it in the same broth and seethe well again ; then cleanse it through a cloth. Then take two parts of the juice and the third of honey boiled and skimmed, and seethe well together. And each day give the sick three spoonfuls fasting.

1002 For the evil in the stomach. Take the root of fennel and the root of ache ; stamp them together and temper them with white wine, and give the sick to drink.

1003 For evil at the breast. Take ambrose (wood-sage) and horehound, of each equally much. Stamp them and temper them with wine, and drink it three days fasting.

1004 Hyssop is a mild grass (herb) and healeth the breast if it be stamped. And temper it with stale ale or with water and drink fasting.

1005 A good drink for all wounds. Take a portion of red cabbage, and red nettle crop, and the broad briar, daisy, and the crop of hemp, of all equally much. When it is stamped, [take] the red may, and as much of the may as of all the other herbs. And stamp each by itself, and make them then into small pellets and dry them, and let them not come in the sun nor in the wind. And give the sick to drink at morn three spoonfuls, and at even two spoonfuls, and he shall be whole.

1006 Thighs that ache, or sinews that be stiff of going (movement). Take brooklime, horehound, St. John's-wort, and prepare them in the manner of a plaster with sheep's tallow and swine's grease and horse-dung, and lay thereto all hot.

---

[1] The dots indicate that the word should be d eleted. *Cf.* § 236.
[2] Reducing dislocations is meant.

1007 The þrote that is sore of syknes and namely when the þrote is [fo. 88 *recto*] streite   Tat (*sic*) woderofe stamp it ⁊ drynke þe juys wᵗ gode ale

1008 ffor þrist take the rote of loueach and stamp itt and temp it with watir and drynk it

1009 ffor þorns   Tak egromoyn gander muke and the rote of the rose stampid togedir with vynegre wex hare grese and hors grese of ech lich moch leid in a pleistre will draw out a thorn or a stubb where it be in the flesshe ⁊ euᵊlemonge drynk the juyse of egrmoyn for ach

1010 To staunch þrist   Tak of fenell ij pties ⁊ hony iij pties and seth hem togedir in wyn to the thyknes of hony and do pep þ⁹to and þ⁹of ete ich day iij sponefull till thou be hole

1011 a Drynk to dryue out the thorne or stubb in the flesshe Stamp sanycle and howsleke ⁊ leues of betayn and menge the juse with stale ale ⁊ giff the syke to drynke

1012 A gode watir for alkyns syknes   Tak clow gillofre juybibbis and macis of ech an vnce of comyn d̄j and vnc⁹ longe pep a quartron of sugre candy ij vnc⁹ of safron a dragme and make poudre of all thies thynges and lat still it

1013 yoxe hold both thyn handys in hote waᵗ or ale and it wyll away

1014 Anoþ⁹ for yoxynge take sauge Rue comyn and pep of ich lich moch and seth hem togedir and ete a sponefull of clarified honyé at morow ⁊ euen

1015 Anoþ⁹   Tak sauge ⁊ stamp it and temp it wᵗ eysell ⁊ streyn it and temp it wᵗ eysell ⁊ streyn it ⁊ drynk it and it shall slake //

1016 Anoþ⁹   Take smerwort ⁊ stamp it ⁊ medle it with gode wyne and it will distroy [fo. 88 *verso*] the yoxynge if þᵘ drynk it

1017 ffor the ȝelow yuell   Take þe rote of rede nettils and take out the juyse and Juyse of celidone and drynk it with stale ale

1007 The throat that is sore of sickness, and especially when the throat is straight.[1]   Take woodruff, stamp it and drink the juice with good ale.

1008 For thirst.   Take the root of lovage, and stamp it, and temper it with water, and drink it.

1009 For thorns.   Take agrimony, gander's dung, and the root of rose, stamped together with vinegar, wax, hare's grease and horse-grease, of each equally much, laid in a plaster will draw out a thorn or stub where[ever] it be in the flesh.   And between whiles drink the juice of agrimony for ache (*i.e.*, to ease the pain).

1010 To quench thirst.   Take fennel two parts and honey three parts, and seethe them together in wine to the thickness of the honey, and put pepper thereto, and thereof eat each day three spoonfuls till thou be whole.

1011 A drink to drive out the thorn or stub in the flesh. Stamp sanicle and houseleek and leaves of betony, and mingle the juice with stale ale, and give the sick to drink.

1012 A good water for all kinds of sickness.   Take cloves, walflower, cubebs and mace, of each an ounce, of cumin half an ounce, long pepper a quarter, of sugar candy two ounces, of saffron a drachm.   And make powder of all these things and distill it.

1013 Hiccough.   Hold both thy hands in hot water or ale, and it will away.

1014 Another for hiccoughing.   Take sage, rue, cumin, and pepper. of each equally much, and seethe them together, and eat a spoonful of clarified honey at morn and eve.

1015 Another.   Take sage and stamp it, and temper it with vinegar, and strain it and drink it, and it shall abate.

1016 Another.   Take smearwort and stamp it, and mingle it with good wine.   And it will destroy the hiccoughing if thou drinkest it.

1017 For the yellow-evil (jaundice).   Take the root of red nettles, and take out the juice, and juice of celandine, and drink it with stale ale.

---

[1] Narrow, or closed up through tonsilitis or similar affections.

1018 Anoþ⁹ Take a man⁹ of spycerye þat men call turmentyne and grate it as small as gynger and drynk þ⁹of thries and be hole

1019 All bitt⁹ thynges conforten the stomak All swete thynges febyll it rostyd thynges bene drye All raw thynges noyen the stomake who so will kepe continuall helth kepe his stomake that he þat he (*sic*) put nat to moch þ⁹in when he hath appetite ne take no thynge in to hit when he hath no nede and þen contynuell helth will syw

1020 ffor the goute Take sothernwod wormod and rw añ ꝳ j and seþe hem wᵗ easy fyre in an nw drye pot of oyle of olyue and a quarte of gode malnesy or tyre tyll the wyne be wastid ꝫ þen streyn it thorow a fayre cloth and enoynt the sore there with ꝫ be ware thow come nat nere the fyre but raþ⁹ warme the oyntement

1021 ffor þe pynne or þᵉ webb Take A sponefull of hony oþ⁹ of the hyffe and streyn it ꝫ put it [in] a sawcer and take the gall of a shepe or of an hare as moch of the one as of the oþ⁹ ꝫ medle hem to ged⁹ ꝫ put it in a glasse ꝫ take a sponefull of hony and halue a sponefull of woman mylk of the yong woma⁹ the bett⁹

1022 A medecyn ffor the goute and ach þat swellith Take A qrte [fo. 89 *recto*] of oyle of olyfe and a quart of juys of beries of þe wod bynd ꝫ þis wodbynd leues be nat ragut but they bene like a mannys hert gedre thies beries bitwene the ij festis of our lady and put boþe Jusis togedir in dowble glasse and shak heme wele togedir and sett it in a pitt A ȝerd with in the erth but lat it be open saue lay A burd apon the glasse for the rayne and lat it stand in the erth ix days and ix nyghtes the x day take it vpe ꝫ it will last xij monythes

1023 A medecyn for the actua passio Tak byldres that grow in small bruks ꝫ mylk and brane and seth all thies togedire to the bildres be ryght soft and then make a bagge of lynnen cloth and put þᵉ pleystre þ⁹in and lay it all hote to the actua passio

---

¹ A sweet wine, also called Metheglin. *See* 242.
² Serrate or dentate.
³ *See* note to § 385.

1018 Another. Take a manner of spicery that men call turpentine, and grate it as small as ginger, and drink thereof thrice and be whole.

1019 All bitter things comfort the stomach. All sweet things enfeeble it. Roasted things are dry. All raw things annoy the stomach. Whoso will keep continual health, [must] keep his stomach so that he put not too much therein when he hath appetite, nor take anything into it when he hath no need. And then continual health will ensue.

1020 For the gout. Take southernwood, wormwood and rue, of each a handful, and seethe them on an easy fire in a new dry pot of oil of olive, and a quart of good Malmsey or Tyre,[1] till the wine be wasted. And then strain it through a fair cloth, and anoint the sore therewith. And beware thou come not near the fire, but rather warm the ointment.

1021 For the pin or the web. Take a spoonful of honey from the hive and strain it, and put it [in] a saucer. And take the gall of a sheep or of a hare, as much of the one as of the other, and mingle them together. And put it in a glass, and take a spoonful of honey and half a spoonful of woman's milk, the younger the woman the better.

1022 A medicine for the gout and ache that swelleth. Take a quart of oil of olive, and a quart of juice of the berries of the woodbine, and [of] this [kind of] woodbine, the leaves be not ragged,[2] but they be like a man's heart. Gather these berries between the two feasts of Our Lady,[3] and put those juices together in a double glass, and shake them well together. And set it in a pit a yard within the earth, but let it be open, save for laying a board upon the glass to [keep off] the rain. And let it stand in the earth nine days and nine nights : the tenth day take it up, and it will last twelve months.

1023 A medicine for the Actua Passio.[4] Take bilders[5] that grow in small brooks, and bran, and seethe all these together till the bilders be right soft. And then make a bag of linen cloth, and put the plaster therein, and lay it all hot to the actua passio.

---

[4] *Cf.* §§ 173, 1056.
[5] *Sium angustifolium.* L., = *S. erectum*, Hudson.

1024 A medecyn ffor Akynge of bonys   Take the gall of a
bull and enoynt the sore place þᵒ wᵗ ꜩ he shall be hole vt
pᵬ ẽ)

1025 ffor þᵉ same   Take colrage or ellis the juys of colrage
and enoynt the sore þᵒwith

1026 ffor ach þat suellith   Take the leues of alþᵒ the leves
of white welow and þᵉ leves off poplere and boyle hem in
rennyng watiꝛ a myle way than take hem out.and grynd
hem in a morᵗ ꜩ fry it with swyns grese and make þᵒof a
pleysᵗ ꜩ [fo. 89 verso] lay it all hote to the sore

1027 ffor the lyũ)   Tak iiij sponefull of watir of rosys and
a sponefull of white wyne ꜩ dj sponefull of saundres ꜩ medle
thies togedᵒ) and lay on a double cloth of lynnen of the
brode of a hand and it (sic) on the ryght side on the lyuere

1028 ffor the splene   Take the rotis of ferne that growith
on an oke and schrape heme or payre hem ꜩ dry hem in the
sune ij days ore iij and stopp youre chekyns or youre
capons with iiij or v rotis and make grewell or browes of
the brothe ꜩ ete þᵉ broþe or þᵉ gruell

1029 Anoþᵒ   Tak hertis tunge v or vj leues ꜩ stop youre
capon or youre chekyn with hē ꜩ make gruell and browes
þᵒoff and ete it

1030 To make ydromell   Take a galon of rennynge waᵗ ꜩ
a pynt of clarified hony and boyle hem wele togedir a myle
way ꜩ scome it clene and streyne it ꜩ put it in an erþen
pot ꜩ lat stand ij days or þe drynk it ꜩ when it is cold tak
a quantitee if soure levyn as grete as a costard ꜩ put it
þᵒin

1031 To make clarified whey   Take a galon of whey ꜩ set it
ou) the fire till it be leuke hote ꜩ then tak þᵉ white of vj
eggs and swynge it wele till it be short and put it in the
whey and þen sett it douñ and stirre it wele togedir and
þen boyle it agayn and when it begynnyth to boyle kest
þere in a cup full of white wyne ꜩ [fo. 90 recto] than tak it
down and lat it kele and when it is cold let the whey renne
thorow a cloth in to an erthen pott

1024 A medicine for aching of bones. Take the gall of a bull, and anoint the sore place therewith, and he shall be whole. *Ut probatum est.*

1025 For the same. Take culrage (water-pepper) or else the juice of culrage, and anoint the sore place therewith.

1026 For ache that swelleth. Take the leaves of alder, the leaves of white willow, and the leaves of poplar, and boil them in running water a mileway.[1] Then take them out and grind them in a mortar, and fry it with swine's grease, and make thereof a plaster, and lay it all hot to the sore.

1027 For the liver. Take four spoonfuls of water of roses and a spoonful of white wine, and half a spoonful of sanders. And mingle these together, and lay it on a double cloth of linen of the breadth of a hand, and [lay] it on the right side of the liver.

1028 For the spleen. Take roots of fern that groweth on an oak, and scrape them or pare them, and dry them in the sun two days or three. And stuff your chickens or your capons with four or five roots, and make gruel or browse[2] of the broth, and eat the broth on the gruel.

1029 Another. Take hartstongue five or six leaves, and stuff your chicken or your capon with them, and make gruel and browse and eat it.

1030 To make hydromel. Take a gallon of running water and a pint of clarified honey, and boil them well together a mileway.[1] And skim it and clean it and strain it, and put it in an earthen[ware] pot, and let it stand two days before thou drink it. And when it is cold, take a quantity of sour leaven as large as a custard, and put it therein.

1031 To make clarified whey. Take a gallon of whey and set it over the fire, till it be lukewarm, and then take the white of six eggs and beat it up well till it be short (light), and put in the whey, and then set it down and stir it well together. And then boil it again, and when it beginneth to boil, cast therein a cupful of white wine. Then take it down and let it cool, and when it is cold, let the whey run through a cloth into an earthen pot.

---

[1] *See* note to § 297.
[2] A soft food.

1032 ffor ach of bones a gude oyntement   Take sothernwod wormod lauandre floures reede rose flours camamyll
sauge riall þat will nat sede of ech an handfull grynd heme
small in a mortare as vert sawce ꝫ put hem in a pot full of
oyle de olyfe and put þ⁹to a pynt of aqua vite and let hem
stand iij days and boyle it wele vp þe space almost of an vnce
and streyne itt

1033 A medecyn ffor the flyx   Tak culid dunge a quantite
and seith wᵗ a galon of galon (sic) of rennynge watire and
lett it in to a potell and set youre fete þ⁹jnne and lat it nat
passe the ankelys and vse this onys or ij as þe thynk and
sett þȯ fete þ⁹in till it be almost cold

1034 ffor Stiches   Take the seede off sowþistill and ete it
first and laste a littell quantitee

1035 ffor the dropsie be it hote or cold for to hele any man
þat eũ shall be hole sykyrely   Tak wormod petymorell
ffethirfoyle spurge walwort rote of ach halue   a pound
ffenell ysop sauge smalach auence mynt welle cresses
heyhone endyue lyuerwort the mydle bark of the ydell
tre of ech of thies a quarͭ ꝫ wasshe heme clene and the rotis
and grynd hem wele in A morͭ ꝫ put hem in an erthen pott
þᵗ was neũ ocupied [fo. 90 verso] and do þ⁹to ij galons of
white wyne and a galon of gode wort þat is nat chaungid
and seþe hem till thei com till a glou þen tak it doun

1036 A medecyne for the fyre of saynt Antony ꝫ for a
mormall and for all vnkynd sores   Tak wormod and jue
lich moch and dry it in the sonne or ellis on a tyle but nat
to moch and mak poudre þ⁹of and strew apon þe sore and
make a pleistre than of soure douȝe tempid with stale ale
and lay on the sore and chaunge it twyes on a day and at
eũy tyme wasshe away this pleistre with holy waͭ

1037 A gode medecyn for the Jawndis   Tak iij angylltwacches ij of hem slyt ꝫ wasshe in rynnyng watir ꝫ tak an
angyltwacch hole ꝫ stampe thies iij togedir and ix bladis
of saferon þ⁹to ꝫ a peny wyȝt of white sope of the best of
castell sope ꝫ stamp all thies togedir ꝫ temper it with

---

¹ A green preparation made of juices and crushed herbs.
² The text has *ounce*, a manifest error.

1032 For ache of bones, a good ointment. Take southern-wood, wormwood, lavender flowers, red rose flowers, camomile, sage, [penny]royal that will not seed, of each a handful. Grind them small in a mortar as vertsauce,[1] and put them in a pot full of oil of olive, and put thereto a pint of aqua vitæ. And let them stand three days, and boil it well up the space of almost an hour,[2] and strain it.

1033 A medicine for the flux. Take pigeon's dung a quantity, and seethe it with a gallon of running water, and let it [boil down] to a pottle (two quarts). And set your feet therein, and let it not come above the ankles. And use this once or twice, as thou thinkest [fit], and set thy feet therein till it be almost cold.

1034 For stitches. Take the seed of sowthistle and eat it first and last a little quantity.

1035 For the dropsy, be it hot or cold, for to heal any man whatever [that] he shall be whole securely. Take wormwood, pettymorell, feverfew, spurge, walwort, root of ache, half a pound ; fennel, hyssop, smallage, avens, mint, well-cress (watercress), horehond, endive, liverwort, the middle bark of the elder tree, of each of these a quarter. And wash them clean also the roots, and grind them well in a mortar ; and put them in an earthen[ware] pot that is newly used (a new pot), and put thereto two gallons of white wine and a gallon of good wort that is not changed.[3] And seethe them till they come to a glue, then take it down.

1036 A medicine for the fire of St. Anthony,[4] and for a mor-mal and for all unkind sores. Take wormwood and ivy, equally much, and dry it in the sun or else on a tile, but not too much ; and make powder thereof, and strew [it] upon the sore. And make a plaster then of sour dough tempered with stale ale, and lay on the sore ; and change it twice a day and every time wash away this plaster with holy water.

1037 A good medicine for the jaundice. Take three earth-worms, two of them slit, and wash in running water ; and take an earthworm whole, and stamp these three together, and [put] nine blades of saffron thereto, and a pennyweight of white soap of the best [quality] of Castile soap. And

---

[3] Fermented, or changed in colour.
[4] Erysipelas.

rennynge wat̃ ꝰ lat the syke drynk þᵉoff iij mornynges ꝰ
iff it do hym gode vse it leng⁹ and iff the lust nat stamp
þᵉ sope wᵗ the medecyne þ⸗ may payre it small in the medecyn
when it is made and this medecyn is gode for all mañ
of Jawndis ȝalow bak (sic) and grene

1038 To knaw waters of man or womā ꝰ the watir be rede
grauellye it betokenyth syknesse in the reyns and iff be white
grauellye it is the spice of the stone ꝰ of the bleddyre and
iff it be fatt aboue the wat̃ þᵗ is wastynge

1039 A medecyn ffor a bocch Tak smalach and stamp
[fo. 91 recto] it in a mort̃ small and tak barowȝ grese that
hath hangyd in the roffe and pyke out all the skynnes
clene and stamp it with smalach as small þᵗ it be nat sene ꝰ
make a pleistre þᵉof and chaunge the pleistre eũ as it drieth

1040 ffor the ffelon Tak rw a quantitee and as moch of
salt ꝰ stamp hem togedir and lay to þᵉ felon and it shall sle
it

1041 ffor the palasye Take the woll of a blak shepis fleese
and lay it in watir iij dayes and wasshe it wele in þᵉ same
watir and boyll it till it be wastid ꝰ tyll it be þik and medle
it with the iij part of turpentyn

1042 ffor þᵉ postyme in the hede ffor the mygrayn ffor
waterynge eyȝen ffor the toth ach ꝰ for to festen the teth
in a mannes hede Take a penyworth of peletre of spayn
as moch of spiknard greyns longe pep round pep of ech lich
moch so þat thei be as moch in quantitee as the peletre
spiknard afore sayd ꝰ mak þis in powdre and tak a littell
posnett ꝰ put all thies poudres þᵉin and than tak vynegre
ꝰ mustard as moch as woll resonably stepe and mele the
seid poudres ꝰ sett it apon the fyre and lat boyle and iff it
wex anon dry put þᵉto mor vynegre and mustard and all
way as it boylith stirre it wele togedir and when it waxith
thik put þᵉto ij sponefull of hony and stirre it oũ the fire
till it wex thyk agayne and þen take fro the fire ꝰ stire it
till it be cold ꝰ put it in a bledd̃ and vse it as I haue
[fo. 91 verso] tawght you as oft as ȝe haue nede

stamp all these together, and temper it with running water, and let the sick drink thereof three mornings. And if it do him good, use it longer ; and if it last not, stamp the soap with the medicine ; thou mayest pare it small into the medicine when it is made. And this medicine is good for all manner of jaundice, yellow, black and green.

1038 To know waters (urine) of a man or woman. If the water be red [and] gravelly, it betokeneth sickness in the reins, and if it be white [and] gravelly, it is a species of stone in the bladder, and if it be fat (greasy) above the water, that is wasting.

1039 A medicine for a botch. Take smallage and stamp it in a mortar small ; and take barrow's grease that hath been hung in the roof, and pick out all the skins clean, and stamp it with smallage so small that it be not seen, and make a plaster thereof. And change the plaster ever as it drieth.

1040 For the felon. Take rue a quantity and as much of salt, and stamp them together ; and lay to the felon, and it shall slay it.

1041 For the palsy. Take the wool of a black sheep's fleece and lay it in water three days, and wash it well in the same water, and boil it till it be wasted and till it be thick, and mingle it with the third part of turpentine.

1042 For an imposthume in the head, for the migraine, for watering eyes, for the toothache, and for to fasten [loose] teeth in a man's head. Take a pennyworth of pellitory of Spain, as much of spikenard, kermes, long pepper, round pepper, of each equally much, so that they be as much in quantity as the pellitory [and] spikenard aforesaid. And make this in powder, and take a little bag and put all these powders therein. And then take vinegar and mustard, as much as will reasonably steep and mingle the said powders.[1] And set it upon the fire, and let [it] boil ; and if it wax anon dry, put thereto more vinegar and mustard, and alway as it boileth stir it well together. And when it waxeth thick put thereto two spoonfuls of honey, and stir it over the fire till it wax thick again. And then take [it] from the fire, and stir it till it be cold, and put it in a bladder and use it as I have taught you, as oft as ye have need.

---

[1] Meaning, as much as they will absorb.

1043 A soũene medecyn for madnes and ffor men þat be travailid wᵗ wikkyd sprets   Vpon mydsomõ nyȝt be twyx mydnyȝt and rysynge of the sonne gedre the fairest grene leves on þᵉ walnot tre ꝫ apon the same day bitwene the sonne rysynge ꝫ the goynge doun distill þᵒoff a watir in a stillatory bytwyx ij basyns ꝫ this watir is gode iff it be dronken for the same maladye

1044 A medecyne for the pestilence   Take diteyne phili- pendula and turmentyn of each lich moch ꝫ bray hem togedir ꝫ tempere hem with ale or with wyne and drynk þam

1045 ffor the piles or emerauntes in the fundement   Tak vnsett leke and an erb that is cald clyvers that yonge gese eten ꝫ a quantitee of may butʳ ꝫ stamp hem in a mort̃ ꝫ þen lay hem on a lynnen cloth and hold to þᵉ fire ꝫ as hote as the syke may suffre it lay it to his fundement ꝫ than bynd it vp þᵗ þᵉ pleist̃ fall nat away ꝫ he shall be easid wᵗin iij or iiij days

1046   An oþᵒ   Tak an egg and rost it hard and then tak it and cleue it in two ꝫ þan take the oyle of rosys ꝫ temp the same halue the yolk beynge wᵗ in the same halue white of the egg wᵗ the same oyle of rosis so þᵗ þᵉ halue yolk be lyk j wid and as hote as the syk may suffre lay it to the foundment and bynd it vp ꝫ wᵗ [in] iij days he shall be hole

1047 ffor a man that may nat here   Take rue and stamp it ꝫ wrynge out the Juyse or streyn it ꝫ put [fo. 92 recto] it in a pece ꝫ mak it lewk warme ꝫ put in the ere ꝫ lat lye on the othir side

1048 A dreggþe ffor the siatica and oþᵒ syknes   Tak the seyd of anneys comyn caraway ffenell watir cressis ich an vnce of pion sede an vnce the beries of bayes two dragms of nutmuges small schredd an vnce ꝫ d̄j gyngere maces clowes lich moch ij dragms of licoresse that sufficeth to make all this swete in dreggþ which do þᵉ vse morow and eve

1049 Vse anoþᵒ if the lust dialanga dracumino diaȝin sebri ilich moch

1043 A sovereign medicine for madness and for men that be troubled with wicked spirits. Upon midsummer night betwixt midnight and rising of the sun, gather the fairest green leaves on the walnut tree, and upon the same day between sunrise and its going down, distill thereof a water in a still between two basins. And this water is good if it be drunken for the same malady.

1044 A medicine for the pestilence. Take dittany, philipendula (dropwort) and tormentil, of each equally much, and bray them together, and temper them with ale or with wine, and drink them.

1045 For the piles or hæmorrhoids in the fundament. Take an unseeded leek and a herb that is called cleavers (goose-grass) that young geese eat, and a quantity of may-butter, and stamp them in a mortar. And then lay them on a linen-cloth and hold [it] to the fire ; and as hot as the sick may suffer it, lay it to the fundament ; and then bind it up that the plaster fall not away. And he shall be eased within three or four days.

1046 Another. Take an egg and roast it hard, and then take it and cleave it in two ; and then take the oil of roses, and temper the same half the yolk and half the white of the same half-egg,[1] so that the half-yolk be liquid, and as hot as the sick may suffer it, lay it to the fundament, and bind it up. And within three days he shall be whole.

1047 For a man that may not (cannot) hear. Take rue and stamp it and wring out the juice or strain it, and put it in a piece [of wool] and make it lukewarm, and put in the ear, and [let] him lie on the other side.

1048 A drug for the sciatica and other sickness. Take the seed of anise, cumin, carraway, fennel, watercress, each an ounce ; of peony seed an ounce ; the berries of bay, two drachms ; of nutmegs small-shredded an ounce and a half ; ginger, mace, cloves, equally much, two drachms ; of liquorice [as much as] sufficeth to make all these sweet in a drug, which do thou use morning and evening.

1049 Use another if thou wilt. Dialanga dracumino diazinsebri,[2] equally much.

---

[1] This passage has been somewhat paraphrased.
[2] These corrupt and barbarous words are probably borrowed from alchemy.

1050 Also take the polipodion ferne of an oke and galyngale and seth this in gode and fresshe rede wyne a potell to a quart and then streyn þt wyne ꝫ vse it when hym lust

1051 ffor the blody flyx   Take the floures of eldir and lay it in iij ours in vynegre and then take it out ꝫ stamp it ꝫ drynk it ꝫ medle it wyth wyne or ale þe quantitee of a sponefull so to drynk it and to kepe it for all the yere put it in vynegre iij ours and then lay it on dryynge ꝫ so to make ther of poudre for all the ȝere ꝫ to drynk it in man̊ afore seid

1052 ffor the Emerauntis   Tak wå myntes and dry hem and after wardys take iij or iiij coles of grene asshene wodde ꝫ put hem wt in a close cheyre and lay the seid dried myntes vpon the coles and so sytt apon the close cheyre and lat the fume passe vpward   And iff a man be wastid vse poudre of myntis in his potage and þe watir of the same in his drynke

1053 A medecyn [fo. 92 verso] ffor the pestilence   Tak v croppis off ruw iff it be a man ꝫ iff it be a woman leue oute ruw for ruw is restauratife to a woman and wastynge to a man ꝫ tak þan þer to v croppis of tansey ꝫ v littell bladys of columbyns and a grete quantitee of marigold flours pull of the small chides fro the croppis þat is lyk safron chyves and if thou may nat get the flour tak the leues than must ȝe haue more of marigold then of all the oþ⁹ then take an egge that is new layd and make an hole on eythire end and blow out all that is with in it and lay it to the fyre and let it rost till þat it may be ground to poudre but brenne it nee and than take a quantitee of good triacle and bray all thies erbis sam with goode ale but streyn hem nat but lat the syk drynke hem iij euen and morow iff thei hold it thei shall haue lyue

1054 ffor to dryfe oute a boch or a sore of a mannys or womans bodye Tak v leues of an erb callid mylfoyle ꝫ stamp hem small and temp hem wt stale ale or with white wyne and put þ⁹to a quantite off triacle and giff the syk to

1050 [Another].   Also take the polypodion fern of an oak
and galingale, and seethe this in good and fresh red wine,
a pottle to a quart, and then strain that wine and use it
when he desires.

1051 For the bloody flux.   Take the flowers of elder and lay
it for three hours in vinegar, and then take it out and
stamp it; and dry[1] it, and mingle it with wine or ale the
quantity of a spoonful.   So to drink it and keep it for all
the year; put it in vinegar three hours then lay it out to
dry, and so to make thereof powder for all the year, and to
drink it in the manner aforesaid.

1052 For the hæmorrhoids.   Take watermint and dry it,
and afterwards take three or four coals[2] of green ash-wood,
and put them within a close chair, and lay the said dried
mint upon the coals, and so sit upon the close chair and
let the fumes pass upward.   And if a man be wasted, use
powder of mint in his pottage, and the water of the same in
his drink.

1053 A medicine for the pestilence.   Take five crops of
rue if it be a man, and if it be a woman leave out rue, for
rue is restorative to a woman and wasting to a man ; and
take then thereto five crops of tansey and five little blades
of columbine, and a great quantity of marigold flowers
full of the small chives from the crops that are like saffron-
chives.   And if thou mayest not get the flowers, take the
leaves, then must thou have more of marigold than of all
the others.   Then take an egg that is new laid, and make a
hole in either end, and blow out all that is within.   And lay
it to the fire and let it roast till it may be ground to powder,
but burn it not.   Then take a quantity of good treacle, and
bray all these herbs therein with good ale, but strain them
not.   And let the sick drink them three evenings and
mornings.   If they (the sick persons) hold it, they shall have
life.[3]

1054 To drive out a botch or a sore of a man or a woman's
body.   Take five leaves of a herb called milfoil, and stamp
them small with stale ale or with white wine.   And put thereto a quantity of treacle and give the sick to drink, and let

---

[1] The text has " drink," which is out of place here.
[2] Glowing brands.
[3] Understand here, " but if they cast it up, they shall die."

drynk and let hem vse this iij days the first day v leues the
secund day iiij leues   The thrid day iij leves stampid and
streynyd w^t triacle afore seid and lay to the same sore when
it is comen owt   A ʒolk of an egg clene purid and the eldist
chese that ʒe kan get and schrape it small and thyk vp þe
ʒolk [fo. 93 *recto*] þ⁹w^t ꝛ lay it to the sore and chaunge it
oft ꝛ it shall draw itt and breke it and mak hyme hole

1055 The toth ach   Tak a cloue of garlyk and cleue it in two
and tak oute the pith ꝛ stopp that full of grete salt and lay
to the soor toth and to the gommes

1056 ffor the actua passio   Take a pynt of nw grete ground
mustard a pynt of·fyne vynegre a pynt of bene floure and
a peny worth of fenycreke and bray it small and medle all
thies togedir and make a pleistre and lay it to the sore
cold with out fire

1057 To take away the ach take erssmert a grete quantite
and stamp it and take the Juyse ther of and wasshe the sore
ther with bi the fyre ꝛ if the skynne be hard that he may
not fele the flesshe but as þou it were dede   Take the drasse
þ⁹off with the Juyse and lay it to the sore

1058 ffor the palasie   Take ambrose and mylfoyle and the
leues of senvey þat men make mustard with ꝛ croppis of
rede nettill and sauge of ech lich moch and lett still hem in
may and vse that same wat amorow by tyme iij sponefull
and also at euen last the same and this shall awoyd the
palasie

1059 ffor the eyʒe syght   Take euꝛose ꝛ pympnoll also the
floure of turmentyne and strawberies when thei bene ripe
off ech lich moch and still hem and put the watir in a glasse
and enoynt his eyʒen at eue and at morow by tyme and þ^is
shall kepe the sight

1060 ffor all manꝛ yuelles that ben [fo. 93 *verso*] in man or
woman   Tak the rotis of elenacāpana   And the rots of
radich and the rotis of turmentyne and also the levys of
bursa pastoris and the levys of pleletre of spayne of euꝛ ich
euꝛ off thies lich moch and make hem in poudre and vse
hem in powdre and vse hem at euen ꝛ at morow and this
[is] gode for all manꝛ yuellis in the bodye this same medecyn
shall avoyd the colyke and the stone and a postym and

him use it thus three days : the first day five leaves, the second day four leaves, the third day three leaves, stamped and strained with treacle aforesaid. And lay to the same sore when it hath come out a yolk of an egg clean purified, and the oldest cheese that thou canst get ; and scrape it small, and thicken up the yolk therewith and lay it to the sore. And change it oft, and it shall draw it and break it and make him whole.

1055 [For] the toothache. Take a clove of garlic and cleave it in two, and take out the pith and stop it full of great salt (rocksalt), and lay to the sore tooth and to the gums.

1056 For the actua passio. Take a pint of new large ground mustard, a pint of fine vinegar, a pint of bean-flour, and a pennyworth of fenugreek. And bray it small, and mingle all these together, and make a plaster and lay it to the sore cold, without fire.

1057 To take away the ache. Take horsemint a great quantity and stamp it, and take the juice thereof, and wash the sore therewith by the fire. And if the skin be so hard that he may not feel the flesh, but as though it were dead, take the dross thereof with the juice and lay it to the sore.

1058 For the palsy. Take ambrose (wood-sage) and milfoil and the leaves of senvey that men make mustard with, and crops of red nettle and sage, of each equally much. And let them be distilled in May, and use the same water next day early three spoonfuls, and also last [thing] at evening. And this shall avoid the palsy.

1059 For the eyesight. Take eufrasia (eyebright) and pimpernel, also the flower of tormentil, and strawberries when they are ripe, of each equally much. And distill them and put the water in a glass and anoint his eyes at eve and at morn early. And this shall keep the sight.

1060 For all manner of evils that be in man or woman. Take the roots of elecampane and the roots of radish and the roots of tormentil, and also the leaves of bursa pastoris (shepherd's-purse) and the leaves of pellitory of Spain, of each and every of these equally much. And make them into powder and use them in powder, and use them at even and at morn. And this is good for all manner of evils in the body. This same medicine shall avoid the colic and the

x 2

oþ⁹ syknes and supfluitee and also the cardiacle and avoyd the flemme for to maynten the strynges off the hert and pryncipally for the eʒe sight

1061 ffor the colek   Tak may butt\^r þe mountenance of an nott v blades of safrone and kytt the safrone small and medle w\^t þe butt\^r and put it in nauell of the syke ꝫ to tak þe erþe that is apon a þresschold the mountenaunce of the pawme of a mannys hand and ley it on colis of fyre ꝫ sprynge þ⁹on drestis of gode ale and turne it and sprenge þ⁹apon till it be hote thorow and then tak it vp and lay it in a lynnen cloþe and bynd it to the navell and lay it oꙋ the butture and safrone and so put in þe navell and he shall be hoole

1062 ffor the stomak take ij handfull of myntis and v croppis off wormod and schred hem small and crommes of soure brede and put hem in a panne ꝫ menge hem wele w\^t vynegre and hete it hote ꝫ lay it on a lynnen cloth ꝫ mak p⁹off a bagge [fo. 94 *recto*] and lay it to the stomak and when it is cold tak it out of the bagge and hete it agayne and lay it to the stomak and when it is cold hete it agayne and lay it to [the stomak] ꝫ it shall make an hole stomake

1063 ffor the mygreyne take a pynt of vynegre halue a pynt of mustard and an vnce of frankencens and make a pleistre þ⁹off and lay it in the nek and thei shall be hole w\^t in iij or iiij tyms and it be leid to mesurable hote

1064 Anoþ⁹   Tak d̄j an vnc⁹ of gyng⁹ d̄j vnc⁹ of nutmuges a q̄rtron of an vnc⁹ of clowes jd wiʒt of spiknard jd wiʒt of anneys a q̄rt of an vnc⁹ of elenacampana d̄j vnc⁹ of licoress ꝫ j vnc⁹ of sugure ꝫ bete hem altoged꙰ in poudre ꝫ medle hem togedir and lat the syk vse this poudre first and last a sponefull in his potage or drynk a sponefull at onys and he shall be sekyrly hole w\^t in iiij days ffor this medecyne vsid galien the gode philosophir   And this p⁹vyd apon my lord John Duk of somerset in the lent tyme when he went oꙋ the see   Also ete this poudre first and last byside oþ⁹ receytis

---

¹ John Beaufort (1403–1444), first Duke of Somerset, grandson of John of Gaunt.   Created Duke, 1443 : Captain-General in Aquituine

stone and an imposthume and other sicknesses and super-
fluity, and also the cardiacle, and avoid phlegm, to maintain
the vessels of the heart, and principally for the eyesight.

1061 For the colic. Take may-butter of the amount of a
nut, five blades of saffron, and cut the saffron small, and
mingle [it] with the butter. And put it in [the] navel of
the sick. And take the earth that is upon a threshold to
the amount of the palm of a man's hand, and lay it on coals
of fire, and sprinkle thereon dregs of good ale. And turn it
and sprinkle it thereupon (*i.e.* on the fire) till it be hot
through, and then take it up and lay it in a linen cloth and
bind it to the navel. And lay it over the butter and saffron,
and so put on the navel. And he shall be whole.

1062 For the stomach. Take two handfuls of mint and
five crops of wormwood, and shred them small, and crumbs
of sour bread ; and put them in a pan, and mingle them well
with vinegar, and heat it hot, and lay it on a linen cloth ;
and make thereof a bag and lay it to the stomach. And
when it is cold, take it out of the bag and heat it again, and
lay it to the stomach ; and when it is cold, heat it again, and
lay it to the stomach. And it shall make a whole stomach.

1063 For migraine. Take a pint of vinegar, half a pint of
mustard, and an ounce of frankincense. And make a
plaster thereof and lay it on the neck, and thou shalt be
whole within three or four times, if if be laid to fairly hot.

1064 Another. Take half an ounce of ginger, half an ounce
of nutmegs, a quarter of an ounce of cloves, one pennyweight of spikenard, one pennyweight of anise, a quarter of
an ounce of elecampane, half an ounce of liquorice and one
ounce of sugar. And beat them all together into powder,
and mingle them together, and let the sick use this powder
first and last, a spoonful in his pottage, and drink a spoonful
at once, and he shall be securely (certainly) whole within
four days. For this medicine used Galen the good philosopher. And this [was] proved upon my Lord John, Duke
of Somerset,[1] in the Lent-time when he went over the sea.
Also eat this powder first and last beside (instead of) other
receipts.

---

and Normandy, 1443. He was recalled in 1444 and is said to have
committed suicide. *See* Introduction, § II.

1065 Jtm̄   Take a halpeny worth of comyn and breke
it to poudre and boyle it in cow mylk þᵗ it be thyk ꝫ make
þꝫof a pleistre and lay it apone the sore as hote as he may
suffre it and it will cesse the rage anone but knyt it fast to
the hede

1066 Anoþꝫ   Tak an egge newe layde and a penyworth of
saunders and make it thyk as [fo. 94 *verso*] papp and lay it
on the temple on the sore syde and let it lye ther iij ours
and do so iij tymes when the grevaunce begynnyth to ragge
and on warantise he shall receyue hele

1067 fforto distroy the pestulence   Take dragance turmentill pympnoll tansay sprigonell beteyn v leuyd grasse
burnell scabiose ruddis femytory of ech an handfull Seynt
John wort ditayne Columbyne dogfenell waꝫ myntis
astrologia longa fethirfay Ruw grete clotes knotfelon
Centorye rosemarye Elenacampana philipendula of ech
halue an handfull watirlely planteyne lyꝯwort stichwort
danndelyon Morsus Diaboli Milfoile rosis Borage langedebefe.
Endiue ssowthistill off ech an handfull   Then distill a waꝫ
off all thies erbis or ellis kep the substance of all thies erbis
and dry hem in to poudre and when tyme is vse thaym wᵗ
sugure as it plese you //

1068 Anoþꝫ ffor the pestulence   Tak turmentill Scabiose
Maydenhere ruddis mathis pympnoll of ech ij handfull
tansay a handfull feþꝫfoy ꝳ j beteyn ij ꝳ daundelyon
ij ꝳ all thies erbis shall be small ground and then the must
take ꝺj a q̄rtron of triacle and as moch of bool armoniake

1069 ffor a man þᵗ is syk in his stomake   Tak comyn a
pound and bray it in a morꞇ and tak þᵗ same and gode
stale [fo. 95 *recto*] ale and seth hem togedir and skomme it
wele and when it is wele boylid take it fro the fire and lat
it renne thorow a streynoure or thorow a lynnen cloth ꝫ lat
the syk drynk the licoure lewk warme and the drass of the
same comyn so boylid to be put in a bagge of lynnen cloth
shapyn lyke and hert ꝫ to be leid to þe stomak of theyme
þᵗ is syk as hote as thei may suffre

1070 ffor wynd in the sydes   Take camamyll an handfull
an oþꝫ of wormod ij handfull of grene brome and stamp

1065 Item.   Take a halfpennyworth of cumin and break it
to powder, and boil it in cow's milk that it be thick ; and
make thereof a plaster and lay it upon the sore as hot as he
may suffer it, and it will cease the rage (pain) anon, but knit
it fast to the head.

1066 Another.   Take an egg new laid, and a pennyworth
of sanders, and make it as thick as pap, and lay it on the
temple on the sore side.   And let it lie there three hours,
and so do three times when the grievance beginneth to rage,
and on warranty he shall receive healing

1067 For to destroy the pestilence.   Take dragance,
tormentil, pimpernel, tansey, sprignel, betony, five-leaved
grass, burnet, scabious, reeds, fumitory, of each a handful ;
St. John's-wort, dittany, columbine, dog-fennel, watermint,
aristolochia longa, feverfew, rue, great cloves, matfelon
(knapweed), centaury, rosemary, elecampane, philipendula
(dropwort), of each half a handful ; water-lily, plantain,
liverwort, stitchwort, dandelion, morsus-diaboli (devil's-bit-
scabious), milfoil, roses, borage, bugloss, endive, sowthistle,
of each a handful.   Then distill a water of all these herbs,
or else keep the substance of all these herbs and dry them to
powder, and when time is, use them with sugar as it please
you.

1068 Another for the pestilence.   Take tormentil, scabious,
maidenhair, red madder, pimpernel, of each two handfuls ;
tansey a handful, feverfew one handful, betony one handful,
dandelion two handfuls.   All these herbs shall be small
ground, and then thou must take a half a quartern of treacle
and as much of bol-ammoniac.

1069 For a man that is sick in his stomach.   Take cumin a
pound, and bray it in a mortar ; and take the same and
good stale ale and seethe them together, and skim it well.
And when it is well boiled, take it from the fire, and let it
run through a strainer or through a linen cloth, and let the
sick drink the licour lukewarm.   And the dross of the
cumin so boiled [is] to be put in a bag of linen cloth, shaped
like a heart, and to be laid to the stomach of him that is
sick, as hot as he may suffer it.

1070 For wind in the sides.[1]   Take camomile a handful,
and another of wormwood, two handfuls of green broom,

---

[1] This recipe is a duplicate of § 965.

hem small togedir than tak a bagge that will go fro the navell
to the reyns and thies maters cowchid abrode and brochyd
in the bagge somwhat brode that will lygge abrode on the
womb and then take a gode porcion of malews and buyle
heme in a pot full of clene rennynge watir to it be thorow
hote ꝛ than plunge the bage in the water and þen qewys
out the waꝛ ꝛ all hote lay it on the wombe till it com to þe
reyns ꝛ when it is cold hete it in the same waꝛ

1071 To avoyd wynd þᵗ is cause of colek   Tak comyne and
anneys of ech lich moch and lay it in white wyne to
stepe and keꝰ it oꝰ with wyne and lat it stand still so iij
dayes [fo. 95 verso] ꝛ iij nyghtes and than lat it be taken
oute and lat it be taken out and layd apon an asshen bord
for to dry ix days and to be turnyd emonge and at the ix
days end take and put it in an erthen pott ꝛ dryed oꝰ
the fyre ꝛ þen mak powdre þ⁹of ꝛ þen ete it in potage or
drynk it ꝛ it shall void wele the wynd þᵗ is cause of colek

1072 ffor the Emerauntis   Tak an handfull of nettyls and
bray hem and wrynge out the Juys ꝛ drynk it ꝛ take the
pomys þ⁹off and lay to þe emerauntis ꝛ bynd it þ⁹to and he
or she þat hath theym shall be hole wᵗ in short tyme þis
is pvid truw

1073 xxxijᵗⁱ euell days þ⁹ ben in the yere with out those
þᵗ bene notid in the kalendare who so weddyth a wyffe
in any of those days he shall nat longe haue joy of hyre ꝛ
who þᵗ takyth any grete jurney shall neꝰ come agayn or
som infurtune shall fall hym ꝛ he þat begynnyth any grete
warke shall neꝰ make end þ⁹off and he þat lattyth hym
blode shall son dey or neꝰ be hole

1074 Janyꝰ þe first day þᵗ ij iiij v x xj xv
     ffeꝰ iij þe first þe vij ꝛ x

March ij þe ij ꝛ xj	August ij xx xix
Aprile ij xvj ꝛ xxj	Septembₐ ij vj vij
May iij vj xv xx	Octobₐ j vj
June ij iiij ꝛ vij	Nouēbₐ ij xv xix
Julle ij xv ꝛ xx	Decembₐ iij vi vij ix days

and stamp them small together.   Then take a bag that will go from the navel to the reins, with these substances laid flat and spread out in the bag somewhat widely that will lie across the womb.   And then take a good portion of mallows, and boil them in a pot full of clean running water, till it be thoroughly hot.   And then plunge the bag in the water, and then squeeze out the water, and all hot lay it on the womb till it come to the reins, and when it is cold, heat it in the same water.

1071 To avoid wind that is the cause of colic.   Take cumin and anise, of each equally much, and lay it in white wine to steep, and cover it over with wine, and let it stand still so three days and three nights.   And then let it be taken out and laid upon an ash-board for to dry nine days, and to be turned about.   And at the nine days' end, take and put it in an earthen pot and dried over the fire, and then make powder thereof.   And then eat it in pottage or drink it, and it shall void the wind that is [the] cause of colic.

1072 For the hæmorrhoids.   Take a handful of nettles and bray them and wring out the juice.   And drink it and take the pomice[1] thereof, and lay to the hæmorrhoids, and bind it thereto.   And he or she that hath them shall be whole within a short time.   This is proved true.

1073 [Dies Nefastæ].   Thirty-two evil days there be in the year without those that be noted in the calendar.   Whoso weddeth a wife on any of those days, he shall not long have joy of her.   And who that taketh any great journey, shall never come [back] again, or some misfortune shall befall him. And he that beginneth any great work shall never make end thereof.   And he that letteth him blood shall soon die or never be whole.

1074 [List of Dies Nefastæ].
January, the first day, the 2nd, 4th, 5th, 10th 11th, 15th.
February, 3 [days] ; the first, the 7th and 10th.

March, 2 ; the 2nd, and 11th.	August, 2 ; 20th, 19th (*sic*).
April, 2 ; 16th and 21st.	September, 2 ; 6th, 7th.
May, 3 ; 6th, 15th, 20th.	October, 1 ; 6th.
June, 2 ; 4th and 7th.	November, 2 ; 15th, 19th.
July, 2 ; 15th and 20th.	December, 3 ; the 6th, 7th,
	[and] 9th days.

---

[1] This word is still used in the West of England for the residue of apples after the juice has been extracted for cider.

APPENDIX

MEDICAL PRESCRIPTIONS FROM A MANUSCRIPT OF THE TUDOR PERIOD.

(*MS. Dawson*, 19.)

The manuscript from which the following medical prescriptions were taken is a commonplace book containing 36 folios of stout paper measuring 37 × 26·5 cm., and it was used by various members of the Purevey (or Purefoy) family.[1] The dated entries range between 1526 and 1561, and they are written by various hands. Most of the entries are in the handwriting of John Purevey, who writes sometimes in English and sometimes in Latin. On the first folio he has written some particulars of his family, from which the following table can be reconstructed :—

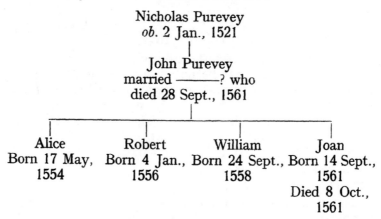

Nicholas Purevey
ob. 2 Jan., 1521

John Purevey
married ——? who
died 28 Sept., 1561

Alice	Robert	William	Joan
Born 17 May, 1554	Born 4 Jan., 1556	Born 24 Sept., 1558	Born 14 Sept., 1561 Died 8 Oct., 1561

John Purevey's wife, whose name is not stated, died a fortnight after the birth of her youngest child.

The first four folios of the book are filled on both sides with accounts, mainly for the sale of velvet and other kinds of cloth, from which it may be inferred that John Purevey was a merchant. These accounts range in date from 1526

[1] The MS. was in an elaborately-tooled red leather wallet, which I gave to the Victoria and Albert Museum.

to 1543.   Folios 5 to 13 are devoted to the medical and
veterinary recipes which are here published.   The remainder
of the book contains particulars of lands and other property,
mostly in the counties of Essex and Hertford, with details
of the tenants and rentals, and copies of documents relating
thereto.   After some blank folios, there is a neatly written
" Order of Study."   This takes the form of a tabulated
system of philosophy, written in Latin and Greek, and
apparently based on the works of Aristotle.   Finally, on
the last folio, are entered particulars of swans belonging to
John Purevey, with diagrams of the marks or " nicks " on
their beaks by which he identified them.

The medical recipes are typical of the remedies that were
popular at the time.   All will be found very similar to those
set out in much greater profusion in M., and some are actual
duplicates.   It has not been considered necessary to tran-
scribe these into modern spelling : they are therefore printed
just as they stand in the original, but explanatory notes
have been added wherever necessary.

Some interesting names occur.   No. 35 was used by Sir
Anthony Browne, No. 39 by the well-known lawyer Nicholas
Barham, and No. 43 by Sir Christopher Haydon.   Particulars
of these persons will be found in the notes.

The prescriptions, which are written by several different
hands, are not numbered in the manuscript.   The numbers
have been affixed to them to facilitate reference.   Judging
by the handwriting and other evidence of date, it appears
that the recipes were written out about 1560 to 1580, during
the reign of Queen Elizabeth, and therefore rather more
than a century later than the manuscript M.

MEDYCYNES FOR DIUERSE DISEASES.

1. ffirst for a plurysye.

Take a good draughte of the water of borage & melt in
asmuche as a beane or a litle lesse of metridatū[1] and blood
warme giue it hym to drynke and at iij severall tymes
after mydnight, and put in a bagge gyneper[2] beryes beaten
small and temp them a litle wth vineger not to well & lay
to the place of the side that the stiche is in and alwayes
kepe the brest warme.

---

[1] Mithridatum, Pennycress.   [2] Juniper.

2. A thynne syrope for the longes.[1]

Take faire rennynge[2] water a galon put to it hartes tonge maydonhere,[3] vyolet leaves, purselane buglosses jsope[4] & the rote of briscus,[5] the rootes of red ffennell, rootes of borage the buddes of the flowers also, a good quantytie of Lettuse endif and Southystill.[6] reasons of the sonne[7] & the stones picked oute, good licoryce pared and the stones beaten flatt penedes[8] and white sugar candye, a sauser full of anyssedes boyle all theise together till thre ptes be wasted[9] and then strayne it and Drincke it when ye liste.

3. The thycker syrope for the coughe.

Take a pinte of englisshe honey & clarifie it cleare then take a handfull of Rue & asmuche of sage & asmuche of arke[10] bet it together & presse the jewse in to the honey & let m boyle together & as it boyleth put in to it vj sponefull of water of rosemarye flowers a litle quantitye of longe pepp[11] & boyle them together tyll it looke of the coloure of the honey & drinke it when ye go to bed & in the night when the coughe dothe trouble you somtyme wth a lycorise stycke frised[12] & dipped in the syrope & let the pacyent sucke thereof.

4. A medycyne for a whote[13] ffever.

Take vj greate handfull of borage stalkes & flowers, wasshe them cleane & drye them in a fayre cloth & put them in a morter there put to them a sponefull of good white vineger then stampe the vineger and borage verye smale then strayne the jewse into a fayre vessell & sett on a chafyngdisshe wth a softe fyre & then under nethe wilbe a yelowe water then strayne it agayne in to a faire vessell

---

[1] Lungs.   [2] Running, or stream-water.
[3] Maidenhair.   [4] Hyssop.
[5] Bruscus, Butcher's Broom.   [6] Sow-thistle.
[7] Sun-dried raisins.
[8] Penides, or Pennet, barley sugar.
[9] *I.e.*, let three-quarters evaporate.
[10] Apparently an abbreviation for Archangel, the popular name of several plants, *Angelica, Lycopus, Lamium*, etc., possibly *Ache* is meant.   [11] Long pepper.
[12] Beaten and splayed out like a brush.   [13] Hot.

throughe a faire cloth & put to it so muche sugar as will make it swete & then sethe it tyll it syrope[1] then put it in a faire glasse & drinke it fastinge everye morninge.

5. An oyle for the plurysye & whote fever.

Take purslane water xij sponefull or more iij or iiij sponefull of rosewater a great sponefull of good saunders[2] iiij ounces of the oyle of vyoletts a quarter of a sponefull of white vineger or oyle of semphire[3] & beate all these together & then take flex and make a plaister & lay it to yo[r] right side somewhat warme.

6. ffor ache in the hed.

Take and seth verveyne & of bittanyne[4] & of wormwood & thorou[ly] wassh the hed of y[e] pacyent & then make a plaister aboue on the molde[5] of this manner. Take y[e] same herbes when they ben sodden & wringe them & grinde them smale in a morter & temp them w[th] y[e] same licoure agayne & put thereto whete branne for to kepe in the licoure & make a garlond of a kercheff & bynde y[e] pacyete[6] his hed & ley y[e] plaister on the molde w[th]in the garlonde as whote as y[e] pacyēt[6] may suffer it & bynde the hed w[th] a volup[7] & set a cappe aboue & thus do iij tymes & the sicke shalbe whole on warrantyes.[8]

7. To make a purgacyon.

Take lawrell & make pouder thereof & temp it w[th] honey of either like muche.

8. ffor stinkinge breth through the nose.[9]

Take red myntes and rue of either like quantytie & wringe the juyce in to the pacyent his nostrelles at night upon he goeth to bed.

---

[1] Thickens, like syrup.
[2] Sanders, or sandal-wood.
[3] Samphire, or glasswort.
[4] Betony.
[5] A.-S. *molda*, the top of the head.
[6] Patient.
[7] *Voluper* (O.F. *enuoluper*), a head-wrap or woman's cap.
[8] Certainly.
[9] *Cf.* M., § 623.

9. A good medicyne for the tothake of the wormes.[1]

Take henbane sede & leke sede & powder of mintes & lay them on a glowynge tylestone & make a pipe of Latten y^t ye nether ende be wyde so that it may owclose the sedes & powder & holde yor mouth uppon the one end of the pipe so that the ayre may go in to the sore tothe & y^t will kill the wormes & out away the ache.

10. ffor greate thirste a good medycyne.

Take ye roote of sanacle & tempe it wth water wel stamped & drinke it iij nightes & ye shall amend.

11. ffor the prlouse[2] coughe a good medycyne.

Take sawge, rue & comyn & pouder pepper & beate them together & put them in honey & make a lettuarye[3] & use a sponefull at even & an other in the morninge.[4]

12. ffor the chyne coughe[5] a good medycyne.

Take the roote of horselene[6] & the roote of conforye[7] of ech like muche & grind them smale in a morter & seth them in faire water till thone[8] half be wasted.   Then take the other half & ye thirde pte of honey & boyle it & sky͞me it & put them together and make thereof a Lectuarye & put it in a box & use thereof v or vj dayes a good quantytie at ones & he shalbe whole.[9]

13. ffor evel in the back.[10]

Take ashe egremoyne & moushyre[11] & stampe it together & put thereto barowes greace [12] & eysyll[13] & fry them well & make a plaister & lay it to ye backe of ye pacyent as whote as he may suffer it.

---

[1] Duplicate of M., § 912, and *see* note thereon.
[2] Parlous, perilous, persistent.   [3] Electuary.
[4] Duplicates, M., § 190 ; *Harl.* 2378 (Henslow, *op. cit.*, p. 101).
[5] Whooping-cough.
[6] Ellenium, Elena Campana. *See* Dioscorides, *De Materia Medica*, i, 27.   Horshelne or Horseheal = Elecampane or Scabwort.   *Cf.* M., § 196.
[7] Comfrey.   [8] Obsolete contraction for *the one*.
[9] Earlier duplicate, *Harl.* 2378, *loc. cit.*
[10] Duplicate of M., § 998.   [11] Mouse-ear.
[12] Fat of a barrow-hog.   [13] Vinegar.

14. for costetyvenes.[1]

Take maues[2] & mecurye[3] & seth it wth a pece of porke & make thereof potage & let ye pacyent eate thereof well & drinke therwth white wyne or whey & y^t shall make him solible.[4]

15. for the flux.

Take hencressen[5] and croppes of woodbynes that beare honey socles stampe them & temp them in warme wyne[6] red / and giue the pacyent to drinke & let him eat iij dayes every daye firste v leekes wth . . . bred[7] y^t is whote and no drinke but red wyne warme & he shalbe whole. And let the sycke haue a stewe w^t a sege[8] & make thereunder a little charcole fyer & let it be closed wth a clothe downe to the erth that no hete may passe but even up unto his foundement & let him syt bare on the stole as ofte as fytte tyll he be whole.

16. for one y^t may not holde his water.[9]

Take the clawes of a gote & brene them & make powder thereof & let hym use it in his potage a sponefull at ones.

17. for a fever quotidyan.

Take feverfew & smalage of ech like muche & stampe them & temp them wth water & strayne them & giue the sicke to drinke when the fyt comyth uppon hym a good quantytye & so shalbe whole wth in iij tymes drinkynge.[10]

---

[1] Costiveness.   [2] Mallows.

[3] The herb, not the metal, is meant.

[4] Soluble, *i.e.*, with bowels open. There is a duplicate of this remedy in *Sloane* 521, and M., § 186.

[5] Shepherd's Purse.

[6] The stroke after " red " indicates that it should be read before " wine."

[7] The blank is left for a Saxon word the writer did not understand. The duplicate text in MS. *Sloane* 521 has " ӡerf," a mistake for " þerfbred," unleavened bread.

[8] A tree-legged stool.   [9] Duplicate of M., § 731.

[10] An almost identical recipe in MS. *Sloane* 521 (Henslow, *op. cit.*, p. 135).

18. for bytinge of an adder.

Take centory & stampe it and temp it wth his owne water
& giue the sycke to drink and it is as good to beaste as
man.[1]

19. ffor ache in the hed.

Take ffennel & Rewe seth them well in water & wassh his
hed & make therof a plaister in manner as is aforesaide.

20. for the opulation[2] of the spleene.

Make a posset with whyte wyne & take the curde & then
sethe in the drinke a quantytye of tyme & hartstonge of
eche alyke & strayne it & drinke it wth sugar.

21. ffor the stytche.

Take a lytle hanfull of mynte asmutche of wormewoodd
asmutche of camemell[3] & a lyke of tyme choppe all together
small.   Then take a rowfe tyle[4] & make it redd hott & take
it from the fyre & put in the erbes w^thin the halowgh
thereof stere them up and downe wth a knyfe & pore iij or
iiij sponefulls of sake[5] amoungts them & then caste in a
quarter of a handfull of wheat branne then put all in a
lynen bagge & lay the same to the place as whotte as the
pacient may suffer it yf this helpe not w^thin ij or iij
dressyngs it is no outward stytche.

22. for the stone in the bladdar.

Take a handfull of Jucy beanes[6] growing upon sallow
or wyllowe yf you canne gett suche washe it not but wype
it & let it lye steping in a pint of aqua vitæ by the space
of fortnyght then drinke the quantytye of a sponefull by
the space of iij wekes evenyng & mornyng & eate not in ij
howres after.

---

[1] Duplicate in MS. *Sloane* 521 (Henslow, *op. cit.*, p. 136).
[2] Oppilation, obstruction.   [3] Camomile.
[4] Roof-tile.   [5] Sack, Canary wine.
[6] Ivy berries.

23. for A Strangulyon.

One potell of malmesey one handfull of vnsett tyme and tyme of the molehill[1] one handfull of pcelley[2] and of pceley seede j ozce brusced halff a handfull of Camamell bruse all these and so brused putt theym all in the malmesey. Then sethe theym and in the same sethynge put asmuche butter as an hene ege and putt thereto ol of Safrone brused[3] boyle well together untyll halff of all be consumed then Strayne theym and so drynke ytt even and morowe blowde warme and when that ys don make more. / in anywyse kepe you solable[4] w[t] a Clyster or suppositor.

24. for to make A Clyster.

Take Camomell and malowes of eche one handfull. Small lavender & lavender stike & Betes of eche half one handefull. Anysede half one ounce. Comyn sede halff an ounce boyle all these in ffayre water w[t] mutton & veale a long tyme w[t] iiij sponefull of honye · then Strayne theym and take a pynt of the same Decokcion & putt in to ytt a Dram or ij of Salte · and v sponefull of Salet Oyle and so mynister ytt.

[imedyatly drynk brath[5] on some thyng ells take ij ouncs & eat it ones very wote & then fast Di ower[6] after & then take a brath or one egge wh wyll make you solable.][7]

25. ffor the Collyke.

Take halffe a shete of whyte pap strike of [all][8] that all w[t] Salett Oyle and then strowe thereof grose peper and so ley to you[r] belye from the navell.[9]

---

    [1] Perhaps Hillwort (*Thymus serpyllum*).
    [2] Parsley.   [3] Oil or juice of bruised saffron.
    [4] Keep the bowels open.   [5] Broth.
    [6] Half an hour.
    [7] The terminal paragraph in square brackets is added by a later hand. In the same handwriting the word " Wryght " is written in the margin against Nos. 23 and 24, which are bracketed together. Both, therefore, were obtained from a person named Wright.
    [8] Crossed out.
    [9] This obscurely worded recipe is evidently for an adhesive plaster, made by sprinkling pepper upon a sheet of paper dipped in salad oil.

26. for the Strangurye.

You must use pouulder[1] of Zedhoryny[2] Bowes in drynke of whyte wyne or Bennysse[3] eury mornynge next your harte and then fast one howre after in anywyse, and so drynke ytt to bedwarde[4] ij howres after Sup.

27. medysyn for a measyll[5] sowe.

take one q̅rte of Newe mylk from the Sowe put theyto whote Embres takyng away all coles & gyve the same to yo[r] Sow to eat ones a Weke p̅r p̅bat[6] & ofterne.

28. An other.

iij apells rosted putt them full of brymstone & lett yo[r] hogge eat them iij dayes together & it wyll heale yo[r] hogge p̅bat.[6]

29. A medycyne for to scower the Syknes[7] Deuysed by ․ ․ ․ ․ [8]

take ij pyntes of ynglysh honey, j ℔. of turpyntine of Venys Di̅[10] pynte of the juyse of lemens myngell all thes together & Styll them in a lymbyk[9] glasse w[t] a soft fyer & there wyll come bothe oyll & water stepe them seurall in ij glasses & iij tymes in euery weke take one draught of whyte wyne or red & with Di̅[10] sponefull of the frsed (aforesaid) water & somuche of the oyll & [then drynk it luke warm & be fastyng iij howres after].[11]

---

[1] Powder.   [2] Yellow Zeodary.
[3] Bind on.   [4] Towards bed-time.
[5] Middle-English *mesel, masel*, a leper, but used for a sick or miserable creature, and especially for a disease of swine caused by the larvæ of *Taenia solium*.
[6] *Per probatum*, "as proved."   [7] Plague.
[8] An illegible word.   [9] Alembic ; *cf.* D., § 40.
[10] *Dimidium*, half.
[11] The words in square brackets are written in the margin, there bring no room for them at the foot of the page. The whole recipe is very badly written and extremely difficult to read.

30. Maister Cesars[1] purgacon.

Take polipody of the oke[2] iij drames, Alexandria souc[r] vj
drames, annesede ij dame di—ginger one drame ; putt all
these all nyghte in a pynt of clene condet[3] water, & in the
mornyng sethe them in the same water vntill the thyrde
pte be consumed, streyne ytt and take iij or iiij ouncs of
the same joyse & putt one ounce di of manna vnto ytt &
streyne it agayne and take it blode warme.

31. To purge the Stomacke of fleame.[4]

Take fennell roots iiij or v pselye[5] roots vj or vij beinge
cut ij ynches longe wth the pithes taken out of them take an
ounce of alicompana[6] roots, ij roots of succary,[7] v stickes of
lickerise brused, xij figgs cut euery one in iiij peces iiij ounces
rasins broken wth y[r] stones taken out, of anhesede an ounce,
a handfull of jsoppe, manipulū[8] a handfull ix crops of horehounde, iij vnces of hony, Boyle all these in a gallen of
runninge watr till it be consumed to a qrte, then streane
yt & giue yt to the pacient, at eue vj spongefull & likewise
in y[e] morning blodde warme.[9]

32. A p[r]seruatiue againste the plage.

Take ij [ounces][10] pounde of figges, ij handfull of rew, lx
wallnutts, & blanche thē, & beat euery one seuerall vntyll
they be small, then beat them altogether & put them in a
boxe & in time of plage take the quantitye of a wallnutte
at once fastinge in the morninge.

33. for one alredy infected wth ye plage.

Take ij onyons & cut of the topps, then make a hole in
ether of them wth inne, fill them wth triacle & pep[11] & so

---

[1] Aldemare Cæsar (died 1569), medical adviser to Queens Mary
and Elizabeth.
[2] " Oak-fern," *Polypodium vulgare.*
[3] Conduit.   [4] Phlegm.
[5] Parsley.   [6] Elecampane.
[7] Chicory.   [8] *Manipulum,* "handful."
[9] There is a somewhat similar prescription " For the best and to
clere a mañys voys " in MS. *Sloane* 521, fo. 237 *verso*, and *cf.* below
Nos. 34 and 37.
[10] Crossed out.   [11] Pepper.

roste them in the fire whilest yt be softe, then take them
out & make them cleane, wch first beings stamped, afterwarde must be streyned with iiij spoynefull of vinegar and
likewise of cleane water, then let the pacient when yt is
mayde bloode warme drinke yt, & lay some of yt strened
to the sore.

34. A ppreparatyve.

R/ iij or iiij fennell roots the pythe beynge taken oute
& vj pcelye[1] rots ye pithe likewyse taken oute iii or iiij
stickes of lycoras brosed, halfe a handfull of great reasons[2]
the stones taken oute. A quantytie of Annys seade jsope[3]
halfe handfull boile all thease in iij pynts of water till the
water be consumed to a pynte then take it and strayne it.
Then take of it iij sponefulls evenynge and mornynge iij
daies together yf you take a purgacon take yor purgacon in
ye mornynge yf you take pills for ye Rume[4] take them at
viij of the Clocke at nyght, and none of yor p'peratyfe.

35. for the stone in the back Justyce Browne.[5]

Take plantayne fetherfewe[6] garden tansey and houselyke
of eche alyke quantytye and stampe all these to gether &
strayne them then take the joyse and put to yt bene floure
asmuche as shall make yt thicke & then take iij or
iiij Sponefull of hony & claryfye them in the fyre and that
'so done put in the saide joyse wth the floure into the hony
& boyle them on the fyre all together vntyll·theye be styffe
to stryke them on a playster when youe wyll vse this
medecyne youe muste take a duble clothe that shalbe a
quarter of a yarde broade and as longe as wyll go rounde
aboute youe and strike this plaster vpon it as hote as you
can & so sow it rounde aboute youe and that youe must
weare ij dayes & a nyght or ells ij nyghtes and adaye before
youe take yt of the plaster must lye agenst yor kydnes on
eury syde of y^r rydge of yor backe when youe feele payne
and Ache ther.

---

[1] Parsley.   [2] Raisins.
[3] Hyssop.   [4] Rheum.
[5] Sir Anthony Browne, appointed Justice in Eyre, 1545 ; died
1548.
[6] Feverfuge or feverfew.

36. for the Strangury Robt penrodock.[1]

Take whyte wyne a quantytye and of styllyd mylke a more quantyty ad therto a portyon of Suger & gyng[r]. Drynke thys mylke warme mornynge or evenynge forseinge that you vse not this after the furst second or thyrd tyme passynge ones eury weke or xiiij dayes.

37. A dredgge to purge the ffleame.[2]

And to do this take an ounce of lycoras fayre scraped and cut smalle, of Annessed an ownce, careway sede an ownce ffennell sedde half an ownce, Colyander[3] half an ownce, Comminge[4] sedd half an ownce cleane ffanned Enula campana root halfe an ownce, A rryse rotte[5] a quarter of an ownce, Gynger half a quarter of an ownce, ffoxe lunges[6] one & a half.

Sevyrcandye[7] a quarter of a pounde, white sevger[8] a quarter of a pownde, beat all thess to[gether][9] powlder and myxe them together ; so put them in a boxe and kepp it drye then in the eatinge take a quarter of a spovnefull eveninge and mornynge or an aple rosted and take the pappe of the same and deppe it in the poulder affore saide.

38. A medecyne to stay the opennes[10] of the Raynes.

Take a quart of malmesey and the yolkes of iiij egges put into the same in thorder of a cawdell makinge put thereunto di oz. of beaten sinamome and two pennywo[r]th of long mace beaten to powlder & put in the same malmesey w[th] the egges and sethe the same from a quart to a pynte and take vj sponefull thereof every mornynge levke warme and faste after in the space of ij howres or iij.

---

[1] Robert Penruddock, the person from whom the recipe was obtained.
[2] Phlegm.   [3] Coriander.
[4] Cumin.   [5] Orris-root.
[6] According to Sextus Placitus : " Vulpis pulmo, ex vino nigro datum suspiriosos emendat " (*Liber Medicinæ ex animalibus*, ii, 5). Dioscordies (ii, 41) ascribes the same virtue.
[7] Sugar-candy.   [8] Sugar.
[9] Crossed out.   [10] Open-ness, " running of the reins."

39. for the stone vsed by Sygeannt Barram.[1]

Take a pottell of mylke and as muche of white wyne put
to gethers, then rake ij[d] worthe of anyeseedé as muche of
Colyander seede, as muche of gromewell seede, and half as
muche of commene seede, beate them all to to powlder and
put them into the mylke and wyne   And so still them all
to gethers.

Memord. a powder to be dronck wth the saide drynck
so dystilled made of wylde tyme.

40. An Aqua composita vsd by doctor Stevens.

Take A gallon of of (sic) good gascon wyne then take
gynger gallengale Cynamon nutmeges [cloves, Annesseds
ffennell sed][2] carawa sed & graynes every of them a like
moche that is to say of every of them   A Drame then take
sage mynte Redd roses tyme pellytory Rosemarie wilde
tyme cammamell lavender of every one a handfull then
bray the spyces small and bray the herbs and put all in the
wyne and let it stand so xij howers stiringe it dyvers tymes,
Then still it by lymbecke[3] and kepp the first water by it
self for it is best then kepp the second for it is good /

The vertu of this water is it comforteth the vitall spiritte
helpeth inwarde deseases that come of could and Againste
the shakeinge of the palsey, it curethe contraction of
Synnewes helpeth the conseption of baren women it killeth
the wormes in the belly it cureth the could coughe it comforteth the Stomake very moche cureth could dropsey it
helpeth the stone in the bladder and in the Raines and
who so ever vseth this water ever amonge[4] and not often
it p[r]se[r]uyth[5] him in good lykinge and shall make him seme
yonge very longe in this wat[r] Doctor Steven p[r]serveth his
lyff very longe fyve years longer then the phsuns[6] supposed
he could / it is accompted excellent /

---

[1] Serjeant "Barram," or Barham, is Nicholas Barham, a well-
known lawyer. He was called to the Bar at Gray's Inn, 1542;
Serjeant-at-Law, 1567; M.P. for Maidstone, 1563. Barham con-
ducted the prosecution of the Duke of Norfolk for conspiring with
Mary Queen of Scots against Elizabeth, and of Higford, the duke's
secretary. He died in 1577 of gaol fever, contracted during the
trial of Jencks, a disaffected Roman Catholic.

[2] These words are added above the line.   [3] Alembic; cf. No. 29.

[4] Read "ever and anon," i.e., from time to time.

[5] Preserveth.   [6] Physicians.

41. To Dissolve fflewme[1] & other infermyties in the stomake.

Take xv handsfull of jsope and ij handfulls of rewe and stampe them smale and strayne once the juce of them & put therto one quart of englishe honnye half a pounde of figge doatts[2] and stampte them smalle and put them to the serope wth a penneworthe of the p[r3] of licora wth a quantyte of Anneysedde and ffennell beaton to poulder and one pynte of Romney[4] Then take a cleane potte and put in all the stuffe and sete over the ymbers and coles and let it stand their ij howers styllinge and boylinge softly and then strayne yt into a cleayne vessell and vse to take therof evenynge and morninge when you fell yo[r] stomacke not well a good spovnfull it wyll dissolve fleame conserv the longes and harte and sease the coughe And causeth delyverance of the wynde and kepeth the lyver ffrom infections and kylleth all maner of wormes / p[rt] / [5]

42. A medysen for the Colde & yellows of A horse.

Take Turmeryk ij sponefull[6] . . . ceyk j $\overline{oz}$ long pper $\overline{di}$ $\overline{oz}$ Anysede 1 $\overline{oz}$ lycoras j $\overline{oz}$ bays $\overline{di}$ $\overline{oz}$ greyns $\overline{lb}$ Jnglysh Saffron ijd [butter as much as an egge][7] myngell all together being betyn in pouder & searchet[8] take of [eache][9] All so myngeled one sponefull & put it to strong Ale being one $\overline{qrt}$ & gyve it yo[r] horse when it is still & Cover it w[t] A dysh vntyll it be cold luke warme.

43. A p[r]cyous medysen for the stone vsed by S[r] Xpfr heyden Knyght[10] my self & many others.

R7 the sedes of gromell[11] Saxyfrage & Smallage of eche ʒ iij & beat them all to powder & then seares them fyne put

---

[1] Phlegm. [2] Dates. [3] Powder.
[4] Rumney, a sweet and heavy white wine. [5] Probatum.
[6] Throughout this prescription the quantities are written above the names of the respective drugs.
[7] These words are also added above the line.
[8] Sifted. [9] Crossed out.
[10] This is the Sir Christopher Heydon who died in 1593 and to whom there is a monument in the church of Baconsthorpe, Norfolk. His son Sir William Heydon was the father of the well-known Sir Christopher Heydon, the writer on Astrology, who died in 1563. As the second Christopher was not knighted until 1596, it must be his grandfather who is here alluded to.
[11] Gromell, or Grey Millet.

therto of good Suger ʒ ix & myxe all together then take viij
sponefull of whyte wyne Buysh wyne or Sakk being luke
warme & putt therto one ʒ of the forseyd powder & so
dryng it fastyng every xiiij days first yᵗ you fast ij vhers[1]
after evry tyme yᵗ you Do the same walkyng Rydyng or
Doing what you lyst after & so god wyllyng you shall
never be trvbled wᵗ the Stone. pbat[2] est.[3]

44. A medysen for any wound of A horse yf ther be no bone broken.

tak bakon broth one gallon or ij put therto, choppyd
nettles as many as you can holde in bothe yoʳ hands after
the quantyte of the broth take of vnslake lyme to a gallon
d̄i peck & somewhat lesse of Bay salt to a gallon one pynt
ynglysh honey d̄i pynt yf ther be ij gallons of broth cleave
A Styk & put on that A cloth wherwᵗʰ you may set it on &
this Do other ones A Day or wyse.

45. ffor the Bott [in sheep].

take red sage erbe of grace[4] lauender cotten of eche
xxᵗⁱ leaues small pepeʳ graynes tryacle bay solt tarr strong
Ale one quart and a litle svte[5] boyle all these together in the
ale & geue[6] to euery shepe ij sponnfolles. Allso let them
blood in the in side of the tayle iij or iiij ynchis.

46. ffor turning round in the heade [of sheep].

Red sannders one halfpeny worth wine vinigere in euery
eare ij sponefulles stoped full of wooll ty a ragg abowt his eare
one night & one daye knock him a bowght the roote of the
horne at nigh vndo the cloth agayne.

---

[1] Hours.   [2] Probatum.

[3] For somewhat similar fourteenth century medicines for stone
see MSS. *Harleian* 2378, and *Sloane* 2584 (Henslow, *op. cit.*, pp. 97,
130).

[4] Several different plants have been called *herba gratia dei* by the
old herbalists. Probably the Rock-rose (*Helianthemum*) is here
meant.

[5] Suet.   [6] Give.

CPSIA information can be obtained at www.ICGtesting.com
Printed in the USA
LVOW10*0227070815

449227LV00007B/37/P